SEEKING ASYLUM

International Studies in Human Rights

VOLUME 37

The titles published in this series are listed at the end of this volume.

SEEKING ASYLUM

Comparative Law and Practice in
Selected European Countries

by

HÉLÈNE LAMBERT

Lecturer in European and International Law
University of Exeter
United Kingdom

MARTINUS NIJHOFF PUBLISHERS
DORDRECHT / BOSTON / LONDON

Library of Congress Cataloging-in-Publication Data

```
Lambert, Hélène.
    Seeking asylum : comparative law and practice in selected European
countries / by Hélène Lambert.
      p.   cm. -- (International studies in human rights ; v.37)
    Originally presented as the author's thesis (doctoral--University
of Exeter, 1992)
    Includes index.
    ISBN 0-7923-3152-4 (acid-free paper)
    1. Asylum, Right of--Europe.  2. Refugees, Political--Legal
status, laws, etc.--Europe.   I. Title.  II. Series.
KJC5202.L36   1994
342.4'083--dc20
[344.0283]                                                  94-35316
```

ISBN 0-7923-3152-4

Published by Martinus Nijhoff Publishers,
P.O. Box 163, 3300 AD Dordrecht, The Netherlands.

Sold and distributed in the U.S.A. and Canada
by Kluwer Academic Publishers,
101 Philip Drive, Norwell, MA 02061, U.S.A.

In all other countries, sold and distributed
by Kluwer Academic Publishers Group,
P.O. Box 322, 3300 AH Dordrecht, The Netherlands.

Printed on acid-free paper

Printed in the Netherlands

For Theo

TABLE OF CONTENTS

FOREWORD

In 1992 Hélène Lambert was awarded the degree of Doctor of Philosophy in Law by the University of Exeter for a thesis produced under my supervision. Dr. Lambert's Examiners were in no doubt about the quality of the thesis and made a strong recommendation in favour of publication. This book is the result. But, while the book is derived from the thesis it is a new work. It has not only been substantially recast and rewritten for publication, but also incorporates further research which adds Germany and Sweden to the four jurisdictions considered in the original study.

The human and political problems presented by refugees and asylum are acute and are not improving. This is reflected in international concern and the existence of a treaty framework. The emergent body of refugee law is an amalgam of international, regional and national rules and procedures. But, it is national law and practice, particularly with regard to immigration, which in reality determines an individual's right to asylum. The key to a true appreciation and understanding of the plight of refugees and the extent of their current rights therefore lies in national law and practice. This comparative study of the relevant law and practice of six European states is a major and challenging contribution to that appreciation and understanding. It is a timely work which has no existing parallel in terms of its focus and range. Dr. Lambert's comparative and critical analysis and exposition also supplies some essential groundwork for the development of common law and policy in this vital area within the enlarged European Union.

It gives me particular pleasure to welcome and commend this book.

John W. Bridge
Professor of Public Law
University of Exeter

ACKNOWLEDGEMENTS

I wish to express my gratitude to John Bridge for his consistent help and support in the development of this work. My sincere gratitude is extended to Theo Farrell for all his assistance, encouragement and support.

I also wish to acknowledge the help and kindness of Marie-Odile Wiederkehr, from the Council of Europe, for arousing my interest in the topic six years ago, Istvan Pogany, Pierre Soler-Couteaux, Houssam Chamseddine, Viola Bensinger, and Lindy Melman.

A special note of thanks to all the people in Belgium, Sweden and Switzerland who gave of their time for interviews. In particular Mrs. Lavry (for the Regional Representative of the UNHCR, Brussels) who kindly organised my meetings in Brussels with Mr. Bossuyt (General Commissioner for refugees and stateless persons), Mr. Von Arnim (UNHCR), Mr. Jaeger (CBAR), Mrs. Semoulin (CIRE), Mrs. Biackso (CSP), Mr. Lefebvre (President of the Appeal Commission), Mr. Depelchin (OCIV), Mr. Ramakers (Cabinet of the Secretary of State for Social Emancipation) and Mrs. Conard (for the Appeal Commission) in Brussels. Thanks also to Mr. Gonczy, Mrs. Grosjean and Mrs. Perrelet (OSAR), Mrs. Della Croce and Mr. Clement (CSP), in Lausanne, Mr. Köfner and Mr. Buss (UNHCR), in Geneva and, Mr. Fischerström (Aliens Appeals Board), Mrs. Ulfvebrand (Swedish Red Cross), people from the Agency for Advisory Service and Mrs. Singer (UNHCR), in Stockholm.

I am, finally, most grateful to the following organizations for giving me grants which made this research possible: the University of Exeter for the Jonathan Young Scholarship and a University grant, the Council of Europe, and the Nuffield Foundation.

ABBREVIATIONS

A/...	–	Documents relating to the work of the UNGA
A.J.D.A.	–	Actualité Juridique de Droit Administratif (F)
All.E.R.	–	All England Law Reports (UK)
AsylVfG	–	Asylverfahrensgesetz (D)
AuslG	–	Ausländergesetz (D)
BGB	–	Bundesgesetzblatt (D)
B.R.C.	–	British Refugee Council
BVerfG	–	Bundesverfassungsgericht (D)
BVwG	–	Bundesverwaltungsgericht (D)
B.Y.I.L.	–	British Yearbook of International Law
C.A.	–	Court of Appeal (UK)
C.B.A.R.	–	Comité Belge d'Aide aux Réfugiés (B)
C.E.	–	Conseil d'Etat (F)(B)
C.E.D.R.I.	–	Comité Européen pour la Défense des Réfugiés et Immigrés
C.E.R.E.	–	Consultation Européenne pour les Réfugiés et Exilés
C.I.R.E.	–	Centre d'Initiation pour les Réfugiés et Exilés (B)
Cmnd.	–	Papers presented to Parliament by command of Her Majesty (UK)
CoE	–	Council of Europe
C.P.A.S.	–	Centres Publics d'Aide Sociale (B)
C.P.R.R.	–	Commission Permanente de Recours des Réfugiés (B)
C.R.A.	–	Commission des Recours en matière d'Asile (CH)
C.R.R.	–	Commission de Recours des Réfugiés (F)
C.S.P.	–	Centre Social Protestant (B)
C.T.D.	–	Convention Travel Document
E/...	–	Documents relating to the work of the Economic and Social Committee of the UN
E.C.	–	European Community
E.C.H.R.	–	European Convention of Human Rights and Fundamental Freedoms
E.C.R.E.	–	European Consultation on Refugees and Exiles
E.F.T.A.	–	European Free Trade Association
E.L.R.	–	Exceptional Leave to Remain (UK)
E.T.S.	–	European Treaty Series
E.U.	–	European Union
E.Z.A.R.	–	Europäische Zeitschrift für Allgemeines Recht (D)

F.F.	–	La Feuille Fédérale (CH)
F.T.D.A.	–	France Terre d'Asile (F)
H.C.	–	House of Commons Papers (UK)
H.L.	–	House of Lords (UK)
I.C.L.Q.	–	International and Comparative Law Quarterly
I.J.R.L.	–	International Journal of Refugee Law
Imm.A.R.	–	Immigration Appeal Reports (UK)
I.R.	–	Information Rapide (F)
J.O.R.F.	–	Journal Officiel de la République Française (F)
(J.O.)		
J.P.	–	Jurisprudence (F)
JuS	–	Juristische Schulung (D)
L.	–	Législation (F)
M.B.	–	Moniteur Belge (B)
M.N.S.	–	Migration News Sheet
M.R.G.	–	Minority Rights Group
N.G.O.	–	Non Governmental Organisation
NJW	–	Neue Juristische Wochenschrift (D)
NVwZ	–	Neue Zeitschrift für Verwaltungsrecht (D)
O.C.I.V.	–	Overlegcentrum voor Integratie von Vluchtelingen (B)
O.F.P.R.A.	–	Office Français de Protection des Réfugiés et Apatrides (F)
O.J.(E.C.)	–	Official Journal (of the European Communities)
O.S.A.R.	–	Office Suisse d'Aide aux Réfugiés (CH)
OVG	–	Oberverwaltungsgericht (D)
Q.B.	–	Queen's Bench Division (UK)
R.A.	–	Recueil Analytique de la Chambre des Représentants et du Sénat (B)
R.D.E.	–	Revue du Droit des Etrangers (B)
Rec.	–	Recueil Dalloz Sirey (F)
R.O.	–	Recueil Officiel des Lois Fédérales (CH)
R.S.	–	Recueil Systématique du droit fédéral (CH)
SFS	–	Svensk Författnignssamling (S)
S.I.	–	Statutory Instruments (UK)
SIV	–	Statens Invandrarverk (S)
S.O.U.	–	Statens Offentliga Utredningar (S)
(Sö)		
S.R.	–	Summary Records of the meetings of the various UN bodies
T.E.U.	–	Treaty on European Union
U.K.I.A.S.	–	United Kingdom Immigrants Advisory Service
U.N.G.A.	–	United Nations General Assembly
U.N.H.C.R.	–	United Nations High Commissioner for Refugees
U.N.T.S.	–	United Nations Treaty Series
VG	–	Verwaltungsgericht (D)
VwGO	–	Verwaltungsgerichtsordnung (D)
W.L.R.	–	Weekly Law Reports (UK)
Z.D.W.F.	–	Zentrale Dokumentationsstelle der Freien Wohlfahrtspflege für Flüchtlinge (D)

CHAPTER ONE

INTRODUCTION

With some 18.2 million in the world today,[1] refugees have been a continuous feature of international life in the present century, with the greatest number being located in Africa, Asia, the Middle East, South America and Eastern Europe. However, the majority of them remain in their own region, finding refuge in neighbouring countries. Less than ten per cent of them actually reach Western Europe.[2] Rarely are these recognized as refugees and granted political asylum (territorial asylum) in Western Europe.

The situation of being a refugee is, and should, remain a situation of exception. Refugees are by definition aliens. They constitute a specific category of migrants. As a rule, the concept of a right to stay and a right to work generally applies to immigrants. More specifically, refugees are normally granted permanent political asylum and the status of refugees which in turn implies the right to stay in the country of asylum and the right to work. Political refugees as displaced persecuted persons have existed since Antiquity[3] but it is only during the twentieth century that they have been the subject of specific international, regional and national legal concern.

1. The Definition of the Term Refugee

The most important instrument dealing with refugees is the United Nations Convention relating to the Status of Refugees and Exiles signed in Geneva

---

[1] This figure does not include displaced persons falling under the United Nations High Commissioner for Refugees (UNHCR) mandate whose number is currently estimated at between 20 and 40 million. UNHCR, *The State of the World's Refugees, The Challenge of Protection*, Penguin Books, 1993, iii. The class of persons within the mandate of UNHCR includes not only convention refugees as defined in the 1951 Convention/1967 Protocol (*infra*) but also large groups of persons, who are internally or internationally displaced because of an invasion, a war or a civil war and, who are unable to avail themselves of the protection of the government of their state of origin.

[2] H. Arnold, "The Century of the Refugee, A European Century?", *Aussenpolitik* 42(3), 1991, pp. 271–80.

[3] M.R. Marrus, *The Unwanted: European Refugees in the Twentieth Century*, Oxford University Press, 1985. UNHCR, *The State of the World's Refugees, op. cit.*, p. 33.

on 28 July 1951.[4] For the first time a general definition of the term refugee is adopted at an international level. Article 1A(2) of the 1951 Convention, as completed by the 1967 Protocol,[5] provides that a refugee is

> any person who owing to a well-founded fear of persecution for reasons of race, religion, nationality, membership of a particular social group or political opinion, is outside the country of his nationality and is unable, or owing to such fear, is unwilling to avail himself of the protection of that country; or who, not having a nationality and being outside the country of his former habitual residence, is unable, or owing to such fear, is unwilling to return to it.

This definition depends entirely on whether the asylum seeker is successful or not in showing individual persecution on specific grounds, the emphasis being on political persecution. The general spirit of the 1951 Convention[6] is that every person is entitled to freedom from persecution and that s/he will receive recognition and assistance from the international community in order to effect that freedom. The drafters of the 1967 Protocol missed the chance they had to widen the terms of this worldwide accepted definition although the timelessness was unique. It was already evident that Third World refugees would become a problem and the adoption of a Protocol would have led to less difficult political discussion in the General Assembly of the UN.[7] However, since the signature and ratification of a Protocol is left to the discretion of a state, many states, in particular, those in Europe and North America, may simply have refused to take such a forward step. Thus, the substantive content of the 1951 Convention definition remained unchanged but legal discussions emphasized the appearance of two trends of thinking: on one hand, a doctrine in favour of legal changes in the existing definition,

---

[4] Further referred to as the 1951 Convention (189 UNTS No. 2545, p. 137; *Collection of International Instruments concerning Refugees*, published by the Office of the UNHCR (Geneva 1988), p. 10). See also, the Statute of the UNHCR, GA Resolution 428(V) of 14 December 1950 (UN Doc. A/1775 (1950); *Collection*, p. 3) and the Protocol relating to the Status of Refugees of 31 January 1967, further referred to as the 1967 Protocol (606 UNTS No. 8791, p. 267; *Collection*, p. 40). By June 1993, 113 states had signed both the 1951 Convention and the 1967 Protocol, 3 states were party only to the 1951 Convention and 4 only to the 1967 Protocol. See, UNHCR, *The State of the World's Refugees, op. cit.*, p. 167.

[5] The 1951 Convention covers only those persons who have become refugees as a result of events occuring before 1 January 1951. In 1966, the General Assembly of the UN (UNGA) recognized the desirability of equal status for all refugees covered by the Convention, irrespective of the dateline (UNGA Res.2198(XXI)) and the 1967 Protocol simply removed both the time and geographical limitations. Although the Protocol is often referred to as 'amending" the 1951 Convention, in fact it does no such thing. It is, strictly speaking, an independent instrument and not a revision within the meaning of Article 45 of the 1951 Convention. P. Weis, "The 1967 Protocol relating to the Status of Refugees and some questions of the law of treaties", 42 BYIL (1967), pp. 39–70.

[6] In this book, the 1951 Convention will be taken to mean the 1951 Convention as completed by the 1967 Protocol.

[7] UNHCR, *Draft Protocol to the 1951 Convention: Analysis of the Present Position*, Internal Memorandum, 26 May 1966.

which dominated the Third World,[8] on the other hand, a doctrine in favour of a widening of the interpretation of the 1951 Convention, in particular its definition, which clearly prevailed in Western Europe. Asylum policies in Europe were elaborated in the early 1950's. They are largely based on the individual approach of persecution adopted in the 1951 Convention. This basic principle has remained in place and, therefore, each asylum application is considered on a case-by-case basis and is decided on its own merits with reference to the reasons or grounds put forward by the applicant.

2. The 'Right' of Asylum

The second crucial outcome of the 1951 Convention is the corollary that no person should, or can, be forcibly repatriated (*refoulement*) to his own country, the source of his fear of persecution. The principle of *non-refoulement*, as embodied in Article 33 of the 1951 Convention,[9] constitutes the cornerstone of the protection of refugees and, thus, creates a specific law of refugees, besides human rights, immigration law and international law. Refugee law, therefore, now exists as a branch of international law in parallel with, and rooted in, humanitarian law and human rights.[10] The major and outstanding constraints within the terms of the 1951 Convention are that an individual must have crossed a national border in order to achieve official recognition as a refugee and that his[11] fears of persecution be well-founded. Besides providing a legal definition of the term refugee and a protection against *refoulement*, the 1951 Convention sets out the minimum guaranteed rights granted to a person recognized as a refugee and the obligations attached to this status.[12] However, in neither the 1951 Convention nor the 1967 Protocol is there a specific reference given to asylum, which remains a concept

---

[8] Article I(2) of the 1969 Organisation of African Unity (OAU) Convention Governing the Specific Aspects of Refugee Problems in Africa (1001 UNTS No. 14691) provides that

The term *refugee* shall also apply to every person who, owing to external aggression, occupation, foreign domination or events seriously disturbing public order in either part or the whole of his country of origin or nationality, is compelled to leave his place of habitual residence in order to seek refuge in another place outside his country of origin or nationality.

A similar definition is incorporated in other regional instruments, ie, in the 1985 Cartagena Declaration by the Organization of American States, in Latin America.

[9] Non-refoulement also constitutes a fundamental right within the meaning of the ECHR. *Altun* case, 3 May 1983, European Commission of Human Rights, application no. 10308/83, *Decisions and Reports*, 36, p. 248 et seq., CoE, Strasbourg, 1984.

[10] J. Patrnogic, *International Protection of Refugees in Armed Conflicts*, reprinted by UNHCR Protection Division from *Annales de Droit International Medical*, July 1981, para.4. See also, J. Patrnogic, *Promotion, Dissemination and Teaching of International Refugee Law*, International Institute of Humanitarian Law, Villa Nobel, San Remo, Italy, February 1984; Shamsul Bari, *Le droit des réfugiés en péril?*, in REFUGIES, August 1989, p. 23–25.

[11] This book will refer to asylum seekers and refugees in the male gender. This is because ALL legal instruments, to which I make extensive reference, regrettably do likewise.

[12] Article 7(1) proposes, as a minimum standard, that refugees should receive at least that treatment which is accorded to aliens in general.

rather than a recommendation embodied in the text of either document. Nor does either instrument refer to the procedures of access to the status of refugee. Contracting Parties are, therefore, free to interpret the terms of the Convention/Protocol and to set up their own national procedures, subject to various instruments. These are, among others, the Handbook on Procedures and Criteria for Determining Refugee Status,[13] Conclusions on the International Protection of Refugees,[14] various Conventions, Recommendations and Resolutions adopted within the Council of Europe (CoE) and the European Union (EU), in particular the European Convention on Human Rights and Fundamental Freedoms (ECHR)[15] and its Protocols. Both United Nations (UN) and European Conventions and Protocols are intended to be legally binding within the territory of the Contracting States. The position of conventions in international law is that Contracting Parties are obliged to bring their domestic provisions into accordance with the international obligations. The UN requests formal statements from Contracting States regarding the procedures for implementing conventions and concerning any reservations made to certain articles. Although there are no legally binding instruments as regards political asylum[16] the practice of states is normally to grant asylum as a sovereign right to recognized refugees. As Simpson has stated "asylum is a privilege conferred by the state. It is not a condition inherent in the individual."[17] The key protection afforded to a refugee in international law is the right to seek asylum and the guarantee that he shall not be forcibly repatriated. However, the expulsion of aliens is equally a sovereign right of states. In practice, therefore, the rights of the 1951 Convention only apply once a refugee has been granted permanent asylum. Temporary asylum does not usually entitle a refugee to the full social and economic benefits embodied in the main provisions of the 1951 Convention. Theoretically any person who fulfils the criteria of the 1951 Convention is a refugee. In practice, he can only benefit from that status once it has been recognized by a potential country of asylum. This situation often creates 'refugees in orbit'.[18] Furthermore, in practice, it is increasingly common for asylum seekers to be authorized to remain in a country on political and humanitarian grounds, or on humani-

---

[13] Office of the UNHCR, Geneva.

[14] Adopted by the Executive Committee of the UNHCR Programme; Office of the UNHCR, Geneva.

[15] Rome, 4 November 1950; 213 UNTS 223; ETS No. 5; Basic Documents V.1; *Collection* p. 274.

[16] Declaration of Territorial Asylum adopted by the UNGA on 14 December 1967, Resolution 2312(XXII), UN Doc. A/RES/2312(XXII), Basic Documents III.6, *Collection* p. 57. The CoE has failed, until now, to adopt a text on this matter despite recent attempts by the Committee of Experts in Human Rights to design an additional Protocol on Asylum to the European Convention on Human Rights and Fundamental Freedoms.

[17] J.H., Simpson, *The Refugee Problem*, Oxford University Press (1939), p. 230.

[18] Individuals who present themselves at a port of entry but are refused admission and are sent back to their port of exit which may not be their country of origin, where once again they are refused entry.

tarian grounds alone. In such cases, they are not recognized as 'convention refugees'.[19] In Scandinavian countries, for example, they are called 'de facto refugees' and benefit from a particular status. In other countries, such as the United Kingdom, Switzerland or Germany, they are no more than tolerated persons with no legal status.

3. Refugees as a Problem for States

It follows from the UNHCR Statute that there are two kinds of refugees. First, the Statute recognizes refugees who are part of a mass movement provoked by invasion, oppression or war. In this case, groups are usually recognized as refugees according to the Statute of the UNHCR and programmes are set up in the countries of refuge, by the Governments, to accept a quota of refugees.[20] Second, the Statute sees refugees as individuals who claim to have escaped persecution in their own country. Unlike 'quota refugees', who are automatically recognized refugees, individuals are also covered by Article 1A(2) of the 1951 Convention. Thus, they may only be recognized as refugees if they are successful at showing a well-founded fear of persecution on political grounds. Although a few references may be made to quota refugees, this study will mainly stress an individual approach to the concept of refugee and the right of asylum.

South-North migration trends since the Second World War had been welcomed as an opportunity to use cheap labour. However, in the early 1970's, Europe plunged in an economic recession. As a result, European states adopted restrictive immigration policies to stop labour coming in. Policies towards refugees had remained quite liberal, however, and migrants started to use asylum procedures instead of the restrictive immigration ones in order to enter Western Europe. It is only in the mid–1980's that, as the whole asylum legal system was put under such considerable pressure, European states realised the scale of the problem they were to deal with. Jonas Widgren sees four aspects to this problem. "The constant growth of the annual number of formal asylum applicants in Europe ... the growing phenomenon of irregular movements of asylum seekers ... the emergence of large-scale flows of non bona-fide asylum

---

[19] A convention refugee is a refugee within the meaning of the 1951 Convention.

[20] The term 'quota' refers to the number of places which a country makes available to the UNHCR as a planning figure for selection from different camps. The country in question fixes the number of places and selects the individual persons for transfer. For example, 21,300 South-East Asians refugees were accepted for resettlement in Britain between 1979 and 1989 (D. O'Keeffe and R.W. Piotrowicz, "National Report: Asylum Law in the United Kingdom", Paper presented at Trier, March 1992, p. 4). As another example, Sweden receives refugees for resettlement under an annual quota of 2,000. During 1991, 1,222 refugees from Vietnam, Iran, El Salvador and Iraq were accepted (Swedish Ministry of Cultural Affairs, *Immigrant and Refugee Policy*, 1992, p. 25). However, Sweden has recently decided to refuse convention status to quota refugees in UNHCR camps; they will be given a lower status instead (MNS, March 1994, p. 8).

seekers ... the rapidly raising state costs for the processing of an ever growing number of cases."[21]

It has, indeed, become more and more difficult to distinguish between genuine refugees,[22] economic refugees,[23] de facto refugees[24] and displaced persons.[25] Responsibility to accept refugees and to provide them protection and a dignified status is assumed by many different organizations. Clearly Contracting States do bear the greatest part of the responsibility. Refugee law, although a branch of international law, is above all a matter of national law and policy strongly connected with immigration law. In essence, refugee law depends on the respect and interpretation by each state of European and international refugee instruments.

4. Book Outline

This book is not about showing that refugees are a class known to, and defined, by international law. This is already a well recognized fact. The aim of this book is to examine the effectiveness of relevant international and European provisions in six European states. To this end, I will examine the refugee law and practice in these states and will give an appraisal on the level of protection offered in each of these countries.

In this book, I identify six separate issues. A first chapter looks at admission procedures for asylum seekers (the emphasis is on first instance proceedings). A second chapter deals with the rights of appeal against rejected applications. A third chapter concentrates on the burden of proof and rules of evidence. A fourth chapter looks at protection against 'refoulement' and living conditions during the pre-asylum period. A fifth chapter discusses the situation of 'de facto' refugees and 'humanitarian grounds' refugees, and a sixth chapter analyses the status of convention refugee.

The six countries which this book will examine are: Belgium, the Federal Republic of Germany, France, Sweden, Switzerland and the United Kingdom. Obvious differences, not to mention discrepancies, exist amongst the national legal systems and practices in these states. Broadly speaking, the United Kingdom has always had a restrictive policy towards refugees. France and Germany have recently adopted stricter policies in place of their previous

---

[21] The European Conference on Reception of Asylum Seekers", Final Report, "Opening address" by J. Widgren, 1991, p. 14.

[22] A genuine refugee is by definition a convention refugee.

[23] They are usually escaping from economic harship in their home country (ie, Ghana, Zaire).

[24] A de facto refugee can be a genuine refugee who for various reasons is refused convention refugee status. Very often, however, a de facto refugee is a person who does not fear persecution exclusively on political grounds but such fear is also based on humanitarian grounds.

[25] Such persons are not covered by the 1951 Convention but they fall under the mandate of the UNHCR. They may be protected against *refoulement* and allowed to remain in the territory of a member state on humanitarian grounds.

liberal ones. Switzerland and Belgium (for their size) accept a disproportionate number of refugees, regardless of their policies. Of all the six countries, Sweden is the most unique; its law is restrictive but because of its welfare tradition, its practice is not.

From an international law perspective, all the six states are Contracting Parties to the UN refugee instruments and are members of the CoE. Belgium, France, Germany and the United Kingdom are also members of the EU but only Belgium, France and Germany are currently parties to the Treaty of Schengen.[26] Ways of solving the problem of refugees are presently being tackled at the European level. It is often argued that national attempts have proven inadequate and that solutions need to be found through increasing cooperation between the members states of the EU and/or the CoE. The purpose of this book is not to discuss solutions at a regional or international level but to analyse the way Belgium, France, the Federal Republic of Germany, Sweden, Switzerland and the United Kingdom are currently dealing with refugees and asylum seekers. Nevertheless, the possibilities for a harmonized asylum policy in Europe will be discussed in the concluding chapter.

---

[26] The Federal Republic of Germany, Belgium, France, Luxembourg and the Netherlands signed on 14 June 1985 the Treaty of Schengen on the removal of their internal frontiers. On 19 June 1990, the same five countries signed the Additional Schengen Convention in pursuance of the Schengen Agreement of 1985; Italy signed the Convention on November 1990 and, thus, became the sixth country of the "Schengen Group", followed most recently by Spain and Portugal.

CHAPTER TWO

ADMISSION PROCEDURES FOR ASYLUM SEEKERS

"The most important legal problems concerning refugees are directly or indirectly related to the question of asylum. In the absence of a universal instrument on asylum – indeed there is not even a generally accepted definition – there exists much dispute on the obligations of States to receive refugees and the legal consequences arising from the reception of refugees, be it for permanent asylum or merely on a temporary basis. Further legal problems result from the lack of generally accepted criteria for the granting of asylum and the determination of refugee status".[1] Although a clear distinction exists in international law between the right of asylum and the recognition of refugee status, all European states have now recognized the essential purpose of the 1951 Convention and have accepted that "the criteria for recognition of refugee status also serve as the criteria for the grant of asylum in the sense of residence and protection".[2]

Procedures for determining refugee status and for granting asylum in Europe are not yet harmonized and the case-study of Belgium, France, Germany, Sweden, Switzerland and the United Kingdom will illustrate the extent to which national procedures available to asylum seekers vary between these states.

The aim of this chapter is to discuss the most important aspects of the asylum procedure in these countries. In each case, the emphasis is on the first instance procedure. Section one will describe the existing national legal provisions dealing with asylum and refugees. Section two will analyse the asylum procedure, mainly until a first instance decision is taken, and section three will look at the degree to which the UNHCR is involved in the procedure.

1. Relevant Domestic Provisions

The Executive Committee of the High Commissioner's Programme recommended that states parties to the 1951 Convention put a stress on formal proce-

---

[1] *The Encyclopedia of Public International Law*, published under the auspices of the Max Planck Institute for Comparative Public Law and International Law, vol. 8, p. 455.

[2] G.S. Goodwin-Gill, *The Refugee in International Law*, Clarendon Press, Oxford, 1985, p. 54.

dures for the determination of refugee status, rather than referring to informal or ad hoc arrangements.[3] Wherever possible, those procedures should be regulated by law to provide a full protection to asylum seekers against *refoulement*. In all six countries under review provisions concerning the determination of refugee status and the granting of asylum are mainly based on statutes.

1.1. *International Refugee Treaties in the National Legal Systems*

In Belgium, there is no express reference to the right of asylum but the 1951 Convention was incorporated into Belgian Law by the *loi portant approbation de la Convention Internationale Relative au Statut des Réfugiés*, which was promulgated on 26 June 1953.[4] In France, it is said that the principle of the right of asylum is laid down in the Preamble to the 1958 Constitution[5] and binds the authorities according to the terms and restrictions defined in French statutes or in the international conventions incorporated into French law.[6] The Federal Republic of Germany ratified the 1951 Convention and the 1967 Protocol.[7] The fundamental subjective right to asylum is provided in Article 16 of the Basic Law (*Groundgesetz* or GG), as amended in 1993. It is on the basis of this provision that the whole legal system for the protection of refugees is based. In Switzerland, the right of asylum is laid down in Article 69ter of the Federal Constitution of 29 May 1874.[8] The same instrument, Article 89 of the Federal Constitution, approved the 1951 Convention and its ratification was therefore authorized. Sweden is a party to the 1951 Convention and 1967 Protocol[9] but a general reservation was made concerning the most favourable treatment accorded to aliens. Such treatment is not to include necessarily all special rights accorded to the nationals of other Scandinavian countries. Some more specific reservations were also made to Articles 8, 12(1), 17(2), 24(1)b, 24(3) and 25.[10] In the United Kingdom ,"[a]lthough the Immigration Act states in s.33(5) that the Act 'shall not be taken to supersede

---

[3]   See Conclusions 8 (XXVIII) on the Determination of Refugee Status (1977).

[4]   M.B. 4 October 1953; voted at quasi-unanimity (*Sénat*: 150 votes against 1). For the 1967 Protocol, see *Loi Belge* of 27 February 1969 (M.B. 3 May 1969).

[5]   "Anyone persecuted because of his action for Freedom has a right to asylum in the territories of the Republic". See Goodwin-Gill, *The Refugee in International Law, op. cit.*, p. 15. See also, the intention of F. Mitterrand, President of the French Republic, concerning the Preamble of the 1946 Constitution, in *Le Monde*, 6 January 1989, pp. 1,8.

[6]   Translated from: Conseil d'Etat, section du contentieux, 27 septembre 1985, *Association France Terre d'Asile et autres*, Rec.(1986), p. 278. The 1951 Convention was incorporated into French Law by the *loi autorisant le Président de la République française à ratifier la Convention de Genève* (Law No. 54–290 of 17 March 1954 and Decree of publication No. 54–1055 of 14 October 1954).

[7]   1953 *Bundesgesetzblatt* II, p. 559 (BGB or Federal Law Gazette), and 1969 BGB II, p. 1294, respectively.

[8]   RS 101.

[9]   Sö 1954:55 and Sö 1967:45, respectively.

[10]   *Asile en Europe, Guide à l'intention des associations de protection des réfugiés*, ECRE, 1990, p. 469, para.1.

or impair any power exercisable by Her Majesty in relation to aliens by virtue of Her prerogative', in practice the only powers exercised are statutory ...".[11]

Thus, Belgium, Germany, France, Sweden, Switzerland and the United Kingdom are parties to all international conventions relating to refugees, including the 1951 Convention and the 1967 Protocol. Ratified international treaties are an integral part of Belgian,[12] German,[13] French[14] and Swiss[15] law and their provisions prevail over municipal law, provided the rule of reciprocity is respected. In the United Kingdom, international conventions and agreements are not self-executing and provisions have to be made in municipal legislation for them to become effective in the domestic legal system: 'International obligations contained in the Protocol and Convention on the Status of Refugees are incorporated into the Immigration Rules, but no mention of the European Convention on Human Rights is found in them".[16] The question of whether or not the ECHR should be incorporated into English law has often been raised. In 1988–89, while the Parliament was trying to agree on the spirit of a new Bill of Rights,[17] it was agreed that the ECHR would not be incorporated into English law and that one should be fully satisfied about the system of judicial review[18] developed by judges under the assent of Parliament. However, as stated by Lord Scarman, there is a danger that "if the law is deficient, judicial review will also be deficient".[19] The situation in Sweden is quite similar to that in the United Kingdom. The 1809 Swedish Constitution was repealed by the new Instrument of Government of 1st January 1975. Both instruments affirm the doctrine of Parliament sovereignty and the dualist principle. International law rules need to be incorporated into national law, through Parliament, to be relied upon by individuals before national courts. Furthermore, the possibility of a transfer of powers (the right to make a deci-

---

[11] Ian A. Macdonald, *Immigration Law and Practice in the United Kingdom*, London, Butterworths, 1983, p. 24.

[12] Constitution, Article 68(2).

[13] Basic Law, Article 25. Clearly worded provisions do not need to be transformed or incorporated by Parliament or Government. Federal Administrative Court, 16 October 1990, Collection of Decisions, Vol. 87, p. 11.

[14] Constitution, Article 55.

[15] Constitution, Articles 89 and 113(3).

[16] See *R v. Immigration Appeal Tribunal, ex p. Bastiampillai* (1983), *The Times*, 3 February 89, DC. See also, *R v. Secretary of State for the Home Department, ex p. Sivakumaran and conjoined appeals*, 10 Nov., 16 Nov, 1987, All ER, 1, 1988, p. 195, HL, b : 'The United Kingdom having acceded to the convention and protocol, their provisions have for all practical purposes been incorporated into United Kingdom law. Rules 16, 73 and 165 of the Statement of Changes in Immigration Rules (HC Paper (1982–83) No. 169)(made under s 3(2) of the Immigration Act 1971) provide: ..."; House of Commons Papers, 1982–83, HC 169, vol. 26.

[17] Notice that in the UK "the Government can use its majority in Parliament to do whatever it likes'; Anthony Lester, *How Europe is defending the human rights of the British*, *The Independent*, 18 May 1989, p. 26; Peter Jenkins, *ibid*, p. 27.

[18] See "Judicial review and immigration", *ALL ER Annual Review* 1986, pp. 9–10.

[19] Lord Scarman, *A Bill of Rights could become the conscience of the nation*, *The Independent*, 9 June 1989, p. 20.

sion) to an international organisation or an international tribunal is provided for the first time by the new Instrument of Government. In practice, Swedish courts' decisions are based on national statutory instruments, which embody international conventions, rather than on international rules themselves. Like in the United Kingdom, the ECHR is not directly applicable in the domestic legal system but most basic rights now exist in the new Instrument of Government.[20]

1.2. *National Instruments on Refugees*

Belgium
Like in France, Sweden or the United Kingdom, provisions on asylum and refugees are found in statutes regarding aliens in general. This is not the case in Switzerland, or in Germany to a certain extent, where specific texts exist. The main municipal provisions regarding aliens, and therefore also refugees, are the Law of 15 December 1980 on access to the territory, residence, settlement and removal of aliens,[21] as modified by Law of 28 June 1984 relating to certain aspects of the condition of aliens and creating the code of the Belgian nationality,[22] Law of 14 July 1987,[23] Law of 18 July 1991,[24] and finally Law of 6 May 1993.[25] These statutes have been completed, for their application, by numerous Royal Decrees (*arrêté royal*).[26] Mention should also be made of the Ministerial Decree of 18 May 1993,[27] modifying the Decree of 26 January 1988, relating to the delegation of the Minister of Justice's powers to representative authorities in matters such as access to the territory, residence, settlement and removal of aliens. Delegated authorities are representatives of the local authority, *communal* authorities and police authorities. Finally, as a result of a new provision on the role of the UNHCR Representative (Article 57/23bis of the Law of 6 May 1993), the Representative of the UNHCR adopted a decision relating to the delegation of his powers.[28] The General Commissioner, equally, adopted a Decree relating to the delegation of powers conferred to him by the Law of 15 December 1980.[29]

---

[20] A.Z. Drzemczewski, *European Human Rights Convention in Domestic Law – A Comparative Study*, Oxford, 1983, pp. 135–41.

[21] M.B. 31.12.1980.

[22] M.B. 12.07.1984.

[23] M.B. 18.07.1987.

[24] M.B. 26.07.1991.

[25] M.B. 21.05.1993, p. 11974.

[26] In particular, Royal Decree of 19 May 1993 relating to the functions and the procedure before the Permanent Commission of Appeal (M.B. 21.05.93, p. 11993). Royal Decree of 8 October 1981 on access to the territory, sojourn, settling down and removal of aliens, as finally modified on 19 May 1993 (M.B. 21.05.93, p. 11997). For a more exhaustive list, see for instance, *Asile en Europe, op. cit.*, pp. 188–91; or Jean-Yves Carlier, *Droits des Réfugiés*, Editions Story-Scientia, 1989, pp. 40–1.

[27] M.B. 21.05.1993, p. 12031.

[28] Decision of 13 May 1993, M.B. 21.05.1993.

[29] *Ibid.*

Federal Republic of Germany

'Persons persecuted for political reasons enjoy the right of asylum".[30] The scope of this fundamental individual right to asylum, which used to be without restrictions (Article 16II–2 of the 1949 Basic Law), is now subject to important limitations.[31] Are excluded from the asylum procedure, refugees of war and civil war[32] and refugees coming from a safe third country, that is a country which adheres to the 1951 Convention as well as to the 1950 ECHR.[33] Accelerated proceedings shall apply to all cases of refugees coming from a safe country of origin,[34] that is a country where no persecution for political reasons nor inhuman or degrading punishment or treatment takes place.[35] Shortened procedures will also apply to asylum seekers who have committed serious crimes or have abused existing regulations. A new fingerprinting system is created and new investigating methods applied to combat fraudulent applications. Finally, deportation is facilitated by the systematic detention of asylum seekers coming by plane from safe countries of origin or without the proper travel or identity documents. Despite these changes, the Federal Republic of Germany continues to adhere to the notion of the politically persecuted rather than the notion of refugee as provided by the 1951 Convention. This could well constitute an obstacle to the way of a European harmonization of asylum policies. The fundamental principle of Article 16aI of the Basic Law was developed in the Aliens Law of 28 April 1965 (*Ausländergesetz* or *AuslG*)[36] and in the Asylum Procedure Law of 16 July 1982 (*Asylverfahrensgesetz* or *AsylVfG*).[37] The Asylum Procedure Law is the basic legislation regulating the procedures by which asylum seekers may enter and apply for refugee status in Germany. Further provisions may also be found in other legal and administrative texts of less general scope.[38]

---

[30]   Article 16aI of the Basic Law, as amended in June 1993.

[31]   REFUGEES, December 1993, pp. 38–40.

[32]   They shall, nevertheless, be accorded a temporary right to remain. Bundesministerium des Innerns, "Das Neue Asylrecht – Fragen und Antworten", Bonn, July 1993, p. 16.

[33]   *Ibid*, p. 8.

[34]   *Ibid*, p. 10.

[35]   Joachim Henkel, "Das Neue Asylrecht", NJW, Heft 42, p. 2708.

[36]   1965 BGB1.I. Para.51 guarantees the principle of *non-refoulement*. The Aliens Law 1965 was amended several times, in particular on 1st January 1991. See Federal Minister of the Interior, *Survey of the Policy and Law regarding Aliens in the Federal Republic of Germany*, January 1991 (Translation), Annexes 1 and 2.

[37]   1982 BGB1.I. It was modified several times, in particular in 1984, 1992 and more recently in 1993 by the Asylum Law of 1st July (1993 BGB1.I).

[38]   For examples, Law of 25 June 1969 promoting employment (*Arbeitsförderungsgesetz*, 1969 BGB1.I); Regulation of 12 September 1980 on work permits (*Arbeitserlaubnisverordnung*, 1980 BGB1.I); Law of 29 July 1980 on aid to refugees admitted under humanitarian relief programmes (1980 BGB1.I) See, *Asile en Europe, op. cit.*, pp. 104–5.

France[39]

The main text concerning the entry and residence of aliens in France is the Ordinance No. 45–2658 of 2 November 1945.[40] This instrument has been subject to so many amendments that an attempt to list all of them would seem rather vain. Furthermore, a great number of legislative texts regarding asylum seekers are never published. This is the case, in particular, of ministerial circulars of which only one out of 15 was published during the year 1991.[41] I shall, therefore, mention only the most current and important provisions published in the Official Journal (JO).[42] Ordinance 1945, as modified, was last published in an Annex to Decree No. 91–902.[43] Law No. 92–190 of 26 February 1992 relating to the application of the Schengen Convention, amended further Ordinance 1945 to the extent that it added new provisions on carriers liability and responsibility, as well as new provisions on the expulsion of aliens.[44] Further modifications may finally be found in Law No. 92–625 of 6 July 1992 on transit zones at ports and airports[45] and Decree No. 92–1333 of 15 December 1992.[46] Provisions of the 1945 Ordinance on the position

---

[39] Brief explanation as regards the status of and the relationship between Ordinances, Laws and Decrees in France. The Constitution is hierarchically the supreme instrument, followed by the laws voted by the parliament within the limits set up by the Constitution and in respect of the Constitution. According to Article 38 of the 1958 Constitution, the Government may ask the parliament the authorization to take measures (within a limited period of time) by Ordinances which should normally be the subject of Laws. Such Ordinances are taken in the Council of Ministers after decision of the *Conseil d'Etat.* Decrees are taken by the President of the Republic or by the Prime Minister. According to Article 37 of the 1958 Constitution *"les matières autres que celles qui sont du domaine de la loi ont un caractère réglementaire".* See Jean-Louis Quermonne, *Le Gouvernement de la France sous la Vième République,* études politiques économiques et sociales, Dalloz, 1987, Pp. 355–87.

[40] Relative aux conditions d'entrée et de séjour en France des étrangers et portant création de l'office national d'immigration (JO, 04.11.45; rectificatifs JO, 07.11.45 and 13.12.45; Rec.(1946) L., pp. 24–5).

[41] "This means that the legal framework for asylum seekers is mainly based on texts which have not been published in the official journal". ECRE Country Report, France, 3–5 April 1992, p. 79. See also, FTDA, "Rapport semestriel pour la CERE, juillet à décembre 1991", Paris, 12 mars 1992, p. 6.

[42] Or the *Recueil Dalloz Sirey, Législation* (Rec., L.).

[43] Decree of 6 Sept.1991 (JO, 13.09.91, p. 12058; Rec.(1991)L., p. 214). It includes new Article 35bis, which provides possibilities of detention and guarantees pending the removal of an alien. Decree No. 91–1164 of 12 November 1991 (JO, 14.09.91, p. 14823; Rec.(1991)L., p. 481) provides conditions for the application of Article 35bis, ie, the possibility of appeal against the decision.

[44] JO, 29.02.92, p. 3094; Rec.(1992) L., p. 222. Besides modifying Articles 5,19,22 and 26, it adds a new Article 35ter. See also Decree No. 93–180 of 8 February 1993 relating to the application of Articles 19,20bis and 22 of the 1945 Ordinance (JO, 09.02.93, p. 2129; Rec.(1993) L., p. 235).

[45] JO, 09.07.92, p. 9185; Rec.(1992) L., p. 362. It modifies Articles 5 and 35bis and adds a new Article 35quater. See also Law No. 94–6 of 4 January 1994, in particular Article 32 on the powers of border control officers during detention at the transit zone of airports (JO, 05.01.94, p. 245; Rec.(1994) L., p. 107).

[46] JO, 22.12.92, p. 17522; Rec.(1993) L.,p. 39.

of aliens in France were also thoroughly modified by Laws No. 93–1027[47] and 93–1417[48] of 24 August and 30 December 1993 relating to the control of immigration in France and to the modification of the *Code Civil.*[49] In addition, Law No. 52–893 of 25 July 1952 created the *Office Français de Protection des Réfugiés et Apatrides* (OFPRA).[50] It was modified by Law No. 90–550 of 2 July 1990[51] and Law No. 93–1027 of 24 August 1993.[52] The reform aimed at speeding the proceedings dealing with requests for the status of refugee. Law of 25 July 1952 was completed by Decree No. 53–377 of 2 May 1953 relating to the OFPRA.[53] It was modified, in particular, by Decrees No. 80–683 of 3 September 1980,[54] No. 90–968 of 29 October 1990,[55] No. 91–314 of 26 March 1991[56] and No. 92–732 of 30 July 1992.[57]

Asylum and refugee status are also the subject of a number of ministerial regulations or circular instructions of considerable importance.[58] Newly adopted legal provisions reinforcing fight against illegal employment (work underground) include Law No. 91–1383 of 31 December 1991[59] and Law No. 93–1313 of 20 December 1993.[60] Provisions concerning nationality in the Civil Code and in the Nationality Code were modified by Law No. 93–933 of 22 July 1993,[61] as modified by Law No. 93–1027 of 24 August 1993, in

---

[47] JO, 29.08.93, p. 12196; Rec.(1993)L.,p. 485. See, in particular, Chapter VII on Asylum Seekers.

[48] JO, 01.01.94, p. 11; Rec.(1994) L., p. 72.

[49] Completed by Decree No. 93–1362 of 30 December 1993 (JO, 31.12.93, p. 18559; Rec.(1994)L.,p. 58).

[50] JO, 27.07.52, p. 7642; Rec.(1952) L., p. 284. *L'Office Français de Protection des Réfugiés et Apatrides* is a public administrative establishment attached to the Minister of Foreign Affairs but with a relatively autonomy, which task is to determine the status of refugee.

[51] On the OFPRA and the Appeal Commission. JO, 05.07.90; Rec.(1990) L., p. 289.

[52] See, in particular, Title VI.

[53] JO, 03.05.53; Rec.(1953) L., p. 158.

[54] JO, 04.09.80; Rec.(1980) L., p. 347.

[55] JO, 31.10.90; Rec.(1990) L., p. 434.

[56] JO, 28.03.91, p. 4264; Rec.(1991) L., p. 197.

[57] JO, 31.07.92, p. 10292; Rec.(1992) L., p. 448. New Article 15–1, in particular, provides the possibility for the President of the Appeal Commission to refer a case to a *Section Réunie*.

[58] For instance, Circular Instruction No. 84–15 of 24 June 1984 from the Minister of Justice relating to the civil status of refugees (JO, 09.11.84, p. 10210; Rec.(1984) L., p. 581) and Circular Instruction of 17 May 1985 from the Prime Minister relating to Asylum Seekers (JO, 23.05.85, p. 5776; Rec.(1985) L., p. 310). The latter was amended by Circular Instruction of 26 September 1991 relating to Asylum Seekers' Right to Work (work is in fact prohibited); JO, 27.09.1991, p. 12606; Rec.(1991) L., p. 427.

[59] JO, 01.01.92, p. 15; Rec.(1992) L., p. 74. It reinforces combat against illegal employment as well as against the organisation of illegal entry and residence in France, thereby, modifying Articles 21,25 and 27 of the Ordinance of 1945.

[60] JO, 21.12.93, p. 17769; Rec.(1994) L.,p. 12. Articles 34–36 of the Law, regarding illegal employment, provide modifications to the *Code Pénal, Code du Travail* and Article 21ter is inserted in Ordinance 1945.

[61] Loi No. 93–933 réformant le droit de la nationalité (JO, 23.07.93, p. 10342; Rec.(1993) L., p. 400).

particular Article 32, and Law No. 93–1417 of 30 December 1993. The most recent provisions concerning legal aid are Law No. 91–647 of 10 July 1991,[62] as completed by Decrees of 19 December 1991[63] and 4 February 1994.[64]

Sweden

The Aliens Act of 1st July 1989[65] constitutes the legal basis for the determination of refugee status. It is completed by the Aliens Ordinance of 8 June 1989.[66] Furthermore, relevant provisions may also be found in other laws and decrees.[67] Governments Bills and policy statements by Standing Committees of the Parliament, which are adopted before amending the Aliens Act are also important sources of law. The 1989 Aliens Act was adopted with the aim that it would help speeding up the procedure and that it would create new grounds for refusing refugees but shortly after its adoption, a new proposal for amending asylum and immigration policy was already put forward.[68] Following the general election of September 1991, the new Government decided to withdrew the bill on an "Active Refugee and Immigration Policy", except for one concrete proposal, and in December 1991, it proposed to the Parliament the introduction of a new Aliens Appeals Board by 1 January 1992.[69] Parliament accepted the proposition and the Appeals Board was set up. On 19 December 1991, the new Government also decided to lift the restrictions on the right of asylum introduced by the former Government in 1989,[70] and in 1992 it decided further amendments to the Aliens Act.[71] The Parliament approved an amendment to the Act concerning assistance to asylum seekers

---

[62] Rec.(1991) L., p. 310.

[63] Decree No. 91–1266, Rec.(1992) L., p. 15.

[64] Decree No. 94–117, JO, 11.02.94, p. 2352.

[65] *Utlänningslagen*: *Svensk Författnignssamling* (SFS) 1989 no. 529, which amended the Aliens Act of 5 June 1980 (SFS 1980:376).

[66] *Utlänningsförordning* (SFS 1989:547), as amended by Aliens Ordinance of 1992 (SFS 1992:581). It modifies Aliens Ordinance 1980 no. 377.

[67] For instance, the Act on legal aid (1972:429), the Act on special control of aliens (1991:572) and the Act on introductory remuneration for refugees and certain other aliens (1992:1068). See *Asile en Europe, op. cit.*, p. 491 or Kjell Jönsson and Sten De Geer, 'The rights of asylum seekers and accepted refugees in Sweden", Röda korset, 1993, Annex I. This is the Swedish Report for a new edition of the book *Asylum in Europe* (ECRE, forthcoming 1994).

[68] Government Bill Prop. 1988/89:86. The government at the time proposed new restrictive rules for war resisters and de facto refugees.

[69] Prop. 1991/92:30.

[70] New Aliens Ordinance (SFS 1991:1998) and new Ordinance on Residence Permits for Aliens in Certain Cases (SFS 1991:1999). A decision of the Government of 13 December 1989, in particular, provided that *de facto* refugees were not to be granted a residence permit automatically. Special reasons (ie, a too great influx in Sweden) could prevent granting such permit. See Göran Melander, 'Undocumented Asylum Seekers in Sweden", An Independent Study, 1990, p. 5.

[71] Prop. 1991/92:138.

and others[72] and changes in the Aliens Ordinance were made accordingly.[73] Parliament also approved some changes to the Aliens Act as a consequence of the transfer of responsibility to carry out asylum investigations from the police to the Immigration Board (SIV), which took place on 1st July 1992.

Switzerland

According to Article 69ter of the Federal Constitution of 29 May 1874, the Confederation is competent to legislate on matters of entry, departure, residence and settlement of aliens.[74] On the basis of this provision, the *Conseil fédéral* adopted the Asylum Law of 5 October 1979.[75] It constitutes the most important instrument relating to asylum and refugees.[76] It was modified several times, for instance in 1983, 1984, 1986,[77] and finally on 22 June 1990.[78] These modifications were followed by orders (or decrees, *arrêtés*) of application, in particular, the Asylum Order of 12 November 1980,[79] as modified in 1987, 1988 and 1990.[80] On 20 June 1990[81] an emergency Order (*arrêté urgent*) was adopted, valid for five years. It aimed at accelerating the asylum procedure and, thus, modified quite considerably the Asylum Law of 5 October 1979 as well as the Federal Law on Sojourn and Establishment of Aliens of 26 March 1931.[82] On 22 May 1991, two Federal Orders were adopted which complete the Asylum Law. Asylum Order 1 deals with the procedure;[83] Asylum Order 2 is concerned with assistance and financial

[72] Article 8a of the Act (1988:153).

[73] On 1st July 1992. See ECRE Country Report, April 1992 and October 1992.

[74] RS 101.

[75] RS 142.31; which entered into force on 1 January 1981: ACF of 12 November 1980, RO 1980 1729.

[76] H. Schoeni, "Refuge, Politique des réfugiés, Politique d'asile, Droit d'asile", Office fédéral des réfugiés, 1992, pp. 9–10.

[77] Asylum Law of 16 December 1983 (RS 142.31), which entered into force on 1 June 1984 (RO 1984 532 533; FF 1983 III 807); Asylum Law of 5 October 1984 (RS 142.31), which entered into force on 1 January 1987 (RO 1986 2062 2063; FF 1984 III 705); Asylum Law of 20 June 1986 (RS 142.31), which entered into force on 1 January 1988 (RO 1987 1674 1679; FF 1986 I 1).

[78] RO 1990 1587. It entered into force on 2 October 1990.

[79] RS 142.311; which entered into force on 1 January 1981: RO 1980 1730.

[80] Asylum Order of 25 November 1987 (RS 142.311), which entered into force on 1 January 1988, except for Articles 21–1 and 26–2 which entered into force on 1 July 1987 (RO 1987 1680). It repeals Order of 12 November 1980 (RO 1980 1730, 1982 2027, 1984 534, 1985 1632 1864, 1986 4 ch.I 5 2064); Asylum Order of 3 October 1988 (RS 142.311; RO 1988 1558); and Asylum Order of 2 October 1990 which entered into force on the same day (RS 142.311).

[81] RS 142.31; RO 1990 938, which entered into force the day it was passed as an emergency measure. A referendum was announced but never took place because of lack of a sufficient number of signatures (Article 89 bis 1–2 of the 1874 Federal Constitution). It shall be valid until 31 December 1995.

[82] See H. Schoeni, *op. cit.*, pp. 12–5.

[83] RS 142.311, RO 1991 1138. It entered into force on 5 June 1991. It repealed Order of 25 November 1987.

rules.[84] They constitute the second main source of law on asylum. The Swiss Appeal Commission in asylum matters was created as late as 1991 by a Federal Order of 18 December.[85] Other important provisions exist in the Federal Law on Sojourn and Establishment of Aliens of 26 March 1931[86] and its Decree of application of 1 March 1949, as amended;[87] in the Federal Order on the Internment of Aliens of 14 August 1968,[88] as modified in 1987 and 1990;[89] in the Federal Order relating to Entry and Registration upon Arrival of Aliens of 10 April 1946;[90] in the Order Limiting the Number of Aliens of 6 October 1986,[91] as modified in 1987;[92] in the Federal Law on Judiciary Organisation of 16 December 1943,[93] as modified in 1968[94] and 1978.[95]

United Kingdom
The Immigration Act of 28 October 1971, as modified,[96] is the most impor-

---

[84]   RS 142.312, RO 1991 1166. Most of its provisions entered into force retroactively on 1 January 1991.

[85]   RS 142.317.

[86]   RS 142.20.

[87]   RS 142.201.

[88]   RS 142.281.

[89]   Decree on Internment of Aliens of 25 November 1987, modified by Decree on Temporary Admission and Internment of Aliens of 2 October 1990 (RS 142.281).

[90]   RS 142.211.

[91]   Ordonnance limitant le nombre des étrangers (OLE); RS 823.21, RO 1986 1791.

[92]   Order of 5 October 1987 (RO 1987 1334); Order of 18 october 1989 (RO 1989 2234); Order of 24 October 1990 (RO 1990 1720) and Order of 16 october 1991 (RO 1991 2236).

[93]   RS 173.110, which entered into force on 1 January 1945.

[94]   Federal Law on Administration Procedure of 20 December 1968 (RS 172.021; RO 1969 757), which entered into force on 1 October 1969 (ACF of 10 September 1969). Article 1 (1) of the Law that "the present law applies to the procedure in administrative matters which are ruled by decisions of federal administrative authorities giving a rule on first instance or on appeal". The Asylum Law is quite express and gives the power of decision to a federal authority, in first instance (Article 11 (1) of the Asylum Law 1979 as modified by the Federal Order of 22 June 1990). The intervention of the cantons (Article 15 of the Asylum Law 1979, as modified) is only the result of of a delegation of the federal law and not an ordinary sharing of duties between the cantons and the Confederation. Therefore, authorities in the cantons do not take any decision in first instance but only provide to the Confederation the necessary staff to allow the Confederation to conduct a procedure that is totally under its control. In Philippe Bois, "Procédures applicables aux requérants d'asile", *Revue Suisse de Jurisprudence*, March 1, 1988, p. 78.

[95]   Federal Law of 20 June 1978 (RO 1978 1450; FF 1977 II 1205 III 612).

[96]   Immigration Act 1971, in Halsbury's statutes (1987) Vol. 31, pp. 47–112; as amended by the Immigration Act 1988 with regard to Overstaying and Deportation, Home Office Circular No. 37/1988, in Halsbury's statutes services (1989), Issue 22, Vol. 31, pp. 3–14. The legal bases of immigration control contained in the 1971 Act have been modified by the British Nationality Act 1981, which came into effect on January 1, 1983 (SI 1982/933, in Halsbury's statutes (1987), Vol. 31, pp. 112–79); see also J.M. Evans, *Immigration Law*, Sweet & Maxwell (1983), p. 72. For an enumeration of the relevant provisions of the Act, see, for instance, *Bugdaycay v. Secretary of State for the Home Department and related appeals*, [1987] 1 All ER, HL,954 et seq.

tant legislative instrument dealing with aliens and, therefore, also refugees. It is completed by the Immigration Rules.[97] Many orders and regulations are made under the Act "to deal with such things as the extension of the Act to the Channel Islands and the Isle of Man, entry through the Republic of Ireland, variation of leave to preserve rights of appeal, exemptions from control, registration with the police, and very importantly the Rules of Procedure for immigration appeals, and the service of notice".[98] Immigration Rules are made by the Home Secretary in accordance with s.1(4) and (5) and s.3(2) of the 1971 Act. Despite a controversy on the legal status of the Immigration Rules, it has been made clear that they have the force of law in Appeal Tribunals or even in the High Court.[99] However, "[t]hey give no rights other than those which are subject to an immigration appeal".[100] Changes have been made, and it is said that it is the Rules in operation "at the time of the immigration authority's decision" which are applicable.[101] Since the Statement of Changes in Immigration Rules of February 1980,[102] specific reference is made to the 1951 Convention: "Leave to enter will not be refused if removal would be contrary to the provisions of the Convention and Protocol relating to the Status of Refugees" (paragraph 64).[103] In the last Statement of Changes in Immigration Rules (1993), many detailed provisions on asylum and refugees were added, besides the usual reference to the 1951 Convention and 1967 Protocol, in particular Paragraphs 75A–C and 180A–R. Other relevant instruments are the Immigration Act 1988 on Overstaying and Deportation,[104] the Immigration Carriers' Liability Act 1987,[105] the Immigration Appeals (Procedure) Rules and (Notices) Regulations of 1984,[106] as amended, and the Immigration (Variation of Leave) Order of 1976.[107] A major reform of the asylum procedures started in 1991 when the Asylum Bill 1991 was published along with a draft of the new Immigration Rules

---

[97]   Since 1973, there have been new Statements of changes in Immigration Rules almost every year. For instance, Statement of Changes in Immigration Rules laid before Parliament on 20.02.1980 (HC 394), as amended by Statement of Changes in Immigration Rules laid before Parliament on 09.02.1983 (HC 169), as amended etc. The Statement of Changes in Immigration Rules laid before Parliament on 23.03.1990 (HC 251) was last amended by Statement of Changes in Immigration Rules laid before Parliament on 05.07.1993 (HC 725).

[98]   Ian A. Macdonald, *op. cit.*, p. 24.

[99]   *Ibid*, p. 25.

[100]   *Ibid*, p. 26.

[101]   *R v. Immigration Appeal Tribunal, ex p. Nathwani* [1979–80] Imm AR 9, QB.

[102]   HC 394

[103]   See also, HC 169 (1982–83), paras.16,73 96,134,153 and 165; and HC 251 (1989–90), paras.21,75, 98, 161 and 173.

[104]   Home Office Circular No. 37/1988; see also Halsbury's Statutes Service (1988), Issue 22, Volume 31, pp. 3–14.

[105]   Halsbury's Statutes, Fourth Edition, Current Statutes Services, Butterworths (C), Vol. 31, pp. 1–2.

[106]   Immigration Appeals Rules: S.I. 1984/2041; Immigration Appeals Regulations: S.I. 1984/2040.

[107]   S.I. 1976/1572 as amended by S.I. 1989/1005.

dealing with asylum procedures and a draft of new Appeals Procedure Rules. In April 1992, the Bill was abandoned because of the general elections. It was reintroduced later on that year and finally enacted in July 1993 as the Asylum and Immigration Appeals Act 1993. New Asylum Appeals (Procedure) Rules 1993[108] and new Immigration Rules[109] were adopted as a result. These instruments, along with the 1971 Immigration Act constitute the current legislation dealing with asylum and refugees.

Decisions of tribunals and courts (*jurisprudence*) are also an important source of immigration law. Easy to find as regards Germany,[110] France,[111] Belgium[112] and the United Kingdom,[113] recent decisions are more difficult to get in Sweden.[114] In Switzerland, although access to recent decisions is relatively easy, there are no decisions of the Appeal Commission before April 1992.[115] Both the discretionary power of states in the determination of political asylum,[116] and administrative practices should neither be disregarded as they introduce an element of uncertainty in the sources of law. Finally, provisions of EC law may also be considered as sources of immigration law. The principle of supremacy of EC law over national law is now well recognized. Any provision of EC law applicable in the matter should be the primary source of law. Such supremacy is provided by the written constitutions of Belgium, France and Germany. However, the situation is not so obvious in the United Kingdom. Courts do not have to take into account the provisions of the European Convention on Human Rights,[117] or of international law other than the 1951 Convention and the 1967 Protocol relating to the Status of Refugees[118] when interpreting the Immigration Rules, as long as the domes-

---

[108] S.I. 1993 No. 1661. Laid before Parliament on 5 July 1993, they came into force on 26 July 1993.

[109] HC 725.

[110] Decisions from administrative courts and the constitutional court are reported, for instance, in the *Neue Zeitschrift für Verwaltungsrecht* (NVwZ) and in the *Neue Juristische Wochenschrift* (NJW).

[111] They are reported in, for instance, the *Recueil Dalloz Sirey* and the *Tables du Lebon*.

[112] In for instance, the *Revue du Droit des Etrangers*. The Permanent Appeal Commission was created by the Law of 14 July 1987, therefore, no decision before then exists.

[113] In for instance, *Immigration Appeals Reports*.

[114] The Aliens Appeals Board was created in 1992, therefore, no decision exist before then, except for those taken by the Government. Furthermore, the Appeals Board has had to deal with such a number of cases that it is still, today, making decisions solely on the backlog. No recent decisions are therefore available at the time of writing. However, a book (in Swedish) including all the main decisions taken by the Appeals Board since should be published during the Summer 1994.

[115] Created in 1990, the Commission started sitting only on the 1st of April 1992.

[116] See, for example, A.C. Helton, "The proper role of discretion in political asylum determinations", *San Diego Law Review*, September–October 1985, pp. 999–1020. Although the article refers to the American Jurisprudence, it also applies to Europe.

[117] *R v. Chief Immigration Officer Heathrow Airport, ex p. Salamat Bibi* [1976] 3 All ER 843; *R v. Secretary of State for the Home Department, ex p. Brind*, [1990] 1 All ER.

[118] *R v. Secretary of State for the Home Department, ex p. Thakrar* (1974) QB 684, (1974) 2 All ER 261, CA.

tic provision is clear and unambiguous. However, provisions of EC law must be taken into account, where applicable, especially when in conflict with the 1971 Act or the current Rules.[119] As yet, neither Sweden, nor Switzerland are members of the European Union, they are, therefore, not bound by EC legal provisions. Nevertheless, they both are members of the Council of Europe and, as such, are bound by all the agreements adopted by that organization, in particular, the ECHR 1950 and its Protocols, the European Convention on Extradition,[120] the European Agreement on the Abolition of Visas for Refugees,[121] the European Agreement on Transfer of Responsibilities for Refugees[122] and the Convention on the Rights of the Child.[123]

2. General Features of the Asylum Procedure

National asylum procedures, in order to fully comply with fundamental rights, should include four elements: the protection of the right to be heard, the elimination of arbitrary decisions by referring to precise rules and criteria,[124] the respect of reasonable delays and the protection of human dignity.[125]

The right to be heard includes, first, the possibility for the asylum seeker to present facts and arguments which may influence his case and to comment on any other information in the hand of the competent authority. Second, it includes the time to prepare his presentation and the opportunity to present it orally.[126] Conclusions 30(XXXIV) of the UNHCR Executive Committee[127] recommended that decisions on manifestly abusive or unfounded requests should only be taken after a complete personal interview between the competent authority and the asylum seeker. In all the six countries under review, this decision is usually taken by the police authorities as soon as the asylum seeker has crossed the border. It is regrettable that this first interview arises with immigration officers who are not involved any further in the decision process. Conclusions 8(XXVIII) of the UNHCR Executive Committee[128] also provide that the applicant should be given the necessary facilities to submit his case,

---

[119]   Ian A.Macdonald, *op.cit.*, p. 265 et seq.

[120]   Paris, 13 December 1957.

[121]   Strasbourg, 20 April 1959.

[122]   Strasbourg, 16 October 1980.

[123]   Strasbourg, 20 November 1989.

[124]   This element refers to section 1. of this chapter, as well as to chapter four on burden of proof and rules of evidence, *infra.*

[125]   This element includes, in particular, measures restricting the free movement of asylum seekers as well as, measures regarding social and economic rights. This will be discussed in chapter five, *infra.*

[126]   Jesuit Refugee Service Lawyers Project, "Understanding the Refugee Status Determination Process" (Notes for Vietnamese Asylum Seekers awaiting Refugee Status Determination), IJRL, 1993, pp. 630–46.

[127]   On the Problem of Manifestly Unfounded or Abusive Applications for Refugee Status or Asylum (1983).

[128]   On the Determination of Refugee (1977).

that is, the right to be assisted by an interpreter and a counsel,[129] the right to contact a representative of the UNHCR and/or any other voluntary agency working for refugees.

In recent years, the length of asylum procedures has increased in many European countries owing to huge numbers of asylum seekers (including genuine refugees, war refugees and (il)legal immigrants) and has resulted in a problem that needs to be solved. Everyone seems to agree on the necessity of speeding up the procedures to guarantee protection and certainty about the future for asylum seekers.[130] Conclusions 30(XXXIV) put a stress on allocating sufficient personnel and resources to refugee status determination bodies. The Report on living and working conditions of refugees and asylum seekers[131] and Recommendation (85)1016[132] adopted on the basis of the Report by the Parliamentary Assembly of the Council of Europe, both call upon European states reduce the length of their asylum procedures to at the most one year.

In this section, the emphasis is on the first instance asylum procedure in the legal systems of Belgium, the Federal Republic of Germany, France, Sweden, Switzerland and the United Kingdom. Authorities competent on appeal as well as the procedures are discussed in the next chapter. For each country, I describe the national authorities competent in refugee and asylum matters and I analyse the procedure to be followed by asylum seekers, from the moment they enter the country until the day they are authorized to remain or requested to leave.

Belgium
The Belgian asylum procedure is in two phases. During the first phase, receivability of the application is determined by the Minister of Justice (*Office des Etrangers* or aliens office), the authority competent to deal with asylum matters. Only after access to the territory has been authorized, may the status of refugee or eligibility of the applicant be determined. This second phase is mainly the responsibility of the General Commissioner for Refugees and Stateless Persons (*Commissariat général aux réfugiés et apatrides* or General Commissioner). The General Commissionership was created by the Law of July 1987, within the Department of the Minister of Justice. Appointed by the King for a period of five years, the Commissioner is an independent admin-

---

[129] The right to be assisted by a counsel is also specified in Recommendation(81)16 of the CoE, which provides that the intervention of a lawyer should be permitted "at an appropriate stage" of the procedure, and if possible from the moment the asylum seeker is in contact with the national border authorities until a final decision on his application is taken.

[130] Consultations on this issue already started between the UNHCR and European countries in May 1985 (A/AC.96/INF.174).

[131] Rapporteur Mr. Boehm, CoE, Doc.5380, p. 14.

[132] Adopted on 26 Setember 1985. Text in, for instance, Doc.5930, CoE, 23 August 1988, Appendix IV.

istrative authority and enjoys full autonomy of his decisions.[133] The reform introduced by the Law of July 1987 may be described as positive to the extent that it created two new national authorities, the General Commissioner and the *Commission Permanente de Recours des Réfugiés* to appeal against decisions from the former. It failed, however, to solve the problem of increasing delays in the procedure arising from the continuous number of asylum seekers arriving in Belgium. The procedure was far too complex. While it created new grounds of non-receivability[134] and provided an obligation to give good reasons for all decisions, it also created a new system of appeal. However, the newly created authorities lacked of personnel and the system was prevented from working properly,[135] causing further delays and immoderate costs.[136] At the end of 1989, it was estimated that an asylum seeker whose request was considered admissible, could wait three years for a first instance decision on his status of refugee to be taken. Any appeal from that decision would lengthen this delay considerably. The Law of July 1991 made things even worse.[137] Most of the complex new rules were finally abolished by the Law of May 1993. This last attempt may provide better results regarding delays because it greatly simplify the procedure. It also creates further restrictions for applying to the status of refugee.

The current Belgian procedure may be broadly described as follows. Asylum seekers have eight days to request asylum and the status of refugee, from the day they arrive in Belgium. When such a request is made at the border, police officers transmit the declaration to the Minister of Justice, who must

---

[133] *First Annual Report of the General Commissioner for Refugees and Stateless Persons,* activity year 1988, Brussels, p. 90.

[134] Thus making access to Belgium more difficult and not as automatic as it used to be under the Law of 15 December 1980. Some of these grounds are specific to the Minister of Justice, some others are also of the competence of his representative and of the General Commissioner. The General Commissioner, Mr. Bossuyt, disagreed on such particular prerogatives specific to the Minister of Justice. Interview with Mr. M. Bossuyt, Brussels, December 1990.

[135] The *Commission Permanente de Recours des Réfugiés* faced real problems in the first months of its creation. Two hearings per months were planned but only one sitting at the most could be ensured for several reasons: non appointment or absence of the members required for a hearing, lack of lawyers competent to prepare files etc. It is the responsibility of the Minister of Justice to provide enough members for the *Commission* to sit, but it had not been done properly. Interview with Mr. Lefèbvre, President of the *Commission Permanente*, Brussels, December 1990.

[136] For a survey on the causes and consequences of such delays, see, for instance, *First and Second Annual Reports* (1988 and 1989), *op. cit.,* respectively at pp. 33–46,59–62 and pp. 9,10,14,15,29–41,54–58. The 1989 Report concludes that the year 1989 has been disastrous for refugee's instances. The aliens' office and the General Commissionership have registered such delays that reception's instances (transit centre at the airport, the *Petit Chateau* and the *CPAS*) are extended beyond their full capacity. The collapse of the procedure, particularly the phase of access to the territory, caused a greater attractiveness of asylum seekers and their number doubled during the second semestre of 1989.

[137] *Fifth Annual Report* (1992), *op. cit.,* p. 66.

inform immediately the General Commissioner.[138] The Minister of Justice may refuse access to the territory if the application is manifestly unfounded,[139] if the asylum seeker does not apply for asylum within the eight days time limit, if the asylum seeker is already in the country but apply for asylum only after his residence permit has expired, or if the asylum seeker does not attend interviews or refuse to cooperate with the authorities.[140] The Minister of Justice takes its decision within eight days. When asked to leave the territory, the applicant is provided with either an Annex 11bis (refusal to enter and *refoulement*), 13bis (order to leave territory after refusal to a residence permit) or 13ter (order to leave).[141] The decision of the Ministry of Justice refusing entry to the territory can be subject to an emergency appeal before the General Commissioner.[142] An asylum seeker, who is allowed to enter the territory, cannot be fined because he arrived without the proper documents.[143] He will be provided with an Annex 25.[144] He then have to present himself to the administration of the *commune* where he wishes to take up residence and to the aliens' office located at the reception centre (ie, the *Petit Chateau* in the Brussels area), where he will be interviewed. It is exceptional for an asylum seeker to be interviewed straight away at the border by a representative of the Minister of Justice, unless he entered the territory illegally.[145] Once the administration of the *commune* has registered the asylum seeker, he is given a registration certificate valid for three months.[146] Interviews of asylum seekers take place at the aliens' office (the head office or at the *Petit Chateau*). Fin-

---

[138]   Articles 50 and 51 of the Law of 15 December 1980, as last modified by Law of 6 May 1993. See also Article 71bis of the Royal Decree of 8 October 1981, as last modified on 19 May 1993.

[139]   According to the Article 52 of the 1980 Law, this is the case of a fraudulent application, of an application which is not based on any of the criteria of the 1951 Convention, the asylum seeker has already been the subject of an expulsion order less than 10 years ago, the asylum seeker is coming from one or more safe third countries where he stayed for at least three months (in total), the asylum seeker is in possession of a valid travel document to another country, or finally, the applicant does not provide any serious information to substantiate his fear of persecution.

[140]   Article 52 of the 1980 Law, as modified. Access to the territory is also refused in cases of threat to national security or public order (Article 52bis of the Law).

[141]   Articles 71ter and 75(2) of the Royal Decree of 19 May 1993.

[142]   Articles 63/2 and 63/3(2) of the Law. Article 113bis, ter, quater of the Royal Decree of 19 May 1993.

[143]   Article 53 of the Law.

[144]   Document valid for eight days and attesting that application for the status of refugee has been made. If the asylum seeker fails to register within the time limit of eight days, he may only be subject to penal sanctions. His presence should still be considered as legal. Tribunal Civil Bruxelles, *A. c. Commune de Woluwe-Saint-Pierre*, 17 March 1992; in RDE (1992) no. 68, p. 81.

[145]   This procedure at the border only takes place at the airport of Zaventem. See, *Asile en Europe, op. cit.*, p. 143. However, in some circumstances (sickness, absence of an interpreter, family with young children), the interview may nevertheless take place at the Aliens' Office, although the asylum seeker entered illegally. *Ibid*, p. 146.

[146]   Article 6 of the Royal Decree of 19 May 1993.

gerprinting is commonly used to avoid multiple applications. The interview is recorded on a questioning sheet. Questions are on the personal data of the individual, the route taken to arrive in Belgium and the reasons for seeking asylum in Belgium. An interpreter is provided when necessary, s/he must be independent and trustful,[147] as well as competent.[148] All admissible cases are referred by the aliens office to the General Commissioner. The General Commissioner is competent to recognize or refuse the status of refugee to an applicant.[149] He takes his decision mainly on the basis of a copy of the interview held at the aliens office or at the *Petit Chateau*, the questionnaire completed by the asylum seeker and the lawyer's opinion and suggestions. His decision must be reasoned. He may request assistance from the UNHCR for further information.[150] Decisions of the General Commissioner shall be notified to the individual as well as to the Minister of Justice.[151] The status of refugee is normally refused to asylum seekers who fail to elect domicile, who do not answer to a written notice to attend an interview or, who refuse to cooperate with the national authorities.[152]

Constitutionally, Belgium has been on the move since 1971 and aims at a Federation. These constitutional changes are not yet fully realized and the system operates badly. Centralism is still very present and, therefore, important decisions (the legal aspect of the reception of asylum seekers and refugees) are taken within the government by central authorities (the General Commissioner) while other issues (social and economic reception and integration) are shared between the central government and the executive authorities (Fleming, German and French). While the social reception of asylum seekers is the responsibility of the central authorities and the *municipalités* through the *CPAS (Centres Publics d'Aide Sociale)*, the social reception of refugees is the sole responsibility of the *CPAS*. A similar approach exists in Germany and in Switzerland.

Federal Republic of Germany[153]
The authority competent to deal with asylum applications is the Federal Office for the Recognition of Foreign Refugees (*Bundesamt für die Anerkennung*

---

[147] C.E., *Kaplan c. Etat belge*, 28 January 1992; in RDE (1992) no. 67, p. 13.

[148] To request help from another asylum seeker who has only vague notions of the language spoken by the applicant in order to fulfil the function of interpreter is not satisfactory. C.E. *Manou c. Etat belge*, 19 February 1992; in RDE (1992) no. 69, p. 190.

[149] Article 57/6 of the Law.

[150] Article 57/7.

[151] Article 57/8.

[152] Article 57/10.

[153] The Federal Republic of Germany is composed of Federal States (*Länder*). Competence to decide on asylum and the status of refugee belongs to the Federal authorities. The Länder are nevertheless responsible to provide material assistance to asylum seekers. See generally, *Asile en Europe, op. cit.*, p.80–6.

Ausländischer Flüchtlinge).[154] The Federal Office is based in Zirndorf but has offices in the rest of the territory. The Head of the Federal Office is appointed by the Federal Minister of the Interior. Officers of the Federal Office are not bound by any instructions and their decisions must be taken independently. However, a Federal Commissioner for asylum matters (*Bundesbeauftragter für Asylangelegelheiten*) is present during proceedings to represent the interest of the state.[155]

Aliens without entry documents must apply for asylum at the border. Aliens who have entered the territory illegally must report and apply for asylum immediately either at a reception centre or at the police or aliens authority.[156] In specific cases, the application must be made directly at the Federal Office.[157] Asylum applications made at the border are referred immediately to a designated reception centre. Leave to enter may be refused if the alien is coming from a safe third country,[158] or if he constitutes a threat to public order.[159] Deportation may be ordered and fingerprints and photographs taken. Asylum seekers arriving at an airport must apply for asylum at the border control post. Those coming from a safe country of origin[160] or without any identity paper can be detained within the premises and the Federal Office will be contacted immediately. Counsel assistance is allowed. Leave to enter is refused if the asylum application is manifestly unfounded and deportation may be ordered. If any doubt exists or more time is required concerning an application, the asylum seeker will be allowed to enter the territory.[161] Both this airport-procedure and the provision on refusal of leave to enter to persons coming from a safe third country were introduced by the new Asylum Law of July 1993.[162] Asylum seekers who are already in the country must apply for asylum to the aliens authority or the police of the Land of residence.[163] Interviews on the general profile of each claim are held at the border. Asy-

---

[154] AsylVfG, s.5. The Federal Office is also responsible for issuing deportation orders pursuant to s.50 and s.51-IV of the Aliens Act (AuslG).

[155] S/he is appointed by the Minister of the Interior and may participate in the proceedings and before the administrative courts. S/he can challenge decisions of the Federal Office. AsylVfG, s.6.

[156] AsylVfG, s.13.

[157] S.14(2).

[158] S.26(a) and s.27(1)(2). Safe third countries are EU and EFTA member states as well as Poland and the Czech Republic. See Appendix I, AsylVfG.

[159] S.18.

[160] Ie, EU member states, as well as, Bulgaria, Gambia, Ghana, Poland, Senegal, Slovakia, Czech Republic and Hungary. See Appendix II, AsylVfG.

[161] S.18a.

[162] B. Huber, "Prozessuale Besonderheiten asylrechtlicher Eilverfahren auf Gestsattung der Einreise", NVwZ 1994, Heft 2, p. 138. On the changes which occured in June and October 1992 (acceleration and simplification of the procedure), see M.-E. Geis, 'Neuregelung des Asylverfahrens", JUS 1993, Heft 2, p. 170.

[163] S.19.

lum seekers are obliged to cooperate with the national authorities[164] and, the Federal Office is responsible to establish their identity.[165] An interpreter or translator is available when necessary at all stages of the procedure.[166] Asylum applications, wherever made, are all transmitted to a reception centre[167] and asylum seekers are obliged to register at that reception centre, at the branch of the Federal Office. Fingerprints and photographs are taken.[168] At this stage, access to the asylum procedure is usually denied if the asylum seeker is coming from a safe third country or if he is without the proper identity documents. All other cases are dealt with by the Federal Office, at the Branch Offices.[169] Extensive oral interviews are held by officers of the Federal Office in order to determine whether or not the asylum seeker is politically persecuted. Asylum seekers must appear personally.[170] Hearing may be dispensed in specific cases.[171] At the hearing, the asylum seeker has to provide all documents, facts and information which will help the authority to take a decision.[172] Hearings are not public but the UNHCR can attend.[173] Asylum applications are divided into two categories: requests for asylum according to Article 16aI of the Basic Law[174] and requests for protection against deportation or expulsion to the country of persecution according to para.51 of the Aliens Law.[175] The first instance procedure ends with the Federal Office adopting a reasoned written decision which will be transmitted to the applicant.[176] Negative decisions are usually followed with a deportation order which is subject to judicial review. Immediate departure is normally required when the application is manifestly unfounded or abusive but also on grounds of public order or public safety.[177] In all other cases (political persecution has failed to be shown), the asylum seeker may be allowed to stay at least during the rest of the procedure but his freedom of movement

---

[164] S.15. Non-compliance with the duty of cooperation may result in the application being declared "obviously unfounded".

[165] S.16.

[166] S.17.

[167] S.20.

[168] S.22.

[169] Asylum seekers are given a certificate confirming permission to reside, valid for three months, renewable, as long as the applicant is in a reception centre, its validity is of six months thereafter. AsylVfG, s.63.

[170] S.23.

[171] Safe third country cases or for children under the age of six (s.24).

[172] S.25.

[173] S.9.

[174] War and civil-war refugees are denied asylum, however, they may be admitted to remain temporarily on humanitarian grounds.

[175] It used to be the competence of local authorities to examine facts. These powers were transferred to the Federal Office. ECRE Country Report by ZDWF, Germany, September 1991, p. 9 and October 1992, p. 8.

[176] S.31.

[177] Accelerated procedures are normally decided within one week. Bunderministerium des Innerns, "Das Neue Asylrecht ...", *op. cit.*, p. 13.

and residence will be restricted. Possibilities of judicial review exist before an Administrative Court and the Higher Administrative Court. Legal aid can be requested but is usually granted on the grounds of the applicant's chances of success. However, several organisations exist which can provide legal advice to asylum seekers (ie, the public legal aid offices, the Refugee Council and specialists lawyers working with the UNHCR).[178] An applicant, who is recognized as a person entitled to asylum, will be issued an unlimited residence permit and will enjoy the full status of refugee as provided in the 1951 Convention.[179]

Until quite recently, the whole asylum procedure could last more than eight years because of extensive possibilities of review up to the constitutional court in cases where constitutional guarantees provided in the Basic Law were threatened.[180] Since 1990, the new laws have reduced the length of the procedures, in particular the appeal procedure.[181] While accelerated procedures are usually dealt with within four weeks, in all other cases the average duration with the Federal Office is ten months.[182] On 1 July 1992, for instance, the revised Asylum Procedure Law entered into force and provided that manifestly unfounded applications should be dealt with within six weeks.[183] According to Mr. Norbert von Nieding (Director of the Federal Office before his resignation in July 92), "manifestly unfounded asylum applications do not account for more than 30% of the total. As for the new law [of 1st July 1992], it will not apply to the other 70%, whose applications may now take longer to process since there is still an acute shortage of personnel ... The former asylum law would have been sufficient to deal with asylum applications if the Federal Interior Ministry had granted his office the necessary funds and personnel which he requested many times".[184] The most recent amendment to Article 16II–2 of the Basic Law facilitates the refusal of even more asylum seekers, in particular those coming from safe countries of origin (now subject to the accelerated procedure) and from safe third countries (excluded from the asylum procedure), to enter the territory while still

---

[178] Ron Hooghiemstra, "Comparative Study on the provision of publicly funded legal services to asylum seekers in the 12 member states of the European Community", Immigration Law Practitioners' Association, p. 7.

[179] AsylVfG, s.68. Those protected against *refoulement* according to s.51(1) of the Aliens Law are equally given a permanent residence permit for exceptional purposes (s.70).

[180] The fist instance procedure usually lasts between a few months and three years but it was the appeal procedures which used to take so long. NIDI (Netherlands Interdisciplinary Demographic Institute), "Draft Report on Asylum Seekers and Refugees in Germany", 1 February 1993, Appendix 1, p. 7.

[181] Time limits for appeal were curtailed by the 1992 Asylum Procedure Law, as modified in 1993, and obviously unfounded applications are now subject to accelerated procedures. ECRE Country Report by ZDWF, Germany, October 1992, p. 8; M.-E. Geis, *op. cit.*, p. 170.

[182] *Ibid*, 22/23 September 1990, p. 53.

[183] *Ibid*, October 1992, p. 7.

[184] *Ibid*, p. 9.

at the border. Furthermore, the 1993 Asylum Procedure Law imposes very strict time limits in court proceedings.[185]

France

Like in Belgium, a distinction is made between the authority competent to decide applications for the status of refugee and the authority competent to grant a residence permit, therefore, asylum. The former is the French Office for the Protection of Refugees and Stateless Persons (*Office Français de Protection des Réfugiés et Apatrides* or OFPRA),[186] the latter is the Minister of the Interior,[187] who has delegated his powers to the *Préfet de Police* in Paris and in a few major cities, and to the *Commissaire de la République* in each *département*,[188] as it concerns national security and public order. This distribution of power creates a massive *jurisprudence* on the subject[189] and, one could also argue that it is a source of confusion for individuals applying for the status of refugee and seeking asylum as a result.

Before applying for the status of refugee to the OFPRA, asylum seekers must get a temporary residence permit. Asylum seekers with no visa, with a short term visa or, with a residence permit which has expired, must report to the local police authority (*préfecture de police*), where they will be issued first, a provisional authorization of residence (*autorisation provisoire de séjour*) valid for one month,[190] second, a receipt for residence permit (*récépissé de demande de séjour*) valid for three months and renewable.[191] Asylum seekers with a short term visa or no visa, still at the border (ie, the airport) will be referred by frontier officials to the local police authority where they wish to reside. They will be issued a safe-conduct in order to get there. Only if the

---

[185] AsylVfG, chapter seven.

[186] The French procedure for determining refugee status is organized by the Law No. 52–893 of 25 July 1952, as modified, which set up the *Office Français de Protection des Réfugiés et Apatrides* (OFPRA) and a *Commission de Recours des Réfugiés* (CRR). On the composition of the OFPRA, see, for instance, Goodwin-Gill, *The Refugee in International Law*, op. cit., pp. 173–4.

[187] Who has to consult the Foreign Affairs Minister.

[188] *Asile en Europe*, op. cit., p. 257.

[189] See, for instance, MM. Philippe Waquet et François Julien-Laferrière, "Droit des étrangers", *Rec.*(1986), p. 278 (*Conseil d'Etat*, 27 Septembre 1985). It is clearly said that if the OFPRA is competent to determine whether an applicant is a refugee or not, it does have any power with regard to the admission or stay at the border of any refugees or immigrants in the French territory.

[190] This authorization may be refused if the asylum seeker has already been subject to a deportation order or to a serious criminal conviction, if, having enterred the country illegally, he gives no credible reasons for such action, or if he is coming from a safe third country. However, refusal of the provisional authorization is not automatic. And special consideration must be given to asylum applicants. Finally, this authorization may be renewed, only once, and in extremely limited cases of 'force majeure'. FTDA, *Guide Pratique du Réfugié*, 1992, loose leaflet one, pp. 11–2.

[191] This document can only be obtained after application for the status of refugee has been made to OFPRA.

applicant does not come directly from the country of persecution can frontier officials refuse him entry and return him to a safe third country.[192] Formal application for the status of refugee to OFPRA can only be made after the first contact with local police authorities, during which a first interview is held. Quite short, it aims at checking the identity of the applicant and the non-fraudulent character of the claim.[193] Information is then passed on to the Minister of the Interior and to OFPRA, if the asylum seeker is allowed to enter. The asylum seeker has to fill out two questionnaires, one given to him by the local police and one by OFPRA. A file for each case is open. It will contain the two questionnaire forms, four identity pictures, a copy of the provisional authorization of residence, documents relevant to identify the applicant and all the evidences which may prove persecution. The asylum seeker can contact a voluntary organisation dealing with refugees and seek assistance from a lawyer and an interpreter. Once OFPRA has registered the file, the applicant is given a receipt (*certificat de dépôt*) which is necessary in order to get the receipt for residence permit. OFPRA has four months to notify its decision to the applicant. For many years, decisions of OFPRA were normally taken on the sole ground of the written documents or file.[194] OFPRA has only started to hold interviews in the majority of cases since 1993.[195] If OFPRA recognizes the status of refugee to the applicant, he will be provided with a refugee certificate (*certificat de réfugié*) valid for an initial period of three years (renewable for periods of five years), which normally entails the grant of durable asylum (*admission définitive au séjour*).[196] If

---

[192] The legal situation of refugees at waiting zones of French airports has been subject to severe criticism. The Law of 6 July 1992 legalized the waiting zone (also referred to as transit or international zone). Any alien who is refused access to the territory can be maintained and/or detained within that zone until deportation. During this period of time, the alien can seek assistance from an interpreter, a doctor, a counsel or any other person that he wishes to contact. However, a judge from *Tribunal de Grande Instance* may only intervene after four days and maximum detention may be allowed for a maximum of 20 days (Law No. 92–625 and Decree No. 92–1333; *Bayemy*, Cass. 2e Civ., 9 Feb.1994, Rec.(1994) IR, p. 58). Although officials from OFPRA used to intervene at airports, they have now no power to interview asylum seekers at the border. Police officers are competent to carry out all border interviews. See FTDA, *Rapport Semestriel pour la CERE*, July–Dec. 1991, p. 10 and Jan–June 1992, pp. 6–7.

[193] Pursuant to new Article 31bis of the 1945 Ordinance, as amended by the Laws of 24 August and 30 December 1993, applicants coming from a EU country or applicants whose application is fraudulent, are not allowed to lodge an application with OFPRA.

[194] *Asile en Europe, op. cit.*, p. 267, para.46; *The Guardian*, 14.06.1991, p. 27.

[195] Since 1991, no more backlog exists at OFPRA. Authorities are dealing with current applications. However, in 1992, only about one third of the applicants were interviewed. This number increased to more than a half in the year 1993. *Documentation-Réfugiés, Revue de Presse* No. 204 (December 1992), p. 1 and No. 210 (February–March 1993), p. 1.

[196] The card of resident (*carte de résident*) is given automatically to recognized refugees, by the *Préfet*. It is valid for ten years, renewable, and allows its holder to work in France. It is the role of the *Préfet* to check that the application for the card of residence is not fraudulent as it is his responsibility to refuse such documents to a foreigner (CE (opinion), *Abihilali*, 9 October 1992, Rec.(1993) JP., pp. 251–4).

OFPRA dismisses the request, notification of the decision has to be given to the applicant within four months. An appeal may then be lodged within the month following OFPRA's notification of its negative decision, or within four months of filing the request for recognition of refugee status if no decision has been made by OFPRA within that period.[197] A further appeal (*pourvoi en cassation*) may be lodged against the decision of the *Commission de Recours des Réfugiés* with the Council of State as Supreme Administrative Court (*Conseil d'Etat statuant au contentieux*) within two months following the notification of the decision.

Thus, it can be said that normally the legal procedure of admission of refugees in France should not exceed one year.[198] However, in practice, for incidental administrative reasons such as lack of personnel, delays in the procedure appear already at an early stage.[199] In cities such as Paris, Lyon or Marseille, asylum seekers are not given a provisional authorization to stay or a receipt for residence permit request automatically after their first contact with the authorities. They are often asked to call back for a further appointment, which is contrary to the spirit of circular instruction of 17 May 1985.[200] Such a practice delays, therefore, the remittance of the provisional document to sojourn, sometimes for weeks if the *préfecture* requests attestations of residence or other documents, which are not required by official orders.[201]

Sweden

The Swedish Immigration Board (*Statens Invandrarverk* or SIV) is the competent authority to decide on refugee and asylum matters. It is composed of two persons under a duty to report to the Government. It is based in Norrköping. It is a central authority attached to the Ministry of Cultural Affairs, which is the authority responsible for immigration and immigrant affairs within the Government Chancery. SIV's decisions to grant residence permits are taken not only on the basis of the Aliens Act and Ordinance but also on the grounds of prejudicial decisions setting precedents adopted by the Government and the Aliens Board on a case by case basis (the *jurisprudence*).[202]

---

[197] If the asylum seeker wishes to be personally present at the hearing before the CRR, he will have to make an express request in writing. FTDA, *Guide Pratique du Réfugié, op. cit.,* p. 19. See also, CE, *Auguste,* 26 June 1978, Rec.(1978) p. 336 (asylum seekers must have had the opportunity to be aware of the faculty to be heard).

[198] According to Circular on asylum seekers and the situation of the labour market (26 September 1991, Prime Minister), OFPRA should take a decision within two months and, if the case goes on appeal to the CRR, the whole procedure should end within six months.

[199] See, for instance, "Note regarding the shortage of personnel within OFPRA", in *First Annual Report, op. cit.,* pp. 83–4, which refers to the work of F. Tiberghien and the newpaper *Le Monde.*

[200] Circulaire relative aux demandeurs d'asile (JO, 23.05.85 p. 5776).

[201] *Asile en Europe, op. cit.,* p. 263.

[202] The Aliens Act provides the possibility for SIV and the Appeals Board to refer a case to the Government for decision. Such decisions set out the principles to be followed by SIV and the Appeals Board for the future. This is usually the case of applications for asylum involving

Government Bills and policy statements by Standing Committees of the Parliament, which precede amendments to the Aliens Act, are also a source of reference for SIV authorities.[203] Asylum seekers should address their applications to the local police authority or the border police, as soon as they arrive in Sweden.[204] Basic questions are asked straight away by the police and a brief report is written. All asylum applications must be referred to SIV as a matter of principle. Police authorities may nevertheless, in very rare cases, decide to refuse leave to enter to aliens without the required documents, when it is clear that they are not asylum seekers and that they have no other reasons to be allowed entry into Sweden.[205] However, in cases of doubt, the case must be referred to SIV. Thorough investigations are held at one of the four SIV's clearance centre to which all applicants are sent and it should not last more than four weeks.[206] Since 1 July 1992, SIV is sole responsible for carrying investigations on the credibility of asylum applications.[207] Applicants fill in a form stating the reasons for coming to Sweden and for applying for the status of refugee and/or asylum. An oral hearing should normally follow as a matter of principle provided by the law[208] but in practice it does not in most cases.[209] Strong criticisms by lawyers, the Appeals Board[210] and international organisations have been made against the denial of such a right. This appears to be not only a problem of resources to be solved by the politicians,[211] but also a problem of fear to be overcome by the Swedish

---

national security, terrorism or where a principle needs to be set out (ie, concerning Bosnians and Somalis). SIV has used this possibility to some extent. The Appeals Board has only used it for cases of security or terrorism or to suggest a change of directions in a principle set out some years ago. Interview with Mr. Fischertröm, President of the Aliens Appeals Board, Stockholm, April 1994. SIV is similarly bound by the decisions taken by the Appeals Board.

[203] The Swedish legal system on immigration matters is, therefore, very centralized.

[204] *Asile en Europe, op. cit.*, pp. 471–2, paras.13 and 15.

[205] K. Jönsson, *op. cit.*, paras.10, 13–15. Immediate refusal at the border and expulsion can take place against a person who after a negative asylum decision is under an obligation not to come back to Sweden for at least two years and, who ignores this obligation. Interview with Mr. Johan Fischerström, *op. cit.*

[206] *Asile en Europe, op. cit.*, p. 474, para.26. This is the result of the 1989 reform which introduced a new reception system for asylum seekers in order to speed up the decision process; see European Conference on Reception of Asylum Seekers, *Final Report*, 1991, p. 9 et seq.

[207] Before that date, such responsibility was in the hands of the police. The Swedish Ministry of Culture, *Immigrant and refugee policy*, 1993, p. 33.

[208] ECRE Country Report, Sweden, 3–4 October 1992, p. 123.

[209] A lawyer appointed by SIV for a specific case represents the applicant's interest.

[210] Notice that oral hearings do not usually take place at the Appeals Board either.

[211] Interview with Mr. Fischertröm, *op. cit.*. "We have suggested that there should be an oral hearing in every cases of first instance before a tribune or laymen. In the first instance, SIV should take into account, on one hand the state's interest, on the other hand the applicant's interest. Both sides should be included in the system. As it stands today, the state's interest is not involved at all in the procedure. That means that today, when SIV agrees to grant an asylum seeker the right to remain, that decision can never be brought to the Appeals Board. We think that it is wrong. There should be some person representing the state". *Ibid.*

authorities that interviews may result in decisions based on too much subjectivity rather then objective criteria.[212] Full cooperation with the authorities is necessary to show credibility. Withholding evidence or information, late applications, lack of the proper documents constitute sufficient grounds for asylum seekers to be refused convention status.[213] Cases of irregular entry are not treated less favourably than others. However, detention may be taking place until identity of the person is clear or further evidences found. Asylum seekers are allowed to be assisted by an interpreter as well as a lawyer, free of charge.[214] "Sweden has the principle that no one should be forced to leave the country without the right to consult a lawyer paid from public funds".[215] They can also contact a representative of the UNHCR or any organisation working for refugees.[216] In practice, however, it appears that none of these facilities is provided at the border (unless entry into territory is refused).[217] An interpreter is nevertheless present at the stage of investigation by SIV' officials, but rarely a lawyer.[218] The police, SIV and the Aliens Board as well as interpreters, counsels and lawyers, all have a duty of confidentiality. When the investigation is completed, SIV decides on whether or not to grant asylum and/or the status of refugee. SIV is composed of two persons, one responsible to present the case, the other one to decide.[219] The procedure is secret (no

---

[212]   Interview with Eva Singer, UNHCR, Refugee Law Training, Stockholm, April 1994.

[213]   Statens Offentliga Utredningar (SOU) 1994:54, "Utvärdering av praxis i asylärenden", Summary, p. 32.

[214]   Legal assistance in the form of public counsel is automatically provided to persons who SIV believes may be refused entry in Sweden. SIV, "To Persons Seeking Asylum in Sweden", June 1992. See also, K. Jönsson, *op. cit.*, paras. 26–31.

[215]   Johanna Niemi-Kiesiläinen, "The Asylum Seeker's Rights during the Provisional Asylum Period", in Asyl I Norden (Asylum in Nordic Countries), English Summary, p. 22.

[216]   On the difficult and delicate tasks of interviewing, see Eva Smith, "Recording and Evaluating Evidence", in Asyl I Norden, *op. cit.*, pp. 16–8. The Agency for Advisory Service, which groups Save the Children, Swedish Refugee Council and Amnesty International, since January 1991, deals particularly with helping asylum seekers to obtain strong information and evidences in order to be able to get a residence permit. Their task remains, unfortunately, entirely advisory and often ignored by the officials authorities. Information is usually obtained through organisations like Amnesty and is often in contradiction with that of the Swedish authorities (obtained from Embassies). Interview with the Agency for Advisory Service, Stokholm, April 1994.

[217]   "The possibility of having a group of lawyers at ports of entry has been suggested to the Government several times by UNHCR. Nothing has been established yet." Interview with Eva Singer (*op. cit.*).

[218]   It seems that today, the decision on whether or not an applicant is entitled to a lawyer is taken by SIV, following a short interview by SIV authorities which takes place before the more formal and detailed investigation. 'Ideally' lawyers should be already present during this pre-interview by SIV officials. Interview with Eva Ulfvebrand, Legal adviser, policy-questions, Swedish Red Cross, Refugee Section, Stockholm, Aril 1994.

[219]   According to Mr. Fischerström, *op. cit.*, "ideally, SIV could carry out all the investigations relating to the case, then leave a separate body (ie, a prosecutor), which would represent the state's interest, to look at the case, and then leave a court to decide the case."

public hearing is allowed), so are documents and information.[220] Under the Aliens Act (Chapter 3, Section 1) refugees,[221] war service resisters[222] and *de facto* refugees[223] are entitled to asylum in Sweden as a legal right, that is to say to a permanent resident permit.[224] Exceptions are: threat to national security; special grounds (ie, has committed a crime); arrival from another Nordic country or a country with which Sweden has signed a readmission agreement; arrival from a safe third country;[225] special links with another safe country.[226]

Following the reform of 1989, it was expected that first instance proceedings before SIV should never last more than six months.[227] Today, the waiting time for a final decision on a normal case is between 12 and 15 months.[228] However, in 1992, SIV was still dealing with some cases which would last four to five years because it was overloaded with applications involving mainly Bosnians, for which no decisions had been made yet.[229] Although it is true that no accelerated or 'fast-track' procedures exist as such, SIV usually

---

[220] However, SIV authorities may sometimes give infromation to lawyers if it concerns the individuals in question. Of course, lawyers must keep it secret. Secrecy is total at the Appeals Board and no information can be given to anyone. Interview with Eva Ulfvebrand (*op. cit.*).

[221] A refugee is defined according to Article 1A(2) of the 1951 Convention. Aliens Act (Chapter 3, Section 2).

[222] A war resister is defined as an alien who has deserted a theatre of war or fled from his country of origin or needs to remain in Sweden in order to escape imminent war. Aliens Act (Chapter 3, Section 3).

[223] An alien who, although not a refugee, is unwilling to return to his home country on account of the political situation there, and is able to plead very strong grounds in support of this reluctance. See also Aliens Act, Chapter 2, Section 4 which provides that an alien who, for humanitarian reasons, should be allowed to settle in Sweden, may be issued a permanent residence permit. However, this is not a legal right.

[224] Aliens Act, Chapter 2, Section 2.

[225] Notice, however, that unlike all five other countries under review, cases of safe third countries are examined substantially.

[226] K. Jönsson, *op. cit.*, para.48.

[227] *Asile en Europe*, *op. cit.*, p. 476, para.33.

[228] Interview with Mr. Fischertröm, *op. cit.* "We aim for the end of 1994 at a decision taken by SIV within three months and by the Appeals Borad within three months. So the maximum length could be six months. *Ibid.*

[229] The Swedish Ministry of Culture (1993), *op. cit.*, p. 33. A decision was finally taken by the Government in 1993–94 when a case concerning six Bosnians was referred by SIV to the Government for guidelines. The Government agreed that they should be granted permanent resident permit on humanitarian grounds. Consequently, 40,000 Bosnians were automatically provided a permanent residence permit. A similar decision has since been made concerning Somalis. Some people argued that temporary permits should have been granted instead of permanent ones but the Swedish system did not provided any such possibility at the time. It has also been argued that for a single political body to take such important decisions cannot be right. Interview with Mr. Fischerström, *op. cit.* Proposals for temporary protection should become part of an amendment to the 1989 Aliens Act in July 1994. It seems that it would be used in cases of major disturbances. It would only be granted for one year and would be related to humanitarian status. Interview with Eva Singer (*op. cit.*).

decides quite quickly on clear cases[230] and may order immediate expulsion before a decision of appeal is even reached.[231] Further steps can be taken before the Aliens Board, which is the supreme instance of appeal. Persons granted asylum in Sweden receive permanent residence permits. Persons who are also recognized as refugees may, upon request, obtain a written declaration of refugee status.[232] Those refused to enter are allowed to appeal from such refusal but may have to do so only after having left Sweden. This is the case, in particular, when the application is manifestly unfounded.[233] According to statistics, more than 70% asylum seekers arrived undocumented in Sweden in 1988 and 1989. The Government agreed[234] that "the lack of documents creates problems for countries of asylum to carry out a just and fair refugee policy; lack of documents is an abuse of the right of asylum; criminals and terrorists may make use of the possibility to enter undocumented and may be given residence permits under false names".[235] In cases where removal does not take place immediately or when the asylum seeker cannot prove his identity, police officers are allowed to fingerprint and photograph the asylum seeker.[236] Notice also that Scandinavian countries, including Sweden, are famous to "more or less automatically deport all rejectees".[237]

Switzerland

The Federal Office for Police and Justice (Federal Office or the *Office Fédéral*) is the authority competent to decide whether or not to grant asylum and the status of refugee to an applicant.[238] Proceedings for the granting of asylum and for the recognition of the status of refugee are not distinct. Within the Federal Office the recognition of refugee status and the granting of asylum is precisely in the competence of the Federal Office for Refugee (*Office Fédéral*

---

[230] As an example, a person is coming from Singapore and arrives at Arlanda airport. If it is very clear that this person is not a refugee nor a family member of a refugee, s/he will be sent back back straight away while still at the airport, because in such cases the border police contact SIV authorities by phone or fax and an answer usually follows immediately. In such cases, where it is clear that there is no case, no lawyer is normally called, nor any written decision even taken by SIV (interview with Eva Ulfvebrand, *op. cit.*). Similar practice exist concerning Polish people (interview with the Agency for Advisory Service, *op. cit.*) as well as people coming from another European country (interview with Eva Singer, *op. cit.*).

[231] An appeals against an expulsion order can be made to the Appeals Board. The latter will decide whether expulsion shall take place before or after a final decision. Interview with Mr. Fischertröm (*op. cit.*).

[232] Aliens Act, Chapter 3, Section 7.

[233] *Asile en Europe*, *op. cit.*, p. 472, para.16.

[234] Prop. 1988/98:92. In late 1989, the Government adopted the so-called Absence of Documents Decision, providing the line of decisions to be taken in the future by SIV and the Appeals Board on the matter. This decision contributed to a decline in the number of recognized convention and de facto refugees. SOU 1994:54, *op. cit.*, p. 28.

[235] Göran Melander, *op. cit.*, p. 3.

[236] Aliens Act, Chapter 5, Section 5.

[237] Göran Melander, *op. cit.*, p. 28.

[238] Article 11–1 of the 1979 Asylum Law, as modified.

des Réfugiés or ODR), a new term for the Delegate for Refugees (*Délégué Aux Réfugiés* or DAR). An important observation, however, should be made at this stage regarding the Swiss system of competence. Switzerland is a Confederation of cantons and municipalities. There are 23 cantons, three of which are divided in two half-cantons. All 26 cantons are considered as individual states within the Confederation. About 3,000 municipalities form the basic political units in the Swiss Confederation. They have their own territories, elect their own officials and are self-governing. They are, however, subject to the constitution of the canton in which they are situated. Since Switzerland is a Confederation, only a limited number of functions fall within the competence of the central authorities. The cantons are to a large extent autonomous in questions like public education, employment and taxation. Each canton has its own police. Although the final decision on asylum is taken within the Confederation (the Federal Office)[239] in Bern, the Aliens Police of each canton (*Police des étrangers*) has an important role to play in the process of decision-making. Interviews of asylum seekers are, indeed, conducted by the canton and a written statement or file is then transmitted to the federal authorities.[240] However, and this is important, the authorities of each canton are only used by the Confederation as delegates, the procedure is, therefore, solely a federal one.[241] In no case, may immigration frontier officers refuse entry in Switzerland to an asylum seeker. They must always inform the Federal Office, the sole authority competent to take a decision.

The Federal Order of 22 June 1990 introduced important modifications to the asylum procedure. Beside the usual asylum procedure, an accelerated procedure was implemented which would deal with asylum requests subject to non-entry (*non-entrée en matière*). This new system is explicitly provided by Article 16 of the 1979 Asylum Law, as modified. Article 16 consists in three paragraphs. Paragraph 1 enumerates the cases (a to e) for which an individual request for asylum may be subject to non-entry. Paragraph 2 makes reference to countries in which it has been decided that no persecution is occurring, therefore, requests for asylum made by people who flee from these countries may be subject to non-entry, provided they prove the contrary. Paragraph 3 provides that a decision on the ground of Article 16 paragraphs 1 and 2 has to be taken within six weeks after the day the request has been lodged and reason for it should at least succinctly be given to the applicant. In practice, it appears that the procedure of Article 16 lasts between one day and four weeks. However, such a procedure remains exceptional and for the great majority of cases it is the usual and full length procedure which applies.

---

[239] Article 69 ter of the 1874 Federal Constitution and Article 11–1 of the Asylum Law.
[240] Article 15, Asylum Law.
[241] Philippe Bois, *op. cit.*, pp. 78–9.

An application for asylum in Switzerland may be introduced abroad,[242] at a border check point,[243] or when already in the country.[244] Apart from *réfugiés sur place*,[245] all other applicants must present themselves to one of the four registration centres (Geneva, Basel, Chiasso and Kreulingen). Summary interviews are conducted in the registration centres. Basic questions are asked to the asylum seeker about his identity, travel documents, relatives in Switzerland, relatives who remained abroad, education, work experience, spoken languages, financial situation, political activities, grounds for seeking asylum in Switzerland, police record, travel itinerary before arriving in Switzerland etc.[246] The spouse of the asylum seeker is asked the same questions. Fingerprints are taken. To avoid concentration in registration centres, asylum seekers are then dispatched to the cantons according to regulations of distribution. The report written by officers in the registration centre is transmitted to the canton. The period of time existing between the day the asylum seeker arrives in Switzerland and the day he is interviewed by the aliens police officers in the canton does not usually exceed 20 days.[247] The principal interview takes place at the alien's police of the canton where the asylum seeker was assigned. Are present, the asylum seeker and a lawyer of his choice, the officer in charge, an interpreter when necessary[248] and a representative of a recognized organisation assisting refugees.[249] The asylum seeker is free to refuse or exclude the representative of an organisation

---

[242] Article 13a, Asylum Law. In this case, a preliminary interview is held by Swiss diplomats according to a standard form which will be sent to the Federal Office in Bern.

[243] A brief interview is held by police border officers, according to a standard form which will be faxed to the Federal Office within 24 hours. The asylum seeker's entry will be authorised by the Federal Office if he has the requested identity and travel documents or if it appears that he could be a genuine refugee or at least that he should be protected against refoulement. He has 24 hours to present himself to the designated centre (Ordinance 1 of 22 May 1991, Article 4–3). If the asylum seeker is refused entry, because he is coming from a country with which Switzerland has signed a readmission agreement, he will be ordered to leave the country, provided the UNHCR does not disagree with that decision.

[244] Article 31f, Asylum Law. The Aliens Police of the canton of residence of the asylum seeker (or *réfugié sur place*) is competent to register the application. As regards asylum seekers who entered the territory illegally, they are requested to present themselves, without delay, to the nearest registration centre.

[245] The canton is competent to register their applications.

[246] Article 14, Asylum Law.

[247] H. Schoeni, *op. cit.*, p. 15.

[248] Article 15, Asylum Law. See also Articles 32,33,12-c of the Federal Law on Administrative Procedure of 20 December 1968. Article 26 of the Law on Administrative Procedure also provides the right to consult the file, and Article 65, the right for judicial assistance (see also Article 4 of the Federal Constitution).

[249] Article 15a, Asylum Law. There are seven recognised charity organisations assisting refugees, the main ones are Caritas, Croix Rouge Suisse and Entraide Protestante. The representative usually acts as an observer. However, s/he may ask questions and complete the says of the asylum seekers. Lukas Stucky, "Description du role de représentant de l'oeuvre d'entraide", *Le Jalon*, December 1987, pp. 1–3.

from the hearing.[250] Presence of the representative of an organisation is, however, expressly excluded in decisions of non-entry based on Article 16–1 b,c,e and d (unless the asylum seeker went back to his country of origin).[251] Secrecy and confidentiality are strictly protected.[252] Questions asked concern essentially the reasons for seeking asylum, political and religious activities, military service and contacts with the security services. The asylum seeker's file is then passed on to the Federal Office. Its decision is normally taken on the sole ground of the file. The decision of the Federal Office may be one of the four: the application is subject to non-entry,[253] asylum and temporary admission are refused,[254] asylum is granted[255] or, decision may only be taken after further investigation.[256] Negative decisions are automatically followed by an order of expulsion stating whether or not the asylum seeker may be sent back to his country of origin. In cases where expulsion would be illegal,[257] temporary admission is granted.[258] Possibilities of appeal against a decision of the Federal Office exist before the Appeal Commission (*Commission de*

---

[250] According to Mr. M. Gonczy and Mrs. E. Grosjean (*Office Suisse d'Aide aux Réfugiés* (OSAR), Lausanne), interviewed in December 1990, a real problem exists regarding staffs. With the increasing number of asylum seekers, up to eight or nine hearings per day may take place in the canton, including sometimes Saturdays. Representatives of organisations are snowed under with work and often unemployed, retired people or students are called to do the job. See also the clear and detailed table by W. Stockli, in *Le Jalon*, December 1987, pp. 4–6.

[251] Ordinance 1 of 22 May 1991, Article 14.

[252] The right to be heard is provided by Article 15, Asylum Law.

[253] Grounds for cases of non-entry are: (1)the alien has not clearly requested asylum, (2)the applicant concealed his identity, (3)is coming from a safe third country whether or not an asylum procedure is pending in that country, (4)return in the country of origin, (5)violation of the duty to cooperate, (6)is coming from a safe country of origin. Article 16, Asylum Law. The majority of these cases are dealt with under less than six months.

[254] This is the case for manifestly unfounded applications.

[255] Asylum is granted is the applicant is a refugee according to Article 3 of the 1979 Asylum Law. According to Serge Bodart, when a country chooses to provide its own definition, although very similar to that of the 1951 Convention, risks exist that the national definition may be slightly more restrictive than the one provided by the 1951 Convention. Serge Bodart, *Les autres réfugiés. Le statut des réfugiés de facto en Europe*, Sybidi Papers 8, Academia, Edition et Diffusion, 1989, p. 18. Refugees granted permanent asylum are provided with a residence permit renewable each year for the first five years. Permanent residence permit may be granted after five years.

[256] The Federal Office may conduct a personal interview with the asylum seekers. Procedural guarantees shall be the same as for the interviews in the cantons (Aticle 16, Ordinance 1 of 22 May 1991). Before 1988, a federal hearing in Bern was provided for all asylum seekers. This sytem happened to be too centralized and too slow. Hearings, therefore, became the competence of the cantons. Since 1988, it seems that the Federal Office only hears 60% of the cases, when doubts appear which need to be clarified. Interview with Mr. Gonczy and Mrs. Grosjean (*op. cit.*). Also, in Alain Bovard, "La Procédure d'Asile Suisse", *Documentation-Réfugiés*, Supplément Juridique, 30 Mars/12 Avril 1993, p. 4.

[257] Either contrary to Article 33 of the 1951 Convention (*non-refoulement*) or to Article 3 of the ECHR (inhuman or degrading treatment), or also because civil war exists in the country of destination.

[258] Residence permit is normally granted for less than 12 months.

recours en matiére d'asile).[259] Like other European countries, Switzerland is still trying to deal with an increasing number of asylum seekers. It has, however, managed to reduce considerably the delays in the decision-making proceedings by providing an accelerated procedure but at the costs of many applicants. A thorough hearing with full guarantees seems to be provided only for those who appear as being genuine refugees after a brief contact with the Swiss authorities. Breaches of Articles 33 and 31 of the 1951 Convention may well arise if interviews at the registration centres are not taken with more vigilance. Similar guarantees to those provided in the cantons should be offered.

United Kingdom

All applications for asylum as well as for the status of refugee and wherever made are referred to the Home Office, Immigration and Nationality Department, for decision.[260] Although a technical difference exists between recognition of refugees and the granting of asylum, the decision is taken jointly within the Home Office.[261] Competent authorities can only exercise specific powers which derive from the 1971 Immigration Act and in accordance with its terms. According to s.4(1) of the Act, immigration officers are competent for matters of immigration such as access to the territory, the Secretary of State is competent to decide whether or not to grant asylum and the status of refugee. However, in practice, it is admitted that no Immigration Officer has the right to refuse leave to enter without consulting his superior (Chief Immigration Officer or Immigration Inspector)[262] and all asylum applications must be referred to the Home Office.[263] As for the power of the courts in the decision-making process, Lord Templeman held in *Bugdaycay v. Secretary of State*: "The 1971 Act does not allow the courts of this country to participate in the decision-making or appellate processes which control and regulate the right to enter and remain in the United Kingdom. This also is not surprising. Applications for leave to enter and remain do not in general raise justiciable

---

[259] Created in 1990, its composition and rules of procedures are provided by Ordinance of 18 December 1991. It started sitting on 1st April 1992.

[260] *Asile en Europe* , *op. cit.*, p. 443; see also, HC 251, para.75. Since 1 November 1992, the identity of asylum seekers at the border is carefully checked by the IND, while those already in the country must all go through the screening procedure at the Screening Unit of the Home Office, in Croydon (ECRE Country Report, United Kingdom, 3–4 October 1992, p. 135). Fingerprints are taken as a measure to check multiple applications and social security fraud (Asylum and Immigration Appeals Act 1993, s.3(1)).

[261] *Asile en Europe, op. cit.*, p. 445, para.12.

[262] HC 251, para.78. Two examples may be given to illustrate mistakes that can be done by immigration officers. *R v. Home Secretary, ex p. Minton*, CA, 8 November 1989, in *The Guardian*, 9 Nov. 1989, p. 39 and, *R v. Secretary of State for the Home Department, ex p. Rehal*, CA, 22 June 1989, in *The Independent*, 1 Sept. 1989, p. 15. The UK should consider more carefully Conclusions 30 (XXXIV) on the problem of manifestly unfounded or abusive applications for refugee status or asylum of the Executive Committee of the UNHCR which recommend that immigration authorities at the border should be qualified and specialised.

[263] HC 725, para.75.

issues. Decisions under the Act are administrative and discretionary rather than judicial and imperative. [...] The only power of the court is to quash or grant other effective relief in judicial review proceedings in respect of any decision under the 1971 Act which is made ...".[264]

Entry clearance is issued before the alien arrives in the United Kingdom; leave to enter is issued at his arrival. The holder of an entry clearance is checked at his arrival before being authorized to enter the country and leave to enter may be refused if it appears that the entry clearance was obtained by fraud or that conditions upon admission are no longer fulfilled.[265] Aliens without the required entry clearance are also sent back to the country they are coming from. Aliens, whom an entry clearance is not required, have to convince immigration officers that they fulfil the conditions upon admission provided by the Immigration Rules, before being given leave to enter. Asylum applications made at a port of entry must be referred to the Home Office and no action for removal can be taken before a decision is taken by the Secretary of State.[266] When the request for asylum is submitted after the applicant has legally entered the UK, Home Office officers will interview the asylum seeker. Entry in the country without reporting to an immigration officer (ie, stowaways or deserters) or with false documents or by any other fraudulent means, is considered illegal. The alien will be sent back automatically to the country where he comes from, unless he applies for the status of refugee and can show good reasons to fear persecution if sent back.[267] "A person refused leave to enter following the refusal of an asylum application" is notified of the decision by a letter which must explain the reasons for such decision as well as explain the rights of appeal available.[268] No removal may take place while an appeal is pending.[269] Asylum is usually refused if the applicant is coming from a safe third country,[270] if the applicant fails to cooperate with the Secretary of State,[271] if the asylum application has already been rejected, in the UK or in another country party to the 1951 Convention, and there is no new substantial element.[272]

---

[264] [1987] 1 All ER, HL, 955. See also the opinion of Neil LJ in the same case before the Court of Appeal, [1986] 1 ALL ER, CA, 466.

[265] HC 725, paras.14–16.

[266] HC 725, para.75 and para.180A. Asylum and Immigration Appeals Act 1993, s.6.

[267] He is a convention refugee or should at least be protected against refoulement, HC 725, para.180B.

[268] HC 725, para.75C and para.180N.

[269] *Ibid.*

[270] HC 725, para.180K. A mere stop at the border of a safe third country is sufficient evidence that he should have applied for asylum in that country.

[271] HC 725, para.180F–J. This includes, in particular, the application is not credible, cases of multiple applications, the asylum seeker is undocumented, the asylum seeker is coming from a country where persecution exists but he could have sought protection in another part of the country etc. Cases are decided on an individual basis.

[272] HC 725, paras.180L–M.

Asylum seekers are usually interviewed by immigration officers (at the border) or by Home Office officials (if already in the country). Although interview reports remain at the discretion of the competent authority, decisions to refuse entry in the territory must be referred by immigration officers to their superiors. The formal decision on refugee status remains, however, at the discretion of the central authority, the Secretary of State.[273] Aliens ordered to leave the territory have the right to contact friends or relatives in the United Kingdom, as well as an organisation specialized in refugee matters.[274] In practice, when asylum is refused to an alien at a port of entry, the Home Office will inform the Refugee Unit of the UK Immigrants Advisory Service (UKIAS) before removal takes place. This gives the UKIAS the opportunity to ask questions and advise the alien. Set up in 1970 as an independent body, the UKIAS is funded by the Government and doubts exist, at least in the mind of some refugees, about its independence and confidentiality. The right to legal advice and assistance and the right to choose such advice are important rights which should be protected at all the stages of the procedure. That free representation be solely provided by the UKIAS raises no major problem; but legal advice should never be provided exclusively by one organisation, more or less under the control of the Government. This particular issue raised much controversy in July 1991, following a statement to this end made by the Home Secretary.[275] This was, however, denied shortly after,[276] and no further provision regarding legal aid has been included in the Asylum and Immigration Appeals Act 1993. Thus, at today, free representation continues to be exclusively provided by the Refugee Unit of the UKIAS, referred to as the 'New Refugee Unit' since its restructuration, but legal advice and assistance can also be sought from solicitors trough the legal aid system. The right to an interpreter is also essential for most asylum seekers.[277] To secure confidentiality, it would not be superfluous that in all cases a second interpreter be provided. The right to be heard is as important as the right to be represented and to choose legal advice and assistance.[278] Like in most other countries, this right is often jeopardized in most of the cases subject to the accelerated

---

[273] The Secretary of State usually takes his decision on the basis of the interview and the complementary questionnaire filled out by the asylum seeker.

[274] On the role of voluntary agencies, see, for instance, Simon Field, *Resettling Refugees: the lessons of research*, Home Office Research Study no. 87, pp. 21–6; MRG Report, *The Refugee Dilemma*, Report No. 43, 1985, p. 10; R. Jones, *Vietnamese refugees: a study of their reception and resettlement in the UK*, Research and Planning Unit, Paper 13, London, Home Office, 1982, p. 7 et seq.

[275] Home Secretary, *Official Report*, 2 July 1991, Vol. 94, c.166–67.

[276] During the third reading og the Asylum Bill before the House of Commons. Hansard, Orders of the Day, 21 January 1992, p. 209.

[277] Interpreters are normally selected by the Home Office and only in exceptional circumstances may an external interpreter be called. *Asile en Europe, op. cit.*, p. 450, para.31.

[278] "Most important, in upholding the refusal to leave to enter, the Secretary of State had given the applicants no opportunity to explain their situation. ... Accordingly, the decisions would be quashed", in *Halsbury's Laws of England*, 1986, Vol. 52, p. 287.

procedure, in particular when the application is manifestly unfounded or abusive[279] or the applicant is coming from a safe third country. In such cases, applications may be refused without substantive examination.[280] It is, indeed, to be regretted that because of an increasing number of requests for asylum, the situation of refugees, particularly at airports, is often disastrous.[281] Although it is true that voluntary agencies do help, such help cannot justify the restrictive practices of Governments.[282]

In 1987 the British Refugee Council reported: "The Home Office acknowledges that it takes an average of 53 weeks to deal with an asylum application. But many people wait 18 months and in some cases more than 2 years. This is unacceptable, placing an unnecessarily prolonged period of uncertainty and stress on individual asylum seekers. While BRC accepts and encourages thorough investigation of asylum claims, the Home Office – which has publicly committed itself to dealing with 75 per cent of claims within six months – should be given the resources to do so".[283] In October 1991, the ECRE reported that it took "the Home Office, on average, 16 months to make a first instance decision".[284] In 1992, the staff of the Home Office Asylum Division was finally increased.[285] Legislative texts used to be silent on the details and length of the asylum procedure. The gap was partly closed with the enactment of the Asylum and Immigration Appeals Act 1993 which imposes strict time limits in the appeal procedure.[286]

3. Participation of the UNHCR

Conclusions 28 (XXXIII) of the Executive Committee of the High Commissioner's Programme[287] and Recommendation No. R(81)16 of the Committee of Ministers of the Council of Europe[288] recommended strongly that the UNHCR be involved in the decision-making process but left each state free to specify the form and degree of such involvement. The UNHCR is the only international authority specialized in the protection of refugees.[289] Such pro-

---

[279] Asylum and Immigration Appeals Act 1993, Schedule 2, s.5(3).

[280] For instance, the substance of third country cases shall not be considered (HC 725, para.180K).

[281] As reported in *The Guardian*, 6 November 1989, p. 6.

[282] See generally on the legal and the practice of the British Government, C. Vincenzi and D. Marrington, *Immigration Law – The Rules Explained*, Sweet and Maxwell (1992), Chapter 7.

[283] *Ibid.*

[284] ECRE Country Report, United Kingdom, 5–6 October 1991, p. 106.

[285] *Ibid.*

[286] Asylum Appeals (Procedure) Rules 1993.

[287] Follow-up on earlier Conclusions of the Sub-Committee of the Whole on International Protection on the determination of refugee status, inter alia, with reference to the role of UNHCR in national refugee status determination procedures (1982).

[288] On the harmonisation of national procedures relating to asylum.

[289] On the UNHCR, see, for instance, UNHCR, *Information Paper*, Secretariat UNHCR, Geneva, March 1993.

tection would, with no doubt, be better guaranteed if decisions on the status of refugee at national level, were taken after consultation of the UNHCR and with his/her consent. Most countries of the CoE seem to agree on this point but national practices show some discrepancies.[290] At one extreme, one may find a legal system which allows the representative of the UNHCR to be the sole decision-maker (this used to be the case in Belgium). At another extreme, the role of the UNHCR may be confined to that of a simple adviser with no institutional role and no legal effect attached to his opinion (for instance, in the Federal Republic of Germany, Sweden and the United Kingdom,[291] to some extent). The representative of the UNHCR in the United Kingdom has a consultative role during the first instance of the procedure. His/her role is, however, greater at the stage of appeal. Any notice of appeals involving a claim for asylum is in practice transmitted to the UNHCR branch office in London and "according to the rules of procedure, the representative of UNHCR in the United Kingdom may elect to be treated as a party to any appeal in which the appellant is or claims to be a refugee...".[292] In the Federal Republic of Germany, the role of the UNHCR is usually that of an observer and monitor. He has the right to participate in all interviews at the Federal Office.[293] Most of the time his/her actions concern individuals cases but s/he may also intervene on general issues regarding asylum policies. The situation in Sweden is similar to that in Germany. UNHCR opened its Regional Office for Scandinavian countries in January 1986, in Stockholm. In the past two or three years, it is also dealing with the Baltic States for geographical and political reasons. Its role is traditionally that of supporting asylum seekers and officials in the receiving countries. At first, Nordic countries started mainly as donors. They became important receivers of asylum seekers only in the late 1980s.[294] As a result of an increasing number of asylum applications since 1992, the post of refugee law training officer was created.[295] The role of the

---

[290] C.L. Avery, "Refugee Status Decision Making: The System of Ten Countries", *Stanford Journal of International Law*, 1984.

[291] Louise W. Holborn, *Refugees: A Problem of Our Time. The Work of the UNHCR, 1951–1972*, Scarecrow Press, 1975, p. 256, 263. Advice from the UNHCR may, for instance, be helpful for aliens already settled in the UK who may request asylum later on as it appears that if he may be asked to go back to his country of origin, he may fear there persecutions. Cf. Immigration Rules, HC 251, para.140.

[292] Goodwin-Gill, *The Refugee in International Law*, op. cit., p. 184. See also, the Asylum Appeals (Procedure) Rules 1993, para.8.

[293] AsylVfG, s.9.

[294] Soren Jessen-Petersen, "The UNHCR in the Nordic Countries", in Asyl I Norden, *op. cit.*, pp. 3–6.

[295] The creation of training officers appears to be the result of discussions which took place in 1992 at the European level and concerning the priorities of UNHCR in the future. It was agreed that UNHCR cannot be involved in all individual cases. Instead UNHCR should be able to train lawyers. In November 1993, Eva Singer became first official Refugee Law Training Officer for UNHCR in Sweden (interview with Eva Singer, *op. cit.*).

training and protection officer in Sweden[296] is, firstly, to advise authorities and lawyers about status determination, principles and information on countries of origin,[297] secondly, to deal with problems of family reunification.[298] UNHCR rarely interferes in the decision process. When it does, it is usually as an informal adviser rather than as a law-decision maker.[299] According to the *travaux préparatoires* to the Aliens Act, the Appeals Board has an obligation to consult the UNHCR. This usually happens when a particular situation arises.[300] An intermediary situation is found in France[301] where the UNHCR shares with the national authorities the responsibility of taking a decision. The representative of the UNHCR is present during the procedure of appeal, for s/he is one of three members which compose the *Commission de Recours des Réfugiés*.[302] S/he is also a member of OFPRA and, therefore, attends board meetings during which s/he is allowed to make comments and suggest propositions.[303] In Switzerland, the UNHCR's role is mainly to observe. The law does not provide any involvement of the UNHCR in the normal procedure. His role is, nevertheless, more important in cases of non-entry and at airports. According to Articles 16 to 16c of the Asylum Law[304] and Article 15

---

[296] Theoretically, there is one training officer and one protection officer for the all eight countries. However, in practice, both officers have divided the work so that one (Eva Singer) is responsible for training and protection in the Nordic countries, except Finland, and her colleague is responsible for training and protection in Finland and the three Baltic States. According to Eva Singer, most of her protection work is in Sweden, because both Denmark and Norway have a very strong Refugee Council. 'Thus, UNHCR does not need to do anything with regards to individual cases. We only provide training. As regards Iceland, there was one asylum seeker last year and he was allowed to stay". Interview with Eva Singer (*op. cit.*).

[297] As an example, although, accelerated procedures do not exist as such in Sweden, an asylum seeker coming from a safe first country of asylum (ie, another European country) is normally returned immediately. The decision is taken by police authorities, at the border, after having consulted SIV, within a day or two. The UNHCR is sometimes contacted when authorities require information or advice about a specific country. Interview with Eva Singer (*op. cit.*).

[298] Strictly speaking, cases of family reunification should be dealt with by SIV or the Red Cross, unless the case involves contacting relatives abroad who have no safe access to a Swedish embassy. For reasons of lack of personnel, however, almost all cases are referred to the UNHCR. Interview with Eva Singer (*op. cit.*).

[299] UNHCR never deals directly with an asylum seeker. It is usually approached by lawyers. "At today, there is no case where we have clearly say that this person is a refugee and this person has been rejected. They may not have been given convention status but at least they got a residence permit". Interview with Eva Singer (*op. cit.*).

[300] The Appeals Board, for instance, is now using the concept of internal flight in its decisions (which are binding on SIV) since it was accepted by UNHCR after consultation. Interview with Mr. Fischertröm (*op. cit.*).

[301] Law No. 52–893, art.3 and Decree No. 53–377, arts.9–14.

[302] Law No. 52–893, art.5; Decree No. 53–377, art.15.

[303] The UNHCR carries on a supervision on the OFPRA, as provided in Article 31(5) of the 1951 Convention. See Louise W. Holborn, *op. cit.*, pp. 257–8.

[304] As modified by the Federal Order on Asylum Procedures of 22 June 1990. Article 16 deals with subject of non-entry, Article 16a with rejection without further instruction, Article

of Ordinance 1,[305] the Federal Office for Refugees must consult the UNHCR in cases of doubt. Also according to Article 13d(4) of the Asylum Law, the UNHCR is strongly involved in cases arising at airport.[306] If at an airport, entry into Swiss territory is not allowed and return to a third country is not possible, the asylum seeker may only be directly sent back to his country of origin if both the Federal Office for Refugees and the UNHCR agree that the applicant will be safe from persecution. This provision gives the UNHCR an absolute right of veto because in cases of disagreement between the Federal Office and the UNHCR, the person is allowed to enter the territory and to benefit from the procedure. According to Mr. G. Köfner (statement translated) "this is something we long discussed about and finally agreed on. The idea is not to carry out masses of asylum seekers at the airport but to sort out the manifestly abusive and unfounded cases at an early stage. If there is the slightest doubt on whether there could be something which should be clarified, for instance no documents, for reasons of general human rights these cases will simply go to the procedure".[307] Finally, Article 48 of the Asylum Law provides a general obligation of cooperation between the Confederation and the UNHCR in order to solve the problem of refugees. In practice, the representative of the UNHCR follows carefully most cases. In specific ones he may even be called to make comments. When a disagreement exists between the opinion of the UNHCR and the decision of the Federal Office, the UNHCR will usually continue to intervene in the case. The UNHCR also intervenes to recognize refugees already settled in Switzerland but to whom the Confederation has refused to grant the status of refugee. If the UNHCR recognizes this person as being a refugee, expulsion or *refoulement* to his country of origin may not be carried out by the authorities. Such situations can create problems and the UNHCR has often had to go to Bern to discuss personally an individual situation. This possibility only exists in practice and nothing is provided in the legislative instruments. This kind of power to recognize a refugee only exists at an international level, which means that the Confederation can still refuse to grant the applicant such a status, but would Switzerland try to expel an applicant against the opinion of the UNHCR? However, such cases are exceptional and the UNHCR acts on a very strict basis.[308]

Belgium, finally, offers a quite unusual example. Until 1987, the sole authority competent to determine refugee status and to grant asylum was the representative of the UNHCR. The reform introduced by the Law of 14 July

---

16b with asylum or temporary admission without further instruction and Article 16c with other instruction measures.

[305] Asylum Ordinance of 22 May 1991.

[306] However, these cases represent only 1 to 1.5 % of the total of asylum seekers arriving to Switzerland (in 1989, about 350 persons out of 24000).

[307] Interview with Mr. G. Köfner (Head of Desk) and Mr. H. Buss (assistant legal adviser) at the UNHCR, Centre William Rappard, Geneva, 19 December 1990.

[308] Interview with Mr. M. Gongzy and Mrs. E. Grosjean (*op. cit.*).

1987 changed the situation radically and the power of decision is now in the hands of a national authority, the General Commissioner for Refugees and Stateless Persons. Various reasons were put forward to explain such a fundamental change. First, it was argued that the UNHCR discretionary power could be in contradiction with administrative law. The 1951 Convention, indeed, provides that the UNHCR should be the guarantor of the application of the Convention and not that he should decide solely on individual cases. Could Belgium have been in an exceptional situation for so many years? Second, it was held that concentrating so much powers in the hands of one authority puts it in direct confrontation with various kinds of pressure: from lawyers, non-governmental organizations (NGO) and the government. Even the morally prestigious authority of the UNHCR could not save its representative from all people's bad intentions. Thus, one may say that the UNHCR itself wished to withdraw but one could argue that pressures were so strong that no choice was left. According to the current representative of the UNHCR in Brussels, Mr. Von Arnim, it is a positive step that the UNHCR is not so much involved in the procedure of asylum.[309] The Minister of Justice welcomed gaining more power.[310] Other procedural factors were also involved in favour of the reform. The experience and knowledge of the UNHCR being assumed and unquestioned, decisions were not reasoned nor subject to any appeal. One may finally agree that the reform brought the Belgian procedure into alignment with the other European procedures. Although the reform appeared to be as satisfactory as it could be at the time,[311] important modifications have been made since. When the *Commission Permanente de Recours des Réfugiés* (CPRR) was created, the UNHCR was one of three members composing the authority. He had power of deliberation along with the President of the CPRR and the assessor.[312] As a result of the last reform introduced by the Law of 6 May 1993, the representative of the UNHCR voluntarily withdrew from the CPRR. Instead, he is now able to fully concentrate on selected applications which raise particular problems of protection or matters of principle at all stages of the procedure, including the border and airports.[313] His role is now consultative. He may give oral or written advice to the authorities at the border, to the General Commissioner or to the CPRR. Any decision taken by

---

[309] Interview with Mr. Von Arnim and Mrs. F. Lavry (for the Regional Representative), UNHCR Brussels, December 1990.

[310] Interview with Mr. M. Bossuyt (General Commissioner), *op. cit.* See also, J.Y.Carlier, "Réfugiés Refusés", *Revue des Droits des Etrangers*, No. 41, 1986, p. 183.

[311] Interview with Mr. Bossuyt, *op. cit.*: "what we are doing does not reach the level of what we must do". He meant by this that although efforts have been made through the Law of 1987 they are not sufficient and further actions should be taken. One new law cannot solve all problems at once.

[312] Royal Decree of 30 September 1991.

[313] Decision of the UNHCR of 13 May 1993 and Law of 6 May 1993, Article 57/23bis. He is not, however, competent to intervene during proceedings before the *Conseil d'Etat.*

one of these authorities which would be contrary to the UNHCR advice will have to be expressly justified.[314]

It thus seems that in none of the countries under review does the whole procedure last less than one year, except in cases decided under special accelerated procedures. While in Belgium and France an express distinction is made by the law between the authority competent to grant asylum and the authority competent to decide on refugee status, in Germany, Sweden, Switzerland and the United Kingdom, competence in both matters is concentrated in the hands of one central authority. This appears to be *a priori* more in conformity with recommendations of the Executive Committee of the High Commissioner's Programme[315] and of the CoE,[316] which put a stress on a central authority for decision. However, it does not mean that asylum seekers have a better chance to be granted asylum or to benefit from a wider protection in these countries. Procedural guarantees (ie, the right to be heard, the right to be assisted by counsel and an interpreter, the right to contact the UNHCR or a voluntary organisation) appear to be better guaranteed once the asylum seeker has been authorized access to the territory. Most facilities are, in fact, denied at the border where refugees need them most to be allowed entry in the country and access to the procedure. This practice is common to all countries and shows the present willingness of states to consider fight against illegal immigration a priority over the protection of even the most basic human rights. The laws, relating to the admission procedures of asylum seekers in the six countries under review, have all recently changed to meet this end. On a comparative level, France, and perhaps also Belgium, provides the most detailed, complex and formal refugee eligibility procedure of all.

---

[314] Article 57/23bis.

[315] Conclusions 8(XXVIII).

[316] Recommendation R(81)16. See, A. Swart, "The problem connected with the admission of asylum seekers to the territory of member states", in Proceedings of the Sixteenth Colloquy on European Law, *The law of asylum and refugees: present tendencies and future perspectives*, CoE, Legal Affairs, 1987, p. 84.

CHAPTER THREE

RIGHTS OF APPEAL

It follows from Article 3[1] and Article 13[2] of the ECHR that asylum seekers must be provided with an effective remedy against the decision to refuse their request for asylum.[3] Articles 32(2) of the 1951 Convention and 13 of the International Covenant on Civil and Political Rights (1966) are even more explicit.[4] Both articles provide, in identical terms, that "except where compelling reasons of national security otherwise require, the refugee shall be allowed to submit evidence to clear himself, and to appeal to and be represented for the purpose before competent authority...". Furthermore, Conclusions 8 (XXVIII) of the UNHCR Executive Committee[5] and Recommendation R(81)16 of the Committee of Ministers of the CoE[6] insist on the possibility for the asylum seeker to have his case re-examined. Conclusions 8(XXVIII) leave to the Member States a choice between reconsideration of the decision by the same authority, an appeal to a higher administrative authority and an appeal to a judicial body. Recommendation R(81)16, though not excluding the possibility of review by the same authority, does only refer to it as a measure of last resort. Finally, Conclusions 30(XXXIV) of the UNHCR Executive Committee[7] rightly require that the same opportunity be given to asylum seekers whose applications are considered manifestly unfounded or abusive.

Of the three possibilities suggested, review by the same authority offers the less guarantee, while an appeal to an independent court of law would be much

---

[1] Contravention of the prohibition on *refoulement* is equal to inhuman treatment.

[2] Anyone whose rights under the ECHR are violated has the right to an effective remedy before a national authority.

[3] Article 1 of the Seventh Protocol to ECHR grants aliens lawfully resident in the territory of a state the right to have their case reviewed. The Explanatory Report to the Protocol states explicitly that the provision does not apply to the removal of aliens who have entered the territory unlawfully.

[4] Notice that Article 32 of the 1951 Convention applies only to cases of expulsion, not to *refoulement*.

[5] On the Determination of Refugee Status (1977).

[6] On the Harmonization of National Procedures relating to Asylum (1981).

[7] On the Problem of Manifestly Unfounded or Abusive Applications for refugee Status or Asylum (1983).

more appropriate. As is apparent from the decision of the European Court of Human Rights in the *Klass case*,[8] an effective remedy before a national authority needs not necessarily in all instances be a judicial authority in the strict sense. In its opinion, however, the powers and procedural guarantees an authority possesses are relevant in determining whether the remedy before it is effective. It seems to be an arguable point whether a review of the decision by the same authority can be regarded as an effective remedy. The same applies to an appeal to a higher administrative authority if the decision by the lower authority was based on its instructions.

At today, the situation in the six countries under review can be broadly described as follows: in Belgium and in France, appeals are dealt with by an independent administrative authority, the *Commission Permanente de Recours des Réfugiés* (Belgium) and the *Commission de Recours des Réfugiés* (France) and a further appeal is possible before the *Conseil d'Etat*; in Germany, cases challenging action taken by a government official must be filed in the administrative court system (the Administrative Court of first instance or *Verwaltungsgericht*, the Administrative Appeals Court or *Oberverwaltungsgericht*, the Federal Administrative Court or *Bundesverwaltungsgericht*, in Berlin). Possibilities of further appeal exist to the Federal Constitutional Court (*Bundesverfassungsgericht*), in Karlsruhe. In Sweden, following important changes in the system, a court of appeal for aliens was created in January 1992. In Switzerland, appeals are now dealt with an independent judicial authority, the *Commission des Recours en matière d'Asile*. Finally, in the United Kingdom, appeals are dealt with by an Adjudicator, an independent judicial officer, a further appeal may be lodged before an Immigration Appeals Tribunal.

In this chapter, the emphasis is on the rights of appeal. Possibilities of judicial review are only very briefly mentioned.

1. The Belgian 'Commission Permanente de Recours des Réfugiés'

The *Commission Permanente de Recours des Réfugiés* (CPRR) is an independent administrative authority. It was created by the Aliens Law of 14 July 1987,[9] but started to sit only in June 1989.[10] Before the reform of 1987, the representative of the UNHCR was solely competent to grant the status of refugee. No system of appeal was provided and the *Conseil d'Etat* always refused to challenge decisions of an international body.[11]

---

[8] *Klass and Others*, Euro. Court of H.R. Series A, No. 28(1978).

[9] Article 57/11.

[10] Interview with Mr. Lefèbvre, President of the *Commission Permanente de Recours des Réfugiés*, Brussels, December 1990. See also, *Second Annual Report* (1989), *op. cit.*, pp. 18–9.

[11] J.Y. Carlier, "Réfugiés Refusés", *op. cit.*, p. 183.

1.1. *The Overall Appeal Procedure*

The Minister responsible for authorizing access to the territory (the Minister) is responsible for refusing entry into Belgium to an asylum seeker whose application is manifestly unfounded, who has already been the subject of an expulsion order less than ten years ago, who has stayed in a safe third country for more than three months or in several safe third countries for a total period exceeding three months, who has a valid travel document to another safe country[12] or who is a threat to national security or public order.[13] *Refoulement* may only be carried out after consultation of the Aliens Commission and a request to have the decision reviewed is possible before the Minister.[14] In any case, an urgent appeal (*recours urgent*) against such a decision refusing access to the territory is possible to the General Commissioner, within one or three days from the day the asylum seeker receives notification of the decision.[15] If the General Commissioner uphold the Minister's decision, expulsion will follow. If the General Commissioner disagrees with the Minister's decision, access to the territory will be authorize to the asylum seeker and the General Commissioner will become competent to take a decision on the status of refugee according to Article 57/6 of the Aliens Law.[16] Indeed, according to Article 57/6, the General Commissioner is competent to take decisions relating to the status of refugee. Except for decisions pursuant to Article 63/3 of the Aliens Law (*recours urgent*),[17] decisions by the General Commissioner cannot be subject to an appeal to the *Conseil d'Etat*. The CPRR is sole competent to hear the appeal[18] and all appeals brought before the CPRR have a suspensive effect.

1.2. *Composition and Functions of the CPRR*[19]

The CPRR is composed of at least three permanent French-speaking members (one president and two assessors) and of at least three permanent Dutch-speaking members (one president and two assessors).[20] Members of the CPRR

---

[12]   Article 52 of the Aliens Law, as last modified on 6 May 1993.

[13]   *Ibid*, Article 55.

[14]   *Ibid*, Articles 64–67.

[15]   *Ibid*, Article 63/2. See also, Article 113bis of the Royal Decree of 19 May 1993 relating to the procedure before the CPRR.

[16]   Article 63/2–3, Aliens Law.

[17]   Pursuant to Article 63/3, the Minister responsible for access to the territory can introduce an action for annulment against a decision taken by the General Commissioner if that decision is contrary to the Aliens Law or a Royal Decree. Such action must be brought to the *Conseil d'Etat* (Article 69bis, Aliens Law). See, for instance, *Fifth Annual Report* (1992), *op. cit.*, pp. 16–7.

[18]   Article 57/11, Aliens Law.

[19]   Refer to Articles 57/12–23, Aliens Law.

[20]   *Ibid*, Article 57/12. Following the reform of 1987, the role of the UNHCR within the CPRR became only consultative. It gained full right to vote following the reform introduced by the Law of 18 July 1991. It is only since the entry into force of the Law of 6 May 1993

must be Belgian nationals, doctor or graduate in law or in other disciplines,[21] and have at least 30 years experience. They are appointed by the King, after recommendation by the Minister of Justice, for a period of five years before permanent appointment.[22] Chambers may be composed of three permanent members (one president and two assessors) or of a single permanent member.[23] If the president has strong reasons to believe that the appeal is inadmissible or is manifestly unfounded, s/he may decide the appeal alone. However, if the appeal is admissible and well-founded, the single judge can send the case back to a chamber of three judges.[24]

1.3. *Proceedings before the CPRR*

The procedure of appeal to the CPRR is oral[25] and is usually open to the public, unless expressly requested otherwise.[26] The asylum seeker is present, he has a right to be heard and a right to counsel for his defence.[27] This is usually the first time the asylum seeker is in direct contact with the authorities taking a decision on his case because decisions by the General Commissioner are taken on the basis of files. The CPRR takes a decision on the substance of the first instance decision adopted by the General Commissioner. The Minister and the asylum seeker are both competent to introduce this appeal.[28] The asylum seeker chooses the language (French or Dutch).[29] Appeals must be lodged within 15 days of the notification of the negative decision by the General Commissioner.[30] The introduction of such a short time limit is fully justified to avoid abuses[31] and speed up the whole asylum procedure. Decisions of the CPRR, beside providing full reasoning,[32] must contain specific formal requirements, in particular, the names of the CPRR members who took the

---

and pursuant to the wish of the representative of the UNHCR, that it completely disappeared from the CPRR proceedings. See R.Foucart and G.Vandamme, "La place de la Commission Permanente de Recours des Réfugiés en droit belge", *Documentation-Réfugiés*, Supplement to No. 209, February 1993, pp. 1–4.

[21] Only lawyers may take decisions as single judge.

[22] Article 57/12, Aliens Law.

[23] A single judge is competent for cases brought under article 57/11(2) of the Aliens Law.

[24] Article 57/12, Aliens Law and Article 8, Royal Decree.

[25] Article 57/20, Aliens Law. An interpreter shall be provided when necessary.

[26] *Ibid*, Article 57/19. Confidentiality must be respected.

[27] *Ibid*, Article 57/18. Only documents officially translated may be taken into consideration (Article 13, Royal Decree).

[28] Article 3, Royal Decree.

[29] Article 57/20, Aliens Law. Article 3, Royal Decree.

[30] Article 57/11, Aliens Law.

[31] In particular, an asylum seeker whose refugee status and asylum have been denied by the General Commissioner may remain for indefinite period of time in Belgium until arrested by the gendarmes. If the time limit of 30 days (at the time this interview was carried out) did not exist he could lodge an appeal straight away and remain in the territory until a decision is taken. Interview with Mr. Lefèbvre, CPRR, *op. cit.* The 15 days time limit was introduced by the Law of 18 July 1991.

[32] Article 57/22, Aliens Law.

decision, the names of the asylum seeker, the name of his country of origin, his place and date of birth, the address of his elected domicile in Belgium and the date of the decision.[33] CPRR's decisions are notified to the asylum seeker, the Minister and the General Commissioner.[34] It emerges from a few decisions adopted by the CPRR that it gives a fully independent ruling. Many of its decisions have, in fact, quashed decisions of the General Commissioner, in particular on grounds of political opinion,[35] of religion or membership of a particular social group[36] as these are the most common grounds called upon. Two kinds of decision may be taken by the CPRR upholding decisions of the General Commissioner. It may either be a decision taken in the absence of the applicant[37] or a decision taken because the applicant fails to prove a fear of persecution.[38] Thus, like in other European countries, refugee status in Belgium is denied or withdrawn on the basis of Article 1C of the 1951

---

[33] Article 18, Royal Decree.

[34] Article 19, Royal Decree.

[35] A citizen from Zaire, member of the Union for Democracy and Social Progess, whose passport was backdated (29 March 1990; CPRR/88/478/F009); a citizen from Yugoslavia, whose story of his polical activities and following events arising to his family and, himself in particular, appeared to be likely and plausible, particularly with reference to the 1990 Report of Amnesty International (19 November 1990; CPRR/89/034/FA024). See also, decision of 12 October 1989 (CPRR/88/092/F004) granting refugee status to a citizen of Ghana who gave convincing evidence and details of his collaboration to the *coup d'Etat* in 1986 against the government of Ghana and, of his detention in prison for seven months. In another decision (14 September 1989; CPRR/88/0024/F003), the CPRR acknowledged that physical violence should not be only taken into consideration but also justified personal fears of persecution, in particular by objective elements whose family members were victims. The CPRR also recognized that some intimidating measures are specific to certain political regime (the Seychelles in this case) and provide a sufficient ground to grant asylum if it appears that the applicant is of *good faith* (29 March 1990; CPRR/88/537/F010). Finally, the CPRR quashed a decision of the General Commissioner on the ground, among other grounds, that fears of persecution should be assessed proportionally to the importance of the function fulfilled by the applicant within an opposition political party and according to the real risk run while fulfilling concrete and ordinary tasks (22 June 1989; CPRR/88/0021/F002).

[36] The CPRR agreed that persecutions may not only proceed from official authorities of a country (Turkey in this case) but also from a group of people further to serious acts of discrimination, voluntarily tolerated by official authorities or against which an effective protection by these authorities is impossible. The CPRR went even further by admitting that fear of persecution does not have to be extended to the whole territory of the country of nationality of the applicant (Turkey) but that persecutions against an ethnic or religious group limited to a part of the territory may be taken into consideration. In such a case, refugee status should not be refused on the sole ground that the applicant could have settle in another part of Turkey (8 November 1990; CPRR/90/263/FA015). See also, decision of 15 March 1990 (CPRR/88/515/F007) granting refugee status to a Christian citizen of Syria, whose brother killed by accident a member of a Muslim family. The applicant feared serious retaliation because she was his sister and revenge traditionally occurs against family members.

[37] The asylum seeker gives up the appeal procedure (12 July 1990/CPRR/89/221/D011) or the applicant does not present himself the day of the hearing and fails to answer a request for information (17 May 1990; CPRR/89/050/R071).

[38] For various reasons such as contradiction in the facts set out at the hearing and dubious assertions (13 September 1990; CPRR/88/487/R090); vague or false evidences

Convention as well as on the basis of the Law of 15 December 1980, as last modified in May 1993, particularly Article 52 (access to territory is denied) and Articles 57/10 and 57/17 (the alien fails to elect domicile in Belgium or fails to answer to a notification or a request for information within the time limit). Finally, appeals against decisions of the CPRR are possible to the *Conseil d'Etat*, as Supreme Administrative Court.[39] Such appeals may be introduced by the asylum seeker or the Minister of Justice, within two months of the notification of the decision of the CPRR.[40] Appeals to the *Conseil d'Etat* have no suspensive effect,[41] the asylum seeker will have to wait for the decision outside Belgian territory. Such appeals may only be authorized under the *ultra vires* principle (no review on the merits).[42] Articles 57/11 and 57/23 of the Aliens Law seem to rule out any other possibility of appeal.[43]

2. The German Administrative Court System and the 'Bundesverfassungsgericht'

2.1. *The Court System*

Appeals against a decision by the Federal Refugee Office must be filed within the administrative court system.[44] The court system in Germany is largely decentralised because of the division between Federal and Länder courts. Administrative courts (*Verwaltungsgericht* or VG) are established in each Land. They are regulated by the Administrative Courts Act (VwGO) and may only be approached following a preliminary administrative procedure of objection (*Widerspruchsverfahren*).[45] They are composed of three professional judges and two lay judges. Although, in theory, judges in VG should sit in panels of five, the practice in asylum cases is for a single judge to decide.[46]

(25 October 1990; CPRR/89/098/R099); see also, CPRR/88/225/R036 (2 May 1958) and CPRR/89/093/R087 (12 July 1990).

[39]   Article 57/23, Aliens Law.

[40]   On the concrete applicability of such appeals, see, *Second Annual Report* (1989), *op. cit.*, pp. 20–2.

[41]   With two exceptions: appeal against an order of deportation from the Minister of Justice and appeal against a royal order of expulsion, in which cases the asylum seeker may be allowed to remain in Belgium while waiting for a final decision. However, restrictive conditions must be fulfilled; see, J.Y. Carlier, *Droits des réfugiés, op. cit.*, pp. 69–70.

[42]   This system of appeal is identical to the one existing in France. See also, Articles 69 and 70, Aliens Law.

[43]   The question whether the first instance tribunal should also be competent was raised, nevertheless. See, J.Y. Carlier, *Droits des réfugiés, op. cit.*, pp. 70–2.

[44]   Notice that, according to s.71, AsylVfG (follow-up application), if new information or new evidence exist, a new asylum application can be made to the Federal Office. This possibility exists also in Sweden.

[45]   For details, see Nigel Foster, *German Law and Legal System*, Blackstone Press Limited, 1993, p. 132.

[46]   S.76, AsylVfG.

This possibility was introduced by the 1992 Asylum Law aiming at accelerating and simplifying the asylum procedure.[47] Appeals against a decision by the VG are dealt with a higher administrative court (*Oberverwaltungsgericht* or OVG), usually composed of three professional judges. Further appeal, on points of federal law only, may be heard by the federal administrative court (*Bundesverwaltungsgericht* or BVwG) in Berlin. The BVwG is composed of five, sometimes seven, professional judges. State attorneys are attached to this court, they represent the public interest. Important cases involving a violation of the Basic Law can be brought before the federal constitutional court (*Bundesverfassungsgericht* or BVerfG) in Karlsruhe. The BVerfG is independent from other state organs and from the courts. Its task is that of guardian of the Constitution. It is thus competent to interpret it in order to ensure consistency and uniformity.[48] Two senates of eight judges constitute the BVerfG. Decisions are taken by a majority of six judges. The first senate considers cases involving basic rights. It can hear direct individual complaints. The second senate considers political issues involving disputes between institutions and the government.[49] Like in other civil law countries, there is no rule of binding precedence. However, the rules of the BVerfG are binding rules of law on all courts. Moreover, in practice, lower courts (ie, VG) tend to respect decisions of higher courts (ie, OVG or BVwG), in particular recent ones, thus creating consistency wherever possible.[50] German judges in administrative courts are career judges. They are appointed for life and are independent. However, their independent character is limited to the extent that judges for the state are selected by the Minister of Justice and that considerable pressure exists for their advancement.[51]

2.2. Termination of Residence

Aliens who are not recognized as persons entitled to asylum and who do not hold a residence permit are issued with a notification of deportation by the Federal Refugee Office.[52] In cases where the application is irrelevant

---

[47] M.-E. Geis, *op. cit.*, p. 170.

[48] Constitutional courts exist in all countries with a written Constitution. However, the case of Germany is unique because Article 16a of its Constitution expressly provides a subjective right to asylum along with important limitations. In other countries such provisions are found in statutes (with perhaps the exception of France).

[49] Nigel Foster, *op. cit.*, p. 44.

[50] This is also the case in Belgium, France and Switzerland. The situation is of course very different in the United Kingdom, where the rule of binding precedence and references to old cases is strongly respected. As regards, Sweden, the fact that the Government continues to be strongly involved in the case-law making process makes it a separate case.

[51] M. Fullerton, "Persecution due to membership in a particular social group: jurisprudence in the Federal Republic of Germany", *Georgetown Immigration Law Journal*, Vol.4, No. 3, 1990, p. 394.

[52] S.34, AsylVfG. Notification is not, however, necessary in cases of deportation to a safe third country (s.34a). Aliens with a residence permit cannot normally be deported (s.43) but aliens in reception centres are not issued such documents (s.43a). Deportation may also be

or manifestly unfounded, the alien has one week to leave the country and any complaint against the notification of deportation must be filed within that week to the competent VG.[53] The VG will take its decision within one week following an accelerated written procedure, also called special summary procedure.[54] In such cases, if the VG sustains the complaint, the Federal Office must continue the asylum procedure.[55] On the other hand, if the VG rejects the complaint, there is no further appeal and deportation will take place.[56] In all other cases (the Federal Office denies asylum on other grounds than manifestly unfounded or the VG revokes the recognition), the alien has one month to leave the territory.[57] The aliens authority responsible for the district where the alien is obliged to reside, must be informed immediately by the Federal Office of any deportation decision as well as of any decision having a suspensive effect.[58]

2.3. *Court Proceedings*

Decisions from the Federal Refugee Office denying asylum on other grounds than manifestly unfounded can be challenged in the VG. Actions must be brought within two weeks after the decision was made.[59] Aliens have one months to submit facts and evidence.[60] Decisions from the Federal Office may also be challenged by the Federal Commissioner for Asylum Matters. According to s.6 of the AsylVfG, the Federal Commissioner is appointed to the Federal Office by the Minister of the Interior and is bound by its instructions. S/he can "take part in asylum procedures at the Federal Office and in lawsuits that are brought before the administrative courts. He may bring an action against decisions of the Federal Office".[61] Appeals from the Federal Office's decision have a suspensive effect, except where the application

---

suspended, for a maximum of six months, by the Minister of the Interior for international or humanitarian reasons (s.43a) or for a period of three months, renewable, if there are reasons precluding deportation (*Duldung*, s.41).

[53] According to a ruling by the BVerfG, "one week is sufficient time for an asylum seeker to react to a negative decision transmitted by an official letter and lodge an appeal", in ECRE Country Report, FRG, 3–4 October 1992, p. 5.

[54] S.36, AsylVfG. See also, ECRE Country Report, FRG, 3–5 April 1992, p. 6. Even in a summary procedure, administrative courts are not competent to dismiss the statutory classification of safe third country. They must refer the case to the BVerfG (OVG München, decision of 28.10.1993, NVwZ, Supplement 1/1994, p. 4). See also, B. Huber, *op. cit.*, pp. 138–9.

[55] S.37, AsylVfG. Deportation will, nevertheless take place if the court decides that such action is possible to the country mentioned in the notification (*ibid*).

[56] S.78, AsylVfG. ECRE Country Report, FRG, 3–4 October 1992, p. 8.

[57] Ss.38–39, AsylVfG.

[58] S.40, AsylVfG.

[59] s.74, AsylVfG. However, in cases of manifestly unfounded applications, the decision of the Federal Office may only be challenged within one week.

[60] ECRE Country Report, FRG, 3–4 October 1992, p. 8.

[61] S.6(2), sentence 3.

is manifestly unfounded or the applicant has found protection elsewhere.[62] Appeals against a notification of deportation and against a decision of the Federal Office on asylum must be filed with the same VG. The two actions will be joined and determined in one proceeding. Decisions are normally dealt by one single judge.[63] If the VG rejects the action as manifestly unfounded or inadmissible, no further appeal is possible.[64] In all other cases, a decision by the VG is subject to appeal to the competent OVG but only if authorized by the OVG.[65] Leave to appeal to OVG may only be given if the case raises fundamental questions, if the VG decision goes against the *jurisprudence constante* of a higher court (OVG, BVwG or BVerfG), or if there is a procedural error.[66] Appeal to OVG must be lodged within two weeks after the sentence was served and the application must be filed with the VG.[67] Decisions on such application are taken by the OVG and they do not need to be justified.[68] If the application is rejected, there is no further appeal, the sentence becomes final. If the application is admitted, the procedure of appeal will continue automatically before the OVG.[69] Full access to files by the lawyer is authorized in proceedings under temporary relief.[70] The Asylum Law also provides for the possibility of special arbitration bodies to be created near reception centres.[71]

Decisions by the OVG can be appealed to the BVwG, in Berlin, but leave to appeal will only be given for cases of principle involving important law issues or conflicting issues.[72] Finally, important cases involving a violation of the Basic Law can be brought before the BVerfG, in Karlsruhe. Disputes on fundamental questions between OVG and the BVwG may also be solved by the BVerfG alone.[73] Since the introduction of the airport procedure and the provision on refusal of leave to enter to persons coming from a safe third country were introduced, the BVerfG became *de facto* a second instance of appeal. Problems arose, particularly in the context of remedies, since Article 16aII–3 of the Basic Law allows deportation of aliens coming from a safe third

---

[62] S.75, AsylVfG.

[63] In cases where particular difficulties arise, this judge can still refer the dispute to the panel (s.76, AsylVfG).

[64] S.78, AsylVfG. For a complete analysis of s.78, see Kanein/Renner, *Ausländerrecht*, C.H.Beck'sche Verlagsbuchhandlung, München 1993, pp. 659–73.

[65] S.79, AsylVfG. *Ibid*, pp. 673–4.

[66] S.80, AsylVfG. *Ibid*, pp. 674–5.

[67] It must contain reference to the sentence subject to appeal and the reasons why the appeal should be admitted. S.80, AsylVfG.

[68] See K. Redeker, H.-J. von Oertzen, *Verwaltungsgerichtsordnung. Kommentar*, Verlag W. Kohlhammer, Stuttgart Berlin Köln, 1994, pp. 719–20, paras.19–20.

[69] S.80, AsylVfG.

[70] S.82, AsylVfG.

[71] S.83, AsylVfG.

[72] See, for instance, BVwG, decision of 12.02.1993, NJW 1993, Heft 43, pp. 2824–5 (no leave to appeal is granted when the question has already been answered by both the BVerfG and BVwG and, when the OVG has correctly referred to that *jurisprudence*).

[73] Ie, disputes on the intensity of a persecution, on authors of persecution other than the state, on internal flight alternatives. See, Kanein/Renner, *op. cit.*, p. 664, para.14.

country regardless of an appeal lodged against such decision and s.34aII of the AsylVfG denies interim relief from a deportation order under s.80 and s.123 VwGO.[74] While Dr. Joachim Henkel concludes on the doubtful constitutional character of s.34aII of the AsylVfG,[75] Dr. Bertold Huber argues that s.34aII must be interpreted restrictively so as not to be extended to removals, as understood in the sense used in ss.18,19 AsylVfG.[76] One may conclude that these new limitations will only increase the workload of the B VerfG.

3. The French 'Commission de Recours des Réfugiés'

The complexity of the French system of appeal is largely due to the fact that two authorities are competent to deal with asylum seekers. While the Interior Minister is competent to decide on asylum matters, the OFPRA is competent to grant the status of refugee. Article 5 of the Law of the 25 July 1952[77] creates the *Commission de Recours des Réfugiés* (CRR) and the Decree of 2 May 1953 gives it a double role.[78] The first role of CRR is to decide on appeals against OFPRA's refusal to recognize the status of refugee.[79] Its second role is to advise the Interior Minister concerning refugees' requests relating to administrative measures, ie, expulsion and *assignation à résidence*, taken against them in the light of Articles 31, 32 and 33 of the 1951 Convention.[80]

3.1. *Situations in Which Asylum and/or the Status of Refugee Are Denied*

The Minister of the Interior is competent to order expulsion, the *préfet de police* is competent to order deportation or *refoulement*.[81] An asylum seeker may be *refoulé* if another state is responsible to decide on the application pursuant to the Dublin Convention, the Schengen Agreement or any other international agreement on the matter, or if the applicant is admitted in another state, which is not his country of origin, and in which protection against

---

[74] See, Joachim Henkel, *op. cit.*, p. 2708.

[75] *Ibid.*

[76] B. Huber, *op. cit.*, p. 139.

[77] Law No. 52–893, as modified by Law No. 90–550 of 2 July 1990 and Law No. 93–1027 of 24 August 1993.

[78] Decree No. 53–377, see, in particular, Articles 15–29. Since its modification by Decree No. 90–968 of 29 October 1990, Decree No. 53–377 is now referred to as the "Decree relating to OFPRA *and to CRR*". It was again very slightly amended by Decree No. 91–314 of 26 March 1991 and Decree No. 92–732 of 30 July 1992.

[79] On these *attributions juridictionnelles*, see, F. Tiberghien, *La protection des réfugiés en France*, Presses Universitaires d'Aix-Marseilles, Economica, 1988, pp. 79–178.

[80] Such advisory jurisdiction is in conformity with French administrative law tradition, which allows a wide area of discretion to certain executive authorities, in particular, the Minister of the Interior. On these *attributions consultatives*, see, F. Tiberghien, *op. cit.*, pp. 179–205. Notice that such requests may be made not only against orders of expulsion but also against order of deportation or *refoulement*.

[81] Article 28, 1945 Ordinance (as modified in 1993).

refoulement is guaranteed, or if the application is fraudulent or manifestly unfounded or abusive.[82] In such cases, the asylum seeker is, nevertheless, entitled to apply for refugee status to OFPRA and *refoulement* shall not occur while the procedure is pending.[83] OFPRA will consider such cases in priority over any other cases.[84] A refugee recognized by OFPRA shall be issued a residence permit, except if he constitutes a threat to public order.[85] A residence permit can be withdrawn during the first three years of its issuance, to a refugee who voluntarily find himself in a situation provided by Article 1C(1)to(4) of the 1951 Convention.[86] The decision providing the country to which the alien shall be deported constitutes a separate decision from the one ordering *refoulement*. Appeals against the country of destination in cases of *refoulement* shall have a suspensive effect only if it is brought to the administrative tribunal at the same time as the appeal against the order of *refoulement*. In all such cases of expulsion or *refoulement*, CRR has a consultative role.

OFPRA is only competent to decide on a refugee status application once a decision on access to the territory has been made by the *préfet de police*.[87] In cases where OFPRA denies refugee status to an asylum seeker, an appeal against that decision can be brought to CRR. Article 1D,E,F of the 1951 Convention deals with situations in which the applicant for refugee status, therefore an appellant to CRR, is not entitled to benefit from the status of refugee.[88] However, since CRR was created, its case-law on the subject has increased and decisions of CRR may now be classified into five types of situation which entail the denial of refugee status. The first situation includes cases where the appellant has not lawfully obtained the status of refugee,[89] the second type of situation is when the appellant has another nationality than the one of his country of origin,[90] the third is when the appellant has found a country of protection. For 25 years, CRR refused to grant asylum to a person coming from a third country where he found residence and protection. However, in 1984, the *Conseil d'Etat* disagreed with CRR and quashed a decision[91] which refused to grant the status of refugee to the applicant only

---

[82] New Article 31bis, Ordinance of 1945. The state (Ministry of the Interior) remains, however, free to grant asylum as a matter of discretion.

[83] New Article 32bis, Ordinance of 1945.

[84] Article 2 of the Law of 1952.

[85] Article 15, Ordinance of 1945. In cases of serious threat to public order, an alien may be expelled by the Interior Minister. The procedure of expulsion is provided in Articles 22 to 26 of the 1945 Ordinance, as modified. Special provisions, however, apply to asylum seekers (see chapter VII of the Ordinance).

[86] Article 16, Ordinance of 1945.

[87] Article 2, Law of 1952.

[88] See, F. Tiberghien, *op. cit.*, pp. 102–8.

[89] *Ibid*, p. 109.

[90] *Ibid*, pp. 109–10.

[91] CE ass., *Conté*, 16 janvier 1981 (Rec.(1981), Jurisprudence, p. 250 et seq.). In this decision, the French *Conseil d'Etat* quashed the decision of CRR and opted for a more liberal

because the applicant found protection in a third country. A mere visit to the country of origin does not either normally lead to the withdrawal of refugee status.[92] However, the scope of this *jurisprudence* is now subject to serious limitations since the signing by France of the Schengen and Dublin Conventions, as well as other bilateral agreements on readmission.[93] The fourth situation refers to cases where the appellant loses his refugee status with regard to Article 1C of the 1951 Convention, because he has voluntarily re-availed himself of the protection of the country of his nationality; or has voluntarily re-acquired his nationality; or has acquired a new nationality and enjoys protection of the country of his new nationality; or he has voluntarily re-established himself in the country which he feared persecution; or the circumstances in connection with which he has been recognized as a refugee have ceased.[94] Finally, the straightforward case where the asylum seeker simply does not and cannot satisfy the necessary conditions stated in Article 1A(2) of the 1951 Convention.[95]

3.2. *Composition and Functions of the CRR*

The CRR is composed of three members. Chaired by a judge (a member of the *Conseil d'Etat*, of the *Cour des Comptes*, of an administrative appeal court or of an administrative tribunal), it also includes a representative of the board of OFPRA and a representative of the UNHCR.[96] This is the only example of a non-French authority authorized to be present and to deliberate in the taking of French law decisions.[97] CRR is an administrative jurisdiction and, as such, is subject to a further appeal (*pourvoi en cassation*) to the *Conseil d'Etat statuant au contentieux* (Council of State as Supreme Administrative Court) on a point of law, such as a legal flaw or irregularity in the procedure, misrepresentation of facts or documents.[98] A appeal to the *Conseil d'Etat* must be lodged within two months following the notification of the decision of CRR.[99]

---

view on the matter, that is to say the status of refugee cannot be refused on the sole ground that the refugee has settled in a third country before arriving in the country where he applied for asylum.

[92] F. Tiberghien, *op. cit.*, pp. 110–2.

[93] See, chapter four, *infra*.

[94] F. Tiberghien, *op. cit.*, pp. 112–34.

[95] *Ibid*, p. 83 et seq.

[96] Article 23, Decree of 1953.

[97] See, A.Heilbronner, "La Commission de Recours des Réfugiés", *Etudes et Documents du Conseil d'Etat*, 1978–79, p. 110.

[98] It seems quite rare for the *Conseil d'Etat* to quash a decision of CRR but it has happened, on a few occasions, particularly concerning the "basques espagnols".

[99] F. Tiberghien, *op. cit.*, pp. 176–8.

3.3. *Procedure Before the CRR*

In cases where OFPRA refuses to grant the status of refugee to an asylum seeker, the latter has one month, from the day of the notification of OFPRA's decision,[100] to appeal against such decision to CRR or, four months, from the day the request for recognition of refugee status was filed, if no decision has been made by the OFPRA within that period.[101] This appeal has a suspensive effect.[102] In cases of expulsion or deportation, pursuant to Articles 31–33 of the 1951 Convention, the asylum seeker has one week to request an advice from CRR.[103] Such request has a suspensive effect.[104] The basic procedure for appeals is set out in Decree No. 53–377, as modified.

Concerning appeals against a decision from OFPRA, hearings are public, although closed sessions can be required.[105] The chairman is provided with copies of the appellant's grounds of appeal and the observations of the OFPRA. After a presentation of the case by the chairman, with or without a recommendation, the appellant, alone or through counsel, presents his claim.[106] Given the nature of the case, the standard of proof required of the applicant is less rigorous than in other branches of law. However, CRR has a discretion to grant an oral hearing which may enable the applicant not only to clear up any ambiguities which have emerged from his written submissions but also to show his sincerity. Legal aim may be provided before the CRR but such aid is largely depending on the chances of a successful outcome.[107] To claim the status of refugee, the asylum seeker must show that he is a victim of persecution for reasons of race, religion, nationality, adherence to a particular social group or his political opinions. CRR is com-

---

[100] OFPRA decisions are also notified to the relevant *préfecture.*

[101] Article 20, Decree of 1953; Article 5, Law of 1952.

[102] See, FTDA, "Rapport semestriel pour la CERE", France, July-December 1991, p. 9 (concerning two decisions from the CE of December 1991) and see, IJRL, 1994, p. 121, for an abstract of another decision from the CE, on the matter.

[103] Article 27, Decree of 1953.

[104] Notice that appeals against a decision of immediate refusal at the border must be lodged within the competent administrative tribunal. Such appeals are rare and have no suspensive effect.

[105] Article 23, 1953 Decree.

[106] Since 1978, the *Conseil d'Etat* has decided that, according to Art.5 of the 25 July 1952 Law which provides to the appellant a right to make any oral observations to CRR (see also, Article 24, Decree), the appellant should theoretically always be called before CRR. However, because in practice this would make the procedure too heavy, the *Conseil d'Etat* decided to, at least, always give the appellants the faculty to know and be guaranteed that they have the possibility to be heard (CE, *Auguste,* 26 July 1978, in F. Tiberghien, *op. cit.,* p. 236) but still insist that this possibility is not provided by any statute or decree and therefore the rule is of a general scope (CE, *Prempeh,* 13 November 1985, Rec.1986, IR 283) and, thus, remains at the discretion of CRR. See also, the case *Chandra* of 9 February 1994, in which the *Conseil d'Etat* ruled that CRR must notify the date of the hearing to the appellant and his counsel. However, if counsel never replied that he would represent the appellant, CRR did not have to notify him/her the date of the hearing (Rec.1994, IR 73).

[107] FTDA, *Guide Pratique du Réfugié, op. cit.,* pp. 21–2.

petent to determine the meaning and limits of "persecution". Of necessity its interpretation has been restrictive[108] but it seems not as restrictive as that of OFPRA.[109] CRR commonly questions appellants, and also has the power to ask for supplementary inquiries. The representative from OFPRA may also present the views of the board to CRR.[110] The decision itself is given in public and must be reasoned.[111] The decision and its reasons are then communicated to the appellant and OFPRA. If the decision recognizes the appellant's refugee status, OFPRA is required to issue immediately a *certificat de réfugié*. If the decision withdrawing the status of refugee is confirmed, the applicant has to leave French territory within a month or may be subject to legal proceedings.[112] However, he may be allowed to stay in French territory if he was already settled in France or if he arrived with long term visa. He will then be submitted to the general regime of aliens.

Refugees against whom a measure of expulsion or *refoulement* applies, pursuant to Articles 31–33 of the 1951 Convention, may refer a request to CRR.[113] Such requests shall be immediately transmitted by CRR to the Interior Minister, who has ten days to make any observation.[114] As soon as the Minister has answered the request (or after ten days, if s/he fails to do so), CRR will issue an '*avis motivé*' (a reasoned recommendation) on whether or not the measure shall be annulled. This recommendation will be sent back to the Minister who is sole competent to take the final decision.[115]

4. The Swedish Aliens Appeals Board

On 1 January 1992, the Aliens Appeals Board (*Utlänningnämnden*) was given competence to hear appeals under the Aliens Act and the Citizenship Act.[116] Before then, the Government was the ultimate instance of appeal but a large backlog needed to be taken over. Since its creation in January 1992, the Appeals Board has been working mainly on the backlog. In spring 1992, although the Appeals Board's backlog increased heavily, most cases were dealt with by the autumn. In spring 1993, however, an even greater number of appeals were made against an increasing number of expulsion orders by SIV.

---

[108] See *supra*, section 3.1.

[109] See, for instance, three cases of CRR, quashing decisions of the Head of OFPRA, on the grounds that persecution actually existed. Abstracts in IJRL, 1993, pp. 613–6.

[110] Article 24, Decree of 1953.

[111] *Ibid*, Article 25.

[112] New Article 32bis, Ordinance of 1945.

[113] Article 27, Decree of 1953.

[114] *Ibid*, Article 28.

[115] *Ibid*, Article 29. For a complete analysis of this procedure, see, F. Tiberghien, *op. cit.*, pp. 182–7.

[116] Chap. 7, s.3 of the Aliens Act (1989:529), as amended in 1991 (Government Bill on Active Refugee and Immigration Policy, Prop. 1990/91:195).

In December 1993, the appeal procedure was still congested,[117] and in April 1994, about 8,000 cases were pending concerning 22,000 refugees (including families).[118]

4.1. *Composition and Functions*

The Aliens Appeals Board is composed of a chairman and of a number of laymen to be decided by the Government. There must be an alternate for the chairman. Four of them have actually been appointed by the Government. They come to the Board only once or twice a month and act as chairman. They must be qualified and experienced lawyers.[119] Laymen are third persons appointed by the Government.[120] They are not acting as politicians performing their duties but as "wise" men applying the law. They are supposed to represent the people.[121] At first, they had no vote, but today, they vote like the chairman. According to Mr. Johan Fischerström, Head of the Appeals Board, "it is good to have them, especially when difficult cases involve the mass media. This way it is more difficult for the media or anyone else to be too critical about the justice system."[122] Mr. Fischerström was appointed Head of the Appeals Board on January 1, 1992, by the Government, for a period of six years.[123] He also acts as a chairman besides being president. There are eight chairmen and four alternates. Clear cases are normally decided by one chairman and two laymen. They have one vote each and the majority decides even when the chairman is against the decision. However, whoever disagrees with the decision must make a written statement of his/her dissenting opinion. When a case is difficult, or when the media or any other outside body is interested in it, or also when a case is going to have prejudicial effect on other decisions taken by the Appeals Board or SIV (ie, a reverse of *jurisprudence*), the decision must be taken by two chairmen and four laymen and the Head

---

[117] Informal conversation, on the phone, with Mr. Johan Fischerström (Head of the Aliens Appeals Board, Stockholm), December 1993. See also, the Swedish Ministry of Culture, *Immigrant and Refugee Policy*, 1993, p. 34.

[118] Interview with Mr. Johan Fischerström, (Head of the Appeals Board), April 1994, Stockholm.

[119] Aliens Act, chap. 7, s.3. The Swedish Ministry of Cultural Affairs, *Immigrant and Refugee Policy*, 1992, p. 43.

[120] They are suggested to the Government by Parliamentary political parties in a number which is proportional to the number of Parliamentary members of each party. "This is all very political because some of them are members of Parliament, some others are members of local assemblies throught the country. But this is not new. It always existed in Sweden in the courts system. There are laymen in all the courts, except in the Supreme Court." Interview with Mr. Johan Fischerström (*op. cit.*).

[121] The Swedish courts system has always favoured supervision by the people.

[122] Laymen are very experienced people; they are trained to take decisions and they are keen to apply the law. At present, for instance, among the thirty laymen appointed, one is a retired judge and one is a retired lawyer, both are politicians since their retirement, there is also one female professor of international law, others are doctors in medicine, representative from the union etc. Interview with Mr. Fischerström (*op. cit.*).

[123] He has been a judge for 28 years.

of Board has to be one of the two chairmen. They all have one vote each
and the majority decides. If no majority is reached, the decision will be that
which is most in favour for the applicant. Such solution is quite common in
the Swedish system. Further levels of decisions involving three chairmen and
six laymen or four chairmen and eight laymen are theoretically possible but
in practice it has never happened.[124]

4.2. *Proceedings*

The majority of cases are taken on the basis of written documents. Provisions
on oral proceedings applicable to cases before SIV, are similarly valid in
cases before the Appeals Board.[125] SIV and the Appeals Board should hear
applicants as a matter of principle, such obligation is provided by the law. In
practice, this does not happen very often, though oral hearings seem to take
place more often at the Appeals Board then at SIV. Decisions are taken in
Swedish and hearings are closed to the public and kept secret.[126] Information
concerning asylum seekers and countries of origin are similarly kept highly
confidential and secret in order to protect asylum seekers, their relatives and
their friends against retaliation in the country of origin. Because espionage
seems to be quite common, the Swedish court system is subject to the Secrecy
Act.[127] However, criticism against too much secrecy has been made because
no one, except the Government, SIV and the Appeals Board, is actually able
to know and check what information has been used to decide a case.[128]

Asylum seekers may appeal to the Aliens Board against various types
of decisions by administrative authorities. First, against a refusal to enter
made by a police authority.[129] It is, however, extremely rare for the Appeals
Board to deal with a case concerning an asylum seeker still at the border.
Most asylum seekers are allowed to enter and their case is then examined
by SIV in Norrköping.[130] Second, against a refusal of entry or an order of
expulsion made by SIV and any question of residence or work permits in

---

[124]   Interview with Mr. Fischerström (*op. cit.*).

[125]   Aliens Act, chap. 11, s.1. However, Parliamentary Debates at the time the Board was
created, seem to acknowledge that oral hearings can take place in certain cases before the
Appeals Board and do not have to. Interview with Mr. Fischerström (*op. cit.*).

[126]   It is extremely difficult to get asylum decisions in Sweden as none are actually published
on a regular and systematic basis. The whole practice is very secret (ECRE Country Report,
Sweden, 3–5 April 1992, p. 122). However, the Appeals Board has recently agreed to publish
(in Swedish) certain of the most important decisions on asylum. A copy of this publication
should be available from the Appeals Board by July 1994.

[127]   Notice that secrecy does not exist in every country. In Belgium and France, for instance,
courts hearings are open to the public.

[128]   According to Mr. Fischerström, "we should be able to give some information to the public,
without revealing the names of the persons, because this is the only way corrections can be
made to our information which can be wrong."

[129]   Aliens Act, chap. 7, s.2.

[130]   Cases of immediate refusal and expulsion at the border may only arise if a person is
under an obligation not to come back to Sweden for a period of at least two years following a
negative decision on refugee status, and this person comes back.

connection with it.[131] Third, against the refusal or revocation of the status of refugee or travel documents by SIV.[132] There is no appeal against SIV's decisions in matters concerning visas.[133] Appeal against SIV's decision to refuse entry or to refuse asylum must be lodged within three weeks, from the day the applicant receives a copy of that decision. Asylum seekers are allowed to remain in Sweden while an appeal is pending. However, in cases where SIV finds that "grounds for asylum are manifestly lacking and that there are no other grounds for awarding a residence permit", the asylum seeker will be asked to leave and expulsion will be carried out before any appeal against the refusal of refugee status has been reached.[134] Thus, the asylum seeker will have to wait for that decision outside Sweden.[135] Decisions to retain a ticket or to order detention may also be contested by appeal to the Administrative Court of Appeal.[136] Appeals concerning reimbursements may only be lodged with the Administrative Court of Appeal.[137] Further appeals to the Supreme Administrative Court are possible in such cases. Finally, appeals against an order of expulsion on account of a criminal offence must be made before common courts in criminal proceedings.[138] In most cases, the decision of the Appeals Board is final. However, a further appeal to the Supreme Administrative Court is possible in cases where a mistake on a point of law (not facts) has been made.[139] Such cases must then be referred back

---

[131] Aliens Act, chap. 7, s.3 and s.5. Unless made in connection with a refusal of entry or deportation orders, SIV's decisions concerning work permit or residence permit are final. In autumn 1993, an asylum seeker coming from Kenya was refused entry by SIV while still at Arlanda airport. The media took hold of the story and showed pictures on TV of this person having to go back to Kenya. Just before being deported, the applicant appealed from the decision and the Appeals Board ordered to stop the deportation immediately. He was allowed to stay in Sweden pending the appeal and he was finally granted refugee status. Interview with Mr. Fischerström (*op. cit.*).

[132] Aliens Act, chap. 7, s.4.

[133] Despite the rule that all applications for authorization to stay should be made from abroad, except for asylum, family reunion and persons already living in Sweden, cases (Aliens Act, chap. 2, s.5), only applications made in the country are subject to appeal. Applications made from abroad, ie, from a Swedish embassy, cannot be appealed.

[134] The Swedish Immigration Board (SIV), "To persons seeking asylum in Sweden", June 1992.

[135] This is the only kind of "fast-track procedure" Sweden has. However, an appeal against this decision of expulsion can be made to the Aliens Board, which is competent to decide whether expulsion should be carried out before or after its final decision on refugee status. If the Appeals Board has reasons to think that it will quash SIV decision on refugee status, it will also quash SIV decision of expulsion and such cases will be decided by the Appeals Board in priority to all other cases waiting. Therefore, expulsion to the country of origin while a final decision is being taken may only arise if both SIV and the Appeals Board have quite strong reasons to think that the application in unfounded.

[136] Aliens Act, chap. 7, s.6 and s.7.

[137] *Ibid*, s.9.

[138] *Ibid*, s.8 and s.16.

[139] For example, the Appeals Board has not sent the papers to the asylum seeker for him to comment on.

to the Appeals Board for new decision. Finally, if new circumstances arise and as a result SIV first decision or the Appeals Board negative decision has become wrongful, a new second application can be made to SIV.[140] Strict requirements must be met. First, new circumstances must not have existed or could not be found by SIV or the Appeals Board at the time they took their decision. Second, these new circumstances must be such that they will automatically grant asylum to the applicant.[141] SIV decisions following new applications are not subject to appeal, however, there is no limit as to the number of such new applications, as long as they are allowed to remain in the country.[142]

4.3. *Special Cases Decided by the Government*

Although the Government is no longer the supreme authority to hear appeals against SIV's decisions, it is still competent to deal with important and sensitive cases referred to by SIV or the Appeals Board.[143] While both SIV and the Appeals Board are bound by decisions of the Government, SIV is also bound to respect and apply decisions of the Appeals Board. SIV and the Appeals Board usually refer to the Government cases which require principles to be set for the future, ie, in matters of national security and terrorism. The Appeals Board or SIV may also refer a case to Government if it wishes the Government to change a previous line of *jurisprudence*,[144] or where strong grounds that the matter should be decided by the Government exist.[145] According to Mr. Fischerström, "what is wrong with the existing system [of referring cases to the Government] and we have pointed it out, is that SIV has the possibility to bring a case to the Government. In such a situation, this case will never go on appeal. Furthermore, the case won't have been decided by SIV either but

---

[140] Aliens Act, chap. 7, s.10. As from 1 July 1994, new applications will no longer be made to SIV but to the Appeals Board instead, following a decision of Government. Interview with Mr. Fischerström (*op. cit.*).

[141] This is usually the case if a war has started in the country of origin and no one knew about it at the time or if the applicant has tried to commit suicide in a severe way since a decision was taken and a serious risk continues to exist (SOU 1994:54, *op. cit.*, p. 30). It seems that the taking of tablets does not constitute a serious intention to commit suicide. Interview with Mr. Fischerström (*op. cit.*).

[142] K. Jönsson, *op. cit.*, paras.71 and 73. An order of expulsion following a decision refusing a residence permit must normally be carried out within two weeks. If Swedish authorities have any doubts that the alien will not follow the order, detention may take place. Interview with the Agency for Advisory Service (*op. cit.*).

[143] Aliens Act, chap. 7, s.11. See also, K. Jönsson, *op. cit.*, para.66.

[144] The Government is, however, free to follow such recommendation or to stand by its earlier decision.

[145] Recent examples include the decision on undocumented asylum seekers (1989), the decision on Bosnians (1993) and the decision on Somalis (1994). See for more details on the subject, SOU 1994:54, *op. cit.*, pp. 23–35.

only by the Government. At least when a case reaches us, SIV has taken a decision of first instance."[146]

Thus, to conclude on the Swedish system of appeal for aliens, two points may be made. First, the Appeals Board is not a fully independent authority. If it is in principle independent, in fact, the Government is making certain decisions that the Appeals Board has to follow. Second, the Appeals Board is a quasi-judicial authority.[147] It has elements of both a judicial authority (judges preside and it operates like a court of appeal) and an administrative authority (the administrative rules apply, so that any complaint against the rules of law go to the Supreme Administrative Court and never into the normal court system).[148]

5. The Swiss 'Commission des Recours en Matière d'Asile'

5.1. *Composition and Functions*

The Swiss system of appeal was subject to an important reform following the modification of the Asylum Law in 1990,[149] which created the *Commission des Recours en matière d'Asile* (CRA). The CRA is a judicial authority, based in Zollikofen.[150] It started its work on 1 April 1992.[151] It takes independent decisions in accordance with the law.[152] It is, however, subject to Federal administrative surveillance for matters involving in particular accounts and management.[153] Its decisions are final.[154] It is composed of 29 judges, divided among seven chambers and nominated by the Federation.[155] A single judge is, however, competent to decide cases subject to non-entry, classified appeal with no subject-matter, manifestly unfounded decisions to refuse an appeal and decisions to admit an appeal.[156] The whole procedure before the CRA is

---

[146] Parliament is currently thinking of changing this. Interview with Mr. Fischerström (*op. cit.*).

[147] At the time of its creation, it was strongly argued that "appeals should be handled by the existing system of Administrative High Courts and the Administrative Supreme Court or at least that the new authority should be organised as a court and not as an administrative authority" (ECRE Country Report, Sweden, 3–5 April 1992, p. 121).

[148] Interview with Mr. Fischerström (*op. cit.*) and interview with Eva Singer, UNHCR (*op. cit.*). See also K. Jönsson, *op. cit.*, para.78.

[149] Article 11 of the 1979 Asylum Law, as modified by Federal Order of 22 June 1990 on Asylum Procedure, in force until 31 December 1995. Ordinance of 18 December 1991 relating to the *Commission suisse de Recours en matière d'Asile* (CRA) was adopted on the basis of Article 11 of the Asylum Law.

[150] Article 16 of the Ordinance of 18 December 1991.

[151] *Ibid*, Article 32.

[152] *Ibid*, Article 2.

[153] *Ibid*, Articles 17 and 18.

[154] *Ibid*, Article 1.

[155] *Ibid*, Articles 3 and 9 and Article 11 of the Asylum Law. See also, H. Schoeni, *op. cit.*, p. 18.

[156] Article 10, Ordinance of 18 December 1991.

provided by the Federal Law on the Administrative Procedure.[157] Decisions from the CRA are notified to the appellant in writing and are final.[158] Main decisions of the CRA are published, in particular, in the *'Jurisprudence des autorités administratives de la Confédération'*, however, names of the parties to a case are kept secret.[159] Under the old system, that is before the entry into force in April 1992 of the legislative texts creating the CRA, asylum seekers could only lodge an appeal within the *Service des Recours*, a service which, like the Federal Office for Refugees (the authority which takes the decision) was part of the Federal Department of Justice and Police. The Swiss system of appeal was, therefore, an internal administrative appeal and the *Service des Recours* was in fact very much at the discretion of the Confederation.[160]

5.2. *Proceedings*

Very much like in France and Sweden, the appeal procedure is on paper. The CRA usually takes its decision on the sole ground of the asylum seeker's file. Personal interviews are extremely rare.[161] The refugee has a right to make written representation and the appeal is actually made in writing in one of the three official languages (French, German or Italian). It is to the CRA to then reformulate the appeal in its final form and to transmit the final version to the Federal Office for Refugees for comments. A copy is also available for the asylum seeker to consult, but only after express request.

Asylum may be denied or withdrawn by the Federal Office in the following cases: the asylum seekers did not come directly from their country of persecution (a stay of 20 days in a third country is sufficient);[162] it appears that they have found or may find protection and asylum elsewhere;[163] they are unable to prove any fear of being persecuted or of suffering serious harm according to the definition of refugee provided in Article 3 of the 1979 Asylum Law;[164] it appears that flight from their country of origin or their personal behaviour since the flight constitutes the only ground for being considered as a refugee;[165] they have committed some crimes or constitute a danger to national security and public order;[166] on the basis of Article 16 of the 1979 Asylum Law; asylum has been granted on the ground of forged, wrong or

---

[157] RS 172.021.

[158] Articles 30 and 31 of the Ordinance of 18 December 1991, which refer to Articles 34–36, 61 of the Federal Law on Administrative Procedure.

[159] Article 20, Ordinance of 18 December 1991.

[160] Interviews with Mr. G. Köfner and Mr. H. Buss (UNHCR), Geneva, and Ms. C. della Croce and Mr. B. Clément (Centre Social Protestant), Lausanne, December 1990.

[161] *Documentation -Réfugiés*, Supplement to No. 213, March/April 1993, p. 5.

[162] Article 6, Asylum Law.

[163] Asylum is withdrawn to recognized refugees who went back to their countries of origin, even for a short period, or who left Switzerland for at least three years. Articles 6 and 42, Asylum Law. See also, *Asile en Europe, op. cit.*, p. 509, para.70.

[164] Article 16(a), Asylum Law.

[165] *Ibid*, Article 8(a).

[166] *Ibid*, Articles 8 and 44.

incomplete statements;[167] Article C of the 1951 Convention applies.[168] In all such cases,[169] the asylum seeker has 30 days to lodge an appeal from the day he receives notification of the refusal or withdrawal decision. The Federal Office's decision of notification normally specifies the necessary requirements for appeals. While the appeal is pending the asylum seeker is normally allowed to remain in Switzerland, except in cases subject to non-entry (Article 16) followed by an order to leave or of immediate return (illegal entry from a border country, possible sojourn in a third country or in the country of origin ...).[170] However, in all cases of immediate return, an appeal against the decision of return may be lodged within 10 days (it is indeed a decision on a point of law, *décision incidente*) with the CRA. This appeal may have a suspensive effect as regards matters subject to non-entry, but not in all cases. The decision of the CRA is subject to no further appeal. However, in a very few cases, there may be an exceptional possibility of further revision. The case may therefore be reopened but on very specific grounds only, such as reasons based on legal principles (referred to as *la dénonciation au Conseil fédéral*) or if there is new essential evidences which could have been submitted before but only became available now (*la demande de révision*) or in cases of new developments of new circumstances (*la demande de réexamen*). These exceptional forms of appeal are very rare and do not have any suspensive effect.[171]

6. The British System of an Adjudicator and the Immigration Appeals Tribunal

Rights of appeal in the United Kingdom have been subject to important restrictions since the entry into force of the Asylum and Immigration Appeals Act in July 1993. The new Act, which aims at accelerating and simplifying the asylum procedure, provides shorter time limits for the exercise of the right to appeal and new grounds for refusing possibilities of appeal.

6.1. *Situations Where There Is no Right of Appeal*

Visitors, students (short-term and prospective ones) and their dependents have no right of appeal against a refusal of leave to enter or of entry clearance, in particular no right of appeal exists against the refusal of a visa abroad.[172] Nor is there a right of appeal against the refusal of an entry clearance or to vary leave to enter or remain where the person does not hold proper documents, or does not fulfill the requirements of the immigration rules as

---

[167] *Ibid*, Article 41–1(a).
[168] *Ibid*, Article 41–1(b).
[169] See generally Articles 46 to 47, *ibid*.
[170] *Ibid*, Article 47.
[171] Interview with Mr. G. Köfner, UNHCR (*op. cit.*). See also, *Documentation-Réfugies*, Supplement to No. 213, pp. 5–6 and H. Schoeni, *op. cit.*, pp. 16–7.
[172] Asylum and Immigration Appeals Act 1993, Clause 10.

to age or nationality or citizenship, or seeks to enter/stay in the UK for a longer period of time than that permitted by the immigration rules.[173] Claims without foundation (claims which raise no issue under the 1951 Convention or which are frivolous or vexatious) are subject to special appeal procedures provided by Schedule 2 of the 1993 Asylum and Immigration Appeals Act. In cases where the adjudicator agrees that the claim is unfounded, there shall be no right of appeal. However, where the adjudicator does not agree that the claim is unfounded, the case may be sent back to the Secretary of State for reconsideration. Pursuant to Clause 10(3AA), an Independent Monitor, Lady Anson, was appointed in December 1993, for a period of three years. She has no power to overturn decisions but she will examine refusals of entry clearance where there is no right of appeal. In particular, "she will consider whether the standards required by legislation or administrative practice are being applied correctly and fairly."[174]

6.2. *Right to Appeal and Leave to Appeal*

Appeals against a Notice of Refusal are to be heard by a Special Adjudicator. Parties shall be the appellant and the Secretary of State. The representative of the UNHCR may only be considered as a party if written notice has been given by the UNHCR to the adjudicator.[175] Appeal must be made within ten days after receiving notice of the decision or within two days if the appeal is made under s.8(1) of the 1993 Act (refused leave to enter) or if the claim is without foundation.[176] Appeals may be made under s.8(1)–(4) of the Act. Leave to appeal to the Immigration Appeal Tribunal against a decision of the adjudicator must be requested within five days of getting the adjudicator's decision.[177] No right to apply for leave exists in cases where the adjudicator and the Secretary of State have both agreed that the claim is without foundation. Leave to appeal to the Court of Appeal against a decision of the Immigration Appeal Tribunal must be requested within ten days of getting the Tribunal's decision.[178] Leave to appeal may only be granted against a final decision of the Tribunal and concerning a point of law.

The overall situation provided by the Immigration Act 1971, thus remains. Whether or not asylum seekers whose applications are refused have a right of appeal depend on their immigration status at the time they make their application. If an asylum seeker has a valid visa or entry clearance and is refused entry, he has a right of appeal prior to any action to remove him from the country;[179] and where an appeal would be useless (because in leaving

---

[173] Clause 11, amending s.13 and s.14 of the 1971 Immigration Act.

[174] Foreign and Commonwealth Office, Press Release No. 190, 15 December 1993.

[175] Asylum Appeals (Procedure) Rules 1993, rule 8.

[176] *Ibid*, rule 5.

[177] *Ibid*, rule 13(2).

[178] *Ibid*, rule 21(1).

[179] Immigration Act 1971, s.13(1). Any directions for removal are suspended while the appeal is pending.

the UK in order to appeal, the applicant would have been prevented from returning following a successful appeal, by the law of his country of origin), judicial review and orders of certiorari and mandamus have been granted.[180] However, if an asylum seeker has no valid visa or entry clearance, he is no longer entitled to a right of appeal, even from outside the country.[181] Appeal used to be possible but could not be heard while the passenger was still in the UK.[182]

An asylum seeker will only be given a right to appeal if he applied for asylum before his official leave to stay in the UK expired.[183] No further right of appeal exists until deportation proceedings begin, and this can be rendered useless if an individual is recommended for deportation.[184] Indeed, refusal of asylum results normally from the Home Office's conclusion that the asylum seekers's fear of persecution is not well founded.[185] Asylum may also be refused after consideration of the applicant's credibility and willingness to cooperate with the Secretary of State in order to reach a decision,[186] or if the

---

[180] *R v. Chief Immigration Officer, Gatwick Airport, ex p. Kharrazi*, [1980] 3 All ER 373, CA. When an applicant applies for judicial review at the same time as being under threat of immediate removal, steps must be taken to guarantee the stay of the applicant in the country during proceedings; *R v. Secretary of State for the Home Department, ex p. Mubayayi*, CA (1991) and *M v. Home Office*, CA (1991). See, C. Vincenzi, *op. cit.*, pp. 134–5.

[181] Clause 11, Asylum and Immigration Act 1993.

[182] Immigration Act 1971, s.13(3). *Vilvarajah and others v. UK*, ECHR, 30 October 1991, CoE 45/1990/236 and, *M v. Home Office*, House of Lords, Times Law Reports, 28 July 1993, p. 427.

[183] A person should apply for an extension of time while lawfully in the UK. He would be entitled to remain in Britain for that period if leave is granted; if leave is refused but an appeal has been lodged, he cannot be required to leave the country while the appeal is pending; *R v. Immigration Appeal Tribunal, ex p. Subramaniam*, [1977] QB 190, [1976] 3 All ER 604, CA; see also *Grant v. Borg* [1982] 2 All ER 257, [1982] 1 WLR 638, HL.

[184] Immigration Act 1971, s.15(1) and s.13(4) on deportation ordered by a court. Where a deportation order is made against a person, any pending appeal by that person under the Immigration Act 1971 s.14(1) will lapse (Immigration Act 1971, s.14(5) as introduced by Immigration Act 1988, s.10 Schedule). A person may not appeal against a refusal to revoke a deportation order so long as he is in the UK (Immigration Act 1971, s.15(5)(7)(9) except when he is appealing on the ground that he is not the person named in the order (Immigration Act 1971, s.16(2)) or on the ground that his removal could be contrary to UK's obligations under the 1951 Convention (Immigration Act 1971, s.16(1), Asylum and Immigration Appeals Act 1993, clauses 8(3)(4)). The Immigration Act 1988 brought new provisions with regard to deportation orders; s.5(1)(2) provides that a person who has been in the UK for less than seven years and in respect of whom a deportation order has been made by virtue of the 1971 Act, s.3(5)(a),(c) is not entitled to appeal against the decision to make the order except on the ground that on the facts there is in law no power to make the order. However, the Secretary of State may exempt specified persons (ie, refugees) from the operation of this provision by order; 1988 Act, s.5(2),(3), Immigration (Restricted Right of Appeal against Deportation) (Exemption) (No2) Order 1988, SI 1988/1203. It is for the person in question to prove that leave to enter was last given more than seven years before the date of the decision in question; 1988 Act, s.5(4); and where written notice of the decision in question was given before 1/08/1988, the grounds on which a person can appeal are not affected; 1988 Act, s.5(5).

[185] Statement of Changes in the Immigration Rules 1993, HC 725, 5 July 1993, rules 180B–E.

[186] *Ibid*, rules 180F–J.

applicant is coming from a safe third country[187] or, finally, if the applicant has already been refused asylum in the UK and no substantial changes have occurred since then.[188] The decision is communicated to the asylum seeker or representative in the form of a refusal notice, which also informs him of his right of appeal.[189] The refusal notice is not a notice of intention to lodge a deportation order. Moreover, the latter cannot be undertaken while an appeal is pending.[190] In any event, an intention to make a deportation order carries a further right of appeal,[191] except perhaps in cases where the claim is without foundation.[192] Substantive rights of appeal for all asylum seekers are required where an application is refused by the Home Office. That an asylum seeker can always bring judicial review of the Home Office decision concerning the legality of the decision appears like an essential guarantee because if the decision is quashed upon judicial review it surely gives the applicant what he wants.[193] It is the equivalent of a successful appeal to the Belgian or French *Conseil d'Etat*, or the German Federal Administrative Court, which are neither competent on the merits of a decision.[194]

---

[187] *Ibid*, rule 180K.

[188] *Ibid*, rule 180L.

[189] Immigration Appeals Procedures Rules 1984, as amended by the Asylum Appeals Procedure Rules 1993, see in particular, rule 5. Also, HC 725, rule 180N.

[190] Asylum and Immigration Appeals Act 1993, Schedule 2, s.8, amending s.15(2) of the Immigration Act 1971.

[191] Asylum and Immigration Appeals Act 1993, clause 8(3).

[192] *Ibid*, Schedule 2, s.5(1). However, in cases where the application is rejected by the Secretary of State as being manifestly unfounded on the ground that the applicant (Abdi and Gawe, both Muslim Somalis) is coming from a safe third country (Spain, in this case), it is the duty of the Secretary of State to consider all relevant facts in order to determine the safety of such country and to communicate all relevant materials to the adjudicator. It is then the duty of the special adjudicator "to make a rigorous and truly independent appraisal of the same question on appeal" and not simply to reject the appeal on the basis of Schedule 2, s.(5) of the Act. *R v. Secretary of State, ex p. Abdi and Gawe*, Q.B., Times Law Report, 10/03/1994. A month later, the Court of Appeal quashed the decision because it was not open to the court to impose additional obligations either on the Home Secretary or the special adjudicators and that "the Secretary of State was not obliged to disclose to the special adjudicator all the material which was available to him when he made the decision to refuse asylum ... and the special adjudicator was required to consider the asylum seeker's appeal on the material before him." *R v. Secretary of State, ex p. Abdi and Gawe*, CA, Times Law Report, 25/04/1994. The Court of Appeal has authorized leave to appeal to the House of Lords to both applicants (MNS, May 1994, p. 7).

[193] However, application for judicial review are not always granted, in particular, judicial review is refused where "public law acknowledged no general principle of inconsistency". In the case *R v. Special Adjudicator, ex p. Kandasamy*, for instance, the court (Q.B.) rejected the application for judicial review because the decision of the adjudicator, although treating the applicant differently from another in similar circumstances was not (the applicant, a Tamil, was coming from Sri Lanka via Sweden where he spent a day and a half), in the absence of irrationality, illegality or procedural unfairness to that applicant, susceptible of review." In, the Times Law Report, 11/03/1994.

[194] Goodwin-Gill, *International Law and the Movement of Persons between States*, Clarendon Press Oxford, 1978, p. 265.

The Asylum and Immigration Appeals Act 1993, which govern the appeals procedure is framed to prevent illegal and abusive entry into the country to the detriment of genuine refugees who may arrive with false passports or none at all. For reasons, based primarily on fear, asylum seekers fall under many different categories of the Immigration Act, including illegal entrants, overstayers, "detained pending removal", as well as those who have valid permission to be in Britain. All asylum seekers should have the same right of appeal to an independent tribunal, irrespective of their status at the time of application. As soon as a person applies for asylum, the claim takes precedence over their current immigration status. However, if the application is refused the person reverts to his previous immigration category. If that category (asylum seekers without a valid visa or entry clearance) does not allow for an appeal, the only recourse is further representations to the Home Office (the same authority that made the initial negative decision), although "[o]nly the setting up of a fully independent and impartial tribunal for refugees will safeguard the rights of asylum-seekers".[195]

To conclude, Germany appears the only country to provide a system of appeals for asylum seekers through its general courts system. In all the other countries, a special tribunal or commission has been set up for the matter. While administrative courts in Germany deal with a wide variety of issues, aliens being one of them, tribunals or commissions are much more specialized. They are set to deal with one issue only and their composition often include laymen or non-lawyers with particular expertise in the field or even the representative of a non-national authority (ie, the UNHCR in France and in the United Kingdom). However, the independence of some of the members, vis-à-vis the government, may be questioned (ie, in Sweden). The secrecy of proceedings and the confidentiality of documents is neither equally protected. While Sweden offers extremely high standards of procedural secrecy, France or Belgium provide no secrecy at all and hearings are public. Finally, if it appears that mechanisms of judicial review exist in all the six countries, one must, however, keep in mind that such possibilities are subject to very restrictive grounds.

---

[195] Michael Mayne, *Risks in right of asylum, The Independent*, 18/05/1989, p. 27.

CHAPTER FOUR

BURDEN OF PROOF AND RULES OF EVIDENCE

To be eligible for refugee status, an applicant must have a "well-founded fear of being persecuted" and must not benefit from the protection of his country of origin or of a third country.[1] Proof of persecution is therefore the crucial element in admission procedures and its burden has grown higher and higher in the last few years. Belgium, France and Sweden have incorporated the 1951 Convention into their national legislation and apply directly the definition of refugee as provided by Article 1A(2) of the Convention.[2] The "well-founded fear of persecution" standard is also provided by the laws of the United Kingdom.[3] Until May 1993, Article 16II of the German Basic Law provided that "political persecutees enjoy asylum". The notion of "political persecutee" has always been very similar but never identical (it is in fact wider) to the definition of refugee provided by Article 1A(2) of the 1951 Convention.[4] Article 16II was amended on 26 May 1993 and a new Asylum Procedure Law entered into force on 1st July 1993. Since the constitutional reform, political asylum may only be granted to those who qualify under the 1951 Convention. However, Germany continue to adhere to the notion of "persecution for political reasons" rather than the concept of refugee.[5] Finally, Swiss Law defines refugees as "aliens who in their native country ... for reasons of race, religion, nationality, membership in a particular social group or political opinions are exposed to serious prejudices, or have a well-founded fear of being exposed to such prejudices".[6]

Because Article 1A(2) of the 1951 Convention remains silent on the interpretation of the term "well-founded fear of persecution", reference will be made to national practice, in particular to the decisions of the national competent authorities and courts in all the six countries. *Jurisprudence* concerning

---

[1] Article 1A(2) of the 1951 Convention.

[2] Belgian Law of 15 December 1980, as modified, Articles 48–49; French Law of 25 July 1952, as modified, Article 2; and Swedish Law of 1st July 1989, as modified, Article 2.

[3] HC 251 and HC 725.

[4] Definition which has never been incorparated as such into German legislation. Notice that section 51 of the Aliens Act nevertheless incorporates Article 33 of the 1951 Convention.

[5] Joachim Henkel, *op. cit.*, p. 2706.

[6] Swiss Asylum Law of 5 October 1979, as modified, Article 3.

refugees in Europe is strongly depending on the system of judicial review and appeals of refugee applications in each country. Case-law is not equally developed in all of them. As already discussed, in Sweden, for instance, a system of appeals to an independent authority exists only since January 1992.[7] However, the Appeals Board proceedings are secret and it provides no reasons for its decisions. As a result the *jurisprudence* on the grounds of persecution and on the reasons for a well-founded fear are undeveloped, not to say unreachable to the general public. It used to be the same in Belgium, before the reform of 1987–88 when the UNHCR was the sole authority competent to decide on an application for asylum and refugee status. His decisions were never given reasons and no judicial review was provided.[8] An elaborate system of judicial review, nevertheless, always existed in the Federal Republic of Germany,[9] France and the United Kingdom. Not surprisingly, there are more German, French and British, as well as, more recently, Belgian and Swiss opinions examining claims of persecution than there are Swedish ones.

1. Proving the Existence of a 'Well-Founded Fear of Persecution'

International instruments define the reasons of persecution but remain silent on how the terms "fear" and "persecution" should be interpreted.[10] Likewise no detail is given with regard to the date of persecution nor to the person responsible for such persecutions.

1.1. *Agents of Persecution*

According to general principles of law it is of course for the asylum seeker to put forward evidence,[11] and to give to the authority concerned with his application all documentary or other proof to support his request.[12] However, because of the special situation in which some asylum seekers have to leave their country of origin, it may be impossible for them to submit such evidence. Recommendations from the UNHCR have thus been made to the Member

---

[7] Before then, appeals were the responsibility of the Government or SIV. A similar situation existed in Switzerland until the reform of 1990 which created an independent judicial authority (Article 11(2) of the 1979 Asylum Law).

[8] Law of 15 December 1980.

[9] At the time of writing, references will esentially be made to the *jurisprudence* of German courts as existing before the reform of July 1993.

[10] Goodwin-Gill, *The Refugee in International Law, op. cit.*, p. 38.

[11] Paul Weis, "Le concept de réfugié en droit international", *Journal de Droit International*, Clunet, 1960, p. 986. In France, the Commission of Appeals and the *Conseil d'Etat* have interpreted Article 1A(2) in that way but many applicants have contested such an interpretation (ie, *C.E., Markovic*, 13 mars 1981, requête 18.758 and *C.E., Demir*, 12 juin 1981, requête 25.214; in F. Tiberghien, *op. cit.*, p. 375). In the UK, see, for example, *R v. Secretary of State for the Home Department, ex p. Bugdaycay and related appeals*, [1986] 1 All ER, CA, 463 and 464. In Switzerland, such an interpretation is provided by Article 12a of the Asylum Law.

[12] See, for instance, Article 12b of the Swiss Aylum Law.

States and are to be found in the Handbook on Procedures and Criteria for Determining Refugee Status. Among others the applicant should be given the benefit of the doubt if it appears that no conclusive evidence on the facts backs up his *bona fide* request.[13] Likewise, the competent authority should help the applicant and facilitate his task by using all means at its disposal to hold an inquiry and produce the necessary evidence in support of the request, subject to the respect of the confidential character of the investigation.[14]

As a result of a strict interpretation of Articles 1A(2) and 1C(1) of the 1951 Convention, it is agreed that persecutions which do not directly proceed from public or official authorities of the country of origin should not lead to Convention refugee status. However, it appears that today states are willing to either grant some other kind of status or temporary right to stay, or to interpret the terms of the 1951 Convention in a liberal manner, so as to generally include other authors of persecution. In May 1983, the French *Conseil d'Etat* agreed on a liberal interpretation of the terms of the 1951 Convention, already accepted by the *Commission de Recours des Réfugiés* in 1979, that persecutions do not have to proceed directly from the government.[15] It emerges from the decision in *Dankha* that account should be taken of persecutions proceeding from private individuals if those persecutions are encouraged or allowed by the government and prevent the applicant from the benefit of the protection of his country of origin.[16] However, in January 1994, the CRR refused to recognize Somalis as refugees on the grounds that "without de facto authorities or a Government in place, the nationals of this country are not entitled to refugee status according to the terms of the Geneva Convention".[17] Belgian authorities seem to have continuously favoured a liberal approach, particularly the *Commission Permanente de Recours des*

---

[13] The General Commissioner, in Belgium, admitted that about 80% of asylum seekers are granted the status of refugees on the benefit of the doubt. "It is very rare to be absolutely sure that persecution exists". Notice also that many refugees are recognized within family reunification or quotas. Interview with Mr. M. Bossuyt, General Commissioner (*op. cit.*).

[14] *Handbook on Procedures and Criteria for Determining Refugee Status*, Office of the UNHCR, Geneva, January 1988, pp. 47–8. Recommendation No. 81(16) on the Harmonisation of National Procedures relating to Asylum. See also, for example, the British decision *R v. Secretary of State for the Home Department, ex p. Sivakumaran and conjoined appeals*, [1988] 1 All ER, HL, 193, h.

[15] C.E., Section, 21 mai 1983, *Dankha, Actualité Juridique de Droit Administratif* (AJDA) 1983, p. 481. See also, F. Tiberghien, *op. cit.*, pp. 93–6. It would seem that persecution must be some serious act of state which will include some deliberate omission by the state or passive complicity with other's acts, in A. Heilbronner, *op. cit.*, pp. 111–2.

[16] Such an interpretation is in keeping with the UNHCR Handbook, *op. cit.*, p. 17. See also, *Mademoiselle X.*, Commission of Appeal, 19 September 1991, in *Public Law*, Spring 1993, p. 197.

[17] MNS, February 1994, p. 5. Equally, CRR confirmed a decision of OFPRA refusing asylum to a Japanese applicant, whose persecutions on the ground of membership to a special social group made him loose his job. CRR found no evidence of persecution by the Japanese government, nor even tolerated by it. Abstract in IJRL, 1994, p. 120.

Réfugiés.[18] Likewise, Swiss authorities normally refuse to grant asylum to applicants if it appears that they fear persecution which do not proceed from the state but from non-official groups or groups of individuals, provided the asylum seeker can prove that persecution was covered by the state authorities or that the state was unwilling to offer protection to the person affected.[19] The practice of the courts in the United Kingdom and the Federal Republic of Germany seems equally liberal and can be illustrated as follows. In 1985, the British High Court quashed a decision of the Secretary of State refusing to grant asylum to a Tamil asylum seeker, considering that as regards Tamils, which are a racial minority, the character of personal and individual persecution needs not to be proved and that, in accordance with Paragraph 65 of the UNHCR Handbook, "serious acts committed by the local populace may be considered as persecution if they are knowingly tolerated by the authorities". This case shows clearly that the High Court was willing to grant asylum to an applicant where the reason for persecution was simply membership in the Tamil minority.[20] This approach is similar in the Federal Republic of Germany where courts are willing to grant asylum to Tamils as members of a group subject to persecution not directly stemmed from the authorities.[21] Political persecution needs not always emanate from the authorities of the country of origin, it can also be carried out by third parties (ie, muslims individuals persecuting Yezidis or the Syrian military persecuting a Lebanese); but when the state of origin is unwilling or unable to offer protection, such persecution may be attributable to the state of origin.[22] Finally, the situation appears to present no major differences in Sweden. The state must be found responsible, directly or indirectly, for the persecution.[23] However, following a decision from the Government, both SIV and the Appeals Board have since denied Convention status to refugees whose persecutions are not directly an

---

[18] For instance, in the case of a Turkish asylum seeker, the Commission agreed that persecutions may also proceed from groups of population, purposely tolerated by the state's authorities or against which the state is not able to offer any protection. CPRR/90/263/FA015; CPRR/90/018/F035. However, the Commission, refused to grant the status of refugee to a Jewish Polish applicant who feared persecution from anti-Semite groups on the ground of her membership to the Jewish minority because the Polish authorities have always offered protection to Jewish people against such violent attacks. CPRR/92/180/R668.

[19] Mario Gattiker, *Procédure d'asile et de renvoi*, Document de Travail pour les représentants d'oeuvre d'entraide, OSAR, 1988, p. 20. See also abstract of a decision in IJRL, 1990, p. 650.

[20] *The Queen v. the Secretary of State for the Home Department, ex p. S.J.*, Queen's Bench Division of the High Court; abstract in IJRL, 1991, p. 336.

[21] Decision by the Administrative Tribunal in Berlin, abstract in IJRL, 1991, p. 335. However, the Federal Administrative Court does not recognize Tamils as refugees. See R. Marx, "The Criteria for Determining Refugee Status in the Federal Republic of Germany", IJRL, 1992, p. 159.

[22] Decisions by the Higher Administrative Court and the Administrative Appeals Court; abstracts in IJRL, 1991, respectively at p. 337 and 342.

[23] SOU 1994:54, *op. cit.*, p. 26. Indirect responsibility may occur if persecution took place with the tacit support of the state or when the state is unable to provide protection.

act of the state and have granted de facto or humanitarian status instead.[24] The UNHCR is against such an interpretation of the 1951 Convention and, on several occasions, it has suggested to the Government to change its attitude and to refer to the UNHCR Handbook which cannot be clearer on the subject: agents of a state include other groups of people when the state cannot offer protection or is unable to stop such acts.[25]

1.2. *Grounds of Persecution*

Refugees have to show that the persecution they fear is for one of the reasons provided by Article 1A(2), that is race, religion, nationality, membership of a particular social group and, political opinion.[26] Other grounds of perse-

---

[24] This attitude is the result of the Government position regarding Russian jews, which SIV and the Appeals board are bound to apply (SOU 1994:54, *op. cit.*, p. 27). A similar decision of principle was made by the Government concerning Bosnians in 1993 (it used to be the same for Lebanese), who were all granted a permanent residence permit on humanitarian grounds.

[25] Interview with Eva Singer (UNHCR), *op. cit.* At present, a case is pending before the Appeals Board, concerning a Bosnian who has been granted humanitarian status but who is seeking Convention status. The UNHCR has made a submission in this case. The problem is real because if the Appeals Board allows this Bosnian to be granted Convention status more than 40,000 Bosnians are as a result likely to appeal as well.

[26] Refer to Goodwin-Gill, *The Refugee in International Law*, *op. cit.*, for a clear analysis of each of these grounds at pp. 26–38 and their relation with fundamental human rights at pp. 39–40. See also, UNHCR Handbook, *op. cit.*, pp. 18–20.

[27] Traditionally, the Swedish Government refused to grant asylum to deserters from non-conventional wars, in particular to various armed elements in Lebanon. See P. Nobel, "What Happened with Sweden's Refugee Policies?", IJRL, 1990, p. 266. It also refused rape as a grounds of persecution, ie, for women and children from the Bosnian war zone (MNS, July 1993, p. 6), unless it can be shown that the state is directly or indirectly responsible (MNS, May 1994, p. 12). However, recent developments concerning Bosnians have occured and the Government has now agreed to grant residence permits to applicants on grounds of inhuman conditions (SOU 1994:54, *op. cit.*, p. 31). The Federal Administrative Court in Germany, similarly refuses to grant asylum to asylum seekers from civil war areas (MNS, February 1994, p. 6). While Belgian and British courts accept Tamil applicants, the German Federal Administrative Court does not recognize Tamils as refugees. See R. Marx, *op. cit.*, p. 159. Swiss authorities normally only provide temporary admission to victims of civil wars. See Alain Bovard, *op. cit.*, p. 5. The same applies in France.

[28] Cases of torture are not all recognized as proof of persecution. Impending tortures do not constitute a ground to be granted asylum in Switzerland (interview with C. della Croce and B. Clément, Centre Social Protestant, December 1990). And even when torture actually occured, at first instance it is exceptional that competent authorities have recourse to medical examinations to assert the origin of scars. Yet, a medical examination would sometimes back up the subjective statement of the asylum seeker. See Yves Brutsch, *Memorandum relatif à l'application de la législation sur l'asile à l'intention du Parti Socialiste Suisse*, Geneva, 1990, pp. 10–1. Torture is neither a ground for asylum in Sweden (MNS, July 1993, p. 6) but matreatments by the authorities while prisoners can be a ground for refugee status (SOU 1994:54, *op. cit.*, p. 25). In the Federal Republic of Germany, torture is not usually considered as political persecution, except in cases where the political intentions of the persecutor can be shown. Since 1987, however, the Federal Administrative Court has agreed to consider torture which aims at the extermination of Kurds as of a political nature. See R. Marx, *op. cit.*, pp. 157–8.

cution exist (ie, civil war,[27] torture,[28] criminal attacks[29]) which do not fall under the strict definition of Article 1A(2).[30] Persons subject to such fear of persecution have small chances to be granted the status of refugee but they are usually authorized to remain in the country on a temporary basis; Sweden being probably the only country where permanent residence permit is granted.[31] This is the case, in particular, of most asylum seekers from the former Yugoslavia area, with some distinctions, however, between countries.[32] According to paragraphs 40–42 of the UNHCR Handbook, fear of persecution contains a subjective (feelings, state of mind of the asylum seeker) and an objective element (factual situation) and both elements must be taken into consideration in order to assess the fear of each individual. Surely no state is willing to grant asylum to refugees on the sole grounds of subjective fear. Nevertheless, a practice based on objective and subjective grounds is likely to be more liberal[33] than a practice which would rely exclusively on

---

[29] More than a thousands of gypsies from Poland were denied asylum in Sweden and sent back to their country because of lack of grounds of persecution. Their reason was a local fight between gypsies and Poles resulting from a car accident in which a Pole was killed by a gypsy. ECRE Country Report, Sweden, 5–6 October 1991, p. 94.

[30] Notice that the definition of refugees provided by the 1969 OAU Convention includes victims of a civil strife or any form of instability in the country of origin.

[31] As a result of a decision of Government in 1993, Bosnians were granted permanent right to stay in Sweden for humanitarian reasons. This decision has been subject to criticisms and it has been suggested that refugees coming from civil war areas should be granted only temporary asylum in future. Such proposal is being considered before amending the 1989 Aliens Act any further in July 1994.

[32] In 1992, Sweden refused asylum to most of asylum seekers from Slovenia, Croatia, Serbia-Montenegro and Macedonia but refused to take any decision on asylum seekers from Bosnia-Herzegovina (ECRE Country Report, Sweden, 3–4 October 1992, pp. 120–1). Permanent residence permits were, nevertheless, granted to almost 42,000 Bosnians (this figure does not include family members) after a decision of principle adopted by the Government in 1993. Swedish authorities have always refused a right to remain to Kosovo Albanians, arguing that they do not risk being involved in the war in Bosnia (MNS, Jan.94, p. 7). This "tough attitude towards Kosovo Albanians is an exception in Europe" and has raised many complaints from the UNHCR and other European countries (MNS, Feb.94, p. 7). Notice, however, that people from Kosovo already in Sweden before January 1993 were all granted permanent residence permits, following a decision of Government (interview with Eva Ulfvebrand, Swedish Red Cross, *op. cit.*). British authorities have recently held that Sweden could not be considered as a safe third country for Kosovo Albanians (MNS, Feb.94, p. 8). Since June 1993, Bosnians require a visa to enter Sweden (*Ibid*, p. 5). Switzerland imposes a visa obligation for all asylum seekers coming from the former Yugoslavia, including Bosnia, since 1st December 1993. Germany has recognized Albanians from Kosovo as refugees; but because civil war does not constitute grounds for the granting of asylum, most other groups are granted limited permits to stay or at least a '*duldung*' (ECRE Country Report, FRG, April 1993). The United Kingdom, which used to return ex-Yugoslavs to the country in which they passed through, have finally decided to waive the 'third country' rule for ex-Yugoslavs (ECRE Country Report, UK, 3–4 October 1992, p. 134).

[33] This is the case in Belgium and in France, where the competent authorities do take into account subjective elements but only to a certain extent.

objective elements.[34] If states are legally bound to respect the principle of *non-refoulement*, they are not obliged to grant asylum to refugees and, in most countries, applicants failing to show objective fear of persecution are refused the status of refugee as provided in the 1951 Convention. They may, however, be granted a temporary right to stay or a *de facto* refugee status. In any case, manifestly unfounded or abusive applications for asylum are now subject to accelerated procedures.

Manifestly Unfounded or Abusive Requests

Access to a territory or the right to stay in that territory may be refused if it appears that the asylum seekers's request is manifestly abusive or unfounded.[35] This is the case, in particular, of requests based on personal, family, economical or social difficulties[36] but also requests containing wrong information,[37] or incomplete evidence[38] or, finally, based on forged documents.[39] The loss of travel documents or identity papers should not *a*

---

[34] See the application of the objective theory of fear by British, German and Swiss courts in J. Bhabha and G. Coll (Eds.), *Asylum and Practice in Europe and North America: A Comparative Analysis*, Federal Publications Inc., 1992, pp. 28–9. See also, W. Kälin, "Refugees and Civil Wars: Only a Matter of Interpretation?", IJRL, 1991, pp. 435–51 and R. Marx, *op. cit.*, p. 153, 156.

[35] This is the attitude adopted by most European countries. See, for instance, in Belgium, art.52 of the 1980 Law; in Switzerland, art.16a,b of the 1979 Asylum Law; in Germany, s.18a and s.30 of the AsylVfG; in Britain, rules 180F–G of the Immigration Rules (HC 725); and in France, the practice introduced in July 1992 (Amnesty International, *Europe: Harmonization of Asylum Policy. Accelerated procedures for 'manifestly unfounded' asylum claims and the 'safe country' concept*, November 1992, pp. 9–12). Like in France, Swedish authorities have introduced a similar practice (SOU 1994:54).

[36] The French CRR considers that besides true and real persecutions which affect directly and personally the applicant there exist many other distressful situations which do not reach the threshold of persecution, such as ordinary difficulties in the every day life or at work, constraints or vexation. F. Tiberghien, *op. cit.*, pp. 86, 88 and 101. See also SOU 1994:54, *op. cit.*, pp. 31–2 (with regard to Sweden) and s.30(2) of the German AsylVfG.

[37] See, for instance, the *Ryan* case, in Belgium. According to the opinion given by the General Commissioner to the Minister of Justice's refusal of the right to stay for Mr. Ryan, the Minister of Justice agreed to decide that Ryan's request was abusive and fraudulent because his statements relating to his activities and travels were confused and incomplete. The General Commissioner was more of the opinion that such statements may not necessarily reflect a voluntary attitude to elude Belgian authorities. See also C.E., *Bennani c. Etat Belge*, 17 March 1992, no. 39.015 (RDE, 1992, no. 69, p. 185).

[38] For example, when religion is invoked as a ground of persecution, the status of refugee is normally refused to the person who cannot answer fundamental questions on his belief, such as what particular religion is it and what makes it the subject of persecution. See, in particular, the Belgian decision of the *Commission Permanente de Recours des Réfugiés*, CPRR/90/026b/ R676.

[39] In the United Kingdom, charges against two alleged passports forgers had to be dropped for lack of evidence because the prosecution (the police and immigration officers) refused to reveal any details which could help forgers in improving their technics (MNS, May 1993, p. 4). But see Rule 180G (c) of the 1993 Immigration Rules, HC 725.

priori be considered as a fraud[40] nor as a criminal offence.[41] The lack of an identity or travel documents has, nevertheless influenced the practice relating to refugee determination[42] and the UNHCR Executive Committee has acknowledged the problem.[43] Prosecution for criminal charges is rarely considered as a ground for persecution, except in cases where the penalties are proved to be disproportionate and/or actually based on the political opinion or other opinion of the person concerned.[44]

---

[40] *First and Second Annual Reports, op. cit.*, p. 13 (in Belgium); MNS, December 93, p. 6 (in Germany). Since the airport-procedure (s.18a AsylVfG) was introduced in July 1993, the German BVerfG *de facto* became a second instance authority for many cases of refusal to enter (see B. Huber, *op. cit.*, p. 138). In the case *Yanlik I* (VG Frankfurt, 28.10.93, 10 G 20195/93A), the VG dismissed an application for interim relief to enter the country, because the applicant's application was manifestly unfounded on the grounds of lack of credibility (no identity document). The BVerfG confirmed the decision (04.11.93, NVwZ, Supplement 1994, p. 1) and further clarified the situation. It held "if the refused asylum seeker, after the case has been decided by VG, produces additional documents and offers to prove his identity, this shall not be decided in this proceedings; it would be a matter of remedy to be decided by the administrative court".

[41] Swedish Supreme Court, abstract of decision in IJRL, 1990, pp. 453–4. But in Britain, the House of Lords ruled that asylum seekers without valid travel documents are not illegal entrants if they do not use these documents to try and enter the United Kingdom clandestinely (MNS, June 1993, p. 8).

[42] The situation in Sweden has become very strict since a decision of principle adopted by the Government on 2 November 1989 stating that an Iranian citizen statement about her motives for being without identity and travel document can only lead to the conclusion that she has been in possession of such documents but wilfully get rid of them. "This fact decreases the credibility of the information she has invoked in support of her application for a resident permit". The application was therefore rejected. Göran Melander, *op. cit.*, p. 33. The impact of this decision is even greater today as a result of a line of interpretation adopted by the Appeals Board. As a rule, the absence of documents disqualifies for the convention refugee status, irrespective of the cause and of the persecution grounds. The applicant can only be granted *de facto* status or humanitarian status (SOU 1994:54, *op. cit.*, p. 27). The Head of the Appeals Board, nevertheless, "denies that the lack of documents alone reduces the chances of asylum seekers" (MNS, May 1994, p. 7). Identical practice is provided by the law in Germany, s.30(3)–2 of the AsylVfG.

[43] Conclusions on the Problem of Refugees and Asylum Seekers who move in a Irregular Manner from a Country in which they already found Protection (1989), Para.25.

[44] The Federal Administrative Court in Germany has agreed for many years that criminal proceedings against separatist activities can amount to political persecution if the motive behind such a prosecution is linked to the person's race, religion, nationality, membership to a particular social group or political opinion. Abstract of decision in IJRL, 1990, p. 651. In Sweden, only long incarceration (for instance eight years) is considered as a ground for refugee status and when Yugoslavia broke down and all various new states were created, Sweden was puzzled about what to do with all the drafters coming from areas where no war was going on (ie, all of them except Bosnia). The Swedish authorities then found out that if sent back, none of them were going to be punished (in the sense of inhuman treatment) although they were deserters. The common punishment was fines, police custody or at the worse imprisonment for two years. Under Swedish practice this is not sufficient to be granted a residence permit. Interview with Mr. Fischerström, Appeals Board (*op. cit.*).

Personal or Individual Fear of Persecution
Paragraph 43 of the UNHCR Handbook provides that "these considerations [well-founded fear of persecution] need not necessarily be based on the applicant's own personal experience. What, for example, happened to his friends or relatives and other members of the same racial or social group may well show his fear and that sooner or later he also will become a victim of persecution is well-founded". Most countries follow this recommendation.[45]

Conscientious Objection (for Religious or Political Reasons)
Articles 170 and 171 of the UNHCR Handbook provides that "a deserter may be recognized as a refugee on this sole ground". The General Commissioner in Belgium agrees to think that such provisions only apply to soldiers who are directly involved in armed conflicts. This is also the interpretation which results from the Swedish Aliens Act which provides that asylum is granted to war-resisters,[46] and defines a war-resister as "an alien who has deserted a theatre of war or fled from his country of origin or needs to remain in Sweden in order to escape imminent war service".[47] However, there may be other factors which, combined with desertion, can justify the granting of refugee status,[48] provided no internal flight alternative exists.[49] The important element to look at and to assess is the seriousness of the sanction and its disproportionate character. The same approach exists in France,[50] Sweden[51] and in the United

---

[45] In France: C.E., *Dankha*, 27 May 1983, (AJDA) 1983, p. 481. In Belgium: *Second Annual Report, op. cit.*, pp. 79–80. In Germany: the Federal Constitutional Court held that "a well founded fear of persecution may be based on persecution suffered by other members in the group"; abstract of the decision in IJRL, 1991, p. 99; see also, ECRE Country Report, FRG, 5–6 October 1991, pp. 67–8. As regards, "other members of the family", it seems that the general attitude of the German Courts is to only consider *personal* persecution and not to presume that the spouse of a victim of political persecution would also be persecuted (see M. Fullerton, *op. cit.*, pp. 396–7; interpretation to the contrary in ECRE Country Report, FRG, 22–23 September 1990, p. 54 and judgment from the BVerwG of 31.03.92, C 140.90, JUS 1993, Heft 8, pp. 687–8). In Switzerland, asylum seekers who are members of a social or religious group, which is persecuted as a whole, are released from having to show a personal fear of persecution; Mario Gattiker, *op. cit.*, p. 18. It seems that Swedish authorities only grant convention status to asylum seekers who can show individual and personal persecution. In any other circumstances, *de facto* or humanitarian status is usually granted, provided the applicant can prove a particularly great need for protection.

[46] Chapter 3, s.1(2). War resisters are rarely granted convention status, they normally benefit from *de facto* or humanitarian status.

[47] Chapter 3, s.3. Serbs deserters, for instance, have been refused asylum in Sweden and habe been sent back (MNS, July 1993, p. 6).

[48] On 14 August 1990, the *Tribunal Civil* of Brussels declared admissible the request from a Sri Lankan applicant of Tamil origin who left Sri Lanka to evade military service. The Court held that he was minor and that risks of persecution against the child was real. Abstract in IJRL, 1991, pp. 131–2.

[49] See *infra*, in this chapter.

[50] See F. Tiberghien, *op. cit.*, pp. 349–50.

[51] Only long incarceration (eight years for instance) is considered as an inhuman treatment. This is the practice today. Interview with Mr. Fischerström, Appeals Board (*op. cit.*).

Kingdom.[52] The Immigration Appeals Tribunal in the United Kingdom also admits that South Africans who have strong objections to apartheid may be recognized as refugees.[53] A more restrictive approach exists in the Federal Republic of Germany, where the intention of the persecutor is the sole criterion in order for the asylum seeker to prove persecution. However, in a recent case, the Federal Administrative Court admitted that a deserter from Iraq be considered as a political persecutee because the sanction incurred was probably going to be death penalty.[54] Finally, in Switzerland, conscientious objection or desertion from the military service does not constitute a ground for asylum.[55] This is regrettable but not surprising as the Swiss Government made a declaration not to be bound by Recommendation (87)8 adopted by the Committee of Ministers of the Council of Europe which states that persons with strong and serious reasons for objection may be exempted from this service and do a substituted service instead.[56]

Membership of a Particular Social Group
While the terms 'race', 'religion', 'nationality' are to be understood in their usual meaning,[57] problems arise concerning 'membership of a particular social group'. The UNHCR Handbook defined a 'particular social group' as normally comprising "persons of similar background, habits or social status". A claim to fear of persecution under this heading may frequently overlap with a claim to fear of persecution on other grounds, ie, race, religion or nationality.

---

[52] In the case *P.P.M. v. Secretary of State for the Home Department* (24 May 1984), the Immigration Appeal Tribunal, nevertheless, refused to grant asylum to a Christian citizen of Israel because Israel's requirement of compulsory military service is not excessive and does not constitute persecution against a Christian citizen who opposes service on the ground of his religion. Abstract in IJRL, 1991, p. 128. Similarly, asylum was refused to a citizen of Yugoslavia who feared persecution if sent back to his country because of his failure to perform military service. There was a lack of evidence that such persecution would occur. *D. Petrovski v. Secretary of State for the Home Department*, 22 October 1992, [1993] Imm AR, p. 134.

[53] This is in conformity with UN Resolution 33–165 on the status of persons refusing to serve in military and police forces to enforce apartheid (1978). *Asile en Europe, op. cit.*, p. 450.

[54] Federal Administrative Court, 25 June 1991, BVerwG 9 C 131.90.

[55] See, for instance, a decision of the Delegate for Refugee Matters which states that "fear of punishment for refusing military service is not a ground that justifies asylum"; abstract in IJRL, 1990, p. 650. However, as a matter of exception, it has recently been agreed that deserters from Croat, Bosnian and Serb armies will obtain provisional admission. ECRE Country Report, Switzerland, 3–4 October 1992, p. 127.

[56] Text of the Recommendation is published by CoE. It was adopted by the Committee of Ministers on 9 April 1987.

[57] UNHCR Handbook, paras.68–76. See, for example, the definition of religious persecution given by the Higher Administrative Court in Germany: "religious persecution occurs when acts are aimed at robbing a person of his or her religious identity, or when such acts destroy the minimum religious existence, which includes the possibility to practise one's religion and express one's religious convictions" (referring to the persecution of Yezidis by local muslims for reasons, at least partially, linked to their religion). Abstract of the decision in IJRL, 1991, p. 337.

A few examples of recognized social groups in *jurisprudence* shall be given in order to illustrate this concept. The French *Commission de Recours des Réfugiés* recognized the status of refugee to an applicant of Turkish nationality but of Kurdish origin on the ground that the applicant wrote and song Kurdish poems in order to preserve Kurdish cultural identity.[58] Similarly, the German Federal Constitutional Court (in conflict with the lower competent authorities in asylum matters), has agreed that membership in the Kurdish ethnic group of a Turkish national may rise to a well-founded fear of persecution, in particular if such membership is coupled with prosecution in Turkey for criminal behaviour because torture of the applicant in Turkey may be applied for political reasons.[59] The Administrative Court of Berlin, in conflict with the Federal Administrative Court, has also agreed that Tamils are persecuted as a group in Sri Lanka, therefore, membership in the Tamil population group constitutes a ground for asylum.[60] On a more general scale, members of traditional African groups (ie, the Baganda in Uganda) are recognized as particular social groups.[61] The French Commission of Appeal has also recently recognised that female circumcision is persecution and that women fearing persecution because of their refusal of such a mutilation are to be regarded as a social group. [62] In Sweden, applicants who fear persecution, harassment or serious discrimination due to their sex or sexual tendencies, in other words gay men or lesbians, are usually granted residence permits for humanitarian reasons.[63] However, the British Home Office has not yet accepted that gay men or lesbians belong to a social group. The Secretary of State, indeed, stated that "their only common characteristic is a sexual preference which, if it is revealed at all, is normally only revealed in private. A group cannot be a social group if its only common characteristic is so concealed".[64] However, in a few rare occasions, exceptional leave to remain was granted to gay men coming from countries such as Iran and Argentina.[65] A similar approach exists in the Federal Republic of Germany where homosexuals are not normally granted asylum. Nevertheless, in 1983 the Administrative Court of Wiesbaden agreed to consider Iranian homosexuals as a particular social group because there were enough evidence of their execution as punishment,[66] and in 1993, the

---

[58] *Ibid*, p. 743.

[59] *Ibid*, p. 744. There is however "no automatic right to asylum for Kurds" according to the Administrative Court in Hessen (MNS, Feb.94, p. 6).

[60] IJRL, 1991, p. 335 and R. Marx, *op. cit.*, p. 159.

[61] See generally, the article by M. Fullerton, *op. cit.*, pp. 381–444.

[62] *Mademoiselle X.*, 19 September 1991, in *Public Law*, Spring 1993, pp. 196–8.

[63] ECRE Country Report, Sweden, 3–5 April 1992, p. 123. See also, K. Jönsson, *op. cit.*, para.56.

[64] *R v. Secretary of State for the Home Department, ex p. Zia Mehmet Binbasi*, [1989] Imm AR 595. See also, C. Vincenzi, *op. cit*, pp. 134–5.

[65] Sue Shutter, *Immigration and nationality law handbook*, Joint Council for the Welfare of Immigrants, 1992, p. 63.

[66] M. Fullerton, *op. cit.*, p. 408. See also, decision of the Federal Administrative Court, abstract in IJRL, 1989, p. 110.

High Administrative Court "ruled that homosexuality as a ground for asylum is only relevant in cases of non-reversibility".[67] The Administrative Court of Berlin also refused to consider gypsy people from Romania (Roma) as an ethnic group to which membership gives reason to be granted asylum.[68]

Political Opinion

The difficulty consists in proving that the opinions the asylum seeker hold are not tolerated by the authorities, that such opinions have become known to the authorities[69] and that he may be subject to arbitrary and disproportionate punishment.[70] Although the attitude of French jurisdictions is usually quite liberal, there are also some restrictive decisions taken in the matter where for lack of adequate evidence the court is not prepared to be convinced otherwise. For instance, in the case of *Mac Nair*, the *Conseil d'Etat* held that although the circumstances of hijacking a plane could have had a political ground, it does not imply that legal proceedings which follow from such an act (the fear) constitute a persecution on the ground of political opinion.[71] Similarly, political asylum in Sweden was refused to a Russian couple who hijacked a plane in February 1992.[72] However, asylum seekers who can prove that they "held leading positions in opposition movements [or] have been harassed for an extended period by the authorities" are entitled to convention status.[73] In Germany, for instance, asylum was granted to an Iranian women refugee on the grounds that refusal to enforce Islamic dress codes in the school where she worked was a serious crime in Iran and, therefore, should be assimilated to a political crime.[74]

1.3. *How to Prove a 'Well-Founded Fear'?*

It is a difficult task to appreciate the real worth of each document or evidence given by an applicant to the competent authority, above all since so many applications are made by economic refugees (as opposed to genuine or political refugees) who flee from their country to settle in another country

---

[67] Case concerning an appeal lodged by a Romanian homosexual and refused by the Court. The sanction for homosexuality in Romania is one to five years imprisonment. MNS, March 1993, p. 7.

[68] MNS, April 1993, p. 5 and June 1993, p. 7.

[69] See, however, the attitude of the Federal Constitutional Court in Germany which held that persecution may exist even if authorities in the country were not aware of such activities. Abstract of decision in IJRL, 1993, pp. 118–9.

[70] It is known that, a political activist, in Turkey, faces a greater danger of being tortured during detention and interrogation than a normal criminal. Such torture is an act of political persecution. Decision of the Federal Administrative Court in Germany, abstract in IJRL, 1990, p. 467.

[71] C.E., *Mac Nair*, 18 April 1980, in AJDA 1980, p. 613. See also, CRR, *Apalategui Ayerbe*, 27 March 1983, requête 9.485, in F. Tiberghien, *op. cit.*, p. 361.

[72] MNS, July 1993, p. 12.

[73] SOU 1994:54, *op. cit.*, p. 25.

[74] Judgment by the Administative Court of Ansbach (VG), abstract in IJRL, 1993, p. 611.

where they may get a better standard of living. This is the reason why a few years ago European countries introduced higher standards of proof and more accurate and convincing components of proof are since required. This attitude exists in almost every country in Europe, in particular France,[75] the United Kingdom[76] and Sweden.[77] One could argue that it is fully justified, for if it appears that during the procedure the applicant may be a genuine refugee, theoretically, the concerned authorities should give the applicant the benefit of the doubt or otherwise help him to get enough required evidence.[78]

There is now a general acceptance on the meaning of "well-founded". German[79] and Swiss courts[80] require that there is a "considerable probability" and British authorities that there is a "reasonable degree of likelihood",[81] coupled with strict procedural requirements. Belgian authorities require that there is a "serious possibility".[82] The French CRR require a plausible or reasonable fear in order to grant the status of refugee to applicants. Statements which appear to be sincere although they only constitute satisfactory presumptions are considered as showing reasonable fear.[83] However, French authorities have become more demanding on the procedural aspects of showing a "well-founded fear" and they now tend to rely on stricter evidences.[84] In Sweden, standards of proof have traditionally been very high. Refugee criteria are interpreted in a very restrictive way and rare are asylum seekers who are granted convention status. To be eligible for such a status, one must

---

[75]   J. Bhabha and G. Coll, *op. cit.*, pp. 33–4.

[76]   The case of *Dikko* shows that the Home Office took its decision of withdrawing the right of asylum to Mr. Dikko on the sole basis of a Report by the British High Commission in Lagos to the Home Office, concluding that many of Mr. Dikko's fears were exaggerated (*The Independent*, 12 May 1989, p. 18 and 18 May 1989, p. 27). In another case, *Viraj Mendis* (a Sri Lankan illegal immigrant), was refused political asylum by the British authorities on the ground that "the slim evidence in support of his fear has failed to convince those he had to convince, including the UNHCR". (*The Times*, 19 January 1989, p. 13, see facts, p. 1).

[77]   It seems that while in the past authorities listened to the advice of psychiatrists, they do no longer take into account such advice, even when there is a serious risk of suicide if the person is sent back to his country of origin (MNS, May 1993, p. 6). Moreover, new methods and criteria are now being used to decide on the credibility of an application. In particular, an application for asylum which is not lodged immediately upon arrival in Sweden is likely to fail; also if the asylum seeker was able to leave his country of origin and persecution legally and in possession of all necessary documents and proofs (MNS, Feb.94, p. 7).

[78]   As provided in para.196 of the UNHCR Handbook.

[79]   R. Marx, "The Criteria for Determining ...", *op. cit.*, p. 165. See also , decision of the Federal Administrative Court, abstract in IJRL, 1990, p. 467.

[80]   Article 12a of the Asylum Law. Decision of the Delegate for Refugee Matters, abstract in IJRL, 1990, pp. 649–50. See also W. Kälin, "Just another Brick in the Wall? A Swiss Report on the Use of Computerized Textual Elements in Substantiating Negative Asylum Decisions", IJRL, 1989, p. 83.

[81]   See the House of Lords interpretation in *R v. Secretary of State for the Home Department, ex p. Sivakumaran*, [1988] 1 All ER, 195,198. See also, R. Marx, *op. cit*, p. 166.

[82]   CPRR/91/141b/F087.

[83]   R. Marx, *op. cit.*, p. 167.

[84]   See J. Bhabha and G. Coll, *op. cit.*, pp. 32–3. Also F. Tibergien, *op. cit.*, pp. 88–90.

prove strong individual persecution, on political grounds, directly from the state. As soon as some humanitarian reasons are considered or, circumstances appear not to be so great or, there is a slight doubt about evidence, *de facto* status will be granted instead.[85] It seems that SIV is applying the 1951 Convention definition in a more liberal way than the Appeals Board but it has also been argued that SIV's decisions were often wrongly motivated.[86] Recent methods and criteria are being used to decide on the credibility of an application.[87] These are very strict and are the result of an extensive interpretation by the Appeals Board of the Government decision of 1989 concerning undocumented asylum seekers.[88] To sum up, the objective standard of proof based on probability developed by the German, Swedish and Swiss courts imposes higher expectations and burden of proof on the asylum seeker than does the subjective/objective standard of proof adopted in Belgian or France or even the British objective standard of proof based on likelihood, rather than probability.[89]

1.4. *Past, Present and Future Persecution*

The very terms of the 1951 Convention prompt national jurisdictions to adopt a liberal interpretation on this matter. Indeed, by subordinating the recognition of the refugee status to fears of being persecuted, it allows the applicant to take advantage not only of past or present persecutions but also of a fear of future persecutions.

---

[85] Notice also that refusal or withdrawal of refugee status (convention, *de facto* or humanitarian) is automatic as soon as the applicant is found guilty of crimes or it is discovered that he lied about his identity or nationality. Interview with the Agency for Advisory Service (*op. cit.*). For example, Sweden has recently agreed to reject asylum seekers from Bosnia on the sole grounds of criminal offences (MNS, Dec.93, p. 7 and Feb.94, p. 7).

[86] "At SIV, they have a few standard sentences. If a person has left the country legally, they say that the person is not persecuted. They don't take into account the fact that in most countries of the world, except perhaps Iran, you can leave your country legally". Interview with Eva Singer, UNHCR (*op. cit.*).

[87] As a result of the Ministry of Culture request that an investigation be made on the comparison between the Appeals Board decisions and those from its predecessor (the Government), a report was adopted in April 1994. The investigation concluded that there had been no changes in general. However, a point was made that the Appeals Board is now using methods to evaluate the credibility of asylum seekers applications and there was criticism made about the fact that too much importance was given to these elements. According to such methods, asylum seekers with no passport, asylum seekers who do not apply immediately at the border or asylum seekers whose statements at the border and in the country do not fully match can never be granted convention status. They may however be granted *de facto* status or humaniatarian status, or nothing at all in cases where no serious persecution exists. Interview with the Agency for Advisory Service (*op. cit.*). See also, SOU 1994:54, *op. cit.*, pp. 32–3.

[88] A current report is suggesting taking into account the impact of the behaviour of an asylum seeker on the decision making. "The criteria to use are still very unclear and do not appear legal in any way. Such a report would affect all the Bosnians and we hope that it will not go any further". Interview with Eva Singer, UNHCR (*op. cit.*).

[89] R. Marx, *op. cit.*, pp. 166,168.

Traditionally, the French CRR and the *Conseil d'Etat* have always been quite reluctant to take into account future persecution or threat of being persecuted.[90] The *Conseil d'Etat* has paid particular attention to the fact that the president of OFPRA and CRR take into account the date of the day they rule on the request to appreciate the fear of persecution.[91] Thus improvements of the political situation in the country of persecution since the time of flight are sufficient criteria to deny refugee status to asylum seekers and refugees "sur place".[92] In Sweden, asylum, understood as permanent residence permit, is granted to refugees[93] but also to war-resisters and those with strong refugee-like grounds.[94] Convention refugee status seems to be granted to only a minority of applicants who can prove current persecution. In cases of doubt, the applicant may, nevertheless, be granted *de facto* or humanitarian status. The General Commissioner in Belgium agrees that the date of the persecution is not the only factor to be taken into account; the nature of the fear and the future perspectives of improvement of the situation in that country are also relevant.[95] The CPRR agrees that because decisions on the status of refugee are declaratory, fear of persecution must be appreciated in accordance with the situation as prevailing the day the request was introduced.[96] German courts' practice consists in taking into account the situation in the country of origin the day the last decision on the facts is possible.[97] However, fear of persecution which can seriously be expected in the near future are also often taken into account.[98] Swiss authorities require that the persecution or the fear of being persecuted be present. Therefore, if before fleeing to Switzerland the applicant remained in his country of origin without fears, no account will be taken of his past persecutions. Likewise, a persecution is not considered as present if the day the decision is taken the applicant may be able to return to his country of origin with no more fear of being persecuted. Like in all the other countries, Swiss authorities appreciate the situation the day they take their decisions. The attitude of British authorities is similar. The persecution or fear of persecution must exist at the time the decision is made. This is why scars which are so old that they cannot have been caused by the present regime against which the applicant is complaining do not make him a genuine asylum

---

[90] F. Tiberghien, *op. cit.*, pp. 91–3.

[91] C.E., 26 novembre 1982, *Ferreyra*, requête 34.892; F. Tiberghien, *op. cit.*, p. 246.

[92] Persons who are present in the French territory at the time a crisis arises in their country of origin (ie, a *coup d'Etat*) and who, therefore, cannot return safely or continue to claim protection from that country.

[93] As defined by Chapter 3, s.2 of the Aliens Act.

[94] Chapter 3, s.1.

[95] *Second Annual Report, op. cit.*, p. 82.

[96] CPRR/90/277/R288; CPRR/89/245/R379.

[97] The Federal Administrative Court annulled a decision of a lower court on the ground that the decisive moment to take into account is the situation at the time of the decision by the court, thus the situation in Sudan after 1988, that is after the agreement between Ethiopian and Sudan had been signed. Abstract of decision in IJRL, 1993, pp. 117–8.

[98] BVerwGE 9C286.80, decision of 31 March 1981; EZAR No. 3, 200.

seeker. Likewise, refugees "sur place", such as visitors or students, who apply for the status of refugee at the time their visa or period of study expire may only be recognized as genuine refugees if at the time of their application, the political situation in their home country has remained unchanged since they left.[99]

According to paras.94–96 of the UNHCR Handbook, asylum should also be granted to refugees with post-flight reasons. In all six countries under review, only pre-flight reasons are usually considered as constituting valid grounds of persecution. Post-flight reasons of persecution are normally not examined. However, a distinction needs to be made between objective and subjective post-flight reasons. Objective post-flight reasons are considered grounds for asylum. This is usually the case concerning aliens already "sur place" (already in the country) who become refugees as a consequence of political changes in their home country (ie, a *coup d'Etat*) or other objective reasons occurring after their flight. Subjective post-flight reasons do not, normally, entitle an applicant to asylum and the status of refugee.[100] Subjective post-flight activities include, in particular, political opinions held after departure from the home country but also the illegal departure from the home country[101] or the marriage with a person of a different religion.[102] In most countries, national authorities and courts accept that political opinions, held by the alien "sur place", can be considered as persecution if these opinions are consistent with previous beliefs and behaviour, in particular, if these opinions were already held in the country of origin before departure and were known by

---

[99] "...fear of persecution ... is to be objectively determined by reference to the circumstances at the time prevailing". In *R v. Secretary of State for the Home Department, ex p. Sivakumaran* and conjoined appeals, [1988] 1 All E R at 193, 196.

[100] As already mentioned (*supra*), states refuse to grant asylum and refugee status solely on subjective grounds (acts of persecution which may arise after or are created because of the flight) as opposed to objective grounds (acts of persecution which existed before or during the flight).

[101] This refers, in particular, to the now obsolete concept of *Republikflucht*. Many Eastern European countries strongly penalized illegal departures or non-authorized stays in a capitalist country. Switzerland, for instance, has always refused to grant asylum to this kind of refugees.

[102] The Higher Administrative Court of Mannheim held that the marriage, in Poland, between an Iranian Muslim and a Polish Christian as well as the Christian upbringing of their children constituted a subjective ground of persecution (if the husband was sent back to Iran). However, the BVerwG referring to a basic judgment from the constitutional court (BVerfG) agreed that such a subjective reason may justify asylum in exceptional circumstances. It then agreed that prohibition of marriage because of religion or nationality constitutes a severe infringement of human dignity. Therefore, in this case, asylum could and should be considered and it referred the case back to the lower court. BVerwG, judgment from 06.04.1992, 9C143.90, in JUS 1993, Heft 8, pp. 688–9.

the home country authorities.[103] In any case, if they are not granted the status of convention refugee, they are at least protected against *refoulement*.[104]

2. Proving the Lack of Protection

The text of Article 1A(2) of the 1951 Convention is clear: "... is unable or ... is unwilling to avail himself of the protection of that country; or ... is unable or ... is unwilling to return to it" and should be read in relation to the cessation clauses set out in Article 1C.[105] It can, therefore, be deduced that an applicant who is still protected by his country of nationality before applying for refugee status will not be granted this status. Likewise, if an applicant benefits from the protection of his country of origin after having been granted the status of refugee, the 1951 Convention no longer applies to him. However, an important question arises when the applicant sojourned in or travelled through a safe third country before arriving to the country where he requests asylum. Shall he be considered as being protected by this third country?

2.1. *Non-Protection of the Country of Origin*

The refugee must refuse the protection of his country of origin, it implies that he must not voluntarily claim it, that he must not try to regain his lost nationality, and finally, that he must not go back to settle in his country of origin. If the whole country of origin is considered as a safe country or if only an area of it is, the refugee is normally sent back to that country or area according to the principles of safe country of origin and of internal flight alternative.

In France, an interesting and commendable reversal of *jurisprudence* occurred. Before 1982, CRR and the *Conseil d'Etat* used to agree that an applicant who went back to his country of origin could not make use of previous persecutions. The argument was that in such a situation the applicant did not lose the protection of his country of origin.[106] The French CRR, today, still assimilates to a claim of protection, a demand for a nationality

---

[103] For the case of France, reference may be made to decisions in F. Tiberghien, *op. cit.*, pp. 385–92. In Germany, the Constitutional Court went even further and agreed that activities may be of minor nature and that the authorities of the country of origin need not be aware of such activities (abstracted in IJRL, 1993, pp. 118–9). Moreover, the Constitutional Court held that exceptions to the rule exist, in particular in cases where the expression of a political opinion before flight could not have happened because the applicant was too young (abstracts in IJRL, 1991. p. 739 and IJRL, 1992, p. 259). This interpretation follows from s.28 of the Asylum Procedure Act (AsylVfG).

[104] ECRE Country Report, Germany, 7–9 March 1991, p. 61. In Switzerland, this is provided in art.8a of the 1979 Asylum Law.

[105] See, for example, Paul Weis, "Le concept de réfugié en droit international", *op. cit.*, p. 974 et seq.

[106] See decisions in, F. Tiberghien, *op. cit.*, pp. 96 and 120.

passport, for a passport, for a visa, for being repatriated and more important is the voluntary character of the claim.[107] But, on 3 November 1982,[108] the *Conseil d'Etat* abandoned its *jurisprudence* to the benefit of a particularly liberal solution that is to say that a voluntary return to the country of origin does not exclude in all cases the taking into account of previous activities of the applicant, it must be a matter of fact and there can be no *a priori* assumptions on this point. A similar approach exists in Belgium where the General Commissioner agrees that a period of time of many years in the country of persecution is not a ground by itself to refuse to grant refugee status, as it may be impossible for some refugees to escape, particularly if travel restrictions exist.[109] In Switzerland, on another hand, it is common practice to refuse asylum to applicants who it appears have been persecuted or have feared of being persecuted but who remained in their country of origin or of residence for a while (months or years) and flee to Switzerland only after a certain period of time. They are normally not considered as genuine refugees with an urgent need of protection.[110] The same approach exists in Sweden[111] and in the United Kingdom. British courts agree that a two year gap between the last persecution in the home country (Turkey) and the departure of the applicant is sufficient evidence that the applicant had found a safe area in which to live in his country.[112]

In all the six countries under review, asylum is refused if the applicant is coming from a safe country of origin, sometimes even leave to enter is refused. In Belgium, France, Sweden and the United Kingdom such possibility arises from the practice of the competent authorities.[113] In Germany and Switzerland, countries of origin considered as safe are listed in the domes-

---

[107] *Ibid*, pp. 397–400 and pp. 443–4.

[108] C.E., *Balasubramaniam*, 3 novembre 1982, requête 36.257; *ibid*, p. 246.

[109] *Second Annual Report* (1989), *op. cit.*, p. 82.

[110] Article 16(1)d of the 1979 Asylum Law also provides that applications from asylum seekers, who went back to their country of origin during the time of the asylum procedure, are subject to non-entry.

[111] Applicants may nevertheless be granted a permanent residence permit on de facto grounds or for humanitarian reasons.

[112] *R v. Secretary of State for the Home Department, ex p. Celal Yurekli*, Imm AR [1990], 334.

[113] Art.52(1)7 of the Belgian Law of 18 July 1991, which provided the rule of "double 5%" according to which countries like Ghana, India, Nigeria, Pakistan and Romania were considered to be safe, was abolished following much criticism from the UNHCR and Amnesty International (Arbitration decision of 4 March 1993, M.B. 25.03.1993, p. 6004). Art.52(1)7 now provides that an application is manifestly unfounded if the asylum seeker does not provide any elements that he may fear serious persecution. The situation is similar in France where the recent French Law No. 93–1027 of 24 August 1993 incorporates the provisions of the Dublin Convention and of the Schengen Agreement. As for Sweden, refugees coming from safe countries are usually sent back straight away. In 1993–94, as a result of decisions in single cases, Bulgaria and Romania have been declared safe countries (they are now members of the CoE). Poland, Hungary and the former Czechoslovakia are equally considered safe countries. The Baltic States, nevertheless, remain unsafe. Interview with Johan Fischerström, Appeals Board, *op. cit.* In the UK, rule 180D of the Immigration Rules 1993 (HC 725) provides that

tic laws.[114] Similarly, asylum is refused if an internal flight alternative is available.[115] In the UK, the law explicitly provides that applications for asylum are to be refused if there is a part of the country which is safe and to which applicants can be expected to go.[116] Like most German courts,[117] French and Swiss courts believe that in most cases there is an internal flight alternative for Turkish Kurds in West Turkey.[118] This is also the attitude of the Swedish authorities towards Turkey and Lebanon.[119]

2.2. *Non-Protection of a Third Country*

According to the spirit of the 1951 Convention, refugee status and asylum may only be granted to individuals who do not benefit at all from the protection of any country. This requirement is fully justified, for it guarantees an essential distribution of refugees among states. Therefore, believing that the parties to the 1951 Convention did not wish to encourage a person who has a new country to abandon it in preference for another, national courts have held that where the person has willingly left the country to which he originally fled, he cannot thereupon claim the status of refugee and the benefit of the privileges

---

unfounded applications may be refused without consideration on their substance. This rule, in practice, applies to asylum seekers coming from safe countries of origin.

[114] In Germany, see Art.16aIII–1 of the Basic Law and s.18a, s.29a, Annex II of the Asylum Procedure Act 1993 (on the constitutionality of s.18a, see judgment by the BVerfG, 19.07.1993, NVwZ 1993, 768). In Switzerland, Art.16(2) of the Asylum Law.

[115] For examples of decisions, see IJRL, 1992, pp. 97–101.

[116] HC 725, rule 180I. *R v. Secretary of State for the home Department ex p. D.S. Vigna*, 9 October 1992, [1993] Imm AR, p. 93. The applicant, a Tamil, was deported to the area of Colombo considered as a safe area in Sri Lanka by British authorities, despite a warning from the UNHCR in a confidential memorandum sent to governments in 1992. Notice, however, that deportation was ordered following convictions for importing heroin in the UK.

[117] In a judgment from 21 January 1994, the lower court of Köln (VG Köln, 21 January 1994, 18 K 10458/90) recently held that the West part of Turkey could not be considered as a safe area for Turkish Kurds. The applicant, a Turkish Kurd, was successful at showing fear of individual persecution in East Turkey. The court then considered whether an internal flight alternative existed in the West, in particular in Istambul, and finally agreed that serious discrimination, based on the language spoken by Kurds, existed, particularly in cities, against Kurds and that such discrimination reached the threshold of persecution (no possibility of work, thus, no money, no housing and no food). However, this judgment is not final and is subject to further decisions before the high courts, which have until now always considered the West part of Turkey as a safe area.

[118] ECRE Country Report, Switzerland, 5–6 October 1991, p. 101.

[119] Swedish authorities recognise that the Turkish military is responsible for persecuting Kurds in the South-East area but they agree that these Kurds would not be persecuted by the military in Istambul. However, it seems that the situation is getting more complicated every day and the possibility of internal flight to Istambul as a safe area is now under re-consideration by the authorities. UNHCR has not yet a policy on that. Interview with Eva Singer, UNHCR, *op. cit.* As regards India, the German Constitutional Court recently recognized that although Sikhs in general can evade the civil-war like situation in Punjab by settling in other parts of India, such alternative is not possible for individual Sikhs who are suspected to be members or supporters of militant Sikhs organizations (BVerfG, 02.12.1992, NVwZ 1994, Supplement no. 2, p. 11).

which flow from it. He will simply be a foreigner. Non-protection of a third country traditionally means that the refugee must not have acquired a new nationality, nor must he have received asylum in a country where he enjoyed rights and obligations similar to the ones ensuing from nationality. Today, this concept also means that the refugee must not have had the opportunity to apply for asylum in that third country, irrespective of the length of time spent in that country.

The 'Country of First Asylum' Principle or 'Safe Third Countries' Cases [120]

A refugee is expected to seek asylum in the first country he arrives after fleeing, provided that country is safe from persecution and from *refoulement*. A refugee who, before arriving in the target country, has stayed in a 'first country of asylum' or 'safe third country' may be returned, as a rule, to that country. This principle is applied by almost all countries which have acceded to the 1951 Convention.[121] Such situations have increased since the arrival of thousands of refugees from Eastern and Central Europe, in particular from the former Yugoslavia.[122] They usually first enter a country on the periphery of Western Europe (ie, Austria, Italy or Germany) but may only apply for asylum once they reached their target country (ie, France, Belgium, Sweden or the United Kingdom). Moreover, according to Article 31 of the 1951 Convention, only refugees "coming *directly* from a territory where their life or freedom was threatened" shall not be penalized because of their illegal entry in a country. From the background of this ambiguous reference, European countries have developed a practice excluding from any substantive consideration on the merits the cases of refugees who have found or are deemed to have found asylum or protection elsewhere, or who are considered to have spent too long in transit. These cases are generally known as 'third safe country cases' or 'country of first asylum cases' and have led to the creation of refugees 'in orbit'. However, Article 33 of the 1951 Convention prohibits the *refoulement* of refugees "in any manner whatsoever" to a country where they may fear persecution, which could include return via a third country.[123] The major problem with regard to third country cases rests on the fact that there is not as yet any obligation for member states to ensure that a third country is actually safe.[124]

The Principle in Each Country

Most European countries only examine claims for asylum if the applicant first entered their respective territory after having left his country of origin. No

---

[120] This principle is not to be confused with the concept of 'safe countries of origin'.

[121] On the principle of the country of first asylum, see, for instance, Goodwin-Gill, *The Refugee in International Law, op. cit.*, pp. 52–6.

[122] However, safe third countries cases also exist among refugees coming from other continents (ie, Africa or Asia).

[123] Amnesty International, *Europe: Harmonization of Asylum Policy ..., op. cit.*, pp. 16–7.

[124] *Ibid.*

more permission to enter Belgium, Germany, France, Sweden, Switzerland or the United Kingdom as a second country of asylum is granted. There is no unanimously accepted definition of the term 'country of first asylum', which is one of the reasons for the phenomenon of refugees 'in orbit'. The principle is applied differently in various countries but seems to be closely related to the problem of undocumented asylum seekers.[125]

Belgium

Article 52 of the Law of December 1980 states that the Minister of Justice or his representative will refuse access to Belgian territory to any alien who has not come directly to Belgium but has stayed at least three months in a safe third country[126] or in several safe third countries[127] or who is in possession of valid travel documents to a third country.[128] However, like in Switzerland, Belgium recognizes the principle of a second asylum.[129]

Federal Republic of Germany

Aliens coming from a safe third country can no longer claim a right of asylum. Their application is considered irrelevant.[130] This is now provided by Article 16aII of the Basic Law. It follows from this very restrictive provision that asylum will not be granted to those who enter from a EU member state or from a third country where adherence to the 1951 Convention and the ECHR is secured. Countries outside the EU, to which the above applies, will be determined by decree, subject to the approval of the *Bundesrat*. Article 16aII finally provides that, in all such cases, deportation measures can be carried out regardless of an appeal. The list of safe third countries is to be found in Annex I to section 26a of the Asylum Procedure Act.[131] Section 26a of the Asylum Act is equally a new provision. It basically implements Article 16aII of the Basic Law. S.27 of the Asylum Act on safety from persecution elsewhere remained, however, unchanged. The "protection elsewhere' requirement had long been interpreted as meaning that the asylum seeker must have stayed in a third country at least three months and that durable solutions were available

---

[125] Göran Melander, *op. cit.*, pp. 21–3.

[126] Article 52(1)4. Two examples of *jurisprudence* in, ECRE Country Report, Belgium, 7–9 March 1991, p. 37.

[127] Article 52(1)5. See the *Ryan* case (GC/88/0794/423M/S407/ADEF) in, for instance, *First Annual Report* (1988), *op. cit.*, pp. 69–73.

[128] Article 52(1)6.

[129] Article 49–3 and Article 55.

[130] S.29, AsylVfG.

[131] According to Annex I (AsylVfG), EU member states, as well as Finland, Norway, Austria, Poland, Sweden, Switzerland and the Czech Republic are considered safe third countries. On the classification of the Czech Republic as a safe country, see for instance, VG Regensburg, NVwZ, Supplement 1993, p. 13 and VGH München, NVwZ, Supplement 1/1994, p. 4. As an example of an Hungarian asylum seeker coming from Austria (safe third country) and deported back there, see BVerfG, judgment of 26.10.93, NVwZ, Supplement 1/1994, p. 3.

in the third country.[132] Today, the scope of s.27 is limited to countries not listed as safe third countries. Therefore, an asylum seeker coming from a safe third country will be subject to deportation even if he spent less than three months there.[133] In assessing the "safety" of a country, the *Bundesrat* takes into account the fact that no persecution nor inhuman or degrading punishment or treatment take place in that country. Moreover, this must be the case nationwide and assessment of the situation must be made individually. The German law thus seems to provide criteria which mostly correspond to the Resolution on Manifestly Unfounded Applications for Asylum adopted by the EC Immigration Ministers in London on 30 November 1992.[134] In two recent cases, the Federal Constitutional Court (BVerfG) has, nevertheless, ruled out the safety of Greece as a third country and it has authorised the persons concerned in both cases to apply for asylum in Germany because as far as Greece is concerned, although it is a signatory to the 1950 ECHR, it does return rejected applicants to their country of origin and of persecution.[135] Both decisions have been strongly criticized and described as an "enormous slap in the face" for European integration.[136]

France

The distinction between asylum seekers arriving directly from their country of origin and asylum seekers arriving from a third country is essentially made in practice. Indeed, circular instruction of 17 May 1985[137] distinguishes aliens with a resettlement visa from those without. It is only in practice, usually at an early stage of the procedure, that the competent authorities will actually take into account the fact that the asylum seeker came from a third country, to decide on whether or not to grant the status of refugee to the applicant. In 1981, in the *Conté* case, the French *Conseil d'Etat* quashed a decision of the Commission of Appeals[138] which refused to recognize the refugee status of the applicant, M. Conté, *on the sole ground* that between the day he left Guinea, his country of origin and of persecution, in 1971 and the day he

---

[132] The Administrative Court (VG) of Ansbach, annulled the refusal of the Federal Office for the Recognition of Refugees to grant asylum on the ground that the situation in Pakistan was unsafe and that if the applicant (Iranian national, who left Iran for Pakistan where he stayed for 18 months) was returned there, there was no guarantee that he would not be sent back to Iran. (Abstract of decision in IJRL, 1992, p. 555). See also, the liberal interpretation given by the Federal Administrative Court (BVerwG) in the case of an Eritrean woman who flew from Ethiopia to Germany via Sudan and Italy. The Court accepted her claim for asylum on the ground that "a flight does not terminate merely by passing through, or briefly remaining in a country ... To determine whether a flight has terminated, regard should be had to objective factors ... such as the hiring of a house, setting up of business...". (Abstract of decision in IJRL, 1990, p. 655).

[133] Bundesministerium des Innern, "Das Neue Asylrecht ...", *op. cit.*, pp. 6–9.

[134] Joachim Henkel, *op. cit.*, pp. 2708–9.

[135] NJW 1993, Heft 49, p. 3192; MNS, October 1993, pp. 5–6.

[136] MNS, October 1993, pp. 5–6.

[137] From the Prime Minister, relating to asylum seekers.

[138] See C.E., 16 janvier 1981, *Conté*, in *Rec.*(1981), p. 250.

arrived in France in 1975 to apply for asylum, he resided in Senegal. The *Conseil d'Etat* stated that, firstly, the fear of M. Conté of being persecuted in his country of origin if sent back was real and true, secondly, an applicant defined as a refugee according to Art.1A(2) of the 1951 Convention cannot be refused the status of refugee and, therefore, the right of asylum *on the sole ground* that he has resided in a third country. The *Conseil d'Etat*, therefore, quashed the decision of the CRR, and sent the case back to the CRR, according to the practice of the French administrative appeals system. According to the remarks of M.B. Pacteau on the decision,[139] it appears that the so-called 'third country of asylum' *jurisprudence* has been condemned through this case, even if the applicant was granted the full status of refugee or the one of refugee *de facto* in this third country.[140] However, this may be going too far in the interpretation of the terms of the decision, in particular if an applicant acquired the nationality of the third country.[141] But it is agreed that as in the *Conté* case if the applicant only resided in a country without benefiting from an effective protection in that country he is still a refugee according to the Convention.[142] Today, the right of entry or residence in France is refused to asylum seekers who could find protection in a third country (even in a part of his country of origin)[143] or in another EU country according to the terms of the Dublin and Schengen Conventions.[144] Notice, however, that these EC provisions raise problems of compatibility with the preamble to the 1958 Constitution which grants the right of asylum to all persons persecuted "for their action in favour of freedom" but which nevertheless leaves the legislature free to set the conditions of examining such applications.[145]

---

[139] *Ibid*, pp. 251–3.

[140] This is in perfect harmony with Conclusions No. 15 (1979) of the UNHCR Executive Committee which states that: "Regard should be had to the concept that asylum should not be refused solely on the ground that it could be sought from another State".

[141] See, decisions in F.Tiberghien, *op. cit.*, pp. 239–40 (for instance).

[142] C.E., *Chin Wei*, 27 March 1981, *ibid*, pp. 239–40.

[143] New Article 31bis of the 1945 Ordinance, as amended by the Law of 24 August 1993 and the Law of 30 December 1993. According to this provision, this category of asylum seekers is, nevertheless, allowed to apply for refugee status to OFPRA. This is not the case, however, concerning asylum seekers coming from an EU country; they are not allowed to lodge an application with OFPRA. In a recent instance, eight stowaways from Africa travelled from their respective countries of origin (ie, Liberia and Zaire) to Dunkerque, via Cameroon and Lisbon (notice that the captain of the ship did not manage do get in touch with the Spanish authorities). Their application for asylum was refused on the grounds that they should have applied in Cameroon. Human rights organisations intervened and they were finally allowed to apply for asylum. Following the incident, the Minister of the Interior stated that "he would soon present a Bill aimed at correcting [the failing] effects [of the new laws]" (MNS, May 1994, p. 5).

[144] *Guardian Weekly*, 16/05/93, p. 14; *Le Monde*, 11/06/93, p. 9. New Article 31bis of the 1945 Ordinance. This category of asylum seekers is not allowed to apply for refugee status to OFPRA.

[145] MNS, October 1993, pp. 4–5. After much discussion, both laws on immigration of 1993 were finally declared in conformity with the Constitution. Furthermore, the Prime Minister rejected the idea of amending the Constitution itself.

Sweden

According to the 1989 Aliens Act, asylum may be refused if "4. the alien has otherwise, before coming to Sweden, stayed in a country other than his country of origin and, if returned there, will be protected from persecution or, as the case may be, from being sent to a theatre of war or to his country of origin and also from being sent on to another country where he does not have corresponding protection or 5. the alien has special links with another country and is protected there in the manner referred to in paragraph 4".[146] Since March 1989, asylum seekers (ie, from Lebanon, Somalia and Ethiopia) have been returned to Poland as a safe country of first asylum; the same has happened concerning Iranians Kurds sent back to Russia as country of first asylum.[147] Swedish authorities have also expelled Bosnians asylum seekers to Macedonia because they first stayed there (third country) for a year before coming to Sweden.[148] The problem with the principle of safe countries is that mistakes can happen.[149] However, unlike in the Schengen countries, cases of safe third countries are examined in their substance.[150] As for asylum seekers who passed through another Nordic State, they are returned to that country by virtue of the Nordic Agreement on the Waiver of Passport Control.[151]

---

[146] Aliens Act, Chapter 3, s.4(4),(5). See also, J. Bjällerstedt, "Border Refusal and the Principle of First Country of Asylum", in *Asyl I Norden, op. cit.*, pp. 10–2.

[147] ECRE Country Report, Sweden, 22–23 September 1990, p. 81. See also, P. Bergquist, "L'asile en Suéde", *Documentation-Réfugiés*, 3/12 August 1989, p. 30. Russia has indeed become "waiting-room" for illegal immigrants and asylum seekers (MNS, March 1993, p. 7). A re-admission agreement between Sweden and Russia is currently under negotiations but it is still at a very early stage. The problem is that, according to the UNHCR, at present, Russia is not a safe country of first asylum and nothing can really be negotiated until it becomes one. Interview with Eva Singer, UNHCR (*op. cit.*).

[148] Sweden signed the UN Resolution recognising Macedonia as a state. MNS, June 1993, p. 12.

[149] According to Eva Singer, UNHCR, *op. cit.*, Denmark recently sent back a Tunisian asylum seeker to Italy (safe third country) and Italy just sent him back to Tunis. "So what is a safe country? Our office is trying to find out what happened to him. He actually stayed only one day in Italy and continued to Denmark because he had relatives there. We are now trying to persuade Danish authorities to allow him to come back and have his application examined."

[150] There is no accelerated procedure in Sweden, except in cases of applicants coming from a safe country of origin. Safe third country cases are usually examined by SIV but it is true, perhaps more quickly than other cases raising complex issues. Interview with Eva Ulfvebrand, Swedish Red Cross (*op. cit.*). However, when SIV or the Appeals Board decides to refuse asylum on the ground of safe third country, it must do so within three months. If it fails to base its decision on this ground within the time limit, the asylum seeker must be allowed to stay. The Appeals Board recognizes that there is no rule as such. Sometimes a day or a night spent in a third country is sufficient ground to refuse asylum. Sometimes it is not. The Appeals Board looks at the circumstances of each case, ie, could he have had the opprotunity to apply for asylum there or would he have been granted permission to stay in that country? Interview with Johan Fischerström, Appeals Board (*op. cit.*).

[151] See *infra*.

Switzerland

The Swiss position on this matter is very much the same as in Belgium, except that the time allowed in transit is shorter.[152] Asylum is normally refused if: the asylum seeker, before arriving in Switzerland, sojourned for some time in a third country where he could return, or is able to go to a third country where he has some relatives or close friends, or when the request is made from abroad and he may be admitted in another country.[153] The current practice is that as soon as there is evidence that the applicant has stayed at least 20 days (sometimes even 15 days) in another country before entering Switzerland, Swiss authorities may withdraw asylum. This practice is very much debated, and it seems that the authorities take their decision on a case by case basis for each individual. It has been said that some asylum seekers have sometimes been staying two or six months in another country and yet have been granted asylum, in other cases, 10 days in transit may be sufficient to withdraw asylum. The problem happens to be that about 90% of the people arrive in Switzerland illegally. Those presenting themselves at an airport, a border check point, a registration centre or an embassy are very few (10% at the most). Therefore, it is difficult for the authorities to prove that the asylum seeker actually stayed a few days in another country. Applicants will usually pretend that they arrived earlier and illegally in Switzerland and may only be *refoulé* according to Article 19 of the Asylum Law, if it appears during the full oral examination and investigations that evidences of his sojourn in another country are given. However, like in Belgium, the Law states that a second asylum may be granted to a refugee who was admitted to another country if it is proved that the refugee sojourned regularly and continuously in Switzerland for at least two years.[154]

United Kingdom

Asylum seekers are supposed to arrive without delay from the country in which they fear persecution. In theory, this notion of delay is not precisely determined. However, it is current practice to refuse asylum seekers who are already seeking asylum elsewhere or have had the opportunity to do so.[155] This practice is now enshrined in the laws.[156] Most recent decisions show that the Secretary of State and the Court of Appeal are willing to remove asylum

---

[152] Details on the current practice have been collected during interviews with Mr. M. Gonczy and Mrs. E. Grosjean, OSAR (*op. cit.*).

[153] Article 6 of the 1979 Asylum Law; see also Articles 13c,d, 16(1)c and 19 of the same Law and Articles 2,4,5,14 and 17 of the Asylum Ordinance 1 of 22 May 1991. See also, a decision of the Delegate for Refugee Matters who denied asylum to an applicant (a Jewish Iranian national) because he had the possibility to be effectively protected from persecution in Israel; abstract in IJRL, 1991, p. 132.

[154] Article 5 of the 1979 Asylum Law.

[155] *Asile en Europe, op. cit.*, p. 449, para.29. See also, decision refusing to grant asylum to an applicant (a South African Jew) who could have sought asylum in Israel, instead of the UK (abstract in IJRL, 1991, p. 129).

[156] Rules 180I-K of the 1993 Immigration Rules, HC 725.

seekers without consideration of the merits of their application as soon as the applicant has spent two or even just a night in transit.[157] Immigration officers are nevertheless obliged to be satisfied that this third country to which the asylum seeker is going to be sent back is safe, in particular that it will not return the asylum seeker to his country of origin and of persecution,[158] but such proof is very difficult to bring.[159] Since July 1993, the Asylum and Immigration Appeals Act provides very restricted procedure for appeals in third country cases but also "it specifically denies any obligation on the part of the Home Office to ensure, before expelling the asylum-seeker concerned, that he or she will be readmitted to the third country and will have there the opportunity to seek and, if appropriate, obtain asylum".[160] The attitude of the House of Lords on this question is quite liberal compared to the restrictive interpretation of the Secretary of State, according to the case *Bugdaycay v. Secretary of State for the Home Department and related appeals.*[161] The House of Lords, indeed, allowed the appeal lodged by Hernest Musisi (Ugandan refugee who lived in Kenya for eight years before applying for asylum in Britain) because of strong evidence that if Musisi was to be removed to Kenya (though a signatory of the 1951 Convention) he would be returned to Uganda in violation of Article 33 of the 1951 Convention. Indeed, according to Lord Bridge there may be "varying degrees of danger that removal to a third country of a person claiming refugee status will result in his return to the country where he fears persecution. If there is some evidence of such a danger, it must be for the Secretary of State to decide as a matter of degree the question whether the danger is sufficiently substantial to involve a potential breach of Article 33 of the Convention. If the Secretary of State has asked himself that question and answered it negatively in the light of all relevant evidence, the court cannot interfere".[162] Lord Bridge finally held that, in his opinion (accepted by the other Lords), the decision of the Secretary of State was made without taking into account the fact that, in reality, Ugandan refugees have already

---

[157] *D.Thevarajah v. Secretary of State for the Home Department*, [1991] Imm AR, p. 371; *C.Bouzeid v. Secretary of State for the Home Department*, [1991] Imm AR, p. 204; *K.Karali v. Secretary of State for the Home Department*, [1991], Imm AR, p. 199. See also abstracts of decisions in IJRL, 1992, p. 550, 556–7 and MNS, May 1993, p. 7. If the asylum seeker had the opportunity to make contacts with the authorities in the safe third country and to seek asylum there, his application for asylum shall be denied in the UK. See, *R v. Secretary of State for the Home Department, ex p. Abdi and Gawe*, CA, Times Law Report, 25/04/1994.

[158] Sue Shutter, *op. cit*, p. 67.

[159] Amnesty International, *Europe: Harmonization of Asylum Policy ...*, *op. cit.*, p. 19. An asylum seeker may, nevertheless, be granted asylum if he has strong family ties (ie, a spouse) in the United Kingdom (Sue Shutter, *op. cit.*, p. 65). The presence of two brothers in Britain does not constitute 'substantial links' (*R v. Secretary of State for the Home Department, ex p. T.K.*, [1993] Imm AR, p. 231) nor does the presence of a sister (MNS, May 1993, p. 7).

[160] Amnesty International, *Passing the Buck: Deficient Home Office Practice in "Safe Third Country" Asylum Cases*, 1993, p. 7.

[161] [1987] 1 All ER, HL, 940.

[162] *Ibid*, 952, j and 953, a; on the non-intervention, cf. Statement of Immigration Rules for Control After Entry, r. 3; and see, J.A.G Griffith, *The Politics of the Judiciary*, (1977), p. 97.

been returned to Uganda by Kenyan authorities, thus violating provisions of Article 33 of the Convention. However, in a recent decision of 8 October 1993, the High Court has ruled that the United Kingdom was not in breach of its obligations under the 1951 Convention in sending back asylum seekers to third safe countries through which they travelled before arriving in Britain.[163] In October 1991, the Government stated that the Dublin Convention on the Determination of the State Responsible for the Examination of an Asylum Application will determine its policy regarding safe third country within the European Union.[164] The Secretary of State was already required to refer to the Dublin Convention, in at least two cases.[165] In the case *R v. Secretary of State for the Home Department, ex p. Muboyayi*, the Court of Appeal held that it would not be "unlawful for the Secretary of State, in effect, to implement the Dublin Convention, to which France is a signatory, before it comes into force, if France will accept obligations under or consistent with it".[166] But, in the case *K.Karali and others v. Secretary of State for the Home Department*, the applicants, Turkish Kurds, flew from Turkey to the airport of Amsterdam and continued their journey to Britain. The Secretary of State refused to grant them asylum and decided for their return to the Netherlands. The applicants appealed of the decision, arguing that the Dublin Convention made the United Kingdom responsible for examining their application. The Court of Appeal denied the application of the Dublin Convention not yet into force and upheld the decision of the Secretary of State.[167] Under Article 22, the Dublin Convention will come into force three months after the last signatories has ratified it.

Special Agreements
As a matter of principle, a refugee cannot choose his country of asylum. Accordingly, a refugee who could have sought and be granted asylum in another country should be returned to that country. The principle is to be decided by the state in which the refugee arrives. However, special consideration is to be taken into account when a refugee has a close relative in one of the countries concerned. Such principles are provided by special bi- or multi-lateral agreements as well as by EU conventions.

---

[163] MNS, November 1993, p. 8. Refer also to the ruling by the Court of Appeal on 20 April 1994 (*R v. Secretary of State for the Home Department, ex p. Abdi*) that for the Home Secretary to assert that a third country is safe, in this case Spain, is enough to send back two Muslims Somalis there (MNS, May 1994, p. 7).

[164] ECRE Country Report, UK, 5–6 October 1991, p. 106.

[165] Other examples may be found in Amnesty International, *Passing the Buck ...*, *op. cit.*, Appendix.

[166] [1991] 3 WLR 442.

[167] [1991], Imm AR, p. 199. A similar incident arised concerning two Kurds, who after having spent 90 minutes in the Netherlands waiting for a ferry, arrived to Britain and were deported to the Netherlands. The Netherlands refused to recognize its responsibility and sent them back to the UK, where they were put back in custody (*The Guardian Weekly*, 07.11.1993, p. 11).

A special agreement has been signed between Nordic countries[168] in order to abolish internal borders and to create a free and common labour market. This means that citizens of one Nordic country are free to settle and work or study in any of the others. Under the Swedish Aliens Act, an alien is to be refused asylum if he "has entered Sweden from Denmark, Finland, Iceland, or Norway and can be returned to any of these countries in accordance with an agreement between Sweden and that country, unless it is obvious that he will not be granted a residence permit there".[169] Thus, the question of asylum is to be answered by the country in which the refugee arrives.[170] Special readmission agreements have also been signed between Sweden and the Federal Republic of Germany, according to which an asylum seeker will be returned to the country he first arrived but only if he stayed there for at least two weeks,[171] and between Sweden and France.[172] The Federal Republic of Germany has itself signed readmission agreements with Austria, Denmark, Norway, Sweden[173] and Switzerland[174] and is of course a signatory of the Dublin Convention and Schengen Agreement. Poland is bound by a readmission agreement which it signed in March 1991 with the Schengen countries[175] and, according to which the Polish Government has to take back asylum seekers as well as clandestine immigrants who pass through its territory to reach the Federal Republic of Germany. Difficulties have arisen regarding the application of this agreement by Poland[176] and "deployment of auxiliary force at the borders have begun".[177] A more advanced Treaty was finally signed on 7 May 1993 between the German and Polish Governments allowing Bonn to refuse asylum seekers at its border with Poland and to deport up to 10,000 rejected applicants who arrived from Poland.[178] In order to allow Poland to cope with its responsibility, Germany has agreed to start deportations in only six months time and to pay Poland a total of 120 million DM in 1993 and 1994 to help housing these people.[179] Special agreements have also been signed

---

[168] On 12 July 1957 between Denmark, Finland, Iceland, Norway and Sweden. Sö 1958:24.

[169] S.4(3).

[170] *Asile en Europe, op. cit.*, p. 473, para.21.

[171] *Ibid*, p. 473, para.22.

[172] Agreement of 14 February 1991: Decree No. 91–726 of 22 July 1991 (JO, 28.97.91, p. 10041; Rec.(1991)L., p. 356) or Sö 1991:16.

[173] This is referred to as an Exchange of notes constituting an Agreement concerning Reciprocal Obligation to accept Certain Persons deported from the Other Country, Bonn 31 May 1954, Sö 1954:80. See, K. Jönsson, *op. cit.*, Annex II.

[174] *Asile en Europe, op. cit.*, p. 83, para.20.

[175] A. Cruz, *Schengen, ad hoc Immigration Group and other European Intergovernmental bodies*, Churches Committee for Migrants in Europe, Briefing Paper 12, p. 13. This agreement is on readmission of aliens in an irregular situation. The full text of this agreement can be found, for instance, in the French J.O. of 20 January 1994, p. 1031 or Rec.(1994), p. 136; Decree of publication No. 94–49 of 12 January.

[176] MNS, April 1993, p. 3.

[177] MNS, May 1993, p. 3.

[178] *Guardian Weekly*, 16/05/93, p. 14.

[179] MNS, June 1993, pp. 6–7.

between the Federal Republic of Germany and Romania on 24 September 1992 and the Federal Republic of Germany and Bulgaria on 12 November 1992, according to which the German Government has agreed on financial incentives in exchange for the return of thousands of asylum seekers.[180] Most recently, the Federal Republic of Germany signed an agreement with Croatia. It authorizes Germany to slowly start repatriating certain categories of Croatian war refugees from 1 May 1994.[181] Bi-lateral readmission agreements are also being signed between Poland and the Czech Republic or still under negotiations between Poland and Slovakia, Poland and Ukraine and Poland and Russia.[182] Switzerland has signed a '*refoulement* agreement' with Austria, the Federal Republic of Germany, France and Hungary. While a similar agreement with Romania is expecting soon,[183] one with Sri Lanka was signed in January 1994.[184] Belgium signed bilateral readmission agreements with Ghana, Romania and Morocco.[185] Finally, Belgium, France, Germany and the United Kingdom by acceding to the Dublin Convention and/or the Schengen Convention have accepted that an alien may be returned to a third country if this country is competent to examine the application or if the refugee has closed family ties in that country. In Switzerland, similar principles are provided in Articles 13c,d, 16(1)c and 19 of the 1979 Asylum Law.[186]

The Dublin Convention and the Schengen Supplementary Agreement
On 15 June 1990, eleven EC Member States signed the Convention on the Determination of the State Responsible for the Examination of an Asylum Application (the Dublin Convention).[187] On 19 June 1990, France, Belgium, the Netherlands, Luxembourg and the Federal Republic of Germany signed the Convention on the Application of the Schengen Agreement on the Gradual Abolition of Internal Borders within the EC (the Schengen Agreement).[188] Both treaties provide similar rules for the determination of the state responsi-

---

[180] *The Guardian*, 08/12/92, p. 9. MNS, May 1993, p. 6.

[181] MNS, May 1994, p. 5.

[182] MNS, June 1993, p. 6.

[183] MNS, March 1994, p. 8.

[184] On the basis of this agreement, the Swiss Government will start repatriating more than 10,000 rejected Tamils in May 1994 (MNS, May 1994, p. 7; see also MNS, February 1994, p. 8 and MNS, April 1994, p. 7).

[185] MNS, February 1994, p. 5.

[186] The same attitude exists in Sweden. Notice also that on becoming a new member of the EU, it is very likely that Sweden will sign the Dublin Convention.

[187] Denmark signed it on 13 June 1991. By June 1993 the Convention was ratified by Denmark, Greece, the United Kingdom, Italy, Portugal and Luxembourg.

[188] Italy acceded to the Agreement in November 1990, Portugal and Spain in June 1991. By June 1993, the Agreement was ratified by France, Luxembourg, Portugal, Spain, the Netherlands and Belgium. It is difficult to say when will the Schengen Convention come into force as it keeps being postponed following disagreements on the Schengen Information System. A third Convention on the crossing of external borders is now well on its way, after a blockage, since 1991, because of the dispute between Spain and the United Kingdom over Gibraltar. A. Cruz, *op. cit.*, p. 17; MNS, February 1994, p. 1.

ble to examine an asylum application. These rules are based on the so-called *authorization principle* which provides that the country responsible for examining an individual application is the country which authorized the asylum seeker to enter the common territory of the EU.[189] Exceptions from the rule exist in particular if the asylum seeker has a family member already recognized as a refugee in one of the member states[190] or on humanitarian grounds.[191] Moreover, under both Article 3(5)of the Dublin Convention and Article 29(2) of the Schengen Agreement, the possibility for member states to return asylum seekers to a third country is provided but neither instrument require member states to preliminary check that such third country will be safe and provide effective protection.[192] Conclusions No. 58(XL)1989 of the Executive Committee of the UNHCR on irregular movements accepts that an asylum seeker may be returned to the country of first asylum if the applicant can enter and remain there, is protected there against *refoulement*, and is treated in accordance with basic human standards. During a meeting in November-December 1992, the ministers of the ad hoc Immigration Group adopted Resolution on a harmonized approach to questions concerning host third countries.[193] Although not legally binding, it recommends fundamental requirements to be taken into account in order to determine a safe host third country, in particular, the life or freedom of the asylum seeker must not be threatened, he must not be exposed to torture or inhuman or degrading treatment, he must have been already granted protection there or there must be clear evidence on his admissibility, he must be effectively protected against *refoulement*.[194] Also according to this Resolution, the provisions of the Dublin Convention should only apply if the asylum seeker cannot in practice be sent to a safe host country but if such a third country exists, the asylum seeker may be sent to that country.[195]

Switzerland fearing to "become a safe heaven for criminals, terrorists, illegal immigrants and asylum seekers rejected by the EU" wishes to become a member of the EU in order to participate to the Schengen Agreement and

---

[189] See Articles 5–8 of the Dublin Convention and Article 30 of the Schengen Agreement. See also, M. Kjaerum, "The concept of country of first asylum", in IJRL, 1992, p. 526.

[190] Article 4 of the Dublin Convention and Article 35 of the Schengen Agreement.

[191] Article 9 of the Dublin Convention and Article 36 of the Schengen Agreement. It has also been agreed that Article 29 of the Schengen Agreement (Member States retain the right to process an application for asylum even if under this Convention the responsibility for doing so is that of another Member State) shall be applied only in exceptional circumstances (MNS, October 1993, p. 3).

[192] Amnesty International, *Europe: Human Rights and the need for a fair asylum policy*, November 1991, p. 10.

[193] A. Cruz, *op. cit.*, p. 18. Resolution on Manifestly Unfounded Applications for Asylum, EC Council, Press Notice no. 10518/92 of 30.11.92 (Press 230), Annex I.

[194] See K. Hailbronner, "The concept of 'safe country' and expeditious asylum procedures: a Western European perspective", IJRL, 1993, p. 60.

[195] *Ibid.*

the TREVI Group. [196] A referendum held in 1993 has, however, rejected Swiss membership to the European Economic Area Agreement. Similarly, Sweden has express strong wishes to become a member of the EU on January 1995 and that despite its neutrality policy.[197] Within the ad hoc Immigration Group, a draft parallel convention to the Dublin Convention extending the Dublin rules to third states (in particular, the EFTA member countries,[198] the USA and Canada) has already been prepared. This parallel convention cannot, however, be adhered to by an interested state until after all EU member states have ratified the Dublin Convention.[199]

---

[196] ECRE Country Report, Switzerland, 5–6 October 1991, p. 101.

[197] See for instance, C.B. Hamilton and C.-E. Stälvant, *A Swedish View of 1992*, the Royal Institute of International Affairs, Discussion Paper 13 (1989).

[198] EFTA States: Finland, Norway, Iceland, Sweden, Switzerland, Austria and Liechtenstein.

[199] A. Cruz, *op. cit.*, pp. 16–7.

CHAPTER FIVE

PROTECTION AGAINST 'REFOULEMENT' AND LIVING CONDITIONS DURING THE PRE-ASYLUM PERIOD

The position of asylum seekers during the pre-asylum period concerns essentially the protection of freedom of movement and of social and economic rights. By pre-asylum period one means the period between the day an asylum seeker enters a country and the day a final decision is made on his application for asylum in that country. International legal instruments, such as the 1951 Convention, remain silent on this matter and each state is thus free to act in its own way.[1] In 1985, the Parliamentary Assembly of the CoE[2] invited governments to find and agree on a common standard of treatment for asylum seekers during the pre-asylum period. It even proposed to grant them rights very close to the ones they would enjoy if they were already benefiting from the status of refugee. In practice, the general consensus seems to be that states have strong reservations about granting important rights to asylum seekers because no final decision has been taken yet on the substantive issue of their application.[3] Basic rights, such as the right to liberty and security,[4] are denied in certain countries. In none of the six countries is a right of family reunion provided pending the issue of the decision, except in Belgium.[5] There is no doubt that, in most European countries, the needs of asylum seekers are often not satisfied and their situation is very precarious.

---

[1] Jacqueline Costa-Lascoux "L'insertion sociale des réfugiés et demandeurs d'asile en Europe", *Revue Européenne des Migrations Internationales*, Vol.3, No. 3, Trimestre 4, 1987, p. 153.

[2] Recommendation R(85)1016 on living and working conditions of refugees and asylum seekers.

[3] J. Costa-Lascoux, *op. cit.*, p. 153. Such attitude is not legally justified because according to the UNHCR Handbook (*op. cit.*, p. 9), the determination of refugee status has only a declaratory value. An asylum seeker is, therefore, recognized as a refugee because he is a refugee and he does not become one because of a recognition.

[4] ECHR, Article 5.

[5] Article 10 of the Law of 15 December 1980, as modified, provides a right of family reunification for the spouse and children of an alien authorized to enter Belgium or to stay there. An asylum seeker, whose access to the territory or the right to stay for a minimum of three months is authorized by the representative of the Minister of Justice can, therefore, benefit from the principle of family reunion. See, chapter seven, *infra*.

1. Restrictions to the Free Movement of Asylum Seekers

1.1. *Detention*

The detention of asylum seekers in Europe is directly covered by Article 5 of the ECHR, while Article 31 of the 1951 Convention states that "refugees unlawfully in the country of refuge" shall not be subject to any penalties nor their movements to restrictions. It results from the decisions of the European Commission of Human Rights that there is detention when the person is not allowed to leave the place where s/he has been confined by the state's authorities. The place could be a cell, a camp or even a part of an airport building, as soon as s/he is not free to leave there is detention.[6] However, lawful arrest or detention of an alien is justified by Article 5 of the ECHR when s/he entered a country illegally or when s/he is subject to a deportation order or extradition.

Belgium

The Law of 18 July 1991 added a new Title IIIter and Article 74/5 to the Law of 15 December 1980. Detention of asylum seekers used to be covered by Article 54 of the 1980 Law, which expressly provided that asylum seekers who entered the territory illegally may be asked by the Minister of Justice to stay in a specific place while investigations are made on their requests. Today, Articles 74/5 and 74/6[7] provide that asylum seekers whose application is manifestly unfounded or who entered the territory illegally can be detained for a maximum of two months, in particular in the transit zone of the airport, at the 127 Centre (new Exit 36)[8] and at the Fort of Walem, which is the recently built transit centre situated between Brussels and Antwerp. [9] Asylum seekers arriving by land or sea are requested to go to the reception centre of the *Petit Chateau*, where they are free to move. Thus, those arriving at the airport of Zaventem are subject to less better treatment. They are normally kept in the airport premises, where living conditions are far from reaching human dignity. This practice raises the problem of conformity with Article 31 of the 1951 Convention.[10]

---

[6] See, European Commission of Human Rights, 7 October 1976, Decisions and Reports, pp. 123–6 and the decision of the European Court of Human Rights in the *case Guzzardi* of 6 December 1980.

[7] Article 74/6 was added by the Law of 6 May 1993.

[8] *Fourth Annual Report* (1991), *op. cit.*, p. 49.

[9] The Belgian State has recently been found guilty, on more than one occasion, of detaining asylum seekers in a inhuman and degrading manner in the Fort of Walem. MNS, December 1993, pp. 5–6 and MNS, February 1994, pp. 4–5.

[10] J.Y. Carlier, *Droit des Réfugiés, op. cit.*, pp. 76–7. See also Articles 71 and 72 (as modified by the 1984 Law and 1993 Law) which provide a possibility of appeal to the *Chambre du Conseil du Tribunal Correctionel*.

Federal Republic of Germany

There used to be no legal basis for detention of asylum seekers in Germany, except where the asylum seeker has committed a criminal offence or has entered the country illegally. Article 18 of the German Aliens Law,[11] indeed, provides that aliens who have entered the country illegally (therefore also asylum seekers who do not make it clear that they wish to apply for asylum or who do not make a proper application for asylum) can be detained by the police in premises at the border until deportation. For asylum seekers arriving at Frankfurt airport, such detention takes place at the reception centre C 183.[12] There is now a legal basis for detention measures but very little guarantees against abuses to such drastic restriction are provided.[13] The new asylum legislation, which was adopted during the summer 1993, provides the possibility to have asylum seekers detained at airports transit areas for up to three weeks, if they are coming by plane from safe countries of origin or without valid identity papers.[14] Such a measure is to facilitate deportations. Detention of asylum seekers once admitted to the asylum procedure is also increasingly becoming common practice. Asylum seekers are indeed requested to accommodate in refugee centres and camps in the *Land* in which they lodged their application. Some of these camps are heavily guarded and no one can get out without permission, subject to prosecution and fines, sometimes even imprisonment.[15] Such practice is illegal and can hardly be justified by the fact that asylum seekers need being protected against racist and xenophobic attacks.

France

Detention of aliens, therefore asylum seekers, can only be the result of a written decision of the *préfet* who has to give good reasons for such a measure, ie, absolute necessity. The present law provides for a series of guarantees. Aliens to whom entry is refused at the border may be detained for a maximum of seven days during which period the alien can request assistance from an interpreter, a doctor, a lawyer and may contact any other person of his choice.[16] New Article 35ter and quarter of the 1945 Ordinance[17] relating to the so-called waiting zones at airports allows the police to detain aliens and asylum seekers refused entry for a maximum of 20 days while a decision is made.[18] Judicial intervention by the judge may only be after four days

---

[11] As amended on 1st January 1991.

[12] Before 1989, awaiting for the hearing and admissibility decision was taking place in the transit zone.

[13] R. Marx, "Study on the Treatment of Asylum Seekers at German Airports", 30 March 1992.

[14] S.18a, AsylVfG. MNS, May 1993, p. 5.

[15] S.59, AsylVfG.

[16] *Asile en Europe, op. cit.*, p. 265, para.38.

[17] As inserted by the Law of 6 July 1992.

[18] Decision of the *Conseil Constitutionnel* of 25 February 1992. Detention may not exceed 48 hours, renewable only once, and the *Tribunal de Grande Instance* may decide to extend the

while most of the detainees remain for less than two days.[19] Foreigners are maintained in extremely poor conditions in such zones and the UNHCR and humanitarian associations have still no access to these zones, which are not considered as French territory.[20] Aliens who have entered the country illegally can be prosecuted. The penalty may vary between one month to one year imprisonment and a fine of 2.000FF to 20.000FF.[21] Article 35bis of the 1945 Ordinance[22] provides for the systematic detention of undocumented aliens for a maximum of seven days (ten days in cases of absolute emergency and threat to public order) while waiting for their forced repatriation.[23] The *Tribunal de Grande Instance* shall be informed of such measures after 24 hours of detention. Extremely detailed procedural guarantees are provided, particularly in the Law of 30 December 1993. The detention centres must not be under penitentiary administration and the person concerned must be over the age of 16 and must be able to contact an interpreter, a doctor or a lawyer.[24]

Sweden

Asylum seekers refused entry at the border can be detained for a maximum of two months while their application for asylum is being examined by SIV.[25] Specific measures are provided for children under the age of 16.[26] These are conflicting with the UN Convention on the Rights of the Child, ratified by Sweden, which provides that a child is a person under the age of 18.[27] Detention in Sweden is mainly used as a measure to secure the execution of a decision to remove an alien and an asylum seeker or to investigate the facts of a case (ie, the identity of an asylum seeker).[28] The Swedish Aliens Act, Chapter 10, treats illegal foreigners and asylum seekers (without the proper travel documents and entry permits) as ordinary criminals and detention is more than likely in such circumstances.[29] Like in all other Nordic countries, Sweden uses the services of regular prisons for the detention of foreigners.

---

period of time of eight days, renewable once. See ECRE Country Report, France, 3–5 April 1992, p. 83 and 3–4 October 1992, p. 78. Article 35ter constitutes the only applicable provision (*Cour de Cassation*, 2e, Civ., 9 February 1994, *Bayemy*; Rec.(1994), p. 58).

[19] *Documentation – Réfugiés, Revue de Presse*, No. 210, 16 Feb./1st March 1993, p. 1. See, Decree No. 92–1333 of 15 December 1992.

[20] MNS, March 1993, p. 2.

[21] Ordinance of 2 Novembre 1945, Article 19.

[22] As modified by the laws on immigration of 24 August and 30 December 1993.

[23] MNS, October 1993, p. 2.

[24] MNS, October 1993, pp. 2–3.

[25] Aliens Act 1989:529, Chapter 6 and Aliens Ordinance 1989:547 as amended on 1st October 1990, Chapter 5, s.11–13.

[26] *Ibid.*

[27] The point was raised in a case concerning a West African child of 16, whose application for asylum was refused and who was detained (under Swedish laws) for three months before being deported. MNS, February 1994, p. 12.

[28] Detention for investigation purposes may not exceed six hours. K. Jönsson, *op. cit.*, para.38.

[29] *Ibid*, para.12.

Switzerland

The Swiss Federal Law on Sojourn and Establishment of Aliens[30] authorizes the detention of an alien, therefore an asylum seeker, in order to secure *refoulement* or expulsion on the grounds of illegal entry or rejected claim. The competent authority for removal, usually the canton,[31] may order the detention when the *refoulement* is executory and where there are strong reasons to presume that the alien will escape and become a clandestine. Detention may never last more than 30 days. After 48 hours, however, the canton has to appoint a competent authority (judicial, administrative or penal) to examine the basis of the detention measure. According to the Federal Law on Sojourn and Establishment of Aliens, detention is not contrary to Article 5 of the ECHR because it is pronounced by a judge (magistrate).[32] However, the legality of detention at airports, particularly in transit zones, is not so clear with regard to Article 5 of the ECHR. The issue was raised when an Iranian family was *refoulée* from Frankfurt to Iran via Geneva-Cointrin. Police officers refused to consider the members of the family as asylum seekers although their request was clear. The husband was illegally detained in a cell at Cointrin airport before being *refoulé* to Iran.[33]

United Kingdom

It is common practice to detain asylum seekers at a port of entry and for a short period while investigations are made on the good faith of what they say.[34] Detention appears to take place in Harmondsworth Detention Centre, near Heathrow Airport, in the Beehive (Gatwick), but also in places such as a disused car-ferry, the "Earl William" for instance.[35] Quite recently, it appeared that asylum seekers are even detained at Pentonville Prison, North London, and at the Campfield detention centre, near Oxford, in dramatic conditions.[36] The Statement of Changes in Immigration Rules,[37] however, provides guarantees. If an asylum seeker is detained more than seven days

---

[30] Entered into force on 1 January 1988, modifying the previous Law of 26 March 1931. RS 142.20.

[31] Article 14 of the Federal Law on Sojourn and Establishment of Aliens.

[32] Philippe Bois, *op. cit.*, p. 83.

[33] See Yves Brutsch, *op. cit.*

[34] BRC, *Settling for a future: proposals for a British policy on refugees*, London, The Council, 1987, pp. 7–8. According to the report 'Detention Without Trial" (2 June 1993), "more than 10,000 persons, immigrants and asylum seekers are imprisoned every year, some as long as 18 months", and thus without any trial. They are simply detained. MNS, June 1993, p. 12.

[35] MRG Report, *Refugees in Europe*, October 1990, p. 15.

[36] Nick Holden, "Refugee held in jail tries to kill himself", *The Independent*, 18/04/1991, pp. 6,28. See also Amnesty International, *UK - Unlawful Killing of Detained Asylum Seeker Omasese Lumumba* (November 1993), in which an inquest jury found the killing of Omasese Lumumba while detained in custody at Pentoville Prison as being the result of the 'use of improper methods and excessive force in the process of control and restraint' by the prison members of staff (at p. 5). See also, MNS, April 1994, p. 7.

[37] HC 251 (1989–90), para.88, as amended by HC 725.

while waiting for a decision on his admission, he may ask an Adjudicator or a Court to be discharged on bail. He is also allowed, at any time, to consult friends, relatives, a lawyer, a member of Parliament, the UKIAS or any other voluntary agency dealing with refugees. Clause 6(3) of the Asylum and Immigration Appeals Act (1993) confirms that asylum seekers may be detained once their leave has been curtailed under clause 6(1). The 1971 Immigration Act already provided such possibility concerning people who apply for asylum at a port of entry.[38] Clause 6 extends these existing powers of detention to aliens who apply for asylum after having entered the UK legally (e.g. visitors, students). In July 1992, the Government has indicated that about 300 additional detention places will be made available between 1992 and 1995.[39] The Home Office recently admitted that about two-third of asylum seekers are kept in detention, some of them during the whole period of pre-asylum.[40] That no maximum time limit exists puts an enormous pressure on detainees and such practice should urgently be revised pursuant to the provisions of the ECHR on prohibition of inhuman and degrading treatment. In any case, detention should only be justified in exceptional circumstances,[41] such as the prevention of terrorism.[42]

To sum up, it appears that detention arises frequently at ports of entry, in particular at airports. In all the countries under review, such measure is provided by domestic legislation but only for limited cases and is normally not subject to judicial or administrative review. The detention of asylum seekers has also become increasingly common practice once they have crossed the border and gone through the formalities of immigration officers. On a comparative level, Britain appears to offer the worse treatment in this respect. Furthermore, even if they are not precisely detained, they see themselves in a similar situation. Unable to buy any food or to find any place to sleep, they have to stay at the airport until assistance is provided to them.[43] This assistance may come from voluntary agencies or governments although the latter normally refuse to provide any money or shelter because there is none available. Voluntary agencies face real problems because of the limited capacity of their accommodation centres.

1.2. *Choice of Residence*

Once admitted to the asylum procedure in a country, asylum seekers are able to stay in that country while a decision is pending on their status. Depending on

---

[38] The lifting of detention is an administrative measure provided by the 1971 Immigration Act. It does not delay leave to enter. Halsbury's Statutes (1987), Vol.31, pp. 47–112.

[39] Parliamentary Debates (Hansard) 1 July 1992.

[40] MNS, April 1994, p. 7. Weekly Hansard 1645, 21.02–25.02.1994, p. 148.

[41] *The Independent*, 25/09/1989, p. 21; see also, *R v. Secretary of State for the Home Department, ex p. Swati* [1986] 1 All ER, 717, CA.

[42] On the British government's attitude, see *The Times*, 30/11/1988, Human Rights Law Report and, *The Economist* 03/12/1988, p. 28.

[43] *The Guardian*, "Refugees abandoned at airports", 06/11/1989, p. 6.

each country, an asylum seeker may be housed in a collective accommodation and free to move within the country or may be requested to stay in a refugee camp or centre with restricted freedom of movement. Also the obligation to live in a collective accommodation or camp may be imposed by law or by other means such as lack of financial support.

Belgium

An asylum seeker, authorized to stay in Belgium, is free to choose his place of residence. He must, however, present himself within eight days to the administration of the *commune* where he plans to take up residence. He will be given a model A registration notification, valid for a first three months and renewable each month until a decision is taken by the General Commissioner for Refugees. However, in 1985 a Royal Decree stated the possibility for six *communes* of Brussels to refuse to register new aliens arriving because of an unsafe increase of the population in these *communes*.[44] Royal Decrees of 12,15 and 22 May 1992 renewed the ban on residence or settlement in the original 6 *communes* of Brussels until May 1995.[45] Registration in a *commune* is an obligation[46] that more and more *communes* infringe.[47] The consequences of such refusals to register an asylum seeker may be heavy.[48] Appeal against a written decision to refuse to register an alien is possible to the *Conseil d'Etat*; when the decision is oral, the most effective appeal is a *référé* to the first instance Tribunal.[49] When an asylum seeker has no place to go, he normally remains at the reception centre of the *Petit Chateau*. It accommodates asylum seekers while a decision from the Minister of Justice or his representative is being taken on their right to access to the territory and right to stay.[50] For a much more limited number of asylum seekers arriving at the airport of Zaventem, this waiting takes place in premises of the airport, at

---

[44] Royal Decree of 7 May 1985 (M.B. 15 May 1985). See also J.Y. Carlier, *Droits des réfugiés, op. cit.*, p. 79. Provisions of this Royal Decree have been renewed for 5 of the 6 *communes* of Brussels and apply also to the city of *Liège* in 1990 (Royal Decree of 10 May 1990).

[45] M.B. 15 and 23 May 1992.

[46] Article 74 of the Royal Decree of 8 October 1981, as modified.

[47] MNS, October 1993, p. 3.

[48] In particular, to obtain a temporary authorization to work an asylum seeker has to fulfil various forms. One of them requires that the signature of the asylum seeker be legalised by the *commune*. But to do so, the asylum seeker must first be registered. Therefore, he has an employer, he has the forms, but he cannot have his signature legalised because the *commune* refuses to register him. Interview with Mrs. L. Biackso, Centre Social Protestant, Brussels, December 1990.

[49] J.Y. Carlier, *Droits des réfugiés, op. cit.*, pp. 81–2.

[50] Created in November 1986, its capacity was originally fixed at 300 but has rapidly increased to 500 and more. Alternative solutions had to be found directly through the CPAS (*Centre Publics d'Aide Sociale*) and through accommodation centres of the Red Cross. See, L. Biacsko, "Demandeurs d'asiles en Belgique, les premiers effets de la nouvelle loi Gol", in *REFUGIES, Drames et Espoirs*, Service Oecumenique des Réfugiés du Centre Social Protestant, Dec.1988, No. 25, pp. 15–6.

the 127 Centre, where it would be more appropriate to speak about detention rather than free residence.[51] To avoid excess of people, in particular in the *Petit Chateau*, a distribution programme was created for asylum seekers authorized to stay in Belgium, while a decision of the General Commissioner is taken. This distribution programme provides broadly a quota of one asylum seeker per one thousand inhabitants.[52] Although this quota is reached in some *communes*, it does not allow these *communes* to refuse to register more asylum seekers when circumstances are such that the number of asylum seekers is too high.[53] Indeed, the aim of the distribution programme is not to stop people being admitted in the *communes* but to avoid a concentration of asylum seekers in some ghettos, like in Germany or in France, for instance. Asylum seekers dividing up in the *communes* are supported jointly by the CPAS of the *commune* of residence and a NGO member of the CBAR,[54] which explains the reluctance of some *communes* to accept asylum seekers.[55]

Federal Republic of Germany

Once admitted into the German territory, asylum seekers are allowed to stay until a final decision has been reached on their asylum application. They must first register in a reception centre[56] and they are confined to the *Land* and the administrative and police district within which the centre is located.[57] It is in these reception centres that interviews are held, medical screening carried out[58] and police records checked. Since the 1st of April 1993, asylum seekers are dispatched among 46 main reception camps instead of the hundreds of hostels and refugee centres which existed previously.[59] They are obliged to stay in these camps from six weeks to three months.[60] After usually two or three months, asylum seekers whose application are not ill founded (on

---

[51] See, M.-C. Leroux, "Vivre au 127", in *Bulletin du Centre Social Protestant*, No. 275, Sept.1990. Created in December 1988, its capacity was carried from 28 to 104 beds in March 1990.

[52] See Tetty Rooze, "L'accueil à Anvers et dans les environs", in *REFUGIES, Drames et espoirs, op. cit.*, No. 25, pp. 17 and 18.

[53] ECRE Country Report, Belgium, 5–6 October 1991, p. 48.

[54] The *Service des Réfugiés*, founder member of the CBAR (*Comité Belge d'Aide aux Réfugiés*) in 1968, was integrated to the CSP (*Centre Social Protestant*) in 1976. The CBAR consists of 7 NGO: Belgian Aid to Stateless Persons, Belgian Red Cross, International Aid of Caritas Catholica, Protestant Social Centre, Jewish Social Department, International Liberal Solidarity and, Social Department of Socialist Solidarity.

[55] See, generally, on the reception of asylum seekers, *First and Second Annual Reports, op. cit.*, respectively at pp. 47–52 and pp. 46–9. See, also for more details and figures, *Accueil des Réfugiés*, Bilan 1989, Le Cabinet du Secrétaire d'Etat à l'Emancipation Sociale.

[56] S.22, AsylVfG.

[57] *Asile en Europe, op. cit.*, p. 87, para.39.

[58] S.62, AsylVfG.

[59] S.44–46, AsylVfG. MNS, May 1993, p. 5.

[60] S.47, AsylVfG. It has also been ruled that asylum seekers are not allowed to apply for accommodation in a centre for homeless people. They have to live in the centre to which they have been assigned. Such ruling is to avoid a transfer of costs from the *Land*, that is the state

grounds of public security and public order or because their application is not admissible) are allocated to local authorities according to criteria such as the population levels on the *Länder* and the local districts making up the *Land*.[61] Only close family ties are taken into account when distributing.[62] In the local districts, they are accommodated in community housing from 50 to several hundred rooms.[63] Unlike in reception centres, they are not, strictly speaking, obliged to live there.[64] The local Aliens Police authorities are competent to deliver provisional authorisation to sojourn valid for six months and renewable as often as necessary until a final decision on asylum is reached.[65] Freedom of movement is restricted geographically to the *Kreis* (local authority) where the asylum seeker has been allocated.[66] An asylum seeker may only be able to move out of the restricted area after having sought permission from the local Aliens Police authorities.[67] Soon after the German unification (October 1990), the five "new *Länder*" in former East Germany were placed under an obligation to offer accommodation to 20% of the asylum seekers registered in the Federal Republic according to the criteria of distribution.[68] Soon after, violent attacks from the far right started against refugee housing. These attacks are now also taking place in the Western *Länder* since hundreds of asylum seekers have fled from East Germany to West Germany since the events.[69] The wave of xenophobic attacks reached its climax in September 1992 following the riots in Rostock. In absolute figures, the majority of xenophobic incidents occurred in the Western part of Germany, while in proportion to the inhabitants, two new federal states (Mecklenburg-Vorpommern and Brandenburg) were at the top of the "violence list".[70]

(responsible for asylum seekers), to the local authorities (responsible for homeless people). See, MNS, May 1994, p. 5.

[61] S.48–50, AsylVfG. Town mayors sometimes strongly refuse to admit anymore asylum seekers if they consider that the proportion of asylum seekers according to the population is becoming too high (MNS, May 1993, p. 6).

[62] S.51, AsylVfG.

[63] S.53, AsylVfG.

[64] There may, nevertheless, be some specific requirements, as provided in s.60, AsylVfG. See also, on the application of s.53, judgment by the OVG Berlin of 19.11.1993, NVwZ, Supplement 2/1994, pp. 13–4.

[65] S.63(2), AsylVfG. The Federal Administrative Court ruled on 24.2.93 that Article 28(2) of the Basic Law does not entitle a local community to be released from its obligation to provide housing for asylum seekers whose application for refugee status have been refused but who are, nevertheless, allowed to remain by decision of the Aliens Authority (NJW 1993, Heft 45, p. 2953).

[66] S.59, AsylVfG, states: "The aliens authority in whose district the alien is obliged to stay ...". See also, s.56–57, AsylVfG.

[67] S.58 and s.66, AsylVfG.

[68] ECRE Country Report, FRG, 7–9 March 1991, p. 61.

[69] ECRE Country Report, FRG, 3–5 April 1992, pp. 94–5; 3–4 October 1992, p. 92; and 23–25 April 1993. See also Jörg Alt SJ, "Comments on the Increase in Violent Xenophobic Attacks in Eastern Germany", Paper presented in Geneva, 3 October 1992.

[70] Fact sheet on Germany, last updated 17 February 1993.

France

Asylum seekers are normally free to choose their residence. They can go and see relatives, friends or voluntary agencies (*CIMADE* or *Secours Catholique* particularly). The latter may provide temporary shelter and limited financial support. As soon as the asylum seeker has received a provisional document to sojourn, he is eligible and free to go to a provisional accommodation centre (*centre provisoire d'hébergement*), where stays are limited up to six months. Provisional accommodation centres are managed by local agencies dealing with refugees, coordinated by the association *France Terre d'Asile* and all expenses are financed by the Ministry of National Solidarity. Shelter, food, pocket money, language courses, help to find work and a lasting accommodation are provided by the centres. Centres are scattered in France (around 60 in 1990). National reception centres have been reorganised since determination procedures have been speeded up. [71] Some of the provisional accommodation centres have been converted into so-called reception centres for asylum seekers. Reception centres are functioning as transit centres. The asylum seeker will be housed there for a few weeks until the final decision on his application is taken. Only recognized refugees can apply for accommodation in a provisional accommodation centre which houses but also helps asylum seekers in their integration. Asylum seekers may also choose to live with relatives or friends or, if lucky, some of them may find permanent accommodation by their own means. There are no restrictions on the freedom of movement of asylum seekers and refugees, whether accommodated in reception centres or elsewhere, except on national security grounds.[72]

Sweden

In Sweden, it is mainly the state (SIV) which organizes housing for asylum seekers. All individual asylum seekers (foreigners who request asylum upon arrival and who are not rejected as well as foreigners who request asylum after having already entered Sweden) are transferred to one of the four existing clearance centres (one in each region, North, South, West and East).[73] They stay there (usually for more than a month) until after a full interview by the competent authority, investigations and medical screening have been carried out. Asylum seekers are then transferred to ordinary refugee centres referred to as 'permanent residential centres'.[74] They stay there until a decision on their application has been reached or until they can be received in a permanent accommodation by a local municipality (at least two or three months). There are 26 permanent centres supplemented by temporary residential units when

---

[71] Circular of 19 December 1991 regarding the reorganisation of the national reception centres for refugees and asylum seekers.

[72] New Article 36 of the 1945 Ordinance, as provided by the Law of 24 August 1993.

[73] Refugees transferred to Sweden under the so-called refugee quota have already been granted residence permits and all the necessary preparations for their reception have been made at a refugee residential centre.

[74] K. Jönsson, *op. cit.*, para.24.

necessary. In 1993, more than a dozen of new refugee centres have been opened in southern Sweden in order to accommodate thousands of asylum seekers from Bosnia.[75] The allocation to the local municipalities takes place after negotiations between the Swedish Immigration Board and the individual local authorities.[76] Since May 1988, municipal reception has been confined to holders of residence permits. The asylum seeker must accept the local municipality in which he is placed.[77] The police and social workers are there to help asylum seekers to find accommodation sometimes in hotels or at some friends. Asylum seekers are free to move within Sweden.[78] However, they are strongly advised to remain near the clearance or residential centres because they could be called for interview at any time. During the pre-asylum period asylum seekers receive a "yellow card" which proves that the asylum procedure has started. No authorization to sojourn, even provisional, is given. An asylum seeker may keep his own passport, or if any can claim a provisional passport for foreigners or simply use his yellow card as an identity card.[79] Because of the shortage of housing in certain municipalities (in big cities and universities cities), asylum seekers are sometimes forced to stay on for a long time in refugee residential centres. From 1st July 1994, SIV will be able to delegate to an entrepreneur, an organisation or any other private person, the responsibility of opening accommodation centres for refugees and of taking care of them. The Red Cross seems to be very interested in opening apartments and flats in a newly created village with a centre where people could meet. It would be for asylum seekers and refugees.[80]

Switzerland

Any asylum request has to be lodged at a registration centre (except for requests lodged abroad to an embassy or consulate).[81] Registration centres have been created in 1988. There are four: Cointrin (Geneva), Chiasso, Kreutzlingen and Basel. Originally they were provided to shelter about 30 to 80 asylum seekers for a maximum period of three days. During this stay of a few days in registration centres, asylum seekers are not allowed to leave the centres and they must comply to the rules of the centres (ie, duty to report if no meals required). No further restrictions exist as to the freedom of movement. These centres became quickly insufficient and new transit centres with registration functions were created (Arbedeau, Gorgier, Haltchtetel and Gotzwill, in particular). These centres could only be created because of the entry into

---

[75] MNS, May 1993, p. 12. There are about 22,000 of them in clearance centres awaiting for a decision to be made by the Swedish Government (MNS, June 1993, p. 5).

[76] *Asile en Europe, op. cit.*, p. 479, para.49.

[77] On residential centre activities and municipal refugee reception, see The Swedish Ministry of Cultural Affairs, *Immigrants and Refugee Policy*, 1992, pp. 43–6.

[78] K. Jönsson, *op. cit.*, para.37.

[79] *Asile en Europe, op. cit.*, p. 479, paras. 47–48.

[80] Interview with Eva Ulfvebrand, Swedish Red Cross (*op. cit.*).

[81] Articles 5 and 6 of Asylum Ordinance 1 of 22 may 1991.

force of the new legal provisions, in particular Article 14 of the Asylum Law. To avoid concentration in these centres asylum seekers are quickly assigned to different cantons,[82] in proportion to the population of the canton. This decision is taken by the Confederation and is final.[83] In practice it may create dramatic situations because family ties are interpreted very restrictively. Brothers and sisters as well as husband and wife from a customary wedding may often be assigned to different cantons.[84] Each canton is then allowed to attribute them a place of residence within its territory (usually collective accommodation called reception centres or transit centres), where they will have to remain, but free to move in and out, until a decision on their request is taken by the Federal Office for Refugees.[85] Individual accommodations are very difficult to find and are often very expensive (all the more the asylum seeker is not allowed to work during the first three months). The asylum seeker receives a certificate of asylum request[86] which stands for an identity document and a provisional authorization to sojourn. This certificate is only valid within the limits of the Swiss territory and allows the asylum seeker to move within the canton in which he has been assigned. Authorizations to travel abroad or to move to another canton are given in exceptional cases. The concept of pre-asylum seeker appeared in 1987–88 as registration centres were becoming more and more snowed under with an increasing number of asylum seekers arriving.[87] A pre-asylum seeker is an applicant who arrives at a registration centre, takes a number and has to find shelter elsewhere until his number is called. These are more and more numerous and have to wait to be able to go to a registration centre in circus tents and subway shelters created on the spot by the organizations assisting refugees. At the beginning this situation was described as urgent, now it became a recognized structure. These shelters are normally closed between 9am and 7pm and the pre-asylum seekers are, therefore, on the streets every day with only three Swiss Francs per day to spend. Swiss authorities hope that the new restrictive measures will start to be known in the countries providing the greatest number of refugees and that the influx of new arrivals will decrease.[88] Switzerland, like most of the other European countries, is facing an accommodation crisis. Accommodation centres in the cantons have only a limited capacity and only 30 or

---

[82] Article 14a of the 1979 Asylum Law, as modified. See also Articles 9 and 10 of Asylum Ordinance 1 of 22 May 1991.

[83] Article 14a–3, Asylum Law.

[84] Interview with Mr. M. Gonczy and Mrs. E. Grosjean, OSAR, *op. cit.* See also, Yves Brutsch, *op. cit.*, pp. 6–7.

[85] Article 19–1 and Article 20, Asylum Law. There are, however, exceptions where the asylum seeker will be removed to another country. This is the case if the asylum seeker has been living with relatives in another country or if he did not come directly from the country he fears persecution. Article 19–2 and –3, Asylum Law.

[86] Article 8, Asylum Ordinance 1.

[87] OSAR, *Rapport Annuel de l'Office central Suisse d'Aide aux Réfugiés*, 1989, pp. 15–9.

[88] Remarks collected during the interview with Mr. M. Gonczy and Mrs. E. Grosjean, OSAR (*op. cit.*).

40% of the asylum seekers may find a shelter in these reception or transit centres. Among these, some asylum seekers may stay up to six years. The others either live with relatives or at hotels. In some municipalities hotels are converted and put at their disposal, but resistance from the population is strong. Moreover, nothing in the legislation provides that municipalities have to admit asylum seekers; municipalities are, thus, free to refuse them.

United Kingdom

The laws in the United Kingdom contain no specific provisions. It is admitted that asylum seekers are allowed to stay in the country, in refugee camps or other form of collective accommodation, until a decision is taken on their application by the Home Office or until a decision on appeal has been reached in cases where the asylum seeker was legally admitted to the country.[89] However, delays between the day asylum seekers arrive at a port of entry and the day their claim is recorded by the Asylum Division of the Home Office, are usually quite long; and during such a period of time, asylum seekers may have to sleep on the street or in airport or church halls. In most cases, asylum seekers are granted temporary admission as soon as suitable accommodation is found for them. During the pre-asylum period, advice may be obtained from voluntary organizations such as the UKIAS or the British Refugee Council (BRC). In the London area, these organizations may even provide shelters in the provisional accommodation centres of the BRC. Under the current homelessness legislation, asylum seekers can qualify for permanent housing from a local authority if, like anyone else, they are unintentionally homeless, or threatened with homelessness and in priority need. The problem remains of course that asylum seekers are concentrated in the London area and difficulties arise to find them a permanent shelter. The new Act 1993 has recently restricted the housing right of asylum seekers.[90] It increases the situations where public authorities have no housing responsibilities to them. Under the Act, local authorities may also apply discriminatory criteria for the allocation if they consider it 'reasonable' for asylum seekers to remain in 'temporary accommodation' however inappropriate.

To conclude on this point, it seems that the freedom of movement of asylum seekers authorized to stay while waiting for a decision on their refugee status is subject to little restrictions in the countries under review, with the exception of the Federal Republic of Germany and the United Kingdom. The future of such freedom is, nevertheless, subject to important restrictions contained in the 1990 Schengen Agreement on the gradual abolition of controls at the common frontiers.[91]

---

[89] *Asile en Europe, op. cit.*, p. 452, para.42.

[90] Clauses 4 and 5 of the Asylum and Immigration Appeals Act, 1993.

[91] D. O'Keeffe, "The Free Movement of Persons and the Single Market", *ELR*, Vol.17, 1992, p. 3; D. O'Keeffe, "The Schengen Convention: A Suitable Model for European Integration?", *Yearbook of European Law*, 1991, p. 185; J.J.E. Schutte, "Schengen: Its Meaning for the Free Movement of Persons in Europe", *CMLRev*, Vol.28, 1991, p. 549.

2. Employment, Education and Social Assistance

Belgium

Until October 1993, asylum seekers could obtain a provisional authorization to work, valid during the whole time of the pre-asylum period but only for the specific job that it was asked for.[92] No legal provisions existed preventing an asylum seeker from getting a job but the employment situation was always such that it was almost impossible in practice to find work. As from 1st October 1993, asylum seekers are no longer able to work until their applications are declared admissible. Such a measure is aimed at persons who apply for asylum as a way to get a work permit.[93] A system of compulsory insurance against illness and disability exists which allows asylum seekers to benefit from it if they have been registered for at least six months in a *commune* and are actually living in Belgium. During the period of time when the asylum seeker is not protected by this insurance, medical costs in general are at the charge of the CPAS, likewise with regards to family benefits which are granted by the CPAS. Compulsory education until the age of 18 also apply to asylum seekers and refugees.[94] Judicial assistance is provided to any alien who does not have sufficient means. The UNHCR representative and the bar associations provide a system which allows the asylum seeker (and the refugee) to benefit from the help of a lawyer free of charge.[95]

It is now well known that the reception of asylum seekers in Belgium is subject to two main criticisms. First, the refusal by the majority of *communes* to register asylum seekers present in their district on the municipal register of foreigners. Second, the length of the procedure. The general situation of asylum seekers seems difficult to analyse because of the very complex structure of the most important link concerning the reception of asylum seekers: the CPAS. They have been created by Article 1 of the Law of 8 July 1976.[96] They are public institutions with a legal personality. Their assignments are stated in Articles 57 to 62bis of the Law. The CPAS provides to individuals or families the social aid due from the collectivity, which may be material, social, medical or psychological. The amount or the kind of social aid is not specified in the Law. The CPAS must investigate on a case by case basis to determine the needs of each person or family and grant a social aid according to these needs. The CPAS should intervene as soon as the need is not covered by the national system of social security. Present in each *commune*, their mandate, according to the law, is to help any person

---

[92] See J.Y. Carlier, *Droits des réfugiés, op. cit.*, pp. 119–20.

[93] MNS, October 1993, p. 10.

[94] As no difference of status exists between asylum seekers and refugees on this matter, refer to chapter seven, *infra*.

[95] Reference should generally be made to the work of J.Y. Carlier, *Droits des réfugiés, op. cit.*, pp. 149–60.

[96] This Law has been modified a few times and the best reference book is: L.-M. Bataille and J.-M. Berger, *Aide Mémoire des CPAS*, "Recueil des principales dispositions légales relatives aux centres publics d'aide sociale", Union des Villes et Communes belges.

(therefore, not only aliens or refugees) who is present in the territory of the *commune*, irrespective of the fact that the person is put down on the alien register or the population register of the *commune*. However, in practice, the majority of *communes* do not respect their legal obligation to register asylum seekers.[97] Refusal is used by the CPAS as an excuse for not having to provide social assistance (in order to find accommodation, food, clothes etc.) to asylum seekers. Such practice has been condemned by the *Conseil d'Etat*.[98] The Minister for the Environment and Social Emancipation has continuously pushed the *communes* to accept more asylum seekers and in some cases, CPAS have decided to grant social aid below what should have been expected, thus trying to make these people leave for another *commune*.[99] If all the *communes* were willing to make the system work, the CPAS would provide a comprehensive system of para-social security. The costs of the social aid are indeed repaid in full by the Government (Ministry of Public Health), except for the personnel costs. The distribution programme of asylum seekers appears therefore to be a distribution programme of the costs. One may, however, conclude on this point that generally speaking, it seems that the distribution plan of asylum seekers from the reception centres to the *communes* is quite successful and that in a great majority of *communes* the quota of 1/1000 has exceeded.[100] That way, the problem of reception of asylum seekers may not primarily be a problem situated in the reception centres and then the *communes*, but seems more likely to be a problem related to the length of the procedure. That only 10% of asylum seekers are recognized as refugees and granted asylum is one thing but that it takes from three to five years to reach a decision is a waste of money without long term achievements. Money should be invested in the procedure not in efforts to try to support so many asylum seekers for so many years. Reception and social aid to asylum seekers is not only provided by the CPAS but also by

---

[97] A late report for registration by the asylum seeker (they have eight days from the day of issue of the Annex 26 as a provisional authorisation to sojourn) to the *commune* does not constitute grounds for refusing unconditionally registration. The *commune* must register the asylum seeker. The asylum seeker may however be subject to a fine. *Tribunal Civil*, Brussels, 17 March 1992, RDE, 1992, n.68, p. 81. Also if a *commune* refuses illegally to register an asylum seeker, the *commune* can be found liable to pay damages to the asylum seeker for the prejudice suffered. *Tribunal Civil*, Brussels, 13 March 1992, RDE, 1992, n.69, p. 196. Ten million BF is expected to be spent by the CPAS of Bruxelles in 1994 to cover lawyers fees for legal actions brought by asylum seekers against illegal refusal by the CPAS to provide assistance (MNS, March 1994, p. 5).

[98] Decision of 29 May 1990. See ECRE Country Report, Belgium, 5–6 October 1991, p. 49.

[99] Faced with the reluctances of the CPAS to accept more asylum seekers, NGOs have started to introduce more and more appeals to the *Chambres provinciales de recours des CPAS*, to correct unfair situations in some individual cases. These NGOs group within the CBAR are authorized, since 1985, to claim to the Minister of Public Health the repayment of the costs created by the social aid given by the members of the CBAR, who substituted their action to the failing CPAS.

[100] Interview with Mr.J. Ramakers, Cabinet de Mrs. Smet, Secrétaire d'Etat à l'Emancipation Sociale, Brussels, December 1990. However, see more recently, MNS, October 1993, p. 4.

various organizations specialised in the field of refugees, such as the CBAR, the CIRE and the OCIV.[101]

Federal Republic of Germany

In July 1991, the five year employment ban was lifted. Since then, asylum seekers who are staying at an initial reception centre are not allowed to work while there.[102] However, once they have been accepted in collective accommodations in the *Kreis* (local authority), they can apply for a work permit for a given job but only after that job has first been offered to German or privileged foreigners applicants. Unqualified and poorly-paid jobs used to exist for asylum seekers in Western industrialized cities areas. The situation is now much more difficult because of the high rate of unemployment in the former East Germany. Social security certificates have been introduced, making it more difficult for asylum seekers to work illegally.[103]

Asylum seekers have restricted access to social benefit but only after their application has been pending for a year.[104] Those with no private means are normally given a monthly low-standard allowance to cover for everyday expenses (food, pocket money, hygiene, clothes and transport).[105] In the *Land* of Saarland, social benefits for asylum seekers are distributed in the form of food and pocket money only. The Government of Northrhine-Westphalia decided to use the same measure in its *Land*.[106] Responsibility for the living conditions of asylum seekers in the community homes lies with the *Kreis* and,

---

[101] The CBAR was created in 1968. It coordinates the action of its seven members organizations. In 1987, two other organs of coordination have been created or re-created at the community level: the CIRE (*Centre d'Initiation pour Réfugiés et Etrangers*) which exists since 1954, and the OCIV (*Overlegcentrum voor Integratie von Vluchtelingen*). The members organizations of the CBAR are also members of these two community organs. They all work together and share out the tasks according to the new structures of Belgium. The CBAR coordinates the government's activities and operates a link between the Belgian organizations and the national authorities, the international institutions and the NGOs. The CIRE (French Branch) and the OCIV (Dutch Branch) coordinate the activities of the executives or of the authorities of the province or the *commune*. They mainly deal with integrating recognized refugees in Belgium. These three organs of coordination are normally not directly in contact with asylum seekers or refugees, but their members organizations are.

[102] S.61, AsylVfG. The Federal Minister of the Interior, "Survey of the Policy and Law regarding Aliens in the Federal Republic of Germany", January 1991, p. 65.

[103] An asylum seeker who is given a certicate of application for asylum which also provides a total prohibition of employment must comply with such obligation. S.85 AsylVfG has, however, abolished criminal punishments for infringement of such prohibition, except in cases of secondary application. See, for instance, decision of the BVerfG, 19.2.93 in NJW 1993, Heft 34, p. 2167.

[104] Bundesministerium des Innerns, "Das Neue Asylrecht ...", *op. cit.*, p. 17. The restrictions which the AsylbLG imposes on the right to social aid as well as the principle concerning benefits in kinds laid down in the same statute, are limited to the first year of the asylum procedure (OVG Berlin, judgment of 19.11.1993, 6 S 194/93, NVwZ, Supplement 2/1994, pp. 131–4.

[105] *Asile en Europe, op. cit.*, p. 87, para.45.

[106] ECRE Country Report, FRG, 22–23 September 1990, p. 54.

as a rule, expenditure incurred by the *Kreis* in respect of asylum seekers is reimbursed by the *Land* concerned. This is not, however, the case concerning local authority expenditure on children of asylum seekers in the school system which is not reimbursed. School attendance by children depends therefore largely on the budget and interest of each local school, except in the *Länder* of Bayern and Hessen where school is compulsory for all children with no distinction. Asylum seekers do not normally have access to German languages classes.[107] However, such classes are sometimes provided by humanitarian agencies in a few asylum centres and at a small scale. Asylum seekers have restricted access to national health services but they can benefit from free medical or dental treatment in cases of emergency.

France

Like in Belgium, the situation used to be rather good for asylum seekers, at least theoretically, because in practice the employment market situation has deteriorated for a number of years. Until 1991, asylum seekers with a receipt for residence permit request (but with no other formalities) were allowed to occupy wage-earning employment, if available in any professional sector, according to the regulations. The receipt also enabled asylum seekers to register as job seekers with the National Employment Agency and, if they could not find a job, to receive a special insertion allowance financed by the government, for a total maximum period of one year.[108] Circular of 26 September 1991[109] has abolished work permits for asylum seekers. Asylum seekers, whether accommodated in reception centres or not, no longer have access to the labour market. By way of exception, the Ministry of Social Affairs and Integration has allowed ex-Yugoslavs coming from "disturbed areas" to work if they can find a job.[110] The asylum seeker is also entitled to free medical assistance from the Social Aid Office of the *Mairie* of his residence area. Such assistance stops when an asylum seekers starts benefiting from social security benefits as a wage-earner. In provisional accommodation centres, this free medical assistance is given to asylum seekers on the ground of emergency, without the usual preliminary investigation. Asylum seekers who find accommodation by their own means and who prefer to live independently are more and more frequently refused such a free medical assistance before they actually find a job and become entitled to social security.[111] On arrival in France, asylum seekers normally receive a "waiting allowance". Asylum seekers housed in reception centres receive a daily allowance (pocket money) because food, accommodation and clothes are available to them for free. Asylum seekers who are not living in reception centres receive a monthly allowance. When the asylum seeker has found a job, his employer

---

[107] *Asile en Europe, op. cit.*, p. 88, para.49.

[108] *Ibid*, p. 273, para.75.

[109] On the situation of asylum seekers regarding the labour market.

[110] Circular from 14 September 1992.

[111] FTDA, *Guide pratique du réfugié*, 1992.

has to declare him to the Social Security Institutes. This entitles the asylum seeker to benefit from various social assistance allowances, as any other wage-earner.[112] Since September 1993, nobody can work in France without first being registered with the Social Security Institutes.[113] The special insertion allowance also gives right to specific allowances from the Social Security, such as the partial repayment of care expenses for the asylum seeker and his dependents.[114] Asylum seekers are not eligible for any free training programmes, nor are they entitled to any integration programmes or French languages courses. Some provisional accommodation centres do however provide special courses to familiarize asylum seekers with the French social and professional way of life. Family benefits, which in France may reach important amounts, are kept for aliens with an authorization to sojourn of more than three months, therefore, in practice, only to asylum seekers arriving in France with a long term visa.[115] As soon as the asylum seeker has been given an authorization to stay (provisional authorization to sojourn or receipt for residence permit request), he, his children and other dependents have access to primary and secondary education.[116] As for higher education, it depends on each University. Some of them may refuse to register an asylum seeker who has not fulfilled the pre-registry formality, that should have been fulfilled by the alien in his country of origin. Statutory refugees are, however, exempt from this last requirement. According to Article 3 of the Law of 10 July 1991 and the Decree of 19 December 1991 on legal aid, asylum seekers may be represented free of charge before the Appeal Commission under such restrictive conditions[117] that in fact this Article allows less than 1% of asylum seekers to be represented free of charge.[118]

Sweden

Since 1 July 1992,[119] asylum seekers who are expected to have to wait for more than four months for a decision on residence have been allowed to work while waiting.[120] In practice, none of them can get work because of very

---

[112] *Ibid.*

[113] MNS, October 1993, p. 3.

[114] This right has been subject to some restrictions according to the new immigration law on entry and residence of aliens in France. Charles Pasqua, has indeed introduced a new bill before Parliament in June 1993. One of its provisions aims at abolishing social assistance and protection to illegal foreigners, even if they are working. *Le Monde*, 11/06/93, p. 9. Such provision was declared in conformity with the Constitution by the *Conseil Constitutionel* in August 1993. *Le Monde*, 15–16/08/93, p. 7.

[115] *Asile en Europe, op. cit.*, p. 274, para.78. FTDA, *Guide pratique du réfugié*, 1992.

[116] FTDA, *Guide pratique du réfugié*, 1992.

[117] The asylum seeker must have entered France legally or must hold a residence permit valid for at least one year. ECRE Country Report, France, 3–5 April 1992, p. 81.

[118] *Documentation – Réfugiés, Revue de Presse*, No. 203, 27 Nov./6 Dec. 1992, p. 1.

[119] Aliens Ordinance (SFS 1991:1993), chapter 4, s.4.

[120] ECRE Country Report, Sweden, 3–5 April 1992, pp. 124–5.

high unemployment.[121] Asylum seekers are expected to participate in the everyday running of the residential centre and as soon as they receive wages they have to pay for food and accommodation according to the rules of the centre. During their stay at the residential centres, asylum seekers are offered Swedish language tuitions.[122] Such classes are organized by the local authorities education departments, by various educational associations or under the auspices of the ministries of Labour and Education.[123] Under Swedish law children must be admitted to primary school as soon as they have reached school-age.[124] Normally children start school after a fortnight in a special reception class. Pupils are often taught by teachers who speak their mother tongue. Local authority expenditure on teaching asylum seekers is paid by the SIV.[125] The social security system is only available to foreigners residing permanently in Sweden. As asylum seekers cannot be considered permanent residents, their basic needs are satisfied in clearance and residential centres. All asylum seekers are offered medical screening. They can also obtain free medical and dental treatment, in cases of emergency.[126] Asylum seekers with no private means can apply for financial assistance. Daily allowances are paid by the SIV.[127] The allowance has to cover pocket money, personal hygiene, clothes and transport. A special allowance can be provided for winter clothes. However, asylum seekers who have income and who stay in a residential centre will have to pay certain costs to SIV.[128] Since February 1993, rejected asylum seekers who refuse to apply for a passport to leave the territory will lose their right to housing and to allowances.[129] Once in a municipality, pressure is put on asylum seekers to become self-supporting as quickly as possible. The reception of refugees and asylum seekers is based on the participation of most of the municipalities, so that responsibility is spread out among all of them. The municipalities receive compensation for assistance to asylum seekers.[130] This payment is intended to cover the cost of housing, living expenses and language courses.[131]

---

[121] K. Jönsson, *op. cit.*, para.44.

[122] *Ibid*, para.36.

[123] The Swedish Institute, "Fact Sheets on Sweden", May 1993.

[124] K. Jönsson, *op. cit.*, para.43.

[125] SIV is responsible for the reception of refugees and asylum seekers coming to Sweden, since 1985.

[126] K. Jönsson, *op. cit.*, para.45.

[127] *Ibid*, para.34.

[128] Article 8a of the Law on assistance to asylum seekers and others, as amended in February 1992 (1988:153).

[129] This measure is intended to Ethiopians whose Embassy refuses to issue them with a passport in order to leave, unless they apply for it personally. MNS, March 1993, p. 8.

[130] The present compensatory system came into force on 1st January 1991.

[131] Statens Invandrarverk, "Facts about Immigration", April 1992.

Switzerland

Asylum seekers, to whom a certificate of asylum request[132] was given, are eligible for financial aid from the social departments of the canton. This certificate also entitles them to a provisional authorization to work. However, there is a general prohibition to work during the first three months following the registration of the asylum application and in current practice some cantons even refuse to give the authorization to work for another three months.[133] After the first three months, asylum seekers are normally allowed to get a job.[134] However, they will need an authorization from the canton in which they reside[135] and lucrative activity is limited to the territory of this canton. Asylum seekers are not allowed to exercise an independent activity, they can only be salaried employees. Since 1 January 1992, as soon as asylum seekers receive a work permit and find work, 7% is deducted each month from their salaries to the benefit of the Government in order to guarantee future assistance expenses.[136] Authorization to work ceases as soon as the applicant is refused asylum in Switzerland. As special cases, Bosnian refugees as well as any other refugees from the former Yugoslavia have been allowed to stay and to work under certain conditions.[137] During the period of three months when asylum seekers are not allowed to work, language courses are provided in reception centres (paid by the Confederation). Outside reception centres there is a charge for language courses. Grants for professional training from the Confederation are not normally issued to asylum seekers. School is compulsory and free for children of an asylum seeker until the age of 16. In cases of unemployment, accident or injury, health problems or poverty, various insurances may cover and help asylum seekers. Due to the fact that too many illnesses exist among certain categories of asylum seekers, medical insurances have now become compulsory in certain cantons but only for asylum seekers who have found work.[138] Asylum seekers who are unable to pay their premiums may benefit from social assistance from the municipalities. As long as an asylum seeker resides in a reception centre he will not benefit from any financial aid but will only receive pocket money to cover personal need. Assuming an asylum seeker is not living anymore in a reception centre he may be given material

---

[132] This certificate stands for identity documents and provisional residence permit.

[133] Article 21 of the 1979 Asylum Law, as modified. Notice that Switzerland is less affected by unemployment than France or the United Kingdom. The European Community average percentage of unemployment is about 8.4. France rate of unemployment is about 9%, the UK about 7%, while Switzerland is only about 1%. *The Guardian* (education), 26 February 1991, p. 7.

[134] The Swiss authorities hoped that the decision on asylum would be taken during these three months. The practice proves that decisions are taken after nine months sometimes even three or four years. Therefore, people arriving in Switzerland only with the intention of finding a job still rush.

[135] The authorization is limited to one year and may be extended.

[136] ECRE Country Report, Switzerland, 3–5 April 1992, p. 131.

[137] MNS, June 1993, p. 5.

[138] H. Schoeni, *op. cit.*, p. 19.

assistance from the social department of the canton, if it appears that he needs it.[139] In Geneva, such an assistance is provided by the general hospital, in Lausanne, the provident and social assistance department of the canton, in Zurich, the delegate to the Swiss Central Office for Aid to Refugees. The asylum seeker may not get any assistance if a third person has guaranteed his cost for support or if a relative is financially able to support him. Assistance benefits may be paid back if it appears that the situation of the asylum seeker improves.[140] Generally speaking it may be said that asylum seekers are assisted like Swiss citizens. They cost a lot to the Confederation (0.5 billions of Swiss Francs in 1990)[141] and to the cantons (0.5 billions of Swiss Francs in 1990).[142] 80% of these costs are for assistance.[143] The remainder 20% is for personnel and infrastructure costs.[144] The length of the procedure is the main reason for such heavy expenses on assistance. It is said that only asylum seekers cost so much to Switzerland, as opposed to recognized refugees who are only a few number and who live more by their own means.[145] Integration and social assistance ceases when the asylum seeker's application for asylum is refused, in fact the day the time limit granted by the Federal Office for leaving has expired.

United Kingdom

Unless the asylum seeker had already found a job in the United Kingdom when he applied for refugee status to the British authorities, he will have no permission to work. The Home Office has, nevertheless, recently recognized the possibility for asylum seekers to look for a job six months after they have applied for refugee status.[146] Such permission is not automatic and request must be made in writing to the Home Office.[147] Permission is normally granted. As for public assistance, there is a discretionary payment of income support if the asylum seeker has no other means of support.[148] Assistance is often provided exclusively by voluntary agencies grouped together within the British Refugee Council. They are mainly financed by donations. Only a small part of their financial resources is coming from the Government and the European Social Funds.[149] Asylum seekers with a certificate of temporary admission are in a more advantageous situation than asylum seekers without,

---

[139]   Articles 20a, 20b and 31 et seq., Asylum Law.

[140]   *Ibid*, Article 21a.

[141]   The Confederation reimbursed the cantons their expenses regarding the assistance of asylum seekers. *Ibid*, chapter 4.

[142]   *Ibid*, Article 40a.

[143]   Article 18 et seq. of Asylum Ordinance 2 on Financial Matters of 22 May 1991.

[144]   *Ibid*, Article 4.

[145]   Interview with Mr. M. Gonczy and Mrs. E. Grosjean, OSAR (*op. cit.*).

[146]   *Dossier: vers une harmonisation du droit d'asile en Europe*, Hommes et Migrations, No. 1096, 15 October 1986, p. 43.

[147]   Sue Shutter, *op. cit.*, p. 70.

[148]   *Asile en Europe, op. cit.*, p. 452, para.42.

[149]   Hommes et Migrations, *op. cit.*, pp. 41, 43–4.

as they are allowed to work and to benefit from income support. Until 1992, the Refugee Unit of the UKIAS as well as other voluntary agencies, in particular the Joint Council for the Welfare of Immigrants (JCWI), were competent to give free legal advice to asylum seekers and to represent them (through a person appointed by the agency, a lawyer, solicitor, barrister or any other person with the agreement of the judge), free of charge, before the courts, even before the court of appeal. This system of advice is peculiar to the immigration field. In other field of law a client can only be represented before an appeal court by a person legally qualified to do so and he, personally, has to pay the cost of the representation. He may, however, call on the National Legal Aid Service. On 20 January 1992, the Government decided to withdrew the possibility to have legal representation provided by UKIAS and announced that such competence would be exclusively given to a new agency set up shortly after: the new Refugee Legal Centre.[150] It is independent from the UKIAS.[151] Notice also that lengthy discussions took place following a statement made by the Home Secretary in Parliament (July 1991) on the possibility of abolishing the green form legal aid for asylum seekers.[152] Such undesirable proposal was, however, withdrawn in February 1992,[153] and legal aid was finally removed from the discussions on the Asylum and Immigration Appeals Act 1993.

Social integration and assistance is not provided and protected uniformly in European countries. While in the Federal Republic of Germany[154] and Sweden, an asylum seeker is legally allowed to work, the United Kingdom and Switzerland prohibit such a possibility during the first few months. With regard to France and Belgium, asylum seekers have simply no longer access to the labour market. European countries seem to have agreed on one aspect, which is that priority should be given to "try to shorten the waiting periods for decision of their case rather than create legislation concerning asylum seekers' right to work". It has even been suggested by a few countries that "all European countries should have the same practice, ie, that asylum seekers should not be allowed to work". This could help thwarting the 'pull-factor' effects.[155] As an alternative, an attractive solution seems to be that "asylum seekers should work within the [reception] centers, get suitable salary for that work and also pay for their food and lodging at the center",[156] provided such reception centres exist in the country.[157] The study of these six coun-

---

[150] Planning Group Report, "Legal services for asylum-seekers", 1992.

[151] ECRE Country Report, United Kingdom, 3–5 April 1992, p. 139 and 3–4 October 1992, p. 135.

[152] The Home Secretary Statement of 2 July 1991, HC Deb 194 cc165–67.

[153] HL Deb 535 cc459–60. See also, Sue Shutter, *op. cit.*, p. 75.

[154] Except during the first stay of a few weeks in a reception centre.

[155] Final Report of the European Conference on Reception of Asylum Seekers, 1991, p. 43 (for the quotations) and p. 55.

[156] *Ibid*, p. 53.

[157] This new obligation to work, coupled with an obligation to learn the language, is expected to become law in Sweden as of 1st July 1994 (MNS, January 1994, p. 7). It would thus supersede

tries also reveals that the standard of social protection varies between each country. However, one common tendency seems to be the recent adoption of national measures restricting the grounds for entitlement to free legal assistance and social supports. Furthermore, that almost no direct assistance from governments is provided, except in Sweden, gives to voluntary agencies an important responsibility during the pre-asylum period.

---

the present right to work as an employee while waiting for a decision on an asylum application (MNS, November 1993, p. 6).

CHAPTER SIX

DE FACTO REFUGEES: A LEGAL STATUS OR A MERE TOLERANCE?

Two kinds of refugees may be granted asylum. A first kind includes asylum seekers who may be recognized as refugees within the meaning of the 1951 Convention. Persons in this category are considered to meet the criteria of the 1951 Convention and are normally granted permanent asylum. They are referred to as convention refugees or *de jure* refugees.[1] A second kind consists of asylum seekers who may be granted permanent or temporary asylum but without refugee status. Persons falling in this category are often referred to as *de facto* refugees and refugees for humanitarian reasons. They are usually protected against *refoulement* because there are valid and compelling humanitarian reasons for not returning them to their countries of origin, even though they are not considered to fall strictly within the definition of Article 1A(2) of the 1951 Convention. This category of refugees has generally been defined as including persons who could qualify for refugee status according to the 1951 Convention but who for various reasons are not willing or able to apply for that status[2] and persons falling outside the definition of the 1951 Convention but who nevertheless are unable or, for humanitarian reasons, unwilling to return to their country of origin.[3] Today, this very last category constitutes the majority of refugees in the world, Europe included. In the last decade, displaced persons[4] have fled from Turkey (persecuted Kurds), Sri Lanka (persecuted Tamils), Iran, Iraq, Lebanon, parts of Africa (ie, Ethiopia, Uganda, Rwanda, Somalia), Chile and, last but not least, former Yugoslavia.

---

[1] This category of refugees will be the subject of chapter seven, *infra.*

[2] Such reasons may include personal safety, fear of retaliation against relatives or friends in the country of origin, lack of information or failure to comply with procedural requirements (ie, a time limit).

[3] Goodwin-Gill, *The Refugee in International Law, op. cit.*, p. 17. Certain European states have chosen to interpret Article 1A(2) of the 1951 Convention restrictively so as not to include in the term refugee, persons fleeing civil war, "external aggression occupation, foreign domination or events seriously disturbing public order in either part or the whole of [their] country of origin" (definition of a refugee under Article 1(2) of the OAU 1969 Convention. Refugees coming from countries of origin where such events are taking place may only be granted a residence permit (permanent or temporary) on humanitarian grounds.

[4] As defined in the Statute of the UNHCR.

Article 1A(2) of the 1951 Convention provides that a refugee must be a person who genuinely fears to be personally persecuted on political grounds. It thus follows that a strict interpretation of this provisions precludes refugee status to be granted to persons unable to prove individual fear, persons who do not strictly fear persecution based on political grounds but who have instead strong humanitarian grounds and persons unable to show the link between fear and grounds of persecution.

1. General Observation at a European Level

The concept of *de facto* refugee has sometimes been described as including a broader category of persons than the concept of 'humanitarian refugee'. According to a Report by the Minority Rights Group, "de facto refugees comprise, in addition to humanitarian refugees, several groups of people who are not recognized refugees but are in a refugee-like situation. They may be hidden in other categories of aliens such as foreign students, migrants workers and visitors".[5]

While it is not the normal practice in Europe to try to return *de facto* refugees forcibly to their countries of origin, these persons are not equally protected against *refoulement* because they are not formally recognized as refugees under the 1951 Convention. It has been argued that they live their lives as second class citizens, having difficulty obtaining residence permits and work permits and generally not qualifying for any of the benefits normally extended to convention refugees (ie, free education, housing assistance and vocational and language training) nor to the right of family reunification.[6]

For many years, the CoE has been the principal forum to tackle this issue and to look at improving the situation of de facto refugees in Europe. As soon as 1976, the Parliamentary Assembly of the CoE adopted Recommendation 787(1976) on Harmonization of Eligibility Practice for Refugees under the 1951 Convention. The Assembly noted in its statement that "not all European states parties to these instruments have established a formal procedure for the examination of applications and that the national procedures which have been established do not conform to a single pattern".[7] The CoE was also concerned by the fact that "refugee status granted in one state is not necessarily

---

[5] MRG Report, *Refugees in Europe, op. cit.*, p. 9.

[6] See, in particular, the example of Kurds who have been granted exceptional leave to remain in Britain and who have been seperated from their family, with no decent possibility to make them come over; *The Independent*, 22.08.1990, p. 3. See also, a letter from Dan Jones in *The Independent*, 24.08.1990, p. 22.

[7] Parliamentary Assembly of the CoE, Recommendation 787(1976) on the harmonization of eligibility practice under the 1951 Convention on the Status of Refugees and the 1967 Protocol: *Basic Documents IV.8.* Notice that the Parliamentary Assembly of the CoE adopted the same year Recommendation 773(1976) on the Situation of De Facto Refugees (*Basic Documents IV.7*) but which has never been adopted by the states; see Serge Bodart, *op. cit.*, p. 36.

recognized in other states parties to the same convention".[8] It was therefore recommended that the Committee of Ministers creates an ad hoc committee of experts to examine the harmonization of eligibility practices relating to the status of refugees and to undertake further work on the legal questions relating to international refugees. The work of this committee, known as the ad hoc Committee on Legal Aspects of Territorial Asylum and Refugees, was responsible for the adoption by the Committee of Ministers on 5 November 1981 of the Recommendation (81)16 on the Harmonization of National Procedures relating to Asylum.[9] This recommendation presents a series of principles to ensure that requests for asylum are dealt with effectively and objectively. These include the principle that all asylum requests should be taken by a central authority, that the applicant be given the necessary facilities for the presentation of his case (including the right of representation by counsel and the right to appeal) and that the applicant be permitted to remain in the country until a final decision is made on the asylum request.[10] "Another important development has been the adoption in 1984 of Recommendation (84)1 by the Committee of Ministers. The statement reminds member states that the principle of *non-refoulement* is generally applicable even to persons not formally recognized as convention refugees. This assertion is also relevant to 'refugees in orbit'".[11] Recommendation (84)1 on the Protection of Persons not Formally Recognized as Refugees, adopted on 25 January 1984,[12] refers directly to the situation of *de facto* refugees. Its aim is to guarantee that the principle of *non-refoulement* is applied to all such persons.[13] As stated in the Preamble, the Recommendation is based on the liberal and humanitarian attitude of the CoE member states and, in particular, on their commitment to the principle of *non-refoulement*, already reflected in Resolution (67)14 on Asylum to Persons in Danger of Persecution.[14] The main purpose of Recom-

---

[8] Recommendation 787(1976).

[9] *Basic Documents IV.12.*

[10] On Recommendations 773, 787 and (84)1, see developments by Johan Cels, "European Responses to *de facto* Refugees", in *Refugees and International Relations*, Ed. Gil Loescher and Laila Monahan, 1989, pp. 200–2.

[11] CoE and the protection of the rights of refugees – 1951–1984 – *AWR Bulletin-Wien* – pp. 103–4. 'Refugees in orbit' may be defined as refugees sent from one country to another, and so forth, with no country feeling responsible to examine their request for asylum. This concept appeared because of the absence of criteria providing the state responsible to consider an asylum claim. Goodwin-Gill, *The Refugee In International Law, op. cit.*, pp. 52–3. See also, for background, Paul Weis, "Refugees in Orbit", *Israel Yearbook on Human Rights*, 1980, Vol. 10, pp. 157–66. However, today, all European states have signed the Convention determining the state responsible for examining applications for asylum lodged in one of the member states of the European Union, in Dublin on 15 June 1990. This Convention will enter into force three months after the last member states has ratified it.

[12] *Basic Documents IV.13*; see also the Protection of persons satisfying the criteria in the 1951 Convention who are not formally recognized as refugees, Recommendation R(84)1 and Explanatory Memorandum, CoE, Strasbourg 1984.

[13] Explanatory Memorandum, *op. cit.*, p. 10.

[14] Adopted by the Committee of Ministers on 29 June 1967: *Basic Documents IV.4.*

mendation (84)1 is to specify the scope of Resolution (67)14, namely, that the principle of *non-refoulement* should be applied not only to persons who are formally recognized as refugees under the 1951 Convention but also to other persons in danger of persecution, in particular *de facto* refugees. The Recommendation does not distinguish between the lawfulness or unlawfulness of the entry or residence of the person concerned, but it does take into account the interests of national security and public order of the host country. The exceptions in Article 33(2) of the 1951 Convention, thus, apply to the persons covered by the Recommendation.[15]

Since the ratification of the Maastricht Treaty on European Union, the institutions of the European Union have become involved in the elaboration of a European refugee policy. The Committee on Civil Liberties and Internal Affairs of the European Parliament has recently proposed a draft resolution calling the member states to "adopt a common approach to providing protection to the many refugees who are not covered by the 1951 Geneva Convention".[16] In the final draft of the resolution, as adopted in January 1994, side by side the convention status (or 'A status') is a tolerated status (or 'B status') for victims of war, violence and violations of human rights and it is further provided that the beneficiary of the tolerated status "are under no obligation to leave the Union as soon as they do not fully qualify for protection any more".[17] Moreover, the resolution calls upon the Commission of the Union to "assume greater responsibility and play the full role foreseen in Title VI" of the Treaty on European Union.[18] As a result, the Commission issued its Second Communication on Immigration and Asylum Policies to the Council and the European Parliament, in February 1994.[19] It was, however, adopted "with lukewarm interest" by the European Parliament.[20] The Commission's Second Communication stresses three types of actions to be taken for a long term strategy on immigration and asylum issues. Action is needed on the causes of migration pressure.[21] Action is also proposed regarding control-

---

[15] Art.33(2) "The benefit of the present provision [prohibition of expulsion or return] may not, however, be claimed by a refugee whom there are reasonable grounds for regarding as a danger to the security of the country in which he is, or who, having been convicted by a final judgment of a particularly serious crime, constitutes a danger to the community of that country." See, generally on the problem of *de facto* refugees and stateless persons, MRG Report, *The Refugee Dilemma, op. cit.*, pp. 8–9.

[16] MNS, January 1994, p. 4.

[17] MNS, February 1994, p. 3.

[18] *Ibid.* Notice also that in December 1993, the Commission signed a contract with the UNHCR to formalize the already existing co-operation between the European Community Humanitarian Office (set up in April 1992) and the UNHCR. MNS, January 1994, p. 11.

[19] MNS, March 1994, p. 1. Its First Communication was adopted in October 1991.

[20] MNS, May 1994, p. 2.

[21] In particular, by improving the collection of data and information, by creating an "observatory" for migration and, by applying the Declaration on Principles governing the External Aspects of Migration Policy adopted by the European Council in 1992. MNS, March 1994, pp. 1–2.

ling migration flows (flows of refugees[22] and flows of illegal immigrants).[23] Action is finally needed with the aim of strengthening integration policies for the benefit of legal migrants.[24]

Today there is no doubt that the increasing number of applicants denied refugee status has contributed to the growth of Europe's *de facto* refugee population.[25] This is a disconcerting development as it is believed that an appropriate interpretation of the 1951 refugee definition would have resulted in far more persons being recognized as convention refugees.[26]

This chapter aims at discussing the position of *de facto* refugees in the six countries under review. In Scandinavian countries, such as Sweden or Denmark, a *de facto* refugee status[27] is legally provided. It provides rights almost identical to those granted for convention refugees.[28] In other European countries, such as Belgium, France, Germany, Switzerland and the United Kingdom, there is simply no status attached to this situation. However, unlike in Belgium and France, the legislations of Germany, Switzerland and the United Kingdom provide some kind of humanitarian status for *de facto* refugees, in particular an authorization to stay is legally granted. Such temporary permission is referred to as *Duldung* in Germany, temporary admission in Switzerland and exceptional leave to remain in the UK. Rights attached to these situations are less than those guaranteed for convention refugees and the possibility for arbitrary decisions by the competent authorities is wider. It is not a right but merely a tolerance. In Belgium and France, there is still no legal provision relating to *de facto* refugees. Both countries agree that the 1951 Convention is supposed to cover all cases and that it would be rather useless, if not unfair, to create a status of second category for some refugees. The executive authorities may nevertheless, in exceptional circumstances and arbitrarily, authorize unrecognized refugees to remain.[29]

---

[22] Ie, by elaborating a Convention on family reunification, by approximating or even harmonizing the policies on admission of humanitarian grounds refugees, by harmonizing the application of the definition of refugee in the 1951 Convention, by providing minimum procedural fair standards, by agreeing on the terms of a Convention on manifestly unfounded applications and on safe third countries, by harmonizing the requirements of admission to temporary protection. *Ibid*, p. 2.

[23] Ie, by finally adopting the Convention on the Crossing of External Borders. *Ibid.*

[24] *Ibid.*

[25] *Report on the Problem of Refugees and Exiles in Europe. Vol. II Legal Report*, International University Exchange Fund on behalf of the Working Group on Refugees and Exiles in Europe: Geneva, July 1974.

[26] See, for instance, Gil Loescher, "The European Community and refugees", *International Affairs*, vol. 65, no. 4, Autumn 1989, p. 626.

[27] "B" status in Sweden as opposed to "A" status; "F" status in Denmark as opposed to "K" status. See Serge Bodart, *op. cit.*, p. 44 and p. 48.

[28] *Ibid*, pp. 45,46,48,49.

[29] *Ibid*, p. 12.

2. A Legal Status in Sweden

Unlike most other European countries, Sweden applies the 1951 Convention, Article 1A(2), in a very restrictive way. Only a very small percentage of asylum seekers are recognized convention refugees and are, accordingly, granted the full status of refugees.[30] As an alternative, Sweden offers two 'lower class' status of refugees. Chapter 3, section 1 of the Aliens Act provides that asylum "refers to a residence permit awarded to an alien because he is a refugee, he is a war-resister, or without being a refugee, he is unwilling to return to his country of origin on account of the political situation there and is able to plead very strong grounds in support of this." In addition, chapter 2, section 4(2) of the Aliens Act provides that "a residence permit may be issued to an alien who, for humanitarian reasons, should be allowed to settle in Sweden."[31] "This is not a statutory safeguard in the strict sense, but rather a faculty for the authority issuing permits to grant a residence permit when it is called for on humanitarian grounds."[32] It thus follows from the Aliens Act, that there are four different categories of refugees in Sweden. While the first category refers to refugees as defined in Article 1A(2) of the 1951 Convention,[33] the second category codifies a practice which dates back from the Vietnam war and which has since become obsolete.[34] The third and fourth categories, respectively, include *de facto* refugees[35] and persons allowed to stay for humanitarian reasons.[36] They both are the subject of this section.

De facto refugees could be considered as convention refugees so far as they have serious reasons of being persecuted on political grounds. However, conflicting reasons prevent them from being granted convention status. This

---

[30] Less than 10% in 1992. See ECRE Country Reports on Sweden. In 1993, this percentage was down to 3%, according to Swedish Red Cross sources.

[31] This last provision is to be found under the heading "Further provisions on visas, residence permits and work permits" and not under the heading "Asylum".

[32] The Swedish Ministry of Culture, *Immigrant and Refugee Policy*, 1993, p. 62.

[33] See chapter seven, *infra*.

[34] During the Vietnam war, US war resisters and conscientious objectors were issued a residence permit in Sweden on humanitarian grounds. Sweden constituted an exception in this way. See, Peter Nobel, "The De Facto-Refugee Concept in the Nordic Countries", in *Asyl i Norden*, *op. cit.*, p. 18. Today, this category is down to 0% (ECRE Country Reports on Sweden). The few applicants who are nevertheless each year recognized as war-resisters or conscientious objectors are, in practice, granted *de facto* refugee status.

[35] According to Peter Nobel, strictly speaking, "[d]e facto-refugees should not actually be called refugees according to the Aliens Act, but nonetheless, they are usually called B-refugees by experts and the public. In the new Aliens Law of 1989, the concept "refugee" does still not include de facto-refugees." Peter Nobel, in *Asyl i Norden*, *op. cit.*, p. 19. Though, I entirely agree with this statement, I nevertheless consider the distinction futile and I will thus refer to this third category of refugees as 'de facto refugees'. From 1989 until 1992, this category constituted around 20% of the total of recognized refugees. See ECRE Country Report on Sweden. However, when referring to figures from the Swedish Red Cross, this category seems to be only 4% for the year 1993.

[36] This category is far the most important one, around 60% until 1992, according to ECRE Country Reports on Sweden, 84% in 1993 according to Swedish Red Cross sources.

may be the case for different motives, in particular, reasons which are personal to the applicant, reasons based on doubts concerning the credibility of the application (ie, information appears to be exaggerated or false)[37] or, finally, if the applicant is coming from a country where war or ethnic conflict affects him personally and on political grounds rather than as a general violation of human rights.[38] Persons to whom a residence permit has been issued for humanitarian reasons, are persons who have failed to prove persecution solely on political grounds, but who, nevertheless, are allowed to stay because there are strong reasons to think that they may be subject to inhuman treatment if returned to their country of origin. Applicants in this category include persons coming from countries or parts of countries in which "violations of their human rights [exist] as a set of rules regulating the relation between individual and state"[39] (ie, a war or civil war is in progress[40]), persons who on account of illness or other strong personal circumstances should not be sent back to their country of origin,[41] and persons who have been waiting so long for their case to be decided that they are now fully settled in Sweden.[42]

Although, in theory, the three main categories of refugee status appear to be quite separate, in practice, however, distinction between convention refugee status, *de facto* status and humanitarian reasons status is quite difficult to draw. Quite rightly, one could say that refugees from all three categories benefit, in Sweden, from the rights and duties provided in the 1951 Convention.[43] In particular, they are all issued permanent residence permits;[44] this certainly

---

[37] K. Jönsson, *op. cit.*, para.52. Undocumented refugees are never granted convention status. At the best, if they are convention refugees, they will be granted *de facto* status. This is also the case concerning fraudulent applications. SOU 1994:54, *op. cit.*, p. 27.

[38] For instance, people from East Turkey (ie, christians) were granted *de facto* status. Although they could have find protection in the West part (ie, Istambul), at the time the decision was made Sweden had not yet recognized the principle of an internal flight alternative. Interview with Eva Ulfvebrand, Swedish Red Cross *(op. cit.)*.

[39] Peter Nobel, in *Asyl i Norden, op. cit.*, p. 18.

[40] K. Jönsson, *op. cit.*, para.54. This category includes, for instance, people from Bosnia and Somalia, as well as people who fled from Kosovo and were already in Sweden when the decision of Government allowing them to remain was taken (January 1993). Interview with Eva Ulfvebrand, Swedish Red Cross, *op. cit.* In cases where the author of persecution is not directly the state, humanitarian status is usually granted. However, *de facto* status is not completely excluded in such cases.

[41] K. Jönsson, *op. cit.*, paras.55–56. In particular, if the person suffers from a potentially terminal illness for which health care cannot be provided in the country of origin or the person suffers from a handicap of a serious kind or, the person has seriously intended to commit suicide and strong risks exist that he may try again. SOU 1994:54, *op. cit.*, pp. 28–31.

[42] K. Jönsson, *op. cit.*, para.57. Also, if there are doubts concerning the need of protection of an applicant and this applicant is married to or living with a Swedish person for at least one year, he will be allowed to stay for six months, renewable four times up to two years. If the relation at that stage is still going on, he will be granted a permanent right to stay. Interview with Mr. Fischerström, Appeals Board *(op. cit.)*.

[43] See chapter seven, *infra*.

[44] There is no temporary right to remain in Sweden. Asylum seekers are granted permanent right to stay. There has, nevertheless, been many discussion about creating a temporary right to

constitutes an exception in comparison with other European countries. There are three limitations, however. The first limitation applies to the right of family reunification which is not equally protected; the Government provide legal aid for family members of convention refugees to travel to Sweden, it does not so for *de facto* refugees or humanitarian grounds refugees. Thus, in practice, the right of family reunion is denied to these people, at least during the first few years of their stay in Sweden. The second derogation concerns the status of refugee itself which is not equally protected, in fact, strictly speaking, *de facto* and humanitarian grounds refugees have no statutory safeguards and, it is easier for them to have their residence permit withdrawn than for a convention refugee.[45] The third distinction provides that asylum and residence permit may altogether be refused to *de facto* refugees or persons with humanitarian grounds "if there are special grounds for doing so, and these special grounds include, for example, lack of reception resources."[46] Apart from these three exceptions, the distinction is almost fictitious. To conclude, one may agree that "when war in the former Yugoslavia started, humanitarian 'status' appeared like a good thing. Germany was closing its border. France, the United Kingdom etc. were refusing these people. The problem today is that there is nothing certain about the future. The situation is dragging on and maybe a temporary right to remain should be created. But if the situation in the country of origin is not going to get better, what is the point in giving 'temporary' permissions to stay for forty years! Something more than a convention status is a good thing. One better thing is of course burden sharing."[47] It is in fact very difficult to choose between having a *de facto* status and not having one. Some people argue that if no *de facto* status existed, more people would get convention status but then there is also danger that people would get nothing at all.

---

remain but it seems that many people think it would be a bad idea. The Government believes, indeed, that those who wish to return to their country of origin can go back even if they have been granted permanent permission to stay. Furthermore, it agrees, that those who, in other European countries, are only granted temporary right to remain and who have lived in Sweden for one, two or more years, should be allowed to stay permanently because most of them have married a Swedish person and have children. It would thus be inhuman to ask them to leave. Interview with Mr. Fischerström, Appeals Board (*op. cit.*).

[45] *De facto* status or humanitarian 'status' ceases on grounds of crimes or lies on ones identity. Although such cessation grounds apply also to convention refugees, in practice, more serious crimes or lies must exist for a convention refugee to loose his status.

[46] The Swedish Ministry of Culture, *Immigrant and Refugee Policy*, 1993, p. 62.

[47] Interview with the Agency for Advisory Service, *op. cit.* Following this line of arguments temporary admission seems a good solution in cases where there is a catastrophy and everyone knows when the situation will improve. As regards civil war, nobody knows and cases of temporary admission must, therefore, be revised altogether at specific times, creating much work as well as insecurity.

3. A Mere Tolerance in the Federal Republic of Germany, in Switzerland and in the United Kingdom

3.1. *Federal Republic of Germany: 'Duldung'*

According to s.1(1) and s.3 of the Asylum Procedure Act 1993, persons applying for protection from political persecution pursuant to Article 16aI–2 of the Basic Law are entitled to asylum whereas persons applying for permanent protection against being returned to a state where they fear dangers under s.51(1) of the Aliens Act are refugees within the meaning of the 1951 Convention.[48] Both categories of aliens are covered by the Asylum Act and they both benefit from the legal status of refugee as provided in the 1951 Convention.[49] Refugees or displaced persons admitted under special programmes (quota refugees) have their status defined in the Act on measures in aid of refugees admitted under humanitarian relief programmes and in the Act on the legal status of displaced aliens in the federal territory, respectively.[50]

Apart from these categories of persons, the Alien Law provides that deportation (or refoulement) of an alien may be postponed for a limited period of time for humanitarian, political or legal reasons (*Duldung*).[51] Such possibility is also provided in s.41 of the Asylum Act, in cases where the Federal Refugee Office or the administrative court are convinced that there are reasons precluding deportation pursuant to s.53(6) of the Aliens Act (ie, threat of torture, death penalty or other grounds provided in the ECHR). Suspension is normally granted for a first period of three months, at the end of which the aliens authority may either revoke the permission or grant *Duldung*.[52] Aliens tolerated to stay are distributed within the *Länder* in collective accommodations where their freedom of movement is restricted.[53] Only persons entitled to asylum or persons to whom the conditions of s.51(1) of the Aliens Act

---

[48] During the year 1992, all German courts, without exceptions, agreed that Vietnamese should not be entitled to asylum. However, courts were divided, and still are, as to whether or not they should be protected against *refoulement* according to s.51(1), AulsG. See, ECRE Country Report, FRG, 3–4 October 1992, p. 3.

[49] See, chapter seven, *infra*. A slight difference exists nevertheless. Unlimited residence permit (*Aufenthaltserlaubnis*) is issued to persons entitled to asylum whereas persons recognized as a refugee are issued a residence title for exceptional purposes (*Aufenthaltsbefugnis*). Refer to ss.68,70, AsylVfG. See also, R. Marx, "The Criteria for Determining ...", *op. cit.*, p. 162.

[50] S.1(2), AsylVfG. Quota refugees benefit from the status of refugee like a person entitled to asylum, in particular, they are given an unlimited residence permit and a work permit, they are allowed to social benefits and they are free to move.

[51] S.55, AuslG.

[52] See also s.18(4), AsylVfG, which provides that aliens coming from a safe third country may nevertheless be allowed to enter the country if Germany is responsible for dealing with the asylum application or if the Ministry of the Interior expressly allows such aliens to remain for international or humanitarian reasons or in order to safeguard the political interests of the country. The Minister of the Interior is responsible to suspend deportation for a maximum period of six months. S.43a(3), AsylVfG; ss.53–54, AuslG.

[53] S.50(1), AsylVfG.

apply are free to chose to live somewhere else.[54] The alien is thus merely tolerated in Germany. A temporary residence permit is granted to such asylum seekers on the basis of legal provisions and according to a special procedure.[55] Tolerance or *Duldung* is not a right. There is no status attached to this situation which remains at the discretion of the authorities. In fact, the *Duldung* provides only very limited rights, very similar to those granted to asylum seekers. Family reunification is usually denied to tolerated persons,[56] the right to work, although formally granted, is often denied in practice, social benefits are much lower than for refugees entitled to asylum, the permit to stay is limited to one year maximum[57] and this period of time can only be extended by the Land Minister of the Interior in agreement with the Federal Minister of the Interior, under restrictive conditions.[58]

Because s.14(3) of the Asylum Act expressly excludes war or civil war refugees, the great majority of asylum seekers today cannot apply for asylum. They may only be entitled to a residence permit for exceptional purposes (*Aufenthaltsbefugnis*) pursuant to s.32a of the Aliens Act and their status is not determined by the Asylum Act.[59] Aliens coming from the war countries or civil war areas are normally granted *Duldung*. This is the case, in particular of persons coming from the former Yugoslavia. When they are coming as individuals (as opposed to quotas) they are usually issued with a limited permit to stay or at least a limited protection against deportation (*Duldung*). They are not entitled to family reunification[60] and they are denied the right to work because of a shortage of jobs.[61] This is also the case concerning Vietnamese, since a ruling by the BVerwG in November 1993 that they should be granted a temporary protection against deportation (*Duldung*). However, many administrative courts continue to consider them as refugees under s.51(1) of the Aliens Law.[62]

3.2. Switzerland: Temporary Admission

Provisions on temporary admission are generally found in the law on asylum and in the legislation concerning aliens. Article 5 of the Ordinance limiting the number of Aliens (OLE) provides that asylum seekers, rejected asylum

---

[54] Ss.52(2),58(4), AsylVfG.

[55] S.55,56,94, AuslG.

[56] S.26, AsylVfG, on family reunification applies only to persons entitled to asylum or recognized as refugees.

[57] S.56, AuslG.

[58] S.94, AuslG. Right to stay was recently extended for another 12 to 18 months concerning four categories of Croatian refugees (MNS, March 1994, p. 6). All other Croatian are subject to deportation since the signing of an agreement between Bonn and the Croatian government in April 1994 (MNS, May 1994, p. 5).

[59] S.32a, AsylVfG. S.49(1), AsylVfG, release them from the obligation to live in a reception centre.

[60] ECRE Country Report, FRG, 23–25 April 1993, p. 3.

[61] MNS, June 1993, p. 5.

[62] ECRE Country Report, FRG, 23–25 April 1993, p. 3.

applicants to whom an authorization to stay is refused, aliens admitted to stay temporarily and aliens who are kept in detention shall not be considered as residing in Switzerland (*population étrangère résidente*).[63] Article 14a of the Law on residence and settlement of aliens (LSSE) allows the Federal Office for Aliens to decide that temporary admission should be granted in cases where expulsion or deportation is impossible or not desirable.[64] As regards the Asylum Law, Article 9 provides that in cases of serious international tension or of armed conflict in which Switzerland is not involved, or during peace time if a sudden mass of asylum seekers arrives in the country, Switzerland should grant asylum to refugees as long as the circumstances allow it to do so. The *Conseil fédéral* is competent to take any measures required to face such situations and if permanent asylum is not possible, temporary admission should take place instead.[65] Furthermore, Article 16b of the Asylum Law provides that asylum seekers whose requests have been refused may nevertheless be eligible for temporary admission. This shall be the case if *refoulement* happens to be technically impossible,[66] unlawful[67] or unreasonable.[68] Pursuant to Article 18 of the Asylum Law, the Federal Office for Refugees is competent to decide on the residence rights of these refugees in application of the Law on temporary admission and detention.[69] Thus, it follows that certain categories of aliens, although not formally recognized as convention refugees, are temporarily admitted to stay in Switzerland. They are merely protected against *refoulement* and, for this reason, they are considered *de facto* refugees. Their right to remain is withdrawn as soon as the situation changes in their country of origin, following a decision by the Federal Office that there is no longer any danger of persecution.[70] Asylum

---

[63] Ordinance of 6 October 1986 (RS 823.21), as modified in 1990. See also, Article 13f of the same Ordinance which refers to aliens who are allowed to remain on the grounds of extremely serious personal reasons or of general political considerations.

[64] Law of 26 March 1931 (142.20), as modified.

[65] Article 9 of the Asylum Law of 5 October 1979, as modified in 1990.

[66] For instance, *refoulement* or deportation may be impossible to a country where because of civil war all airports are closed in that country or if the asylum seeker is without any identity documents and the authorities of his country of origin refuse to issue such papers or if the asylum seeker is stateless. See *Documentation-Réfugiés*, Supplement to No. 213, 30 March–12 April 1993, p. 5.

[67] Ie, contrary to Article 33 of the 1951 Convention or to Article 3 of the ECHR. One typical example would be an asylum seeker who is recognized as a convention refugee but to whom asylum is refused because he is unworthy. *Ibid.*

[68] This is the case concerning *"réfugiés de la violence"*, ie, asylum seekers who are not directly persecuted as individuals but who are victims of a general situation of violence, usually a civil war, e.g., Tamils from Sri Lanka, refugees from Lebanon, the former Yugoslavia and Somalia. *Ibid.* However, if it appears that the refugee to whom asylum has been refused can be expelled or *refoulé* to another country or his country of origin, or that he has a travel document which allows him to leave regularly Switzerland, such a temporary admission will be refused to the applicant. Serge Bodart, *op. cit.*, p. 70.

[69] Law of 14 August 1968, as modified on 2 October 1900 (RS 142.281), in particular Articles 1 and 2.

[70] LSEE, Article 14a(3).

seekers admitted to remain temporarily are merely tolerated. They do not benefit from the status provided in the 1951 Convention but they are entitled to the same rights as aliens in general.[71] They are usually allowed to stay for a first period of 12 months. The canton of residence is competent to renew this authorization for a further 12 months and as long as protection is needed. They cannot benefit from the principle of family reunification nor be eligible for a travel document unless there are good reasons to think that their sojourn in Switzerland may last a few years. They are subject to expulsion if they commit a crime or an offence in Switzerland.[72]

The Federal Office for Refugees, or the alien's police of each canton, may also grant a humanitarian permit on particular humanitarian grounds, such as medical reasons, the asylum seeker has been residing in Switzerland for at least four years,[73] or the asylum seeker does not have any travel document. This humanitarian permit becomes a permanent residence permit, after 10 years of residence.[74] It authorizes the reunification of the family and allows the holder to get a job,[75] but only if it has been granted by the canton.[76]

Switzerland has always accepted many seasonal workers from Yugoslavia[77] but this is no longer the case.[78] Since the beginning of the conflict thousands of people have fled from the former Yugoslavia to join parents or friends in Switzerland. At first, most of them were allowed to remain as aliens for more than three months without special authorization and only a minority applied for asylum. In December 1991, the *Conseil Fédéral* introduced a general visa requirement for persons coming from the former Yugoslavia and special programmes have been set up to accept a quota of refugees and children.[79] The visa requirement, which was partially waived concerning Bosnians in

---

[71] With regard to work permit, work legislation, social security and public assistance their rights are the same as the one granted to aliens in general. LSEE, Article 14b. See also, Serge Bodart, *op. cit.*, p. 69.

[72] Interview with Mr M. Gonczy and Mrs. E. Grosjean (OSAR), *op. cit.* See also on the 'status' of refugees temporarily admitted and on the status of aliens, H. Schoeni, *op. cit.*, p. 21.

[73] The canton must, however, be willing to grant a residence permit. H. Schoeni, *op. cit.*, p. 17.

[74] At the end of 1992, out of a total of 109,900 asylum seekers present in Switzerland, 26,700 were convention refugees, 14,800 humanitarian grounds refugees, 5,200 were refugees admitted temporarily, 5,200 were allowed to stay on other grounds, 47,700 had their case still pending and 9,700 were refused and deportation proceedings were pendings (Figures from the Office Fédéral des Réfugiés, February 1993).

[75] *Asile en Europe, op. cit.*, p. 502.

[76] Serge Bodart, *op. cit.*, p. 69.

[77] There were about 200,000 of them in Switzerland in 1992 (H. Schoeni, *op. cit.*, p. 24).

[78] On 13 April 1994, the Government decided to refuse anymore seasonal workers from the former Yugoslvia as from 1995. Those already in the country will not be allowed to change their status of seasonal worker into a more favourable one year residence permit (MNS, May 1994, p. 3).

[79] *Ibid*, p. 25.

early 1992, was reintroduced in December 1993[80] but in March 1994, the Government, nevertheless, agreed to extend the residence permits of 14,000 Bosnians allowed to stay on humanitarian grounds.[81] Like in most other countries, except perhaps Sweden, Kosovo Albanians continue to benefit from a protection against expulsion but probably not for very much longer.[82]

3.3. *United Kingdom: Exceptional Leave to Remain*

The British practice of granting an exceptional leave to remain (ELR) started in 1974 after the massive influx of Greek Cypriots arriving in the United Kingdom, fleeing the Turkish invasion.[83] In 1984, the government officially decided to abolish the distinction between *de facto* and *de jure* refugees and, instead, it agreed to grant refugee status to all successful applicants.[84] However, the distinction remained and ELR continued to be granted to those whom the Home Office accepted have strong reasons for not returning to their own countries, but are not deemed to fall within the scope of Article 1A(2) of the 1951 Convention, strictly read. This practice is not codified in the Immigration Rules and is entirely at the discretion of the Home Office.[85] The Secretary of State may decide, for humanitarian reasons, to authorize individuals or groups of individuals to remain exceptionally in Britain. The basis for such decisions is essentially political. The practice shows that ELR has been authorized to permit a specific number of a particular group entry to the UK (e.g. Ugandan Asians), to permit nationals of a particular country to remain on a temporary humanitarian basis because of events in their country of origin (e.g. Poles after 1981, Kurds and Tamils after 1986, Somalis after 1993, displaced persons from the former Yugoslavia since 1991) or, to permit individuals to remain because of their particular circumstances (e.g. nationals of Afghanistan, Iran, Iraq and Lebanon).[86] An essential concern for those people who are not allowed to settle as such in the UK is the question of

---

[80] MNS, January 1994, pp. 8–9. According to the Office Fédéral des Réfugiés, however, Switzerland has already accepted 85,000 victims from the former Yugoslavia since the conflict started. It seems that in proportion to the population in Switzerland, this figure constitutes a record in Europe and it is to the turn of Italy to now accept its share of the burden (MNS, March 1994, p. 8).

[81] MNS, May 1994, p. 12.

[82] Switzerland has already signed a readmission agreement with Hungary but it is now desperatly looking for a transit country (Macedonia having withdrawn) which would finally accept to repatriate those people who do not fear any danger (MNS, March 1994, p. 8).

[83] Serge Bodart, *op. cit.*, p. 64.

[84] House of Commons, Home Affairs Committee, Race Relations and Immigration Sub-Committee, Session 1984–85, minutes of evidence.

[85] "Britain has in the past granted 'asylum' to victims of persecution quite apart from international treaty obligations. However their status is very similar to that conferred by recognition as a refugee, and all successful asylum applicants are now automatically granted full refugee status. Some persons whose applications for asylum are refused are also allowed 'exceptional leave to enter or remain' in Britain for 12 months at a time. Their status is in a sense that of temporary refugees". Simon Field, *op. cit.*, p. 3.

[86] See Serge Bodart, *op. cit.*, p. 66.

how long should their stay be considered temporary and when does it become permanent.[87] Following the Swedish argument, it would seem just to grant permanent residence permit because it is often impossible to know how long war or repression in the country of origin or residence may last. Like in Germany and Switzerland, the United Kingdom agrees to offer temporary protection against *refoulement* in such circumstances but should the situation in the country of origin changes the choice of whether to go or stay is that of the Home Office and not of the individual. Individuals or groups of individuals allowed to stay on humanitarian grounds are, like convention refugees, issued standard letters by the Home Office, in due course. These letters specify their status and outline the social benefits to which they are entitled. Their rights as regards social security, public assistance and work legislation are the same as those enjoyed by convention refugees.[88] They are granted permission to stay for a period of 12 months, and, thereafter, an extension is usually granted for a further period of three years.[89] They are not entitled to the CTD and are expected to have their national passport renewed.[90] Only in exceptional cases may the Home Office provide travel documentation (Home Office Travel Document). Their case is regularly reviewed by the Home Office and after seven years of residence in the United Kingdom, *de facto* refugees may apply for convention refugee status and request permanent asylum,[91] a status which may only be repealed by the Home Office in exceptional circumstances.[92] Only then may permission be granted for their families to come to the UK. The protection offered is extensive and includes the right to work.

During the last decade, ELR has been used increasingly by British authorities. For instance, in 1985 refugee status was granted to 835 people while 2,331 were granted ELR (mainly Tamils).[93] In 1989, about 4,000 Kurds arrived, escaping from torture in Turkey. A year after, only 320 were recognized convention refugees but 1,099 were granted ELR.[94] During the first six months of 1992, only 3% of the total of asylum seekers were recognized convention refugee, 24% were granted ELR and 73% were rejected (mainly

---

[87] On the concept of temporary refuge, see Goodwin-Gill, *The Refugee in International Law, op. cit.*, pp. 114–21 and pp. 207–9.

[88] Serge Bodart, *op. cit.*, p. 65.

[89] The granting of this three year extention was first introduced in 1 July 1980 (512 HL Official Report, 5th series, 1244–5).

[90] This may constitutes a serious problem in cases where a passport needs to be renewed. The problem was recognized concerning Polish refugees after 1981 and the British government waived the obligation of renewal.

[91] HC 725, rule 180B(c).

[92] *Asile en Europe, op. cit.*, p. 454.

[93] Figures reported at the ECRE annual meeting, Geneva, October 1988. "... the increased use of the Exceptional Leave to Remain (ELR) – rather than asylum – since 1983 does reflect a change in the criteria used by the Home Office. We have documented many cases of asylum seekers granted ELR, who clearly qualify for asylum under the 1951 UN convention" (*The Independent*, 31 August 1989, p. 19).

[94] *The Independent*, 22 August 1990, p. 22.

on the grounds of safe third country principle).[95] As the situation in the former Yugoslavia was getting worse, Britain agreed to waive "the third country principle for ex-Yugoslavs who have simply transited other countries or who have family connections in the UK".[96] Since the entry into force of the Asylum and Immigration Appeals Act, only a small number of asylum seekers are recognized convention refugees, the large majority of them are refused any right to remain, while the rest of them is granted ELR.[97] However, with regard to Somalis and refugees from the former Yugoslavia, they are largely granted ELR.[98]

Although these figures reflect largely the arrival of nationals fleeing conflicts in their countries, they also show British authorities' increasing willingness to interpret narrowly the definition of refugees, as provided in the 1951 Convention. A similar attitude exists also in Germany and Switzerland, as already discussed. Asylum seekers who a decade ago might have been granted full refugee status are now being given temporary residence and protection.

4. The Particular Situation of Belgium and France

In both Belgium and France, the concept of *de facto* refugee has no legal meaning. An asylum seeker is either recognized as being a refugee according to the 1951 Convention or he is refused the status of refugee and he, thus, becomes subject to the status of aliens in general. It is, however, well known that many foreign students who do not formally seek asylum are *de facto* refugees.[99] Aliens who are either temporarily or permanently not in a position to obtain a passport from the authorities of their country of origin and who are, therefore, *de facto* stateless persons or refugees can be issued as a matter of exception the Travel and Identity Document provided for by the 1951 Convention.

In Belgium,[100] Articles 9 and 13 of the Law of 15 December 1980, as modified, authorizes the Interior Minister to authorize an alien to remain in Belgium, temporarily or permanently. Such cases are very exceptional. These authorizations are at the entire discretion of the Minister and the length of

---

[95] ECRE Country Report, United Kingdom, 3–4 October 1992, p. 132.

[96] *Ibid*, p. 134.

[97] For instance, between August 1993 and February 1994, out of a total of 6,000 decisions made, 290 granted convention status, 1,040 granted ELR and 4,670 refused asylum and refugee status altogether (Weekly Hansard 1645, 21.02–25.02.1994, 23 February 1994, p. 270).

[98] Concerning asylum seekers from the former Yugoslavia, out of a total of 155 cases decided, 5 were granted convention status, 100 ELR and 55 were refused. As regards Somalis, out of a total of 760 cases decided, 10 were granted convention status, 615 ELR and 135 were refused. These figures apply for the period between August 1993 and February 1994 (Weekly Hansard, 23 February, p. 270).

[99] *Asile en Europe, op. cit.*, pp. 162–3 (Belgium) and pp. 275–6 (France).

[100] See generally, Serge Bodart, *op. cit.*, p. 12 and J.-Y. Carlier, *Droits des Réfugiés, op. cit.*, pp. 99–100.

such stays is usually not more than three months. In very exceptional cases the Interior Minister may authorize an alien to remain for more than three months or permanently.[101] It thus seems that, unlike in France, the possibility of an exceptional stay in Belgium is legally guaranteed. However, like in France, the practice shows very limited use of this possibility. Since the conflict started in the former Yugoslavia, Belgium has had to face an increasing number of people coming from this area. Between April 1991 and April 1993, most applications for residence permits were refused by the Aliens Office.[102] The General Commissioner, nevertheless, agreed to apply a wide and liberal interpretation of the terms of the 1951 Convention when requested to urgently review the Aliens Office's decision by refugees from Albanians origins, couples of mixte ethnic origins and deserters or conscientious objectors of the federal army.[103] Since October 1991, the General Commissioner has held that due to the particular nature of the conflict, refugees from the former Yugoslavia should at least be protected against *refoulement* and in March 1992, it suggested to both the Interior Minister and the Justice Minister the creation of a 'temporary protected status' for humanitarian reasons which should allow to a temporary residence permit.[104] During the summer 1992, the Interior Minister agreed on the principle of a 'displaced status' for persons fleeing from a war zone in the former Yugoslavia. This 'displaced status' is fully described in a Circular by Mr. Tolback (Interior Minister).[105] It shall be granted to 200 former prisoners and their families automatically, as well as to groups of persons who arrive to Belgium under UNHCR programmes[106] and to persons who escape from a war zone and arrive to Belgium as individuals. Their requests are subject to individual examination by the Aliens Office. Whether the person applies or not for asylum and whether the procedure is pending or has ended, he will only be granted a provisional authorization to stay, along with a work permit, valid for six months if he is coming from a high risk zone, if he belongs to an ethnic or religious minority which is persecuted or, if he is a deserter or a conscientious objector.[107] The *Ligue des Droits de l'Homme* acknowledged the Circular but stated that important uncertainties remained concerning the status, in particular, concerning the

---

[101] *Asile en Europe, op. cit.*, p. 162, para.148.

[102] According to the General Commissioner, 82% of the 1,800 asylum seekers from the former Yugoslavia were notified an Annex 26bis, that is a refusal of residence permit (as at July 1992). *Fifth Annual Report* (1992), *op. cit.*, p. 21.

[103] *Ibid*, p. 19.

[104] *Ibid*, p. 20.

[105] Circular on the status of nationals from the former Yugoslavia present within the Belgium territory, of 23 March 1993, as an answer to several questions asked by NGOs, in particular the *'Ligue des Droits de l'Homme'*, on 12 February 1993.

[106] These persons are registered on their arrival in Belgium. The Aliens Office is competent to issue temporary residence permit valid for six months and renewable.

[107] This is the 'displaced status'. All others are asked to leave the territory, unless an application for asylum was made, in which case, the applicant is allowed to stay until a decision on his status of refugee is reached.

connection between the status of displaced persons and an application for refugee status. Furthermore, the *Ligue* argued that such a status should have a legal basis and that it could and should be based on Articles 9 and 13 of the 1980 Law. That would at least give this status some kind of legal value vis-à-vis neighboring countries such as Germany, the Netherlands, Denmark and Switzerland. As it stands, such status seems to depend entirely on the discretion of the Aliens Office.[108] The practice of French authorities shows a similar attitude towards *de facto* refugees, in particular displaced persons from the former Yugoslavia.

Many years ago, an alien, in France, could also be given the status of *bénéficiaire de l'asile* (beneficiary of asylum) or *asilé* (refugee *de facto*). This applied to an alien who would for personal reasons refuse to request refugee status although he fulfilled all conditions required to that effect, or who did not fulfilled at all the criteria of the 1951 Convention. *Asilé* status was granted discretionary by the Minister of the Interior,[109] and it was distinctly less favourable than refugee status. Prior to the accession of France to the 1967 Protocol, the *asilés* constituted a significant category. Today, this is a most exceptional status, if not completely obsolete.[110] The practice remains, however, that, following a negative decision from OFPRA or CRR, an asylum seeker is allowed to contact the *préfecture* and to explain why he thinks that the return to his country of origin would be contrary to Article 33 of the 1951 Convention.[111] The *préfet* or competent *commissaire de la République* must refer the claim to the Minister of the Interior. The latter is competent to take a discretionary decision on the matter. A temporary authorization to stay may be issued if the Minister is convinced that there are serious reasons, which are not strictly provided by the 1951 Convention, ie, a civil war,[112] preventing *refoulement* to the country of

---

[108] The only possibility of appeal against a refusal by the Aliens Office of the status of displaced persons is a review of the decision by the *Conseil d'Etat*, therefore, an expensive and slow procedure and no possibility of having the facts reviewed.

[109] See, for instance, Serge Bodart, *op. cit.*, p. 12.

[110] *Asile en Europe*, *op. cit.*, p. 274.

[111] In particular, since the adoption by the Interior Minister on 25 October 1991 of a Circular on the *refoulement* of foreigners. Based on the *jurisprudence* of the *Conseil d'Etat* and of the European Commission of Human Rights, the 1991 Circular expressly provides that Articles 3 and 8 of the ECHR must be taken into account before considering any measure of *refoulement* or expulsion.

[112] As a rule, OFPRA and CRR have always refused to consider civil war as a ground for refugee status. However, CRR has often admitted that, despite a state of civil war, official authorities could be at the origin of persecutions of their own nationals. Similarly, it has agreed to recognize refugee status to nationals coming from a civil war country in cases where official authorities were incapable of protecting their nationals against persecutions by non-official milices. However, in such cases, refugee status applicants will still have to prove a personal fear of persecution or, if a group, that that group has a well-recognized individual fear of persecution (see, F. Tiberghien, *op. cit.*, pp. 98–101). This is the case, in particular of refugees coming from the former Yugoslavia who have had to apply individually to OFPRA. OFPRA decisions vary according to each individual cases. The process is time consuming but those

origin.[113] Such cases are rare. Persons in such a situation are *de facto* refugees. It is a political decision which is entirely at the discretion of the Interior Minister. There is no status attached to the situation of being a *de facto* refugee. The only right the person has is that of being protected against *refoulement* until the situation improves in his country of origin. One may, however, question the scope of Article 2 of the Law of 25 July 1952 which provides that OFPRA recognizes the status of refugees not only to persons defined in Article 1A(2) of the 1951 Convention but also to persons falling under the UNHCR mandate, pursuant to Articles 6 and 7 of its statute. Article 6 reads as follows: "The competence of the High Commissioner shall extend to ...". A note is attached to the word 'competence'. It adds to the list of refugees as defined in Articles 6 and 7 of the statute, "other categories of persons finding themselves in refugee-like situations, have in course of the years come within the concern of the High Commissioner in accordance with the subsequent General Assembly and ECOSOC Resolutions". One could genuinely expect from OFPRA and CRR to include these persons in the legal scope of their competence, instead of leaving them subject to the political discretion of the Interior Minister. With regard to refugees coming from the former Yugoslavia, the French Government has accepted only a very small quota. As to the rest of them, the great majority has not requested asylum or refugee status because they have been taken care of by family members or friends.[114] The others have had to apply for the status of refugee to OFPRA. During the year of 1992, OFPRA refused to decide on applications made by persons of ethnic minorities, couples of mixte ethnic origins and deserters/conscientious objectors on the ground that the situation in their country was too confusing. When it finally agreed to consider these cases, it did not follow UNHCR recommendations concerning deserters and it recognized refugee status only to deserters from a nationality different from that of the recruiting army. However, it finally agreed to grant refugee status to all Muslim Bosnians persecuted by Serbs milices.[115] One may thus conclude that *de facto* refugees, defined as persons temporarily protected against *refoulement* by the Interior Minister, still constitute an exception in France. Not many refugees from civil war countries are accepted to remain *de facto*. They are either refused refugee status and therefore asylum (ie, Somalis) or they are granted convention status on a case by case basis and their families are allowed to joined them (ie, certain categories of persons from the former Yugoslavia).

In conclusion, the question remains whether the growing use of an exceptional and temporary authorization to stay can be considered a positive step. It

---

recognized are finally granted the full status of convention refugee. Somalis, on the other hand, have all been refused the status of refugee because there was no de facto authorities or a Government in place in Somalia, therefore, there could not be a fear of persecution created, encouraged or tolerated by the authorities of that country (MNS, February 1994, p. 5).

[113] FTDA, *Guide Pratique du Réfugié, op. cit.*, first leaflet, p. 23.

[114] CERE, Rapport Semestriel, Janvier à Juin 1992, p. 4.

[115] *Documentation-Réfugiés*, No. 208, January–February 1993, p. 1.

is generally accepted that although the rights of a *de facto* refugee are precarious, as it appears at least in Britain, Germany and Switzerland, the increasing application of such 'tolerance' indicates, nevertheless, a positive development. It constitutes a derivative solution towards the narrowness of the 1951 Convention definition and its restrictive interpretation by the governments. However, a better solution to the problem would be a wider interpretation on the terms of Article 1A(2) to include displaced persons covered by the UNHCR mandate or at least the existence of a permanent legal status. If it is true that the tolerance *de jure*, which is provided in the law of the Federal Republic of Germany, the United Kingdom and Switzerland, has the advantage of legalizing the situation of its *de facto* refugees, it has the disadvantage to offer only limited rights. Because the Belgian and French systems allow a more liberal and extensive interpretation of the 1951 Convention, a larger number of refugees appear to be protected by the convention status. In both systems, therefore, recourse to tolerance *de facto* seems to be restricted to extreme cases of emergency, such as the dramatic and lasting conflict in the former Yugoslavia. I agree to think that the solution to the problem of *de facto* refugees or humanitarian grounds refugees is to be found in the Scandinavian systems.[116] According to the Regional Representative of the UNHCR in Belgium, this is the solution towards which at least Belgium should tend.[117] It corresponds to a new reality that no one can ignore, a reality which is created because of imperfections in the 1951 Convention recently highlighted by the changes in human situations. Idealists would certainly like to see all such people granted the status of convention refugee. Pragmatists should be satisfied with a status not far from it. It would be useless to blame the 1951 Convention and a mistake to try to change it. One should be wise and keep what is already there and certain. However, an agreement on a harmonized humanitarian status within Europe is not only politically but also economically and socially desirable in order to prevent the disappearance into hiding of refugees who have been allowed to remain only temporarily.

---

[116] Notice that the United States recently adopted such a status: special protected cases. Interview with Mr Von Arnim, Representative of the UNHCR (*op. cit.*).

[117] *Ibid.*

CHAPTER SEVEN

THE GRANTING OF REFUGEE STATUS AND OF DURABLE ASYLUM

All proceedings for asylum end with a final decision on whether or not the asylum seeker shall be granted a permanent residence permit. Asylum seekers recognized as convention refugees are granted durable asylum as well as the status of refugee provided by the 1951 Convention.[1] While the 1951 Convention creates rights for refugees it also establishes obligations. Unlike rights, which are described in detail, obligations are defined in simple words: "every refugee has duties to the country of his refuge". Refugees, therefore, have to conform to the existing laws and regulations as well as to measures taken by the authorities for the maintenance of public order (Art.2 of the 1951 Convention).

The purpose of this chapter is to discuss the full status of asylum seekers who have been recognized as convention refugees within the meaning of the 1951 Convention and, who have, therefore, also been granted permanent asylum. Although the main body of the 1951 Convention contains specific provisions with regard to the status of recognized refugees, the matter is largely left at the discretion of states' governments. However, recommendations and declarations, mainly from the UN and the CoE, exist in an attempt to harmonize and regulate national practices. The General Assembly of the UN, for instance, adopted a Declaration on the Human Rights of Individuals Who are not Nationals of the Country in which they live, on 13 December 1985.[2] "The specific rights listed include the right to life and security of person; the right to protection against arbitrary or unlawful interference with privacy, family, home or correspondence; the right to be equal before the courts; the right to retain one's own language, culture and tradition; freedom from torture or cruel, inhuman or degrading treatment or punishment; and the right to medical care, social services, education, rest and leisure".[3] The Parliamen-

---

[1] I wish to remind that convention refugee status and permament asylum is granted not only to 'spontaneous' refugees as individuals but also to 'quota' refugees as groups taken under a programme. The first category alone is discussed in this book.

[2] UNGA Res.40/146, 13 Dec. 1985.

[3] Arthur C. Helton, "Asylum and Refugee Protection in Thailand", IJRL, 1989, pp. 43–4.

tary Assembly of the CoE, the same year 1985, adopted Recommendation (85)1016 on living and working conditions of refugees and asylum seekers.[4] Former texts of a more general scope on social rights are also to be taken into account as pointed out by the report on living and working conditions of refugees and asylum-seekers.[5] The report mentions the 1950 ECHR, its first and fourth Protocols,[6] the 1961 European Social Charter,[7] the 1972 European Convention on Social Security,[8] the 1966 International Covenant on Civil and Political Rights[9] and the 1976 International Covenant on Economic, Social and Cultural Rights[10] and, finally the Charter of Paris for a new Europe.[11]

1. Particular Situations

Besides situations in which the status of refugee is granted in accordance with the principle of family reunification, there exist other alternatives for being granted asylum, particularly in Belgium and Switzerland.

1.1. *'Second Asylum'*

Provisions as regards 'second asylum' exist in the legislation of Belgium and Switzerland. Article 5 of the Swiss Asylum Law, as modified,[12] states that asylum may be granted to a refugee who has been accepted in another country, if he has resided regularly in Switzerland for at least two years.[13] In Belgium, Article 49–3 of the 1980 Law, as modified,[14] provides the possibility for an alien already recognized as a refugee in another country to stay and live in Belgium. It is for the representative of the Minister of Justice to give the authorization to stay, but it is for the representative of the UNHCR (for requests before 1 February 1988) or the General Commissioner for Refugees and Stateless Persons (for all requests after 1 February 1988) to grant the status of refugee, that is to say to confirm the status granted in another country. For that the refugee must have stayed in Belgium regularly, continuously and without a limited reason, for at least 18 months.[15] Article 55 of the 1980

---

[4] *Doc. 5930* of the CoE, 23 August 1988, Appendix IV.

[5] Draft recommendation presented by the Committee on Migration, Refugees and Demography, Parliamentary Assembly of the CoE, *Doc.5380*, 26 March 1985.

[6] 213 UNTS, p. 223.

[7] ETS No. 38.

[8] ETS No. 78.

[9] UNGA Res.2200A(XXI), 16 Dec.1966. UN DOC.A/6316(1966).

[10] *Ibid.*

[11] Paris, 21 November 1990. Text in, I.Brownlie, *Basic Documents on Human Rights*, 1992, pp. 474–86.

[12] RS 142.31.

[13] Six months abroad constitutes sufficient ground for the refugee to lose the benefit of this provision. Article 1 of Ordinance 1 on Asylum Procedure of 22 May 1991.

[14] By Royal Decree of 13 July 1992.

[15] Article 93 of the Royal Decree of 8 October 1981, as modified.

Law also provides a similar provision, except that in such cases the refugee recognized in another country does not leave voluntarily but is compelled to do so, for instance because of political changes in that country. The representative of the Minister of Justice may only refuse to give the authorization to stay and live in Belgium to such refugees on the ground of public order or national security. The previous requirements with regards to having their status of refugee confirmed by the competent authority also applies.[16]

1.2. *Family Reunification*

1.2.1. *General Human Rights Instruments*

Unity of the family is considered as a human right and, therefore, protected by several multilateral legal instruments. Examples of such provisions are: Art.12 of the Universal Declaration of Human Rights, which proclaims that "no one shall be subjected to arbitrary interference with his ... family" and Art.16(3) of the same document, which states that "the family is the natural and fundamental group unit of society and is entitled to protection by society and the State".[17] The International Covenant on Civil and Political Rights uses the same idea by asserting in its Art.17 that "no one shall be subjected to arbitrary or unlawful interference with his privacy, family,..."; Art.23(1) reiterates the principle governing family rights promulgated in Art.16(3) of the Universal Declaration on Human Rights and (2) adds that "the right of men and women of marriageable age to marry and to found a family shall be recognized".[18] Finally, Art.8(1) of the European Convention for the Protection of Human Rights and Fundamental Freedoms provides that "everyone has the right to respect for his private and family life,...".[19]

"Even if they are taken together, these international and regional provisions do not amount to evidence of a right to family reunification in general international law. They do, however, establish the widespread acceptance of the moral or political proposition that States should facilitate the admission to their territories of members of the families of their own citizens or residents, at least when it would be unreasonable to expect the family to be reunited elsewhere. Thereby, they influence the content of bilateral agreements and domestic law. Indeed, the special position of the family, as a fundamental unit of society entitled to the protection of the State, is the subject of explicit constitutional provisions in at least fifty countries",[20] such as Article 6 of the German Basic Law and Article 22 of the Swiss Constitution.

---

[16] Article 94 of the Royal Decree of 8 October 1981. See, generally, J.Y. Carlier, *Droits des Réfugiés, op. cit.*, pp. 95–9 and, *Asile en Europe, op. cit.*, pp. 160–1.

[17] New York 1948.12.10, A/RES/217 (III), UN Doc. A/810 (1948).

[18] New York 1966.12.16, UNGA RES.2200(XXI), UN Doc.A/6316 (1966).

[19] Rome 04.11.1950, 213 UNTS 223. See also, Arthur C. Helton, "The Proper Role of Discretion in Political Asylum Determinations", *op. cit.*, pp. 1015–6.

[20] Richard Plender, *International Migration Law*, Martinus Nijhoff Publishers, Second revised edition, 1988, pp. 366–7.

1.2.2. *Specific Instruments on Refugees*

A great number of refugees resettled in European countries find themselves separated from other members of their families. This is the case, in particular, of many unaccompanied children coming, for instance, from South-East Asia whose parents are still living in Vietnam, Cambodia or Laos.[21] It also occurs that husbands and wives, brothers and sisters, grandparents and grandchildren are separated because one of them remained in the country of origin with sometimes no means at all from each other for a long time. Family reunion is a basic factor for many refugees to preserve their cultural and religious identity.[22] Where various members of the same family are admitted to different settlement countries, it is generally fairly easy for them to rejoin one another. Nevertheless, they often lack the means to travel far and in their case, financial assistance could with advantage be envisaged. But besides this, they need advice and guidance about their admission to another settlement country, help which they may find in voluntary agencies. The problem arises more seriously when refugees already settled in a country of permanent asylum ask for and wish members of their family still in refugee camps in a country of temporary asylum to rejoin them. It becomes even harder when those family members are still in the country of origin, prevented from leaving by a policy hostile to legal emigration.

"Members of the immediate family of a refugee should, in general, be considered as refugees if the head of the family is a refugee ...", therefore, rights granted to a refugee are extended to members of his family.[23]

The Final Act of the United Nations Conference of Plenipotentiaries on the Status of Refugees and Stateless Persons (which adopted the 1951 Convention) contains the following recommendation:

"The Conference,

---

[21] The particular problems raised by unaccompanied refugee children will not be further elaborated in this study because of a lack of space and time, but references on the subject may be found in, for example, IJRL, 1989, pp. 199–219 and pp. 257–9 (UNHCR Executive Committee, Conclusions XXXVIII on Refugee Children, 1987); E.M. Ressler, N. Boothby and D.J. Steinbock, *Unaccompanied Children: care and protection in Wars, Natural Disasters and Refugee Movements*, Oxford University Press, 1988 and; REFUGEES, 'World Summit for Children", and the adoption of the first UN Convention on the Rights of the Child, No. 78, Sept.90, pp. 35–41.

[22] However, the right of freedom of religion is one of the rights particularly well protected by the 1951 Convention and is excluded from any reservation (Art.42). Under Article 4 of the Convention, a Contracting State is obliged to afford to refugees at least the same freedom of practising their religion and teaching their children as it accords to its own nationals of the same religion. Article 4 reads as follows: "The Contracting States shall accord to refugees within their territories treatment at least as favourable as that accorded to their nationals with respect to freedom to practise their religion and freedom as regards the religious education of their children".

[23] Official commentary of the Ad Hoc Committee on Statelessness and Related Problems, UN Doc.E/1618, p. 40; Goodwin-Gill, *The Refugee in International Law, op. cit.*, p. 150n.

"Considering that the unity of the family, the natural and fundamental group unit of society, is an essential right of the refugee, and that such unity is constantly threatened, and

"Noting with satisfaction that, according to the official commentary of the *Ad Hoc* Committee on Statelessness and Related Problems the rights granted to a refugee are extended to members of his family,

"Recommends Governments to take the necessary measures for the protection of the refugee's family, especially with a view to:

"(1) Ensuring that the unity of the refugee's family is maintained particularly in cases where the head of the family has fulfilled the necessary conditions for admission to a particular country;

"(2) The protection of refugees who are minors, in particular unaccompanied children and girls, with special reference to guardianship and adoption".[24]

This recommendation is the only provision found about the protection of family reunification in the main instruments dealing with refugees and their protection. The 1951 Convention, indeed, does not include the principle of family reunification. Nor does it include special provisions on unaccompanied refugee children.[25] The same definition and status apply to all individuals, regardless of their age.[26] "Whether or not a refugee family can be reunited is therefore determined by national asylum and admission criteria or immigration policies, which may or may not allow inclusion of UNHCR's recommendations and guidelines".[27] The UNHCR and the CoE (through its Commission) have always promoted and carried out protection of the family as a major point of the law of refugees. A great number of their texts and documents refer to this concept and set out for states an obligation to respect the principle of family reunification. A few years ago, the UNHCR made more recommendations for states on the basis of positive actions to be taken to guarantee refugee families' reunification. In 1977, the Executive Committee of the Programme of the UNHCR adopted Conclusions No. 9 (XXVIII) on Family Reunion[28] and affirmed that a coordination action should exist between the UNHCR and governments, intergovernmental and non-governmental organizations, with regard to guarantee the reunion of families of refugees. In 1981, in response to the problem of the boat people, the Executive Committee of the Programme of the UNHCR adopted Conclusion No. 24 (XXXII)

---

[24] The Conference met at Geneva from 2 to 25 July 1951. The Final Act was signed on 28 July 1951; UN Doc. A/Conf. 2/108, UN Publications Sales No. 1951. IV. 4 at p. 8.

[25] The UNHCR *Handbook, op. cit.*, paras.213–9, nevertheless, recommends that account should be taken by the competent authorities of the fact that their mental development and maturity is that of a child.

[26] In cases where minors are accompanied with a parent, their status will be determined according to the principle of family reunification.

[27] REFUGEES, no. 95, 1994, p. 7.

[28] *Conclusions on the International Protection of Refugees* adopted by the Executive Committee of the UNHCR Programme, published by the Office of the UNHCR, Geneva 1990, p. 19.

on Family Reunification.[29] Included in the recommendations of the Committee are provisions encouraging countries of origin to grant exit permits to family members of refugees, and asylum countries to apply liberal criteria in identifying family members to be admitted and to grant family members the same legal status as the head of the family who was designated a refugee. The European Union has also declared the protection of the principle of family reunification within the territory of its member states, though in a rather restrictive manner. Indeed, the Convention Determining the State Responsible for Examining Applications for Asylum Lodged in One of the Member States of the European Community, signed at Dublin on 15 June 1990,[30] provides that "application shall be examined by a single Member State, which shall be determined in accordance with the criteria ... set out in Articles 4 to 8 ... in the order in which they appear" (Article 3(1)). Thus, the first criteria to be taken into account by the 12 member states of the Union is the right of family reunification. Article 4(1) of the Dublin Convention provides that "where the applicant for asylum has a member of his family who has been recognized as having refugee status ... in a Member State and is legally resident there, that State shall be responsible for examining the application". Article 4(2) carries on defining who has to be considered as family members: the spouse of the asylum seeker, their unmarried children under 18 years of age, their father or mother where the asylum seekers are themselves unmarried children under 18 years of age. Finally, Article 9(1) emphasizes that "any Member State, even when it is not responsible under the criteria laid out in this Convention, may, for humanitarian reasons, based in particular on family or cultural grounds, examine an application for asylum ...". These provisions are in conformity with international requirements regarding the protection of refugees and, in particular, with Article 8 of the ECHR on the right to family life. However, it is quite clear that the right for family members to be reunified is only granted to recognized refugees. Asylum seekers, tolerated aliens and *de facto* refugees are still denied such a right, yet considered as a basic human right.

Finally, mention may also briefly be made to existing practices concerning health standards, practices which were unforeseen by the 1951 Convention. Contracting States have all adopted a very restrictive and rigid policy with regard to health standards[31] and have often said that refugees do not satisfy those standards. The argument has serious consequences for any developed country which is willing "to admit the sick, old and unskilled".[32] The application of the principle of family reunification is sometimes thwarted on the basis that one member of the family does not fulfil the standard required. "A recent case illustrates the kind of trading that can occur. A family granted asylum as

---

[29] *Ibid*, p. 55.

[30] *Bulletin CEE* No. 6–90, p. 165. As at June 1993, six member states have so far ratified it: Denmark, Greece, Italy, Luxembourg, Portugal and the United Kingdom.

[31] In the UK, for instance, see the 1990 Statement of Changes in Immigration Rules, paras.17(c) and 80–3 (HC 251).

[32] MRG Report, *The Refugee Dilemma, op. cit.*, p. 9.

recognized refugees was precluded from entering the host country (Australia) when it was found that one member of the family was mentally retarded".[33] Recognized standards and co-ordinated actions on this point could be taken between States to guarantee refugees a safe country were they would settle with all the members of their family and with no restrictions. Belgium and Switzerland, for instance, have already made special arrangements to receive a number of old, sick or handicapped refugees.[34] Special measures for their admission as regards the accommodation and nursing staff they might need have been adopted.[35]

1.2.3. *National Instruments*
Belgium

Articles 10 and 15 of the Law of 15 December 1980, as modified,[36] states that the spouse and minor children (under 18 years of age) of an alien authorized to stay in Belgium are also allowed to stay as long as they live with him.[37] Article 9 of the same Law[38] provides that an alien who does not fulfil the conditions of Article 10 may, nevertheless, be allowed to stay exceptionally by the Representative of the Minister of Justice. To benefit from Article 10 minor children must be at the charge of the refugee and have the same nationality as him.[39] The authorization to stay is valid one year and renewable.[40] Family

---

[33] *Ibid.*

[34] Article 22 of the 1979 Swiss Asylum Law. Article 10bis, para.2 of the Belgian 1980 Law, only refers to children of aliens. However, admission of handicapped refugees is a well settled practice in Belgium. A quota is negotiated and granted each year by the Government. It is generally 25 cases in addition to their family. Most of the refugees benefitting from the quota are South East Asians. Handicapped refugees in general do not raise any particular problem, except cases of serious mental disease because these cases cannot most of the time be cured and they constitute therefore a heavy financial burden for the Belgian Government. These quotas exist beside the framework of family reunification. Interview with Mr. Von Arnim (Representative of the UNHCR) and Mrs. F. Lavry (for the Representative), *op. cit.* In Sweden, the Government has recently asked the Appeals Board and SIV to "show greater consideration to handicapped and very sick children when deciding on asylum applications" (MNS, March 94, p. 12).

[35] From 1947 the Confederation grants asylum to old, sick and handicapped refugees. Special homes are created for them. See *Points de repère. Cinquante ans d'aide aux réfugiés*, OSAR (1986), p. 13.

[36] By the Law of 28 June 1984, relating to some aspects of the condition of aliens and creating the Code of the Nationality. See, in particular, J.Y. Carlier, "Réfugiés Refusés", *op. cit.*, p. 162.

[37] The *Conceil d'Etat* has ruled that while applications for asylum must be decided on an individual basis, such practice cannot undermine the principle of family reunification. Therefore, an asylum seeker and her young daughter may not be expelled on the sole ground that her application was rejected by the UNHCR. She is entitled to stay until a final decision on the application lodged by her husband is made. CE, 24 April 1992, No. 39227, RDE, 1992, n.68, p. 66.

[38] As modified by Royal Decree of 13 July 1992.

[39] This last requirement is also valid for the spouse, who should neither be separated from the other spouse. *Asile en Europe*, *op. cit.*, p. 159, para.133.

[40] Article 13 of the Law of 15 December 1980, as modified by the Law of 6 May 1993 and Article 15 of the same 1980 Law, as modified by the Law of 28 June 1984.

members of a refugee who request to be recognized as refugees receive a model A registration notification whose length of validity is the same as the document of the refugee,[41] this is valid also for members of the family of a refugee recognized under Article 55 of the Law of 15 December 1980, as modified.[42] Since the Law of 6 May 1993, aliens who enter the country to reunite with family members and who have the proper documents will be automatically registered in the *commune* of residence and receive a temporary residence permit while waiting for the decision of the Aliens Office. The Aliens Office must take its decision within a maximum period of 12 months, renewable once for three months. This period should allow the Office to verify that the spouse and children do live together.[43] All provisions relating to refugees are also valid for those assimilated to refugees under Article 57 of the 1980 Law.[44]

Federal Republic of Germany

Permission for family reunification is granted by the *Land*. The spouse and unmarried children under 16 years of age normally have an unconditional right to family reunification with a refugee who has been entitled to asylum. They are normally issued with a residence permit, provided they live with the person recognized as entitled to asylum. However, some *Länder* may impose financial and housing requirements. Asylum seekers and persons with *Duldung* (tolerance) have no right of family reunification, except in very rare cases on humanitarian grounds. The so-called 'family asylum' was introduced in July 1992. Section 26 of the Asylum Procedure Act, as last amended in July 1993, provides that the spouse and children of a person granted asylum shall be recognized as persons entitled to asylum. However, restrictive conditions must be met. Regarding the spouse, the conditions are that they were already married in their home country, that the spouse has applied for asylum before or at the same time as the other spouse and that there is no reason to withdraw asylum.[45] Regarding the children, the conditions are that they were under 16 and unmarried at the time of applying or that they were born in Germany after the person was granted asylum and that the application is made within one year after birth.[46]

France

Recognized refugees by OFPRA receive a certificate of refugee (*certificat de réfugié*) normally valid for an initial period of three years and renewable

---

[41]   Article 88 of the Royal Decree of 8 October 1981, as modified.

[42]   In particular by Royal Decree of 13 July 1992. See also Article 94 of the Royal Decree of 8 October 1981, as modified.

[43]   MNS, June 1993, pp. 2–3.

[44]   As modified by Royal Decree of 13 July 1992. See also Article 95 of the Royal Decree of 8 October 1981, as modified.

[45]   S.26(1), AsylVfG.

[46]   S.26(2), AsylVfG.

for periods of five years. OFPRA also recognized the status of refugee to the members of the family. The refugee, their spouse and children (up to the age of 19) are entitled to an authorization to sojourn and work valid for ten years and renewable.[47] However, since 1990, refugees and their families have to produce a medical certificate along with their application for an authorization to sojourn[48], unless they have been staying in a reception centre and have already been subject to medical screening.[49] It is for the refugee to request the OFPRA to issue a refugee certificate to each of his children and to his spouse. The spouse is normally recognized as a refugee, unless she is the national of a different state in which she fears no persecution. The head of the family will have to show that he possesses sufficient means to provide for the family and that his presence or that of members of the family would not constitute a threat to *ordre public*.[50] The principle of family unity also implies that a woman who has been recognized as a refugee because of her marriage to a refugee, both of the same nationality, loses her quality of refugee if she gets divorced. Moreover, because of her divorce she may again benefit from the protection of the country of her nationality, if the fear of being persecuted (if sent back to the country of origin) concerns only her ex-husband who remains a genuine refugee.[51] But a refugee who has been married to a French national for at least six months is immune from deportation from France, as are children under 18 years.[52] The issue of the refugee certificate normally entails an *admission définitive au séjour*, ie, the grant of durable asylum. Specific procedures for family reunification apply to groups or 'quota' refugees, in particular for refugees from South-East Asia.[53] They are granted temporary asylum as a matter of course. Those who wish to obtain a formal recognition of their status of refugee must apply to OFPRA and most of them do so. In the case of a negative decision a quota refugee retains his residence rights. Notice that the principle of family reunification for immigrants is subject to restrictions since September 1993. Mr. Barreau, Minister of the Interior indeed claimed that the right of family reunification is abused "to bring children not belonging to sponsoring families or additional spouses".[54] Provisions of the new law on entry and residence of foreigners in France (June 1993) approved by the *Conseil Constitutionel* in September 1993, provide that only aliens who have been residing in France for at least two years (instead of one) and who have

---

[47] Law No. 89–548 of 2 August 1989 and Law of 17 July 1984, Article 15(5).

[48] Decree No. 90–583 of 9 July 1990.

[49] Circular 92–19 of 6 July 1992 from the Ministry for Social Affairs.

[50] The French *Conseil d'Etat* held that no deportation order could be made against a polygamous wife, on the ground of *ordre public*, even though her husband was living in France with the other of his two wives and her children. In *Minister of the Interior v. Montcho*, 11 July 1980, *Recueil du Conseil d'Etat*, 1980, p. 315.

[51] F. Tiberghien, *op. cit.*, p. 136, *Giro*, 4 juin 1981, requête 11.335.

[52] Law No. 81–973 of 29 October 1981, Article 5, amending Ordinance 45–2658 of 2 November 1945, Article 23.

[53] FTDA, *Guide pratique du réfugié*, 1992.

[54] MNS, May 1993, p. 2.

sufficient financial means may be allowed to have their spouse and children joining them.[55] These new provisions do not intend, however, to apply to refugees. Like in other countries, asylum seekers are not entitled to family reunification.

Sweden

'Second immigration' in Sweden allows persons married to or living with a refugee to be granted a residence permit. The relationship must be established in order to benefit from a permanent residence permit. The holder of a permanent residence permit does not need a work permit. It is thus common practice for husband/wife, cohabitant (even if homosexual), unmarried children of foreigners and, therefore refugees, to be granted residence permit for permanent settlement.[56] Permits are also issued to elderly parents of refugees. However, the polygamy and marriage between minors are not accepted. Family members allowed to stay on the principle of family reunification become refugees and are normally granted the same rights and duties as refugees recognized according to Article 1A(2) of the 1951 Convention.[57] While the Swedish Red Cross is very much involved in tracing, the UNHCR is responsible for many other aspects of family reunification, in particular cases abroad. For instance, following SIV decision that Somalis (as well as Iraqis or Liberians) should apply for family reunification at a Swedish Embassy or Consulate, the UNHCR got involved because the Swedish Consulate in Mogadishu was closed in 1991–92. So not one direct application to Stockholm could be accepted and family members had to apply to the Swedish Embassy in Nairobi and face a waiting period of about a year before receiving any decision on their application.[58] However, following a recent decision of Government (March 1994) in four cases setting a precedent, Somalis are now granted permanent residence permit on humanitarian grounds and can, thus, be joined by their immediate family members (spouse and children under 18).[59] The same situation applies to Bosnians, following an identical decision of Government in 1993. It is, nevertheless, important to point out that being granted residence permit on humanitarian grounds, these refugees are not entitled to any financial assistance from the Government. They must pay for their families to travel to Sweden.[60] Thus, in reality, the right of family reunification is denied to Somalis refugees. The situation as regards Bosnians appears to be more complex. The Government has agreed, as a matter of

---

[55] New Chapter VI relating to aliens and family reunion, as inserted in Ordinance 1945 by the Law of 24 August 1994.

[56] The Swedish Ministry of Cultural Affairs, *Immigrant and Refugee Policy*, 1992, pp. 25–6. See also, K. Jönsson, *op. cit.*, para.59.

[57] *Asile en Europe, op. cit.*, p. 481, para.59.

[58] ECRE Country Report, Sweden, 3–5 April 1992, p. 120.

[59] MNS, April 1994, p. 12.

[60] Interview with Eva Singer, UNHCR (*op. cit.*). However, "so many complaints have been made that the Government is currently looking into the problem."

exception for Bosnians, that family members could actually apply for family reunion before the Bosnian, who is already in Sweden, is given permission to stay,[61] but it has limited the scope of the principle of family reunification to only very close members.[62] It is still too early to say whether any derogation will apply to Somalis.

Switzerland

The principle of family reunification is provided in Article 7 of the 1979 Asylum Law, as modified, which states that asylum is granted to the spouse and minor children of a refugee. Article 3–3 of the Asylum Law also states that the spouse and minor children of a refugee are recognized as refugees. When family members enter Switzerland during the admission procedure, their case is processed with that of the asylum seeker. For those who remained in the country of origin or of residence, a special request must be made to the Federal Office for Refugees. If the Federal Office authorizes the reunification, instructions are given to the Swiss diplomatic authorities to prepare all travel documents necessary to the members of the family for their entry in Switzerland. In exceptional circumstances, less closed members of the family may be authorized to enter Switzerland, it is in particular the case of handicapped or old people.[63] In cases of family reunification provisions of Article 6 of the Asylum Law relating to admission in a third country do not apply.[64] In the same way as the government may admit old, sick or handicapped refugees, it grants asylum to groups of refugees within the frame of a quota system.[65]

United Kingdom

Applicants recognized as refugees are issued a standard Home Office letter setting out the relevant conditions of stay and entitlement to statutory benefits. Since November 1991, a photograph of the asylum seeker is attached to the letter[66] and fingerprint evidence are also used.[67] The principle of family reunification is strongly adhered to although there is no formal procedure for it. After the head of a family has been granted asylum, visas are issued, on request, for the wife[68] and dependent children (as a matter of principle, under 18 years but special cases may arise[69]) and, under more rigorous conditions,

---

[61] Interview with the Agency for Advisory Service (*op. cit.*).

[62] Despite the derogation to the strict rule that family reunion is only allowed once refugees have received their permission to stay, Swedish authorities have refused applications for family reunification to "uncles, aunts, brothers, sisters and cousins", thus limiting considerably the extent of the principle of family reunification (MNS, March 1994, p. 12).

[63] Article 7–2 of the Asylum Law. Article 3 of Ordinance 1 on Asylum Procedure.

[64] Article 7–1 of the Asylum Law.

[65] Article 22 of the Asylum Law. In 1987–88, for instance, 200 Iranians were granted asylum according to the quota system. See *Asile en Europe*, *op. cit.*, p. 500.

[66] Sue Shutter, *op. cit.*, p. 69.

[67] Clause 3, Asylum and Immigration Appeals Act 1993.

[68] HC 251, para.50.

[69] HC 251, paras.53–55.

the fiancé or fiancée,[70] parents and grandparents, and other relatives.[71] In cases where national documentation is not available, the British authorities will issue declarations of identity to facilitate travel. Persons coming to the UK in the framework of family reunification with a refugee in the UK, obtain the same status of refugee as the family member they have joined.[72]

In all the countries under review, close members of the family of a recognized refugee are allowed to be reunited. While such right is provided in the legislation of Belgium, Germany, France and Switzerland, in Sweden and the United Kingdom, family reunification is a matter of practice. As discussed in the previous chapter, asylum seekers are generally denied such a right. The European Union policy (Article 4 of the Dublin Convention) merely reconciles the national attitudes and objectives on this matter of not only its member states but also of third countries already in the queue to join the Union, in particular Sweden and Switzerland.

2. The Status of Convention Refugees

A person who has been granted asylum and who has been recognized as a refugee will enjoy the full benefits of that status, including the rights and duties, provided for by the 1951 Convention.[73] These provisions offer states a large measure of flexibility which can range from treatment on an equal basis with nationals to the more limited rights accorded to other foreigners. Article 5 of the 1951 Convention also authorizes states to grant other rights (non designated in the Convention) to their refugees.[74] The rights stated in the 1951 Convention are, in fact, considered as a minimum standard.

2.1. *Residence Rights and Their Protection*

A basic freedom is freedom of movement. The 1951 Convention grants to refugees the right to choose their place of residence and to move freely within the territory of the accepting state, subject to such regulations as are applicable to aliens in general, in the same circumstances. The intent of Article 26 is to assimilate refugees to aliens in general. Quota refugees, arriving in the country of residence within a programme, may, nevertheless, be required to settle in a specific area or even in camps for a while. It has been acknowledged that such requirements do not conflict with the freedom of movement in Article 26.[75] Article 26 also expressly requires that the refugee be in the country legally.

---

[70] HC 251, para.47 which refers to the primary purpose rule. See, for instance, Rick Scannell, "Recent developments in immigration law", *Legal Action*, February 1993, p. 20.

[71] HC 251, para.56.

[72] Sue Shutter, *op. cit.*, p. 73.

[73] Chapters I to V of the 1951 Convention.

[74] Article 5: "Nothing in this Convention shall be deemed to impair any rights and benefits granted by a Contracting State to refugees apart from this Convention".

[75] Summary Records of the meetings of the Conference of Plenipotentiaries, SR.11, p. 16.

This provision should nevertheless be interpreted in the light of Article 31 of the 1951 Convention which provides that "no penalties shall be imposed by Contracting States on *bona fide* refugees coming directly from the country of persecution, provided they present themselves without delay to the competent authorities and show good cause for their illegal entry or stay into the country of refuge". Although nothing in the 1951 Convention provides that states are bound to grant political asylum to refugees, in the practice of most countries, persons recognized as convention refugees are, as a matter of principle, entitled to asylum. Therefore, the status of refugee leads to asylum and the provisions on expulsion and *non-refoulement* (Articles 32 and 33 of the 1951 Convention) are oblique references to the question of asylum.[76] As opposed to Articles 31 and 32, Article 33 omits to specify whether or not the refugee has to be *in* the country, *lawfully or unlawfully.* Thus, the mere presence of the refugee at the border shall protect him from being *refoulé* to any country where he may fear persecution. Both Articles 32 and 33, however, provide limits to the principle of *non-refoulement* and non expulsion on the grounds of national security and public order.[77] Furthermore, Article 33 does not prohibit the return (*refoulement*) of refugees to countries where they may fear no persecution.

Also, according to Article 1C of the 1951 Convention, a refugee can lose his status of refugee if he has voluntarily re-availed himself of the protection of the country of his nationality, or has voluntarily reacquired his nationality; or has acquired a new nationality, or he has voluntarily re-established himself in the country which he feared persecution; or the circumstances in connexion with which he has been recognized as a refugee have ceased. Furthermore, Article 1F of the 1951 Convention provides "exclusion clauses" based on the personal conduct of the refugee.[78] According to general principles of law and to UNHCR recommendations such clauses, whether cessation or exclusion

---

[76] Article 32(1): "The Contracting States shall not expel a refugee lawfully in their territory save on grounds of national security or public order".

Article 33(1): "No Contracting State shall expel or return (*refouler*) a refugee in any manner whatsoever to the frontiers of territories where his life or freedom would be threatened on account of his race, religion, nationality, membership of a particular social group or political opinion". This is the so-called prohibition of expulsion or return (*refoulement*) which constitutes the cornerstone of international refugee law. See, for instance, Goodwin-Gill, *The Refugee in International Law, op. cit.*, p. 71 et seq.

[77] Article 33(2): "The benefit of the present provision may not, however, be claimed by a refugee whom there are reasonable grounds for regarding as a danger to the security of the country in which he is, or who, having been convicted by a final judgment of a particular serious crime, constitutes a danger to the community of that country". For Article 32(1), see note above. Notice that the principle of *non-refoulement* is declared without exceptions in the 1969 OAU Convention (Organization of African Unity Convention Governing the Specific Aspects of Refugee Problems in Africa, 1001 UNTS 14691).

[78] The status of refugee must be withhold to persons who have committed "a crime against peace, a war crime or a crime against humanity, ... a serious non-political crime outside the country of refuge prior to his admission ... guilty of acts contrary to the purposes and principles of the United Nations".

ones, must be interpreted restrictively. However, states have sometimes agree on a wide interpretation of such provisions.[79]

Belgium

According to Article 26 of the 1951 Convention, a refugee is free to take up residence and free to move within Belgian territory. However, Article 22 of the 1980 Law, as modified, provides that a refugee may be assigned to one specific place for reasons of public order or national security. In any case, a change of residence must be stated to the administration of the *commune* where the refugee lives and to which he wishes to move.[80] According to Article 56 of the 1980 Law, a refugee may only be returned or expelled from Belgium for reasons of public order or national security. A return order proceeds from the Minister of Justice after an opinion given by the Consultative Commission of Aliens; an expulsion order proceeds from the King. Both measures must be taken according to Articles 20 to 26 of the 1980 Law, and in no case may return or expulsion takes place to a country where the refugee fears persecution. It seems that *refoulement* or expulsion of recognized refugees on the ground of public order or national security has never occurred.

Federal Republic of Germany[81]

Persons entitled to asylum are free to settle and move anywhere in Germany. Section 46 of the Aliens Act[82] provides a list of grounds for expulsion (serious crimes, illegal prostitution and illegal consumption of drugs). Aliens having a right of unlimited residence, recognized refugees and asylum seekers, as well as persons married to a German enjoy special protection from expulsion.[83] Furthermore, section 51 of the Aliens Act[84] prohibits deportation of an alien to a country in which "his life or freedom is threatened by virtue of his race, religion, nationality, membership of a particular social group, or political opinion".[85] Thus, only in cases of serious threat to public order or public

---

[79] This is particularly the case of Sweden as regards exclusion clauses (MNS, April 1994, p. 6). See also the discussion on the safe third country principle and safe country of origin principle, chapter four, *supra.*

[80] Royal Decree of 1 April 1960, M.B. 30 April 1960.

[81] On the 1st of July 1990, the Governments of the FRG and of the GDR signed an agreement on the abolition of the individuals controls at their common German border. According to Article 12 of this agreement, the GDR is undertaking to apply Article 33 of the 1951 Convention in the same way as the FRG. ECRE Country Report, Germany, 22–23 September 1990, p.52.

[82] 9 July 1990 (Federal Law Gazette I, p. 1354).

[83] Section 47(3) of the Aliens Act.

[84] The wording of Article 51 is very similar to the wording of Article 33(1) of the 1951 Convention. On the principle of *non-refoulement* in Germany, see R. Marx, "Study on the Treatment of Asylum Seekers at German Airports", 30 March 1992.

[85] The country still remains divided concerning the deportation of Vietnamese, who for the majority of them where migrants workers in Eastern European countries before arriving to the FRG. Asylum in the Federal Republic is unanimously refused by the courts. However, while some courts have ruled that deportation to Vietnam was contrary to section 51, other courts, in particular the Federal Administrative Court, ruled that Vietnamese should not be protected

security may a recognized refugee be expelled.[86] However, entitlement to asylum may expire[87] or be withdrawn[88] and an alien in such situation will simply become subject to the less favourable regime applicable to aliens in general. The Aliens Law of 1st January 1991 has transferred power of expulsion from the *Länder* to the Federal Government (the Federal Office for Recognition of Foreign Refugees).[89] Application to have the order withdrawn can be made (within one month) to the same authority. If the competent authority decides to maintain the order, an appeal is possible before the administrative tribunal. Such appeals have usually a suspensive effect, except in cases where public order or security is endangered.[90] A further appeal may be introduced before the administrative appeal court and finally to the constitutional court.[91]

France

Refugees are guaranteed not to be returned to the country from which they have fled, but, in certain circumstances (if there is a serious threat for public order),[92] expulsion to a third country and according to carefully defined procedures[93] is possible. In particular, and, in perfect conformity with Article 32(2) of the 1951 Convention,[94] the review of the legality of an order of expulsion on grounds of national security or public order is possible and

---

from deportation because they are allowed to return voluntarily to Vietnam with no fear of persecution under a reintegration Treaty of 9 June 1992. ECRE Country Report, FRG, 23–25 April 1993.

[86] Section 48(1) of the Aliens Act.

[87] In particular, if the alien has voluntarily re-availed himself from the protection of his country of origin or has voluntarily regained his nationality or the nationality of a third state. See s.72, AsylVfG.

[88] In particular, if the conditions on which asylum is based have ceased to exist, or if asylum was granted on the basis of incorrect information or lies. The alien has one month to contest such a decision. See s.73, AsylVfG.

[89] ECRE Country Report, Germany, 3–4 October 1992, p. 89.

[90] In which case the order of expulsion must be executed immediately. Only an appeal, before the administrative tribunal, using the summary procedure (*référé* or *Eilverfahren*) is permissible against such a decision.

[91] See chapter three, *supra*.

[92] Article 23 of the Ordinance of 2 November 1945, as modified. The Minister of the Interior is competent to order expulsion.

[93] Articles 24 to 26 of the 1945 Ordinance. The new law of August 1993 on foreigners, however, has abolished any kind of protection for foreigners with strong ties in France. The Minister of the Interior has now complete discretion in matters of expulsion on urgency grounds and procedural guarantees have become inexistent. See MNS, April 1994, p. 1. Such practice has been strongly criticized by the National Human Rights Committee. *Ibid*, p. 2.

[94] Article 32(2): "The expulsion of such a refugee shall be only in pursuance of a decision reached in accordance with due process of law. Except where compelling reasons of national security otherwise require, the refugee shall be allowed to submit evidence to clear himself, and to appeal to and be represented for the purpose before competent authority or a person or persons specially designated by the competent authority".

competence was given to the Administrative Tribunal.[95] On another hand, consultative competence to examine appeals and to make recommendations was given to the *Commission de Recours des Réfugiés*.[96] The Minister of the Interior, however, is not bound by such opinion. French practice may thus be summarized as follows. Firstly, expulsion or *refoulement* of recognized refugees in France may only occur if the refugee represents a serious and real threat affecting some fundamental interest of the state.[97] However, like in other countries, withdrawal of refugee status is possible, in particular if the refugee voluntarily regained protection from his country of origin or elsewhere, or re-acquired his lost nationality, or obtained his status unlawfully.[98] He will then be submitted to the general regime of aliens, therefore, allowed to stay only if he remained in France for some time.[99] Secondly, an order of expulsion can only be based on the present and individual conduct on the person concerned.[100] This liberal interpretation reached its climax in 1988 with the French *Conseil d'Etat* interpreting the terms of Article 33 of the 1951 Convention to include extradition as well.[101] Therefore, not only expulsion and *refoulement* but also extradition may be prohibited to the country where the refugee would fear persecution.[102] The same attitude was also clearly adopted by the Swiss Federal Court.[103] Finally, Circular Directive from the Minister of the Interior of 25 October 1991 on the removal of foreigners emphasized the fact that Articles 3 and 8 of the ECHR as well as the principle of proportionality must be taken into account when carrying out the removal of foreigners.[104]

Sweden

Convention refugees in Sweden receive a permanent residence permit as well as a certificate of refugee, valid for three years and automatically renewable.[105] Although, in theory, an alien convicted of a crime punishable

---

[95] Article 22bis of the 1945 Ordinance.

[96] Article 5 of the Law of 25 July 1952.

[97] Law No. 81–973 of 29 October 1981.

[98] See F. Tiberghien, *op. cit.*, pp. 114–34.

[99] Since February 1994, Chileans' refugee status has expired because of the recent changes in Chile. Their return will be decided on an individual basis. Similar decisions were taken concerning refugees from Poland, Czechoslovakia and Hungary in 1991 and refugees from Capeverde and Benin in 1992. See MNS, March 1994, p. 6.

[100] *Ministry of the Interior v. Dridi*, C.E., 21 January 1977, Rec.(1977), p. 527, note Laferrière.

[101] *Bereciartua-Echarri*, C.E., 1st April 1988, Rec.(1988), p. 135.

[102] For an overview of the traditional French position on this matter before this decision, see F. Tiberghien, *op. cit.*, pp. 201–3.

[103] Decision from the Federal Court of 18 December 1990 concerning a Hungarian national, granted asylum in Switzerland but requested by Hungary on account of suspicion of having committed a criminal offence which happened before arriving in Switzerland to seek asylum.

[104] ECRE Country Report, France, 3–5 April 1992, p. 81. See also the *Diouri* case, C.E., 11 October 1991 (Moroccan refugee allowed to return to France after order of expulsion overturned).

[105] K. Jönsson, *op. cit.*, para.84.

by more than one year's imprisonment can be deported by court order,[106] in practice, a convention refugee is never expelled (*refoulé*) to his country of origin before his status as a refugee has ceased in accordance with Article 1C of the 1951.[107] A particular gross criminal offence, seriously threatening public order and safety, is necessary for a refugee to be deported.[108] Convention refugee status can also be withdrawn if it was granted on the basis of false information.[109] In ordering deportation, the court takes various elements into account:[110] the status of the person concerned,[111] his family situation[112] and the length of his stay in Sweden.[113]

Switzerland

A refugee may only be expelled if he is or appears to be a danger to national security or public order (ie, he committed a serious crime).[114] In such cases, asylum lapses with the execution of the judicial expulsion. There is no need for a separate revocation of refugee status by the Federal Office for Refugees.[115] Criminals may be extradited to countries with which Switzerland has concluded extradition treaties, except in cases where offences of a political, military or fiscal character are involved.[116] Like in France, the Swiss Federal Court has agreed that Article 33 of the 1951 Convention should be interpreted as prohibiting *refoulement* as well as extradition to a country where the refugee may fear persecution.[117] Finally, grounds for withdrawal of refugee status are those provided in the 1951 Convention.

---

[106] Aliens Act 1989:529, Chap. 4, s.7 and 8. See also the Act on Special Control of Aliens 1991:572.

[107] *Asile en Europe*, *op. cit.*, p. 483, paras.71–2.

[108] Aliens Act, Chap. 4, s.10. K. Jönsson, *op. cit.*, para.95.

[109] Aliens Act, Chap. 2, s.9 and 10. As an example, a Tunisian national, who was born and raised in Lebanon, entered in Sweden in 1987. He was 'advised' by friends to lie about his nationality and hide the fact that he was Tunisian because he would have much better chances to be granted asylum if Lebanese. In 1993–94, he got involved in some kind of troubles and his true identity was discovered. His residence permit and status of refugee was withdrawn and he is now awaiting deportation, despite the fact that both his children were born in Sweden and speak only Swedish. Interview with the Agency for Advisory Service (*op. cit.*).

[110] K. Jönsson, *op. cit.*, para.94.

[111] For instance, an alien who arrived in Sweden before he was 15 years of age and who has lived in Sweden for at least five years may not be deported for a criminal offence.

[112] A refugee married to a Swedish may have less chances to be deported.

[113] The holder of a residence permit for at least one year and who has lived in Sweden for at least three years may only be deported on exceptional grounds. *Asile en Europe*, *op. cit.*, p. 483, para.74.

[114] Article 44 of the 1979 Asylum Law, as modified.

[115] Decision from the Federal Court (*S v. Graubünden*, 20 May 1992) concerning a recognized refugee (Pole) sentenced to three months and five years expulsion from Switzerland for breaches of traffic regulations.

[116] Article 45 (principle of *non-refoulement*) of the 1979 Asylum Law.

[117] *Supra*, in note 103. A new law facilating the deportation of aliens who have no right to be in Switzerland will enter into force in July 1994. See MNS, April 1994, p. 4.

United Kingdom

Section 3(5)(b) of the Immigration Act 1971[118] gives to the Secretary of State for the Home Department power to make a deportation order against an alien when he deems this action conducive to public good.[119] No right of appeal exists against a deportation order made on national security or political grounds,[120] except to contest the country of destination.[121] Other grounds on which a person may be deported from the United Kingdom are conviction,[122] breach of conditions or unauthorized stay[123] and deportation of members of families.[124] Nevertheless, the Immigration Rules provide that a deportation order will not be made against a person if this would imply his return to a country where he is unwilling to go to or is due to a well-founded fear of being persecuted.[125] This is simply the application of Articles 32 and 33 of the 1951 Convention. Since the entry into force of the 1988 Immigration Act on Overstaying and Deportation, immigration officers, of the rank of inspector, are competent to make deportation orders.[126] However, a positive step was taken when the question whether the judiciary has the power to enforce orders addressed to the Government ministers was raised and positively answered.[127]

In all the six countries under review, *refoulement* and expulsion of foreigners (including rejected asylum seekers) commonly occur. Nevertheless, recognized refugees seem to be immuned from such measures, except in extremely rare cases of serious threat to national security or public interest and according to strict procedural guarantees. While the principle of *non-refoulement* appears to be reasonably well respected,[128] the cessation clauses

---

[118] See also sections 5(1)–(4) of the Act.

[119] See, as an example, *The Independent*, "Nine Iranians to be deported" in the interest of national security, 02/02/90, p. 1.

[120] HC 251, para.157. However, a right of appeal exists against a deportation order made on other public good grounds, to the Immigration Appeal Tribunal (para.159).

[121] HC 251, para.160. See also the Asylum and Immigration Appeals Act 1993, s.8(3)(4).

[122] HC 251, para.164. Appeal is only possible against the recommendation of the court, to a higher court (para.157). Since the case *R v. I.A.T., ex p. Muruganandarajah* (European Court of Human Rights, 1986), British practice has been to allow appeal against deportation, even where there has been a court recommendation following a conviction.

[123] HC 251, para.166. Appeal is possible to an Adjudicator and further to the Immigration Appeal Tribunal (paras.158 and 159).

[124] HC 251, para.168 et seq. Appeal is possible directly to the Immigration Appeal Tribunal (paras.158–9).

[125] HC 725, para.173. Also HC 251, para.161 provides that special provisions, particularly Articles 32 and 33 of the 1951 Convention, must be taken into account when dealing with refugees.

[126] This practice was held to be legal by the House of Lords, provided written records of such decision be kept and decisions involving persons in the UK for a long time be referred to the Home Office. *Oladehinde and Alexander*, Imm. A.R., 1991, 111.

[127] *M v. Home Office and Another*, Times Law Report, 2 December 1991, Court of Appeal; *Times Law Report*, 28 July 1993, House of Lords. See also ECRE Country Report, United Kingdom, 3–5 April 1992, pp. 140–1.

[128] Since the conflic started in the former Yugoslavia, many refugees have apply for asylum for reasons of conscientious objection and the suffering of civilians. Although the majority

provided in Article 1C of the 1951 Convention seem to have gained a new ground: the refugee has not lawfully obtained the status of refugee.

2.2. *Identity and Travel Documents*

These rights are provided by Articles 25, 27 and 28 of the 1951 Convention dealing respectively with Administrative Assistance, Identity Papers and Travel Documents[129] as well as Articles 32 and 33 which protect refugees against expulsion and *refoulement.*

Article 25 deals with administrative assistance in general but is not applicable to the issue of identity papers and travel documents since special articles deal with these matters. The documents covered by Article 25 are those relating to the position of the refugee and his family (birth, marriage, adoption, death or divorce) or of the refugee himself (education and professional certificates). These documents are normally issued by the authorities of the state from which the refugee flew from. On account of his flight, he normally cannot obtain these documents from the competent authorities who regard him as a traitor. It is thus the responsibility of the country of permanent asylum to arrange that the documents be delivered by its own authorities or by an international authority (the UNHCR, for instance). Such documents will be considered as substitutes and will be given credence in the absence of contrary evidence.

The identity papers with which Article 27 deals are for internal use, as opposed to the travel documents to be used for journeys abroad. An identity paper is either a certificate of identity (identity cards used, for instance, in France) or a substitute for a passport in countries with a passport system (the United Kingdom, for instance). Such papers are issued by the Contracting States authorities to "any refugee in their territory".

In order to give refugees the possibility of travelling abroad, the Contracting States undertake to issue to refugees lawfully residing in their territory, special travel documents (Article 28 and Schedule). The Convention Travel Document (CTD) should be used in place of a national passport or identity card by the refugee; otherwise there is a serious risk that he or she will lose refugee status. Contracting States are also required to give sympathetic consideration to the issue of travel documents to refugees who are either unlawfully or temporarily in their territory when they are unable to obtain such a document from the country of their lawful residence. Because the country of first asylum and the country of second asylum often have divergent views with regard to the issue of travel documents, the CoE has adopted the European Agreement on the Transfer of Responsibility for Refugees in

---

of them are not recognized as convention refugees in either of the six countries, Bosnians, at least, seem to be protected from being *refoulé*. See ECRE Country Reports, Belgium (October 1992, p. 51), FRG (April 1992, p. 89 and April 1993), France (October 1992, pp. 75–6 and pp. 82–3), Sweden (April 1992, p. 119 and October 1992, p. 120), Switzerland (April 1992, p. 131 and October 1992, p. 127) and United Kingdom (October 1992, p. 134).

[129] See also Schedule to the 1951 Convention, para.1 to 16.

1980. The agreement lays down the conditions in which the responsibility for issuing a travel document is transferred from one country to another when the refugee changes his place of residence.[130] Another relevant instrument in this context is the European Agreement on the Abolition of Visas for Refugees (1959)[131] which facilitates greatly the movement of refugees between CoE Member States. Indeed, the real advantage of a CTD is to enable the holder, for example, resident in a state party to the Agreement on the Abolition of Visas for Refugees, to travel up to three months, without a visa, to any other Contracting State.[132]

Belgium

Applicants who are recognized by the General Commissioner for Refugees as being refugees are issued with a certificate of refugee.[133] Appeal against such a decision is possible to the Minister of Justice. The *commune* can then issue a certificate of registration at the Alien's Registry. The certificate of refugee has the general aspect of an identity card but is not one; light blue, it bears the photograph of its holder. With his certificate of refugee, the refugee must go to the administration of the *commune* where he took up residence which will provide him with a registration certificate to the alien's register. This document allows the refugee an unlimited stay and has to be endorsed each year and renewed after three years. It is only after five years of regular and continuous stay that a refugee is entitled to request a settlement authorization and is provided with a new document: the identity card valid for five years and renewable every five years.[134] A refugee recognized by the General Commissioner must surrender his national passport, instead the refugee is issued with a CTD, valid as a passport, by the passport department in each *province*. Its validity is for two years, and may be used to travel in any country, except the country of origin.[135] The refugee is allowed to come back in Belgium at any time during the validity of his travel document.[136]

---

[130]   Belgium signed it on 16.10.1980 but has not ratified it yet; the FRG signed it in 16.10.1980; France has not signed it yet; Sweden signed and ratified it on 01.12.1980; Switzerland signed it on 16.11.1980 and ratified it on 13.01.1986; the UK signed it on 16.10.1980 and ratified it on 01.10.1986.

[131]   Strasbourg, 20 April 1959: 376 UNTS 85. It has been ratified by all six countries.

[132]   Generally on the Convention Travel Document (Article 28), see Goodwin-Gill, *The Refugee in International Law, op. cit.*, pp. 154–8.

[133]   Article 57/6(4) of the Law of 15 December 1980, as modified. This Article gives competence to the General Commissioner to issue documents directed at Article 25 of the 1951 Convention. See *Fifth Annual Report* (1992), *op. cit.*, pp. 38–43.

[134]   Article 15 of the Law of 15 December 1980, and Article 31 of the Royal Decree of 8 October 1981.

[135]   However, travels to the country of origin are permitted for humanitarian reasons, such as serious illness or the death of a close family member. The refugee can claim the protection of his country of refuge when visiting his country of origin in such circumstances.

[136]   Articles 85–87 of the Royal Decree of 8 October 1981.

Federal Republic of Germany

Individually recognized refugees are granted a residence permit for an unlimited period[137] while quota refugees, mainly from South-East Asia and South America, are granted a residence permit of a limited period, renewable.[138] No particular certificates of refugee are issued but mention of their refugee status is made on CTD.

France

Upon delivering a refugee certificate, OFPRA informs the *Commissaire de la République* (new title of *préfet*) where the refugee resides. Convention refugees are granted the *carte de résident* which is valid for ten years and is renewable upon the renewing of the refugee certificate by OFPRA.[139] As it takes usually a while for this card to be issued, the *Commissaire de la République* will, in the meantime, renew every six months the refugees' *récépissé de carte de séjour* with the mention "has applied for the status of refugee".[140] Refugees and their family members must present a medical certificate in order to receive the *carte de résident*.[141] Upon recognition of refugee status in France, OFPRA withdraws the asylum seeker's national passport.[142] The refugee may then obtain a CTD from his *préfecture*, valid for two years, which enables the refugee to travel to all countries except the one of his nationality or of previous habitual residence.[143] The refugee who holds one of the three kinds of *carte de résident* may return to France throughout the period of validity of the CTD, and in such a case he does not need a French re-entry visa. Normally, the validity of the right to return may not be limited to less than three months.[144]

---

[137] S.68, AsylVfG. This permit provides an increased guarantee against expulsion, which can only be ordered on grounds of serious threat to public order or security (s.27 of the Aliens Act).

[138] S.15 of the Aliens Act.

[139] Article 16 of the Law of 17 July 1984. Although a new bill on entry and residence of foreigners was approved by Parliament on 18 June 1993, it does not modify the status (rights and obligations) granted to refugees with a permit of residence. If the ten year residence permit may become more difficult to obtain for immigrants (they must have entered France legally), it can only be withdrawn from refugees on the ground of Article 1C of the 1951 Convention (ties with country of origin). See MNS, June 1993, p. 3 and July 1993, p. 2. *Guardian Weekly*, 16/05/93, p. 14.

[140] FTDA, *Guide Pratique de Réfugié, op. cit.*, pp. 13–4.

[141] Decree No. 90–583 of 9 July 1990.

[142] Details on the matter are set out in, for instance, Circular of 26 June 1984 relating to the civil status of refugees; J.O. 9 Nov.1984, p. 10210; Rec.(1984), L. pp. 581–2.

[143] However, like in Belgium, travel to the country of origin does not automatically entail loss of refugee status. Indeed, "travel to the country of origin may be authorized in exceptional cases particularly for humanitarian or family reasons; in such cases it takes place under the cover of a 'sauf-conduit' specially delivered for that journey, with a validity normally limited to 3 months, on which a visa to and for of equal validity is affixed". Ministerial instruction of 31 October 1973.

[144] FTDA, *Guide Pratique du Réfugié, op. cit.*, pp. 23–4.

Sweden

Only citizens of Denmark, Finland, Iceland and Norway are entitled to settle in Sweden without a residence permit. Any other aliens wishing to remain in Sweden for more than three months must have a residence permit.[145] As a main rule, the Aliens Act states that all applications for permission to stay shall be made from abroad (at a Swedish embassy or consulate), before arriving in country, except for asylum applications, family reunion cases or when the person is already living in Sweden with a Swedish person or intends to marry.[146] Refugees granted asylum in Sweden are granted a permanent residence permit which allows them to live, work and travel in Sweden without any other permission and for an unlimited period of time. A certificate of refugee status is usually granted to a refugee at the same time as his residence permit.[147] In order to travel abroad, refugees are granted a CTD,[148] equivalent to an alien's passport granted to a non-refugee. It is issued by SIV under the 1951 Convention and it replaces the national passport for travel purposes.[149] It can be issued for one or two years. An alien's passport can also be issued by SIV to an alien who is not entitled to a travel document and who is unable to obtain a national passport.[150] Residence permits,[151] certificates of refugee status[152] and travel documents[153] are to be returned to SIV when the holder ceases to be a refugee. A refugee may also lose his residence permit and certificate of refugee if such documents were issued on the ground of deliberately false and incorrect declaration or circumstances.[154]

Switzerland

The status of convention refugees in Switzerland is provided by the law applicable to aliens in general[155] but only so far as no particular provision exists in the 1979 Asylum Law. Asylum seekers granted asylum in Switzerland and thus recognized as refugees[156] are issued a certificate of refugee. They immediately have to present themselves to the alien's police of the canton in which they have taken up residence[157] and ask for an authorization "B" of residence. This authorization, valid for one year and renewable each year, is used as an identity document. It allows a refugee, the holder of the authorization, to take

---

[145]   Aliens Act, Chap. 1, s.3.

[146]   Chap. 2, s.3.

[147]   Chap. 3, s.6.

[148]   Chap. 3, s.7.

[149]   Aliens Ordinance, Chap. 1, s.10.

[150]   *Ibid*, Chap. 1, s.11.

[151]   Aliens Act, Chap. 2, s.9–13.

[152]   *Ibid*, Chap. 3, s.6.

[153]   Aliens Ordinance, Chap. 1, s.13.

[154]   Aliens Act, Chap. 2, s.9 and 10.

[155]   Federal Law of 26 March 1931 on residence and settlement of aliens and decree of application of 1st March 1949

[156]   Article 25, Asylum Law.

[157]   Article 26 of the Asylum Law and Article 19 of the Asylum Ordinance 1 of 22 May 1991.

up residence in the canton which issued the authorization (and temporarily in another canton for a maximum period of three months assuming he does get a job there). A refugee who resides regularly in Switzerland for at least five years may be given a residence permit "C", assuming there are no grounds for expulsion.[158] In practice, refugees may only be granted such a "C" permit after ten years of residence.[159] The "C" permit, like the "B" authorization, are only valid in the canton which issued it. If the refugee wishes to move to another canton he will have to ask for a new permit. Such transfers are not easy to obtain. Recognized refugees are entitled to a CTD which they have to request from the Federal Office for Refugees through the alien's police of the canton.[160] The CTD is valid for three years, during which time the refugee is free to leave the Swiss territory and to come back.[161] National passports belonging to refugees are kept at the Federal Office for Refugees.[162]

United Kingdom

Applicants who are recognized as refugees by the Home Office are given refugee status. A standard letter is sent to them in order to explain the scope of such status (rights and duties). As a rule, refugees are provided with a residence permit valid for four years. It is only after four years in the country that a person may apply for permanent residence. A person who has been granted asylum with refugee status is entitled to a CTD. Applications for CTD need to be made specifically to the Home Office. It is issued for five years once the person has permanent residence. A CTD will be valid for return to the United Kingdom for the duration of the validity of the CTD.[163]

Convention refugees are automatically granted an unlimited residence permit in all the six countries. Passports are surrendered to the national authorities and a CTD is issued instead.

2.3. Civil and Political Rights

Persons recognized as refugees have the same civil rights as the nationals of the state of refuge (with regard to marriage, divorce, change of name and adoption). As regards political rights, refugees are usually treated less favourably than the nationals. They are normally not entitled to vote nor to be eligible for public office. Access to the civil service or to practice a number of professions of a statutory character (chartered accountants, for instance, in France) may be restricted. These rights may, however, be exercised by refugees who have acquired full nationality and citizenship in the country.

---

[158] Article 28, Asylum Law.

[159] This time limit of ten years applies to aliens in general. Aliens Law of 1931, Article 11(5).

[160] Article 1 of Ordinance on Travel Documents for aliens with no documents of 9 March 1987, as modified on 1st October 1990 (RS 143.5).

[161] *Ibid.* Articles 3 and 4. However, a sojourn in the country of origin (country of persecution) may lead to a revocation of the right of asylum, according to Article 1C of the 1951 Convention.

[162] *Ibid*, Article 6.

[163] *Asile en Europe, op. cit.*, p. 455, para.54. See also, Sue Shutter, *op. cit.*, p. 70, 174.

These rights are those provided for by the 1951 Convention. In particular, the Convention grants refugees the right of free access to courts of law in the territory of all Contracting States (Article 16). Refugees are granted the same treatment as nationals in the country of their habitual residence as regards access to courts, legal assistance and exemption from *cautio judicatum solvi*[164] and this assimilation is carried over also to other countries. The right of free access to courts is one of these rights where a reservation from the Contracting States is excluded (Article 42(1)).

Belgium

Refugees residing in Belgium have the same civil rights as Belgian nationals as long as they continue to live in Belgium. However, they are not entitled to any political rights, in particular a refugee has no right to vote and no right to run office for elections.[165] Quota refugees ('invited' refugees through a governmental programme) must sign a document certifying that they will not participate in any political activity.[166] However, the right of association[167] is not restricted for foreigners.[168]

Federal Republic of Germany

Recognized refugees enjoy the full benefits of the 1951 Convention in respect of their civil and political rights. They may exercise these rights (ie, freedom of expression, freedom of assembly and freedom of association) to the same extent as German citizens.[169] In particular, they can become members of political parties. However, they do not have the right to vote nor to run for office at parliamentary elections at any level (Federal, Land, local).[170] This prohibition was recently partly challenged by the Federal, State and Municipal Commissioners for Aliens Affairs. It was proposed that foreigners should be given permission to vote at local elections.[171] The right to vote at

---

[164]   Security for costs and eventual penalty by foreign plaintiff not possessing real property in the country of refuge.

[165]   *Asile en Europe, op. cit.*, p. 168, paras.178–9.

[166]   J.Y. Carlier, *Droits des réfugiés, op. cit.*, p. 165.

[167]   Article 15 of the 1951 Convention provides a right of association to aliens, including refugees, but in general terms. "As regards non-political and non-profit-making associations and trade unions the Contracting States shall accord to refugees lawfully staying in their territory the most favourable treatment accorded to nationals of a foreign country, in the same circumstances". Article 15 is one of the two articles granting refugees the "most favourable treatment accorded to nationals of a foreign country", the other one being Article 17 regarding employment.

[168]   J.Y. Carlier, *Droit des réfugiés, op. cit.*, p. 166.

[169]   The Federal Minister of the Interior, *Survey..., op. cit.*, pp. 33–4.

[170]   Article 28(1) of the Basic Law and Article 20(2) of the Basic Law as interpreted by the Federal Constitutional Court on 31 October 1990 which stated that "it is exclusively Germans that compose the people and that elect its representation". See, the Federal Minister of the Interior, *Survey ..., op. cit.*, p. 36.

[171]   MNS, April 1993, p. 7.

local elections was finally granted to foreigners by a Resolution of 12 June 1993.[172]

France

Law of 9 October 1981[173] on the position of aliens in France, including refugees, has improved their right of association. However, with respect to political activity, the French Minister of the Interior adopted Circular Directive of 12 July 1974 which interpreted restrictively Article 2 of the 1951 Convention dealing with the "general obligations" of the refugee. Since 1974, on being granted durable asylum a refugee had to sign a statement by which he: "undertakes in accordance with the provisions of Article 2 of the Geneva Convention of 28 July 1951 relating to the Status of Refugees, to act in conformity with laws and regulations as well as measures taken for the maintenance of public order, not to support with words or deeds the use of violence for political purposes and generally, not to jeopardize the public credit nor the security of the State." This aimed at stopping certain political activities by some refugees. Circular Directive from the Prime Minister of 17 May 1985 abolishes such a requirement. As a matter of principle, French citizenship is required in order to vote and to run office for election.

Sweden

Aliens with a residence permit, therefore refugees, have very much the same rights as Swedish citizens.[174] They can actively participate in Swedish political activities, in particular since the new immigration policy has been decided by the Parliament in 1975.[175] The main objective of the reform was to increase immigrants' opportunities to influence Swedish political life. Since then, any alien, who has been resident in Sweden for at least three years, has the right to vote and to run for office in local and regional elections but not in Parliamentary elections.[176]

Switzerland

Swiss practice as regards the right to vote is much more restrictive than Swedish one but has some similarities with French legal requirements. Refugees do not have the right to vote nor to run for office in elections or referenda.[177] Moreover, the letter which certifies to the refugee that he

---

[172] MNS, July 1993, p. 7.

[173] Law No. 81–909.

[174] *Asile en Europe, op. cit.*, p. 484, para.76.

[175] Hans Ring, "Refugees in Sweden. Inclusion and Exclusion in the Welfare State", Paper presented at the ECPR Conference, Leiden, 2–8 April 1993.

[176] The Swedish Institute, "Immigrants in Sweden", Fact Sheets on Sweden, 1992. See also K. Jönsson, *op. cit.*, para.98.

[177] A distinction has, however, to be made between cantons. Indeed, in both the canton of Neuchatel and Jura, foreigners legally residing there for the last ten years are granted political rights (right to vote in local elections since 1949 and right to vote and to be elected in local and cantonal elections since 1980, respectively). Voters in the cantons of Vaud and of Geneva

has been granted asylum normally specifies that the refugee is not allowed to exercise any political activity within Swiss territory.[178] In practice, however, this last rule is almost never applied. With regard to all other rights (ie, marriage, divorce) refugees are treated like Swiss citizens.[179]

United Kingdom

It seems that there are no specific rules to this effect in the United Kingdom. Refugees, like asylum seekers, are guaranteed freedom of speech and of association. However, they have no right to vote nor to run office for election.

To sum up the situation on this point, it seems that refugees are granted the same civil rights as nationals of the country of asylum. They are not, however, granted identical political rights. Both the right to vote and the right to run office for elections are subject to important limitations, if not simply refused to non-citizens.[180]

2.4. *Gainful Employment*

Chapter III of the 1951 Convention on "Gainful Employment" provides for "a treatment as favourable as possible and, in any event, not less favourable than that accorded to aliens generally in the same circumstances" as regards self-employment (Article 18) and the liberal professions (Article 19). As for wage-earning employment, the Convention prescribes that refugees must be generally accorded the "most favourable treatment accorded to nationals of a foreign country in the same circumstances" (Article 17).

Article 17 (wage-earning employment) is possibly the most important in the 1951 Convention since without the right to work all other provisions would lose their practical meaning. The authors of the Convention, aware of the need to secure a solid basis for the employment of refugees, suggested that Contracting States should give sympathetic consideration to granting refugees the same rights as nationals, particularly where refugees entered their country under immigration schemes or labour recruitment programmes (para.3). Getting a job is an essential element of integration. It allows refugees to improve their language skills and to get the security of regular wages but many obstacles remain quite insuperable. Before the early 1970s, most immigrants and refugees could find a job. However, the situation has changed since the oil crises of 1970 and 1974 and the majority of refugees are now unemployed, with no real hope of improvement. Statistically, the most hit by the crisis are quota refugees whose number is much higher than the number of individual refugees.[181] As opposed to immigrants, refugees are accepted to remain in a

---

have rejected such possibility respectively in September 1992 and in June 1993. MNS, April 1993, p. 7 and July 1993, p. 12.

[178] *Asile en Europe, op. cit.*, p. 504, para.48.

[179] H. Schoeni, *op. cit.*, p. 22.

[180] *Asile en Europe, op. cit.*, p. 455, para.58.

[181] This is the case, for instance, of the Chileans and the Vietnamese whose asylum has been granted in the United Kingdom under quota refugees programmes, respectively in the years

country because of strong political and/or humanitarian reasons. They do not choose to move because they want to improve their way of life by looking for better jobs and higher wages. This is mainly the reason why refugees are normally satisfied when offered any kind of job even of poor quality, as unskilled workers, labourers or minor employees in service industries. Today, the problem is that even these kind of jobs are refused to them mainly because the demand on the labour market has massively increased during the last twenty years and because of growing feelings of discrimination and racism.[182] Concertive efforts ought to be made in that direction. States, not only need to inform public opinion on their refugee policies, but also they should agree on systematic measures concerning compulsory second language courses and training. Efforts to help refugees finding work are already being made in most European countries of resettlement but more need to be done. Responsibility for such an important task appears to be shared between governments, voluntary organisations and private individuals. Several countries, actually, offer possibilities of vocational training or retraining in order to give refugees an opportunity to work in an area in which they lack of skills. It is, indeed, very difficult for refugees to find a job which meets their wishes and matches their experience. Vocational training aims also at meeting the present requirements of the labour market which may be different from one country to another. Trained or retrained skills need to be provided and advertised for a larger number of refugees. At today, only a small number of them appear to have taken advantage of this possibility.

Generally speaking, convention refugees do not need a work permit to take up a wage-earning occupation. They usually benefit from the same rights of employment as the nationals of all six countries under review. However, there are some exceptions.

Belgium
Salaried employees are entitled to a "B" work permit, valid for one year but only for the job and for the employer it was required for. This "B" permit becomes an "A" work permit after two or three years.[183] The "A" work permit is valid for an unlimited period of time and for all professions except those for which Belgian nationality is required, such as state service or public service. To take up an independent or liberal profession, a professional permit used to be compulsory for all foreigners. However, since 1991, refugees authorized to stay or settle in the Kingdom are exempt from the obligation to hold a *carte professionelle* for the exercise of an independent professional activity.[184]

1974–75 and 1978–79, and who are now, for 50%, still unemployed. See Simon Field, *op. cit.*, p. 34 and MRG Report, *The Refugee Dilemma, op. cit.*, p. 13 and p. 17.

[182] Simon Field, *op. cit.*, pp. 27–35.

[183] Two years for refugees with a spouse and children, three years for a single refugee.

[184] Royal Decree of 14 February 1991.

Liberal professions of a statutory character (doctors, pharmacists, lawyers, for instance), require recognition of diplomas.[185]

Federal Republic of Germany

Upon possession of an unlimited residence permit and of a CTD, refugees are granted a special work permit, which allow them to look for a job and work with no restrictions, such as those imposed generally on foreigners and asylum seekers.[186] However, special authorizations are necessary for certain liberal or self-employed professions, such as doctor, pharmacist and vet. Other jobs require German citizenship. This is the case, for instance of employment in the police force.[187]

France

Recognized refugees by OFPRA are issued a *carte de résident* valid for ten years and renewable. This card constitutes also a permit to work on French territory. Refugees who want to engage in crafts and trades need a *carte de commerçant étranger* (alien's trade card). However, it is a common practice to assimilate refugees with the nationals of states with which France has concluded reciprocity agreements. They are thus treated as privileged foreigners and they usually obtain this trade card without difficulty. The exercise of a liberal profession is not easy, and very often not possible for foreigners in France. Some liberal professions, such as pharmacist, barrister or chartered accountant, require French nationality, others such as physician require a French diploma or at least the recognition that the foreign diploma is equivalent to the French one as well as a special authorization from the Ministry concerned. Thus, refugees who do not yet possess French citizenship have difficulties finding employment in the field they used to work in the country they have fled from.

Sweden

Refugees are automatically granted a work permit when issued a permanent residence permit. The Swedish policy towards an integration of refugees is

---

[185] See, generally on the subject, J.Y. Carlier, *Droits des réfugiés, op. cit.*, pp. 115–128. Notice that EC measures for the recognition of diplomas and abolition of nationality requirements for most of the professions (theoretically in force since January 1993) only apply to EU nationals. At a wider geographical level, the CoE, nevertheless, adopted the European Convention on the Equivalence of Diplomas leading to Admission to Universities (and its Protocol) and the European Convention on the Academic Recognition of University Qualifications. Published under the auspices of the CoE, last edition 1987.

[186] The obligation to give preference to Germans nationals when recruiting, for example. The Federal Minister of the Interior, *Survey..., op. cit.*, p. 30.

[187] In principle, foreigners are prohibited from working in the police force. However, in case "of urgent need of service", the *Länder* are free to recruit foreigners (MNS, June 1993, p. 11). Such new practice has been strongly encouraged by the Federal Minister of the Interior, as a means to combat racism and thus facilitate contact between the police force and foreigners (MNS, April 1993, p. 12).

mainly guided by two factors: finding a job as soon as possible and earning one's own livelihood, on equal terms with Swedish citizens. To this end, refugees have the opportunity to meet a placement officer as well as SIV Officials in order to have their educational qualifications and work experience clearly defined. The Labour Market Administration is responsible for people obtaining easily and quickly employment, education or training leading to employment.[188] Unemployment among immigrants and refugees is almost twice as high as for the total population.[189] Persons with a poor command of Swedish or a poor education find it difficult to find a job.[190]

Switzerland

A refugee who has been granted asylum in Switzerland, or who has been temporarily admitted as a refugee, is allowed to practice a lucrative activity and to change job or profession without consideration to the situation of the job market.[191] The competent authority in matters of employment is the Office for Employment of the canton. Refugees should ask for a work permit at the same time as they make their request for a residence permit to the alien's police of the canton. Holders of a "C" residence permit, however, do not need a work permit. They are allowed to practice any wage-earning employment or self-employed profession. Holders of a "B' residence permit need a work permit. They have to ask the alien's police of the canton for a special authorization (normally granted automatically) if they want to change job, employer or place of work. However, liberal professions may be subject to particular rules. According to Article 29 of the 1979 Asylum Law, refugees are required to take Federal examinations in order to practice a medical profession. As in other countries, some professions are reserved to Swiss citizens, this is the case in particular in the police and judicial sector and for high rank jobs in the public or state services.

United Kingdom

As a matter of principle, refugees do not need a work permit to work. They have the same rights as British citizens.[192] There are, however, some limitations. A refugee cannot get employment in the civil service.[193] In some

---

[188]   K. Jönsson, *op. cit.*, para.99.

[189]   15% of non-Nordic citizens are unemployed, compared with 7.1% of Swedish citizens (MNS, May 1993, p. 12).

[190]   *Ibid.*

[191]   Article 27 of the 1979 Asylum Law. At the end of 1992, there were about 3,400 Bosnians allowed to stay in Switzerland and to work under certain conditions, just as other refugees from ex-Yugoslavia (MNS, June 1993, p. 5).

[192]   Sue Shutter, *op. cit.*, p. 70.

[193]   See Act of Settlement (1700) s.3, British Nationality Act 1981, Schs.7,9 and The Race Relations Act 1976, s.75(1),(5) which 'binds the Crown, but does not invalidate any rule, whenever made, restricting employment in the service of the Crown to persons of particular birth, citizenship, nationality, descent or residence; nor does it render unlawful the publication, display or implementation of any such rules'; *Halsbury's Laws of England*, Vol. 8, para.970.

sectors of British industry, trade union membership is a condition for employment, and this also applies to refugees. As distinct from the system in France, refugees are free to set themselves up in business, provided they comply with national legislation. They are also free to practice a profession provided their qualifications are recognized by the appropriate professional body. As for unemployed refugees they must register with the local office of the Department of Employment which helps those available for work to find employment.

2.5. *Welfare*

Articles 23 and 24 of the 1951 Convention provide that refugees should be given the same treatment as the nationals of the Contracting States with regard to welfare benefits, labour legislation and social security. This is the case in Belgium, Germany, France, Sweden and the United Kingdom where refugees are entitled to a large extent to the same benefits as their own nationals. In Switzerland, refugees are usually treated as the most privileged aliens.

Belgium

The Belgian system of assistance and social security is complex. Unemployment benefits are granted to refugees who are unable to find a job during a certain period of time.[194] Insurance against illness and disability is compulsory[195] and no difference is made between aliens in general and Belgian nationals. The regime of family benefits and of retirement and survival benefits is also generally the same for Belgian nationals and for aliens. On one hand, social aid is granted by the CPAS (*Centre Public d'Aide Sociale*) to any Belgian national or foreigner present in Belgium, therefore, also to refugees and asylum seekers in need. This person does not need to be registered in the *commune* of the CPAS. Social aid includes subsistence allowance, housing allowance, medical treatment as well as clothes and furnitures. Its amount is decided by the CPAS. It is usually equivalent to the MINIMEX or to the minimum income guaranteed to elderly people[196] but it may be increased to include family allowances. Social aid also covers the subscription fee for insurance against illness and disability. If the CPAS refuse to grant social aid, the claimant has one month (from the day of the refusal) or two months (from

---

Text of these Acts in *The Public General Acts and general synod measures*, respectively 1700, chapter 2; 1981, chapter 61; 1976, chapter 74.

[194] J.Y. Carlier, *Droits des réfugiés, op. cit.*, pp. 133–6.

[195] Law of 9 August 1963, as modified.

[196] Minimum income at the charge of the state to any old person whose resources are inadequate. Law of 1 April 1969. This income may also only be granted to elderly or handicapped persons who have resided at least five years in Belgium without a break. This residence requirement was declared (in several judgments by the Labour Court of Brussels) discriminatory against refugees who by definition could not meet this requirement when the status of refugee was granted to them. The Law of 20 July 1991, amending Law of 1 April 1969, has now replaced this five years residence requirement with a less demanding 'real residence' requirement. See ECRE Country Report, 3–5 April 1992, p. 54.

the day of the claim) to appeal before the *Chambre de recours provincial* (local court of appeal). On another hand, the MINIMEX (minimum of existence means) is a minimum resource guaranteed to all Belgian nationals but only to a certain category of foreigners, among them recognized refugees who have resided for at least five years without a break in Belgium before the claim or who have resided at least ten years in Belgium during their lifetime.[197] The Minimex may only be granted to persons whose resources are inadequate and who cannot get such resources through work or benefits.[198] It is concretely an amount of money granted by the CPAS and which varies according to the situation of the applicant. The applicant must be over 21. The Minimex must be requested to a CPAS of the *commune* in which the applicant took up residence. The decision of the CPAS is given within 30 days. It must be reasoned and must specify the amount and mode of payment.[199] An appeal against the decision of the CPAS is possible within one month (from the day of notification by the CPAS) to the *Tribunal du travail* (labour tribunal).[200] Only 50% of the Minimex granted by the CPAS of the *communes* is paid back by the government (Ministry for Social Emancipation) because as it concerns persons living in a *commune* for at least five years, some kind of integration has already taken place, therefore, the *commune* should also bear the responsibility of such costs.[201] However, this limit of 50% does not apply with concern to asylum seekers and refugees. The state reimburses the local authorities the entire sum paid out to refugees.[202]

Federal Republic of Germany

Financial assistance is granted to refugees on equal terms with Germans citizens. This is the case for pension, health and accident insurance, unemployment benefits and child benefits. Social assistance benefits are usually granted in the form of a monthly allowance. They include subsistence allowance (food, pocket money, personal hygiene, clothes, electricity and transport), assistance during sickness or pregnancy and assistance for nursing.[203] Incomes over a certain level are deducted from the monthly social benefits sum. Child and housing benefits are counted as income. Supplementary benefits can be granted on an individual basis, in particular to pregnant women, disabled children (under 16), single mother with a child under 7 or two children under 16

---

[197] J.Y. Carlier, *Droit des réfugiés, op. cit.*, pp. 147–8.

[198] Law of 7 August 1974, as modified, which creates the right to a Minimex. In, for instance, L.-M. Bataille and J.-M. Berger, *op. cit.*, pp. 187–211.

[199] The Minimex is something very mathematical, the amount provided in the Law for each situation is a minimum amount. Interview with Mr. J. Ramakers, Cabinet of Mrs. Smet, Brussels, December 1990. See also, *Les bénéficiaires du Minimex en Belgique*, Secretary of State for Social Emancipation, Bruusels 1988–89.

[200] Article 10 of the Law of 7 August 1974. As regards social aid, an appeal is also possible but to the *Chambre de recours*, Article 69 of the Law of 8 July 1976.

[201] Interview with Mr. J. Ramakers (*op. cit.*).

[202] MNS, October 1993, p. 4.

[203] The Federal Minister of the Interior, *Survey ..., op. cit.*, pp. 38–42.

and, elderly people (over 60) receiving social benefits. Benefits are paid by the local authorities. When settling in a permanent home, social assistance services often give to refugees furnitures or kitchen, bathroom equipment. Refugees with no private means of support are also entitled to a rent and heating allowance.

France

Refugees with a resident permit are entitled to the same benefits as French citizens with regard to welfare, labour legislation and social security. Refugees housed in reception centres are entitled to the same allowances, except for the housing allowance. Unemployed refugees are entitled to integration allowances or to the minimum integration income.[204] Refugees who have worked in France but have lost their job receive unemployment benefits.[205] Any person is entitled to old age insurance if this person has worked in France and has contributed to the national pension scheme. A refugee who has not contributed towards any pension scheme may nevertheless receive a special old age allowance if he has resided in France for at least 15 years, of which five continuous years. Housing allowances for old age refugees are also provided.[206] Refugees have access to the national health system which partly or totally reimburses medical expenses.[207] Finally, refugees with a residence permit valid for more than three months are entitled to family benefits. The legality of entry and residence of the children must nevertheless be justified.[208] Specific conditions (ie, being pregnant or having a child of less than three years old or having several children etc.) must be fulfilled in order to benefit from family allowances. Other allowances may also be payed for social reasons (ie, to handicapped people, to old age persons, to young workers for accommodation etc.).[209]

Sweden

Legal provisions concerning welfare apply without distinction to Swedish citizens and aliens with a residence permit, therefore refugees.[210] Since 1 January 1991, the integration allowance is given in the form of a loan. When refugees are resettled in a local municipality, they have equal right to financial assistance from the local social services as Swedish citizens.[211] In particular, they can obtain financial assistance if they have no means of support. The payment of allowances is administered by the residential centre or the local social assistance office. Social insurance, in Sweden, covers health insurance,

---

[204] FTDA, *Guide Pratique du Réfugié, op. cit.*, (Aides financières aux personnes sans emploi).
[205] *Ibid.*
[206] *Ibid* (Réfugié à l'age de la retraite).
[207] *Ibid* (Se soigner en France).
[208] Decree No. 87–289 of 27 April 1987.
[209] FTDA, *Guide Pratique du Réfugié, op. cit.*, (Les prestations familiales).
[210] *Asile en Europe, op. cit.*, p. 484, para.80.
[211] K. Jönsson, *op. cit.*, para.101.

pension insurance against injury at work etc. In order to be insured, refugees must register at the Insurance Office where they live. One hundred of Immigrant Service Offices are scattered around Sweden to help refugees contacting the proper authorities. Day nurseries and children's leisure centres exist in most municipalities. Parents must pay for child care. Children from the age of four can, however, be sent to part-time pre-schools which are free of charge. Once a child under 16 years of age is registered in Sweden,[212] the mother (or if any the father) is entitled every month to a general child allowance. The mother (or father) must herself be registered in Sweden or be living in Sweden for at least the last six months.[213] All children are subject to health checks at the child centre of the municipality in which they live. School children are given health checks at school. Health care centres or hospitals are part of the national insurance system.[214]

Switzerland

Refugees have usually the same rights as the most privileged aliens (with regard to some complementary social benefits or language courses) and in some cases as Swiss nationals. Rights for refugees as regards social insurance are provided by specific legal provisions, in particular on old age and survivor insurance[215] or disability insurance[216] which are the only two compulsory public systems of insurance.[217] Wage-earning employees, as in other countries, are normally affiliated to complementary systems of insurance by their employer, which usually cover risks of accident, illness and unemployment. The Confederation has discontinued family benefits for refugees since mid–1990.[218]

United Kingdom

Refugees are treated like British citizens. They are entitled to public funds for immigration purposes. This category of benefits includes income support, family credit, housing benefit[219] as well as accommodation for homeless

---

[212] National registration includes such information as personal address, civil status and citizenship.

[213] K. Jönsson, *op. cit.*, para.102.

[214] Swedish Immigration Board (SIV), "When you move to Sweden", leaflet, October 1991.

[215] Assurance vieillesse et survivants (AVS).

[216] Assurance invalidité (AI).

[217] Article 30 of the 1979 Asylum Law, as modified.

[218] Interview with C. della Croce and B. Clément (Centre Social Protestant), Lausanne, December 1990. See also Article 21b of the 1979 Asylum Law, as modified.

[219] See, for instance, Chris Smith "Benefits", CHAR's guide to income support and housing benefit for single people without a permanent home, the housing campaign for single people, 1989; Ian Loveland, "Policing Welfare: Local Authority Responses to Claimant Fraud in the Housing Benefit scheme" and Nick Wikeley, 'Unemployment Benefit, the State and the Labour Market", in *Journal of Law and Society*, Basil Blackwell, Oxford, Vol. 16, respectively No. 2, p. 187 and No. 3, p. 291.

people,[220] although the 1993 Asylum and Immigration Appeals Act provides that asylum seekers with no accommodation should no longer benefit from rehousing as do other homeless people.[221] However, this provision does not apply to refugees. All other welfare benefits are subject to a residence requirement, in particular, National Health Service treatments are free of charge for persons ordinarily resident in the United Kingdom as well as for persons allowed to stay permanently, therefore refugees.[222]

The provisions of the 1951 Convention are quite liberal. They apply to remuneration and overtime payment, hours of work, holidays, restriction of homework, women's and children's work, training, benefits of collective bargaining as well as to social security benefits such as compensation for injury, sickness, old age, and unemployment. There are nevertheless two reservations: states are not obliged to assure to refugees the maintenance of rights acquired elsewhere, and states are reserved the right to make special arrangements concerning such benefits, payments or allowances. Thus, except for these two limitations, once a refugee is a member of the state's labour force, he enjoys the same status and benefits as if he were a national of that country.

2.6. *Education, Vocational Training, Language Courses*

"For many refugees, learning a new language is a top priority. The ability to communicate is the key to many other aspects of life: getting a job, finding accommodation and making friends. But it can be a long and demanding process, both for refugees themselves and for their teachers".[223] The 1951 Convention contains no specific provisions on language tuition and vocational training. Article 22 (Public Education) makes a distinction between elementary education and other forms of education. It provides the same treatment for refugees as to nationals with regard to elementary education[224] but for education other than elementary it applies "treatment as favourable as possible and, in any event, not less favourable than that accorded to aliens". "Education other than elementary education" refers to secondary and higher education which involves access to school, remission of fees and charges, award of scholarships and recognition of foreign school certificates, diplomas and degrees. It is the matter of each state to determine the limit between what is elementary education and what is secondary and higher education. The heading of Article 22, "Public Education", is of considerable impor-

---

[220] See generally, Sue Shutter, *op. cit.*, pp. 129–35.

[221] Clauses 4 and 5.

[222] Sue Shutter, *op. cit.*, pp. 136–40.

[223] REFUGEES, No. 72, Feb.90, p. 17.

[224] According to Art.26(1) of the Universal Declaration of Human Rights, elementary education should be compulsory and free. Therefore, it is natural that refugees should not be treated differently from nationals with regard to elementary education. See "Education: an elementary right" in REFUGEES, No. 78, Sept.90, p. 5; see also comments on the recent Declaration of 1990 as International Literacy Year, in REFUGEES, No. 76, June 90, Dossier.

tance because it restricts its application rather considerably, excluding private schools.[225]

Belgium

School is compulsory until the age of 18.[226] Primary, secondary and higher education, general or technical, is free of charge for refugees and children of refugees; they are exempted from the *Minerval* (supplementary registration fees) but not necessarily from the registration fees. They must, however, have a valid permit to stay and the notification of the General Commissioner.[227] In the Dutch and German speaking regional communities, grants to study in secondary and higher education are provided to refugees and their children. In the French speaking regional community, such grants are only available when the refugee has been granted the full status of refugee for at least one year. This difference in treatment is based on the fact that the majority of refugees settle in the French speaking regions. Study and training period grants are also available from the Minister for Foreign Affairs as well as from the French community, within the framework of professional training courses. Because of the large number of unemployment, refugees may only have access to reorientation courses after a long waiting period. Free language courses for foreigners, and therefore refugees, are organized by the governmental authorities as well as by various non-governmental organizations, mainly the CIRE and the OCIV. The CIRE (*Centre d'Initiation pour Réfugiés et Exilés*) deals with all problems of integration faced by refugees and aliens; it operates within the French community.[228] It is mainly constituted of seven member organizations which are also members of the CBAR.[229] The CIRE collaborates closely with the CBAR and guarantees the link between the collective of its member agencies and the authorities of the regional communities, *communes* and *provinces*. In addition to facilitating the search for accommodation or a job, the CIRE also helps children towards better integration in the education system. Since 1989, the CIRE is in charge of providing language courses in French as well as teaching refugees to read and write in French. At the end of 1990 there were about 400 refugees benefiting from such courses

---

[225] Report of the Economic and Social Committee of the UN, E/1618, comments to Article 22: this provision should "apply only to education provided by public authorities from public funds and to any education subsidized in whole or in part by public funds or to scholarships derived from them".

[226] *Asile en Europe, op. cit.*, p. 170, para.187.

[227] J.Y. Carlier, *Droits des réfugiés, op. cit.*, pp. 162–3.

[228] *Enquête sur l'infrastructure des cours d'alphabétisation et de francais dans la Communauté française*, C.I.R.E., ASBL, under the high patronage of the Belgian Government and the Delegation of the UNHCR in Belgium, January 1989.

[229] "On a tous besoin de vivre quelque part", Réfugiés 89, *Catalogue Audiovisuel*, C.I.R.E., ASBL, under the patronage of the Belgian Government and the Delegation of the UNHCR in Belgium.

in the area of Brussels.[230] However, difficulties arise as refugees usually arrive during any month of the year. Courses start in September and refugees are normally refused to attempt the courses before the following September because of comprehension problems.[231] The work of the CIRE is behind in comparison with the work of the OCIV whose action started as soon as it was created. The OCIV (*Overlegcentrum voor Integratie van Vluchtelingen*) was created in 1987 as an independent body (which is eligible for governmental subsidies) because of a lack of efficient help on the field from the CBAR and the CIRE, in particular in the Dutch and German regional communities. It is also mainly constituted by the seven member organizations of the CBAR but groups also all the people and small organizations who have worked voluntarily for refugees since the mid eighties.[232] The work of the OCIV is, therefore, essentially to support and to stand for people and organizations dealing with refugees. The Headquarters of the OCIV does not actually see refugees nor does it deal directly with refugees. Its position is purely to co-ordinate actions of people in the field and to submit propositions at the political level.[233]

Federal Republic of Germany

Refugee children have the same access to the education system and allowances as German children. The same requirements apply as regards compulsory school attendance. Classes are in German, almost never in the children's mother tongue. School fees are free of charge as well as supplies and books. Access to general or professional higher education is subject to the condition that the refugee holds a diploma or certificate equivalent to the required German one. Public grants or scholarships are financed by the Otto Benecke's Foundation,[234] which also provides free language tuitions for refugee students. Refugee workers are sometimes offered free German tuitions, for at least ten months, directly from their employers. The objective of the Federation is to facilitate as much as possible the integration of refugees, whether children or adults. Integration programmes have focused on young refugees at the stage between leaving school and looking for employment. It has been agreed that at this stage, the two most important factors for integration was a good command of German and regular, practical vocational training programmes. Intensive language courses are thus offered to refugees coupled with vocational training.[235]

---

[230] Interview with Mrs. V. Semoulin, Permanent Secretary of the CIRE, Brussels, December 1990.

[231] *Ibid.*

[232] Interview with Mr. Delpechin, from the OCIV, Brussels, December 1990.

[233] *Ibid.*

[234] *Asile en Europe, op. cit.*, p. 93, para.70.

[235] The Federal Minister of the Interior, *Survey ..., op. cit.*, pp. 18–22.

France

Any child lawfully residing in France, whatever his nationality or status, must go to school between the age of 6 and 16.[236] This principle applies therefore, to refugee children who can go to a public school free of fees (run by the state or a local authority) and which sometimes provides special accelerated classes to teach French to foreign children. Language courses and special resettlement classes for young refugees are essential since many of them have had to interrupt their education, in some cases for several years. It is, therefore, essential for them to be able to readjust their studies but they encounter great difficulties due to a new environment and a new language. A refugee child whose parents reside lawfully in France may obtain, as any other national child, a scholarship from state funds to facilitate his studies from the first section of secondary school onwards. Refugees have normal access to higher education; they are entitled to specific facilities, for instance, they are exempt from pre-matriculation and are treated on the same footing as French nationals with regard to state scholarships.[237] Refugee over the age of 26, normally, no longer meet the criteria for state scholarships.[238] However, several non-governmental organizations dealing with refugees may offer them special scholarships. Refugees, provided they satisfy the prevailing conditions, may also obtain scholarships for retraining or vocational training from the Ministry of Labour. They may also attend vocational training courses, generally after a protracted waiting period. This is a crucial point since successful assimilation of refugees in their country of resettlement depends mostly on the existence of an occupation suited to all refugees of working age. Vocational training or retraining is the only solution where there are not enough jobs offered in the different sectors of the labour market to meet refugees' demand for work, or where refugees are insufficiently skilled to do the job offered. Special tuition and literacy classes in French are available in provisional accommodation centres (*Centres Provisoires d'Hébergement* or *CPH*) where refugees usually stay up to five months maximum after their arrival in the French territory. These language courses are compulsory, of a minimum of 520 hours[239] and are financed by the Ministry of Social Affairs and Integration. Refugees who are not housed in centres can attend free courses organised by *La CIMADE*[240]. These courses are also financed by the Ministry of Social Affairs and Integration.

---

[236] See Law of 28 March 1882 which made primary education compulsory and Ordinance No. 59–45 of 6 January 1959 (J.O. 7 Jan. 1959) which made education compulsory until the age of 16.

[237] Decree No. 79–1214 of 31 December 1979. See, FTDA, *Guide Pratique du Réfugié*, *op. cit.*, (Etudier en France No. 2).

[238] *Ibid.*

[239] Circular of 5 August 1992.

[240] A protestant NGO involved in development aid.

Sweden

Education is compulsory between the age of 7 and 16.[241] At school, refugee children can receive tuition in their home language and in Swedish.[242] Tuition, school books and school meals are free of charge. Students can go to university after secondary school.[243] In some cases, distinctions or high marks are required in order to be accepted to a course. Refugees are entitled to university grants. Adult refugees are also entitled to free Swedish tuitions. It is essential for refugees to have a good proficiency in Swedish in order to find a job. Such courses exist, in particular, in reception centres and are organised by various educational associations in most cities and town. Municipalities receive a lump sum grant from the state in order to cover the cost of housing, living expenses and Swedish language instruction. Since 1986, every immigrant living in Sweden and who has a work permit or is registered in Sweden, is entitled to an average of 700 hours of instruction, in particular to study Swedish new language and new way of life. If the language classes, organised by the municipalities, take place during working hours, leave of absence from work is granted and compensation is payable for loss of earnings.[244] Vocational training are provided for refugees who do not have sufficient professional qualifications or who cannot find a job in the area they are specialised in. Retraining courses in the fields where there is a lack of manpower are popular among unemployed refugees because they can then receive training allowances.[245]

Switzerland

Primary education in Switzerland is compulsory and free of charge until the age of 15.[246] Secondary education is also free and may lead to higher education in a university. Cantons are competent in public education matters and regulations are numerous and various. Refugees' children are admitted to school classes of the canton in which they reside with their parents, at any time of the year. They are usually put in a school class according to their age but may be moved if it appears that the level does not correspond to their ability.[247] Language tuitions may take place for children who need them. However, for adults recognized as refugees and granted a residence permit, because assistance is provided by one of the charity organizations for

---

[241] K. Jönsson, *op. cit.*, para.111.

[242] The Swedish Institute, *Fact Sheets on Sweden*, 1993. In order to cut some expenses, in particular regarding language tuitions, municipalities have the option to refuse to teach refugee children in their native language if groups of at least five pupils cannot be recruited. The Swedish Ministry of Cultural Affairs, *Immigrant and refugee policy*, 1992, p. 34.

[243] K. Jönsson, *op. cit.*, para.112.

[244] The Swedish Institute, *Fact Sheets on Sweden*, 1992.

[245] *Asile en Europe*, *op. cit.*, p. 485, para.86. Special training programmes exist to make better use of the competence of highly educated immigrants. See The Swedish Ministry of Cultural Affairs, *Immigrant and refugee policy*, 1992, p. 33.

[246] *Asile en Europe*, *op. cit.*, p. 506, para.56.

[247] *Ibid.*

refugees present in the cantons, it is for these organizations to decide whether a refugee does or does not need language courses. If he does, the courses are provided by the charity organization and the costs are reimbursed by the Confederation.[248] Vocational training or professional improvement training are available to refugees over 15. Grants are provided by the canton.[249] Higher education at university or polytechnic is open to refugee students. However, education and language requirements are rather restrictive. Refugee students must have a good knowledge of either French or German. If they do not have a diploma from a Swiss secondary school or its equivalent, they must take a special exam or special evening classes for four years. Requirements to be eligible for a university grant vary from one canton to another, in particular, the student normally has to study in the canton of his residence to be eligible.

United Kingdom

Primary and secondary education between the age of 5 and 16 is compulsory for all children in the United Kingdom,[250] therefore refugee children. Education in Britain is controlled in each area by the Local Education Authority (LEA). The LEA is responsible for the placement of children in free local schools. Children of refugees whose income is below a certain amount, qualify for free school-meals,[251] free school-uniform[252] if necessary and sometimes even free travel passes.[253] Primary school refugee children are assimilated into normal classes and in some schools only part-time language courses are held. However, young children learn fast and the problem of language is usually real only at secondary level as language training cannot easily be included in the tight curricula and schedule of secondary schools. Special agencies such as the Save the Children Fund and the Ockenden Venture, however, do provide special language tuition units for those with potential for higher education. Higher education is offered by universities and is open to all suitably qualified candidates. The equivalence to British qualifications is mainly determined by universities and individual colleges themselves. Refugees are entitled to the same award benefits as students ordinarily resident in the UK in further or higher education.[254] Previous study does not disqualify refugees from eligibility for awards as it may do for students ordinarily resident in the UK. Refugees are charged tuition fees for all levels of courses at the home

---

[248] Interview with Mr. M. Gonczy and Mrs. E. Grosjean (OSAR), *op. cit.* See also Article 31 of the 1979 Asylum Law.

[249] Article 33–1 of the 1979 Asylum Law.

[250] Education Act 1944 s.35; Raising of the School Leaving Age Order 1972, SI 1972/444.

[251] Education Act 1980 s.22(1)(a) and s.22(3), substituted by the Social Security Act 1986 s.77(1)(3).

[252] Current regulations are the Education (Provision of Clothing) Regulations 1980, SI 1980/545, reg.3(1), combined with the Education (Miscellaneous Provisions) Act 1948 s.5(6) and (2) amended by the Education Reform Act 1988 s.100(4)(b).

[253] Education Act 1944 s.55(1) and Public Passenger Vehicles Act 1981 s.46(3).

[254] Education Reform Act 1988 PtII ChIII (ss.139–155).

student rate.[255] It is in the reception centres that basic English language tuition is given to refugee adults, but after that period, no further English language courses are available. Different possibilities exist nevertheless through the language training for immigrants' dependents or through evening and vacation courses organized by LEA, home tutoring by volunteers, other vacation courses and vacation schools, university courses, private schools teaching English (which are members of the Association of Recognized Language Schools) and finally, refugee agencies (Save the Children Fund, for instance). Notice also that in many countries, such as Italy, Portugal, Greece, Turkey, Thailand and Austria, basic language courses are already organized for people before they immigrate. It aims to facilitate their resettlement in the new country. General knowledge and information about their future country of resettlement are also provided.

2.7. Housing

Article 21 of the 1951 Convention (Housing) provides that: "As regards housing, the Contracting States, in so far as the matter is regulated by laws or regulations or is subject to the control of public authorities, shall accord to refugees lawfully staying in their territory treatment as favourable as possible and, in any event, not less favourable than that accorded to aliens generally in the same circumstances". Rent control and assignment of apartments is an obligation incumbent not only on the state but also on all other public authorities (ie, *communes*, municipalities). During the first weeks or months of the procedure, most countries in Europe place refugees in provisional and transit accommodation centres. Rare are the refugees directed, after a few days only, to their final destination (flats prepared for them beforehand). States are experiencing great difficulty in providing independent housing, especially low-cost housing. Generally speaking, it is easier to find adequate accommodation (for large families of refugees, in particular) in the rural areas. Nevertheless, only a small number of families accept this solution, since chances of finding employment on the spot are smaller. The distance separating them from other refugee groups of the same ethnic group may also make resettlement in the rural areas inadvisable. Accommodation in the six countries under review is not easily available and has not been so for many years.

Belgium
Belgium remains one of the rare countries where modest accommodation can be found for reasonable prices.[256] Thus, once a refugee has found a job, there should be no real difficulty for him to find decent accommodation. There are also a great number of refugees who arrive within family reunification and, therefore, have accommodation to share, or who are recognized as refugees

---

[255] Education (Fees and Awards) Act 1983 s.1. See also, Sue Shutter, *op. cit.*, pp. 70,74.
[256] *Asile en Europe, op. cit.*, p. 170, para.192.

but go and live with their friends or distant relatives. Refugees who cannot benefit from such support normally arrive at the *Petit Chateau* (or the 127 Centre at Zaventem airport) and from there are distributed into the *communes* according to the distribution programme. In the *communes* it is usually the authorities who provide them an accommodation, or the NGOs members of the CBAR, CIRE or OCIV.

Federal Republic of Germany

Because of a very limited supply of permanent homes, recognized refugees usually remain for some time in collective centres after obtaining a residence permit. While the accommodation of asylum seekers is the responsibility of the *Länder* (Federal States), refugees have to find a permanent home themselves. The German housing market has recently been put under extreme pressure following the reunification and the arrival of a large number of ethnic Germans from Eastern Europe.[257] The accommodation problem is worse in cities and towns than in the countryside and many refugees are temporarily accommodated in hotels and pre-fabricated houses.

France

To rent a council flat in France refugees should, like other residents, approach the relevant municipality or *préfecture*. Refugees may also choose the individual solution which consists in joining relatives or friends already living in the country. A Fund for local settlement of refugees (FILOR, *Fonds pour l'installation locale des réfugiés*) has been established jointly by UNHCR, the French government and refugee-assisting agencies. It helps refugees to settle with respect to furniture and equipment but the means available are limited and refugees are advised to enquire at their sponsoring agencies.[258] Refugees coming from South-East Asia are received by the Red Cross on their arrival at French airports and placed in a transit centre of *France Terre d'Asile* (NGO). *France Terre d'Asile* provides various provisional accommodation centres (*Centres Provisoires d'Hégergement* or *CPH*). If the refugees are entitled to take advantage of this collective solution, their administrative papers and health papers will be issued during their stay at the centre, and literacy and pre-training courses will be provided (e.g. by *La Cimade*, another NGO). The length of their stay in centres is normally three months (renewable only once for two months) and at the end they are on average offered work and accommodation. In urban areas housing chosen by refugees are overcrowded and ghettos have appeared in city centres, where the cost of housing is usually high. The French government, aware of this problem, has been trying to find solutions. In 1977 and 1979 two rural settlements schemes of Hmongs refugees (coming from South-East Asia) were established in French Guyana. The experiment has been a real success, Guyana having a very low population

---

[257] The number of *Aussiedler* (returnees from German descent) is, however, continuing to drop since 1991. MNS, March 1993, p. 2.

[258] FTDA, *Guide Pratique du Réfugié, op. cit.*, (Le logement en France).

density and a climate quite similar to that of South-East Asia.[259] A similar rural resettlement of Hmongs was established in the South-West of France at Port Leucate, in 1979, but was only a partial success.[260]

Sweden

Sweden is divided into 284 municipalities of different sizes (villages, towns, big cities). Nearly all of them receive refugees.[261] Municipalities are quite autonomous. Agreements are being concluded between each municipality and SIV for refugee settlement. Under these agreements, municipalities accept to receive a certain number of refugees. Once a refugee has moved into a municipality, this local authority is responsible for his entire integration (ie, provision of a fully equipped home, language tuition, education, employment services, social services etc.) on the same terms as any other local resident.[262] The costs are met from central government funds. Housing has become more and more difficult to find and increasingly expensive in big cities areas and university cities. It has also become more difficult for single refugees to find accommodation.[263] The number of small flats is limited and single refugees must be ready to share an accommodation.[264] Refugees, therefore, enjoy the same housing standard as Swede but they usually live in more crowded conditions.

Switzerland

As in most European countries, housing raises particular problems in Swiss cities as rents are particularly high and a rental deposit is required. Organizations assisting refugees usually help a refugee who has found accommodation to pay the deposit or other guarantees. These organizations also play an important role in helping refugees to find a place on their own if it appears that they do not have any friends or relatives to go to and live with. In particular, some refugees may remain in an accommodation centre for a period up to six years in big cities such as Geneva, or two years in smaller towns such as Lausanne, because there is no rented accommodation available.[265] Sometimes their employer finds them accommodation or they stay at a hotel, one family in one small room.[266] Small accommodation centres or small converted hotels are open every year to allow refugees to find permanent housing, usually far from the big city centres, in the mountains.[267]

---

[259] MRG Report, *Refugees in Europe, op. cit.*, p. 24.

[260] *Ibid.*

[261] The Immigration Board (SIV), "Facts about Immigration", leaflet, April 1992.

[262] K. Jönsson, *op. cit.*, para.116.

[263] It takes an average of two years and a half waiting for a refugee family to get a permanent home in Stockholm. A single refugee may have to wait up to five years.

[264] The Swedish Ministry of Cultural Affairs, *Immigrant and refugee policy*, 1992, p. 34.

[265] Interview with Mr. M. Gonczy and Mrs. E. Grosjean, OSAR (*op. cit.*).

[266] *Ibid.*

[267] *Ibid.*

United Kingdom

Housing for refugees comes from local authorities, from housing associations or from the private sector. Difficulties with housing have become an important obstacle to settlement and during the past few years this phenomenon can even be described as a crisis, particularly for single people,[268] and black people.[269] Private rented accommodation is scarce and rents are considerably higher than for council accommodation and, therefore, the refugees have little access to this sector until they have had the time to become economically established. "Housing associations are important providers of accommodation for single people of working age and some of the larger associations specialize in providing accommodation for people who have no local connection with area where they wish to reside".[270] Local authority housing is the source of the greater number of houses pledged. It "is normally allocated to those registered on an authority's waiting list. Practically all authorities give preference to local people".[271] However, although the proportion of publicly-owned housing is relatively high, it is more and more difficult to obtain council or housing accommodation in a vacant house of a defined size and location.[272] Unfurnished rented accommodation at a reasonable price is scarce, especially in cities such as London or Birmingham. Financial resources are needed as well as a co-ordinated action between central government and local authorities, voluntary agencies (e.g. Ockenden Venture, Refugee Action, the British Refugee Council) and refugee community groups. Normally, it is said, the central government (Home Office) takes no special measures to make housing available for individuals or "spontaneous" refugees. There is, nevertheless, a situation in which government programmes exist. Where quota refugees have been admitted under a governmental programme, responsibilities and actions for reception are usually more clearly defined. In the case of the Vietnamese,[273] a government programme was set up to share the financial burden by dispersing "clusters" of Vietnamese refugee families all over the

---

[268] Sarah Monk and Mark Kleinman, *Housing*, in "Beyond Thatcherism", p. 121 et seq., edited by Phillip Brown & Richard Sparks, Open University Press.

[269] ECRE Country Report, United Kingdom, 3–5 April 1992, p. 143. Black people are usually housed in less good quality accommodation by local authorities.

[270] MRG Report, *The Refugee Dilemma, op. cit.*, p. 12.

[271] *Ibid.*

[272] New rules require that local housing authorities officials to examine the residence status of all foreigners applying for council (low-cost) housing. This follows a ruling by the Court of Appeal on 7 April 1993, which allowed London Borough to refuse housing to illegal homeless immigrants. See MNS, June 1993, p. 4. Although these new rules may badly affect asylum seekers, they do not concern recognized refugees who by definition are in possession of a residence permit.

[273] In 1975, after the departure of American troops from Vietnam, only 32 Vietnamese refugees entered the UK. The next year, about three times more were given the right to remain and during the last three months of 1978, 450 refugees rescued from boats entered Britain. In January 1979, the British government agreed to admit a quota of 1500 refugees from Hong Kong, Malaysia and Thailand and the same number of refugees were admitted as rescued boat people. In July 1979, during an international Conference at Geneva, the UK agreed to an

UK.[274] In practice, this dispersal policy has failed and the majority of them now live in concentrated communities in specific areas surrounding the major British cities, especially London.[275] Therefore, a solution to this problem could be for central government to provide enough funds directly to local authorities dealing with the greatest number of refugees.[276] Another type of quota refugees were the Ugandan Asians.[277] Less problems arose with their resettlement and housing because a large majority of them found friends or relatives in the UK to support them. However, and to conclude on this point, the resettlement and housing of refugees in Britain is mainly provided by voluntary agencies[278] and the Government does not yet seem ready to financially help these voluntary agencies and local authorities.

2.8. Naturalization

"The Contracting States shall as far as possible facilitate the assimilation and naturalization of refugees. They shall in particular make every effort to expedite naturalization proceedings and to reduce as far as possible the charges and costs of such proceedings". This is the only provision on this subject to be found in the 1951 Convention (Article 34) and it is a rather vague one. The first part of Article 34 could be described as a kind of recommendation to the Contracting States to facilitate "as far as possible the assimilation [in the sense of integration into the economic, social and cultural life of the country] and naturalization of refugees" residing in their countries. No time limit is imposed on this general moral obligation. The second part of the article is a more specific obligation to expedite proceedings whenever an application for naturalization can be or has been made and to reduce the cost involved. Nationality is generally regarded to be similar to citizenship. The question whether or not a person is a citizen of a certain state is, as a rule, to be answered according to the law of that state. Normally, the circumstance that a person emigrates to a state other than that of which he is a citizen does not give him the right to become a citizen of the host country, and the person would, therefore, need to be naturalized. Each state is free to decide who are its nationals; however, this sovereignty may be limited by rules of interna-

---

additional quota of 10,000 Hong Kong refugees. For further developments see, Peter R. Jones, *op. cit.*, p. 3.

[274] "...in the South American refugee programme in 1973–79 government financial assistance was given to the refugee agencies to run a centre and later, as numbers fell, to pay bed and breakfast accomodation, while in the Vietnamese refugee programme large and small centres were established around the country". MRG Report, *The Refugee Dilemma, op. cit.*, p. 13. See also, Peter R. Jones, *op. cit.*, pp. 4–5; and Simon Field, *op. cit.*, p. 40.

[275] Simon Field, *op. cit.*, p. 39.

[276] About 80% of housing was provided by local authorities, the remainder was by associations. See MRG Report, *The Refugee Dilemma, op. cit.*, p. 13.

[277] Simon Field, *op. cit.*, pp. 9,39.

[278] *Ibid*, pp. 9–19.

tional law.[279] On 14 November 1984, the Committee of Ministers of the CoE adopted Recommendation (84)21 on the acquisition by refugees of the nationality of the host country.[280] Considering that acquisition of the host country's nationality constitutes the most effective means of integrating refugees and their children in that country, the governments of Member States are recommended to consider the applicant's refugee status as a favourable element in the procedure for granting of nationality. They should also make use of any possibilities afforded by their legislation so as to facilitate the acquisition by refugees of the host country's nationality (ie, reducing the normally required period of residence). As far as children of refugees are concerned, steps should be taken to ensure that, upon coming of age, acquisition of the host country's nationality be facilitated, regardless of whether they were born in the host country without acquiring its nationality at birth, or whether they were born elsewhere if they have been habitually resident in that country for a considerable length of time. If a refugee parent acquires the nationality of the host country, his minor dependent children present in that country should be able to acquire that nationality at the same time. Furthermore, states which have not yet done so are invited to consider ratification of the New York Convention of 30 August 1961,[281] which aims at reducing the number of cases of statelessness.

Belgium

Legal provisions on Belgian nationality are stated in the Law of 28 June 1984.[282] It creates a new Code of Nationality. This new Code was itself revised by a new nationality Law, which entered into force on 23 September 1993.[283] Belgian nationality may be attributed or gained. Attributed for reasons of the nationality of the father or the mother (Article 8), adoption (Article 9), birth in Belgium (Articles 10 and 11), the collective effect of an act to gain nationality (Article 12) or statelessenes (Articles 8 and 10). In addition it may be gained

---

[279] *Nottebohm Case* (Liechtenstein v. Guatemala), (1955), I.C.J., Rep. 47. "It is for Liechtenstein, as it is for every sovereign State, to settle by its own legislation the rules relating to the acquisition of its nationality, and to confer that nationality by naturalization granted by its own organs in accordance with that legislation." ... "The character thus recognized on the international level as pertaining to nationality is in no way inconsistent with the fact that internationl law leaves it to each State to lay down the rules governing the grant of its own nationality. The reason for this is that the diversity of demographic conditions has thus far made it impossible for any general agreement to be reached on the rules relating to nationality, although the latter by its very nature affects international relations. It has been considered that the best way of making such rules accord with the varying demographic conditions in different countries is to leave the fixing of such rules to the competence of each State" (at pp. 20–3). See also, P. Weis, *Nationality and Statelessness in International Law*, Sijthoff & Noordhoff, Second Edition (1979), pp. 176–81.

[280] No explanatory memorandum has been prepared on this recommendation.

[281] UN Doc. A/CONF. 9/15. The New York Convention on the Reduction of Statelessness entered into force on Dec.13, 1975.

[282] M.B. 12 July 1984.

[283] MNS, October 1993, p. 1.

by option (Articles 13–15), by marriage but under very restrictive conditions (Article 16), because of the possession of Belgian status (Article 17) or by naturalization (Articles 18 to 21). As regards naturalization, the distinction between ordinary naturalization and full naturalization has been abolished. So has the concept of 'Belgian by birth'. Naturalization may be gained by a refugee over 18 who has legally resided in Belgium for at least three years.[284] The new nationality Law of 1993 has also increased the length of the period of time during which a couple have to live together before an application for Belgian citizenship can be made by way of Article 16 (marriage with a Belgium national).[285]

Federal Republic of Germany

Under an old Law of 1913, German citizenship at birth is based exclusively on descent (*jus sanguini*). Thus, the children of an alien born in Germany are not automatically German (no *jus soli*).[286] Generally, aliens may only acquire German citizenship by naturalization after ten years of residence in Germany.[287] Refugees, however, may acquire German citizenship by naturalization after seven years of residence in Germany, provided they are sufficiently integrated.[288] They do not have to renounce their previous citizenship like ordinary foreigners do.[289] As a means to try to combat racism, recent propositions have been made in order to amend the nationality code, in particular to cut the cost for naturalization and to relax the strict rule that citizenship may only be acquired "through birth and blood".[290] It has been suggested that foreigners should be allowed to apply for naturalization after only eight years of residence in Germany and refugees after five years.[291]

France

The Ordinance of 19 October 1945 used to deal with nationality but the system has been thoroughly revised by the Law of 9 January 1973[292] and

---

[284] Notice that this provision is quite liberal as Sweden requires four years of residence, France and the United Kingdom five years, Switzerland six and Germany seven.

[285] MNS, August 1993, p. 8.

[286] As part of a campaign to reform the strict German nationality law, Chancellor Kohl has recently agreed to allow children born in Germany of foreigner parents dual nationality for five years. The condition of five years period has been critised as being too short by the Commission for Aliens Affairs. MNS, June 1993, p. 8; July 1993, p. 7.

[287] An alien married to a German may nevertheless become German by naturalization after only five years of residence in Germany. Relaxed conditions for naturalization for certain catagories of aliens are now provided by the Aliens Act of 9 July 1990, Articles 85–87.

[288] *Asile en Europe, op. cit.*, p. 95, para.77.

[289] *Ibid*, para.78.

[290] MNS, March 1993, p. 8; April 1993, p. 7.

[291] MNS, July 1993, p. 7. The reform of nationality law may not be completed before the end of 1994. It aims solely at easing the integration of resident foreigners in Germany.

[292] Law No. 73–42 of 9 January 1973 (JO, 10.01.1973).

more recently by the Law of 22 July 1993.[293] French nationality may be acquired by any of the five following means: filiation, marriage, declaration, naturalization,[294] and birth and residence in France. Acquisition of French nationality at birth remains principally *jus sanguinis*, as opposed to *jus soli*. Therefore, a person born in France may acquire French nationality if he has at least one parent born in France.[295] Also a child born in France of foreign parents born abroad, but residing in France for at least five years, is French by birth. The restrictive tendency, existing since 1990, has now been confirmed in the new Law of July 1993, which aims at restricting the grounds for obtaining French nationality at birth.[296] These new provisions do not, however, directly affect refugees. They are more specifically directed towards immigrants. Acquisition of French nationality by naturalization requires that the alien, and therefore also a refugee, has resided five years in France before the day he actually applies. This period may be reduced to two years in some cases,[297] or the requirement may be waived altogether.[298] The procedure of naturalization is an administrative one which involves the Minister of the Interior, the Minister of Labour and the Minister of Justice, and lasts about one year. A French national by naturalization has the same rights and duties as any other French national. He may vote at all the elections and be eligible for any office which requires French citizenship. However, any refugee or other alien born in France may acquire French nationality *de jure* or by making the declaration provided by law. In this case, the procedure is of a judicial nature. Finally, like in other matters, refugees should always seek the advice of their sponsoring agencies on questions of naturalization.

Sweden

Like in France, citizenship is based on the principle of descent or of *jus sanguinis*.[299] This means that a child is given the nationality of the mother or of the father if married to the child's mother. Foreigners may become Swedish citizens if they are 18 years of age, have resided legally five years in Sweden and have not been found guilty of committing a serious crime.[300] Stateless persons or refugees can obtain Swedish citizenship after four years of legal residence in Sweden.[301] Children under the age of 18 may become

---

[293] Law No. 93–933 of 22 July 1993 (JO, 23.07.1993).

[294] See FTDA, *Guide Pratique de Réfugié, op. cit.*, (Demander la Nationalité Française).

[295] Law No. 73–42, Art.23, as amended by Law No. 93–933.

[296] MNS, May 1993, p. 8 and June 1993, p. 8. *Le Monde*, 11/06/93, p. 9.

[297] For aliens who have completed at least two years of higher studies with a view to obtaining a degree or diploma from a French university and for aliens who have rendered important services to France, or could do so. Law No. 73–42 Article 63.

[298] Law No. 93–933, Arts.64, 64–1 and 64–2.

[299] The 1984 Swedish Citizenship Act (SFS 1984:682), as amended in 1991 (SFS 1991:1574) and 1992 (SFS 1992:392).

[300] The Immigration Board (SIV), *Swedish Citizenship*, pamphlet, August 1992. p. 2.

[301] *Ibid*, p. 4.

Swedish citizens as dependents of their foreign father or mother.[302] Naturalized Swedish citizens are not allowed to retain their former citizenship. Application forms may be obtained from the local police department and there is no fee to pay for refugees or stateless persons. Applications are then sent to SIV, which is the authority that takes the decision. A certificate of Swedish citizenship is sent to the applicant in cases where the application is accepted. In other cases, an appeal may be lodged with the Aliens Appeals Board.[303] In cases where citizenship is refused, aliens living in Sweden have, nevertheless, the same rights as Swedish citizens as regards social benefits, education etc. The only restriction concerns the right to vote in parliamentary elections which is reserved to Swedish citizens.[304]

Switzerland

Requirements and conditions to be eligible for Swiss citizenship may be obtained from the Swiss central office assisting refugees (*Office central Suisse d'Aide aux Réfugiés*, OSAR) or its member organizations assisting refugees or the authorities in each canton. Swiss procedure for naturalization takes place within the canton. Naturalization may only be requested after at least twelve years of permanent residence in Switzerland, some cantons require even a longer period.[305] Years spent in Switzerland between the age of 10 and 20 and years of marriage with a Swiss national count for double.[306] Naturalization can only be granted by the canton with the agreement of the Federation and the municipality.[307] In June 1993, the Swiss Parliament adopted a new bill which reduces the requirement for naturalization of twelve years residence to six years, leaving the canton still free to require longer delays. The bill also proposes to reduce the residence requirement for the "faster track" naturalization from five to three years, in specific cases. The amount of the fee to be paid may also drop significantly. Any constitutional amendment, which can only happen through referendum, still needs to be examined by Parliament.[308]

United Kingdom

A 700 years tradition of *jus soli* as the only ground for British nationality (the 1948 British Nationality Act only recognized *jus sanguinis* for those born of British parents abroad) ended with the entry into force of the 1981

---

[302] *Ibid*, p. 3.

[303] *Ibid*, pp. 6–7.

[304] The Swedish Institute, "Fact Sheets on Sweden", 1993.

[305] Interview with Mr. M. Gonczy and Mrs. E Grosjean, OSAR (*op. cit.*).

[306] The new nationality code, which entered into force on 1st January 1992, enables the foreign spouse of a Swiss citizen to obtain Swiss nationality through an easier procedure (only five years residence is required). MNS, April 1993, p. 7. This has resulted in the so-called faster track naturalization.

[307] *Asile en Europe, op. cit.*, p. 508, para.67.

[308] MNS, June 1993, p. 9.

British Nationality Act on 1 January 1983.[309] It indeed creates three separate categories of citizenship:(1)British citizenship, is automatically acquired by all those citizens of the UK and the Colonies who had the right of abode in the UK on January 1, 1983. People in the two following categories, do not have an automatic right of abode in the UK any longer.(2)British Dependent Territories citizenship, for instance, from Hong Kong, Bermuda, Virgin Islands, British Antarctic Territories have got a British passport but it does not entitled them settle in the UK.(3)British Overseas citizenship, particularly Asian and Chinese, is a category destined to disappear because the position of British subject can only be passed on to descendants with the authorization of the British Government. It makes amendments to the right of abode under the Immigration Act 1971 accordingly. The term "British subject" is no longer synonymous with "Commonwealth citizen" and, therefore, no longer denotes common nationality status.[310] Foreigners can become British citizens in two ways: naturalization[311] and registration.[312] Naturalization is granted at the discretion of the Secretary of State,[313] who may delegate his functions under the British Nationality Act 1981.[314] Refugees or other aliens[315] who are not Commonwealth citizens nor married to a British citizens can apply for naturalization after five years of continuous residence in Britain.[316] They must also show that they have a 'sufficient knowledge' of English, that they are of 'good character' and that they intend to continue to live in the UK if their application is granted.[317] There is no right of appeal against refusal and the Home Office is specifically relieved of any requirement to give reasons for such refusal.[318] A few refugee adults may also obtain British citizenship by registration on grounds of residence (as opposed to birth) after five years of residence provided they have not had any restrictions or conditions on their stay imposed upon them during at least the past twelve months.[319] However, this procedure is more commonly used for children born in the United Kingdom, but not born British and children born overseas of British parents by

---

[309] In the *Public General Acts and general synod measures*, 1981, Chapter 61.

[310] See generally on British nationality, Sue Shutter, *op. cit.*, pp. 212–31.

[311] Usually applies to adults (over 18 years of age).

[312] Usually applies to children (under 18 years of age).

[313] Section 6 of the British Nationality Act 1981, which entered into force on 1 January 1983. From 1st January 1983, the provisions relating to nationality are repealed by the British Nationality Act 1981, and new provisions are made. The British Nationality Act 1981 makes fresh provision about British nationality. Sections 49, 53 came into force on the 30th October 1981 and the remainder came into force on 1st January 1983; SI 1982/1983.

[314] Sections 43, 44, 45; British Nationality (General) Regulations 1982, reg 14.

[315] For stateless persons, see *Halsbury's Laws of England*, Cumulative Supplement (1990), Vol. 4, para.947F.

[316] Sue Shutter, *op. cit.*, p. 233.

[317] *Ibid*, pp. 233–4.

[318] *Ibid*, p. 235. MRG Report, *The Refugee Dilemma*, *op. cit.*, p. 11. See also generally on the subject, R. Plender, *op. cit.*, pp. 25–9.

[319] Sue Shutter, *op. cit.*, p. 236.

descent.[320] All other children, therefore, children of refugees, may only register at the discretion of the Home Secretary.[321] Although there are no legal requirement as regards residence, the Home Office usually only considers registration of children already living in the United Kingdom for at least five years.[322]

To sum up, at the time of writing, nationality may be gained in Belgium after three years of residence, in Germany after seven, in France and the United Kingdom after five years, in Sweden after four years and in Switzerland after six years. Although a certain willingness towards uniformity seems to exist, national requirements are still far from an harmonized practice.

2.9. *Assistance towards economic and social integration*

Assistance towards economic and social integration is normally provided by specialized agencies or institutions.

Belgium
In Belgium, such assistance is provided by the CBAR, the CIRE and the OCIV. The CIRE and the OCIV, in particular, have undertaken large and varied programmes to make public opinion sensitive to the problems of asylum seekers and refugees. Exhibitions have been held in cultural centres, practical guides have been printed to help asylum seekers on their arrival, to let them know about their rights and obligations in Belgium as asylum seekers and refugees. Audio-visual projects (films) have also been created to make the population sensitive about the countries of origin of the asylum seekers and refugees and to make asylum seekers and refugees sensitive about Belgium as their new country.[323]

Federal Republic of Germany
Integration is promoted by the Federation, the *Länder*, the local authorities as well as by many independent and social groups. Voluntary agencies (ie, German Red Cross and Caritas) have created more than 600 social counselling centres to help foreigners who are beneficiaries of integration aids.

France
Several public and private agencies, such as *France Terre d'Asile*, the *Cimade*, the French Red Cross, the *Secours Catholique*, the Emigrant's Social Aid Service, have been created specifically to deal with the resettlement of refugees, or to assist refugees besides their other tasks.

---

[320] *Ibid*, p. 237.
[321] British Nationality Act 1981, s3(1).
[322] Sue Shutter, *op. cit.*, p. 238.
[323] Information from Mrs. V. Semoulin (CIRE), Mrs. L Biacsko (CSP) and Mr. Delpechin (OCIV), *op. cit.*

Sweden

Several central administrations are responsible for the reception and integration of refugees in Sweden. The most important ones are SIV and the Advisory Council on Immigration Policy with representatives of various immigrants groups. Both are attached to the Ministry of Culture and they deal with permits and citizenship, with general information to and about immigrants, with organising refugee resettlement in agreement with municipalities. The National Agency for Education is in general charge of immigrant education, the National Labour Market Board is responsible for labour market affairs etc. At the municipal level there are about a hundred Immigrant Service Offices. They provide any kind of help and advice in the main immigrant languages.[324] Non-governmental organisations, such as the Swedish Refugee Council or the Swedish Red Cross, also play an essential role in providing help and support.[325]

Switzerland

It is the competence of the *Office central Suisse d'Aide aux Réfugiés* (OSAR)[326] which coordinates the work of the seven other charity organizations (recognized by the Confederation)[327] under OSAR supervision. The OSAR is the official representative of the Confederation. Therefore, in practice, Federal authorities enquire at the OSAR instead of speaking to each of the organizations. The OSAR is a private institution greatly subsidized by the Confederation[328] but also by donations.[329] The organizations assisting refugees and the cantons remain always under the supervision of the Confederation.[330] All the costs spent by the organisations or cantons in assisting, instructing and integrating refugees are reimbursed by the Confederation.[331] Because Switzerland is a Confederation, particular observations may be made. Provisions regarding assistance from the Confederation

---

[324] An advice bureau for asylum seekers and refugees opened in Stockholm at the beginning of 1991, thanks to the initiative of some NGOs. ECRE Country Report, Sweden, 5–6 October 1991, p. 93.

[325] See B.Sjöquist, "The Role of Non-Governmental Organisations in Asylum Work", in *Asyl I Norden, op. cit.*, pp. 22–4. ECRE Country Report, Sweden, 7–9 March 1991, p. 81. For addresses of NGOs, see *Asile en Europe, op. cit.*, pp. 487–8.

[326] The central secretary is in Zurich.

[327] Such as Caritas, Croix-Rouge, Entraide Protestante which are recognized by the Confederation. When recognizing an organization, the Confederation takes a positive decision, in particular it considers the duties and aids given to recognized refugees as stated in the Asylum Law of assistance for refugee, the organization also has to make public its statutes. Interview with Mr M. Gonczy and Mrs. E. Grosjean (OSAR), *op. cit.* See also Article 32 of the 1979 Asylum Law, as modified and Articles 7 and 46 of Asylum Ordinance 2 of 22 May 1991.

[328] Article 34 of the Asylum Law and Asylum Ordinance 2 of 22 May 1991.

[329] About 90% of the expenses of the seven organizations assisting refugees are covered by the Confederation which controls the use of the funds in each individual case. *Asile en Europe, op. cit.*, p. 508, para.69.

[330] Article 35 of the Asylum Law and Article 46 of Asylum Ordinance 2 of 22 May 1991.

[331] See Asylum Ordinance 2 of 22 May 1991.

are set out in the 1979 Asylum Law, as modified, and in the 1987 Asylum Ordinance, as modified. Article 31 of the Asylum Law provides that the Confederation is competent to assist refugees until they receive their residence permit, except in cases of old or handicapped refugees. This assistance duty may be entrusted to charity organizations or to the canton in some circumstances, which will be paid back all costs by the Confederation.[332] According to Article 40a of the Asylum Law, the cantons are competent to provide assistance to refugees with a residence permit, assistance is granted according to the law of each canton. The refugee may choose a charity organization within his canton of residence which will be competent to provide him assistance,[333] according to principles stated in the regulations drew up by the Federal Office.[334]

United Kingdom

Social and economic assistance for integration is delegated by the government to local authorities[335] and voluntary agencies, such as the British Council,[336] the Save the Children Fund and the Ockenden Venture.

The activity of specialized agencies and authorities extend to all the aspects described earlier on, that is to say, legal protection, reception and assistance upon arrival, accommodation and housing, education, employment, naturalization and finally all kinds of economic and social services. It can be said that, generally, a refugee may count on an effective assistance to enable him to solve the problems he is confronted with, although real difficulties exist with regard to employment and housing. Refugees are thus strongly advised to contact one of these agencies and to keep contact with it at least during their first period of resettlement. As a final remark, it is not uncommon that, on arrival in the resettlement country, some refugees may suffer from malnutrition, psychological or physical traumatism and, may need special treatment and care. Mental tension is usually considerable[337] for refugees and it has been acknowledged that the best treatment for depression or other mental disorders needs to come from a specialist personnel, who speak the refugees' language, but rare are the countries providing such personnel in sufficient

---

[332] Cf. also Article 21 and 22 of the Asylum Ordinance of 25 November 1987.

[333] Article 36, Asylum Law. When the organization refuses to allocate assistance benefit to a refugee, the decision has to be written and must be conveyed to the refugee with the grounds for refusal. The refugee may lodged an appeal against the decision within 30 days (Article 28 of the Asylum Ordinance of 25 November 1987). Exclusion grounds with regard to assistance benefit claims are listed in Article 38, Asylum Law. As for provisions concerning the repaid of the benefits to the Confederation, they are set out in Article 40, Asylum Law.

[334] Article 37, Asylum Law.

[335] Some statistics show that local authorities are very slow in providing help and assistance (for health, employment, housing, education etc.) to refugees in need, in particular unaccompanied refugee children. ECRE Country Report, United Kingdom, 3–5 April 1992, p. 143.

[336] See for instance, MRG Report, *The Refugee Dilemma*, *op. cit.*, p. 14.

[337] For examples of serious emotional disturbance and mental illness in the UK, see REFUGEES, No. 74, April 90, pp. 37–9.

number. Alternatives solutions may however be used, in particular by easing contacts with the society in the host country through books and newspapers in the refugees' languages or through small meetings with the local population. No short term answers to the problem of refugees' integration seem to exist and efforts should, therefore, concentrate on long term solutions. In the meantime, public information activities could facilitate the resettlement and integration of refugees in a country.[338] The mass media are already campaigning quite efficiently in countries of origin (ie, Vietnam and Albania). Accurate information is being given to the population concerning the efficiency of the existing restrictive policies and poor living conditions.[339]

---

[338] In Germany, for instance, audio-visual media is being used against racism. See MNS, February 1994, p. 10.

[339] UNHCR, *The State of the World's Refugees, op. cit.*, p. 64.

CHAPTER EIGHT

CONCLUSION

In the past few years, asylum was sought more often by aliens who do not qualify for the status of refugee than by genuine politically persecuted individuals. The cost of an asylum seeker for a country is very high. Unable or unauthorized to work, most asylum seekers are dependent entirely on governmental or charitable aid for social and legal assistance, accommodation and food. Therefore, the longer the asylum procedure, the greater the costs. Belgium, the Republic Federal of Germany, France, Sweden, Switzerland and the United Kingdom have all, without exception, introduced restrictive and deterrent measures with the same intention, to shorten admission procedures and to dissuade potentially new asylum seekers from coming in. The most significant measures apply at the border, before entry in the territory because "where possible, governments prefer exclusion to expulsion".[1] These measures include visas requirements, the 'safe country' principle, carriers liability, detention, fingerprinting and photographing. But steps have also been taken with effect in the country. They include limitations to the right to work, sanctions against employers hiring illegal immigrants and a restrictive interpretation of the definition of refugee as provided in Article 1A(5) of the 1951 Convention.

1. Politics of 'Non-Entrée'

Since the mid-seventies, visas have been extensively required to enter a European country. In most states, visas are now also required for passengers in transit.[2] These requirements were introduced with a double objective, to prevent manifestly unfounded or abusive requests for asylum and to prevent asylum seekers from seeking asylum when they already have found refuge in a third country. According to Recommendation 16(81) of the CoE[3] and Con-

---

[1] UNHCR, *The State of the World's Refugees, op. cit.*, p. 39.

[2] See, in particular, s.12(3) of the Asylum and Immigration Appeals Act 1993, in the UK.

[3] On the harmonisation of national procedures relating to asylum, Committee of Ministers, 5 November 1981.

clusions 8(XXVIII)[4] and 30(XXXIV)[5] of the UNHCR Executive Committee, an asylum seeker can be removed from a country, before a final decision is reached on his case, if his application for asylum is manifestly abusive or unfounded. No further detail is provided on what should constitute a manifestly abusive or unfounded application for asylum and the interpretation of this concept was, thus, left at the discretion of each country. However, in November 1992, the EC Ministers responsible for immigration matters agreed that the concept of 'safety' should be assessed with reference to Article 3 of the ECHR and by looking at whether or not the applicant has actually had the opportunity to apply for asylum in the third country.[6] Today, safe countries of origin cases are no longer examined substantially in any of the six countries under review. The same applies to safe third countries cases, except perhaps in Sweden concerning asylum seekers coming from a third country outside the EU and the scope of the Nordic Agreement. Despite this common tendency, there is still no general legal rule on what is a safe country nor on how long should the stay be in a third country, for an asylum seeker to be refused entry. A rule of law in each country is necessary to create legal certainty. With the exception of Germany, states have not yet incorporated the EC Immigration Ministers interpretation of the concept of 'safety' in their laws (ie, in Switzerland) or, for lack of such legal provisions, in their practices (ie, in Belgium, France, Sweden and the United Kingdom).

To some extent, visa policy in the EU is still a matter of national laws. The Schengen Convention provides the adoption of a common visa policy for short-term visas[7] but visa for longer than three months will continue to be national visas to be issued according to national authorities.[8] As regards the final draft of the Convention on the Crossing of the External Borders of the Member States, which has not yet been adopted,[9] it contains very similar provisions to the Schengen ones relating to the creation of uniform visas.

---

[4]   On the determination of refugee status, 1977.

[5]   On the problem of manifestly unfounded or abusive applications for refugee status or asylum, 1983.

[6]   Resolution on Manifestly Unfounded Applications, London.

[7]   Articles 9 to 17. The Schengen common visa list contains 126 countries (MNS, December 1993, p. 1). Sweden, Switzerland and the United Kingdom are not parties to the Convention. The UK should, nevertheless, soon become a signatory to the External Borders Convention.

[8]   Article 18. Notice that such distinction does not exist in the TEU. Indeed, under Article 100c of the TEU, all categories of visas should be subject to harmonization.

[9]   The adoption of the External Borders Convention was blocked from June 1991 until December 1993 because of the dispute between Britain and Spain over the Rock of Gibraltar but, thanks to the efforts of the Commission, this period seems over now. In December 1993, the Commission proposed to the Council of Ministers a new draft of the Convention, on the basis of Article K.3 of the TEU (MNS, February 1994, p. 1). The European Parliament has since disagreed with the some of the provisions of the new draft Convention and has claimed a greater "role in the application and interpretation of the External Borders Convention" (MNS, May 1994, p. 1). It seems that today very little choice is left to the Council and, therefore, the member states. Sooner or later, the Council will have to adopt the Commission proposal, with or without the European Parliament propositions.

In particular, the distinction between different categories of visas within the common visa policy remains in the External Borders Convention.[10] These provisions have recently been met with strong opposition by the European Parliament.[11]

Because persons without visas still manage to board planes in order to seek asylum, most countries introduced legislation imposing fines on carriers, for each passenger they bring into the country without the proper documents. With the exception of Switzerland, this is the case in all the other countries under review: Belgium,[12] the Federal Republic of Germany,[13] France,[14] Sweden[15] and the United Kingdom.[16] According to Mr. Von Arnim, Representative of

---

[10] *Ibid*, p. 1. A common visa list of 129 countries was annexed to the Convention (MNS, February 1994, p. 1) but Britain abstained from approving it because the list contained 30 Commonwealth countries (MNS, May 1994, p. 1).

[11] MNS, May 1994, pp. 1–2.

[12] Title IIIbis (Articles 74/2–74/4) of the 1987 Aliens Law, as modified, provides that airline and maritime companies will be fined of 1,000BF for each undocumented passenger they carry. The fine shall only apply if at least five passengers are travelling, without the proper documents, at the same time (Article 74/2). It is the responsibility of the carrier to transport the passengers back to the country from which they come from. The carrier is also responsible for any accommodation cost, *in solidum* with the passenger (Article 74/4). On the legality of such provisions, see, J.-Y. Carlier, *Droits des Réfugiés, op. cit.*, pp. 48–50 and Antonio Cruz, "Carrier sanctions in four community states", *Nederlands Juristedblad*, 31 January 1991, p. 180.

[13] According to the Aliens Act, airline personnel transporting undocumented aliens can be fined up to 20,000DM if found guilty of negligence (s.93(5), AuslG). In addition, the company itself will be fined automatically for each undocumented passenger that it carries (s.74(2), AuslG). The company is also responsible for transporting undocumented aliens back to where they departed from (s.73, AuslG) and for paying all the accommodation expenses until departure as well as the return ticket (s.82(3), AuslG). See, A. Cruz, "Carriers sanctions ...", *op. cit.*, pp. 182–3. A similar fine (between 2,100DM and 32,000DM) is now also applicable to ferry transporters coming from Scandinavia (MNS, May 1994, p. 3).

[14] Law No. 92–190 of 26 February 1992 (and Decree No. 93–180 of 8 February 1993) gives effect to the requirements of the Schengen Convention signed by France in 1991 and modifies the 1945 Ordinance accordingly. New Article 20bis of the Ordinance provides a fine of up to 10,000FF for any airline or maritime company transporting undocumented passengers (5,000FF for international road transporters). However, the sanction shall not apply in cases where the asylum seeker is finally admitted in the territory, the application is not manifestly ill-founded, the carrier can prove that the required documents were shown to the authorities on departure or these documents were not manifeslty forged. Rail companies are also responsible for carrying undocumented passengers back to their country of departure (new Article 35ter of the 1945 Ordinance).

[15] Chap. 9, s.2 of the Aliens Act. Although strict sanctions are provided, no fines are actually stipulated. Carriers, who have failed to check the travel documents, are obliged to carry back undocumented passengers. Severe penalties seem to apply also directly against maritime transporters. In March 1994, for instance, the captain of a Russian ship transporting refugees to Sweden was sentenced to 18 months of jail by Swedish authorities (MNS, April 1994, p. 12).

[16] Immigration (Carriers' Liability) Act 1987. The fine is of £2,000 per passenger (ECRE Country Report, UK, 5–6 October 1991, p. 106). See, Anne Ruff, "The Immigration (Carriers' Liability) Act 1987: its implications for refugees and airlines", IJRL, 1989, pp. 481–99, Sue Shutter, *op. cit.*, p. 64 and, A. Cruz, "Carriers sanctions ...", *op. cit.*, pp. 183–4.

the UNHCR in Brussels, "these provisions are useless and aim essentially at upsetting NGOs and the public opinion. The 1944 Chicago Convention, already sanctions airlines through an obligation to pay for the return ticket and hotel accommodation of all passengers without proper documents during the whole time of investigations and, this sanction is effective because the cost may sometimes be significant. Therefore, the supplementary penalty, even if it is £1,000 in the United Kingdom, appears more like an accidental measure than a real sanction. European countries should have correctly applied the Chicago Convention, like they did in the United States, to avoid such controversial reactions and problems today. It is in fact true that since at least 20 years, it is impossible to fly to the United States without proper documents".[17] At a European level, Articles 26 and 27 of the Schengen Convention expressly provide sanctions against anyone who helps or intends to help aliens, for profit, to penetrate into the territory of a member state. In particular, sanctions against carriers bringing passengers without the required identity and travel documents are to be introduced and, the removal of such persons will be at the charge of the carrier. The same principle exists in the Draft Convention on the External Borders.[18] Overall, with regard to visa requirements and carriers liability, EU policies merely reconcile national politics of 'non-entrée'.

In order to accelerate the asylum procedures, the concept of 'safe country' was not the only measure introduced, detention has also become an increasingly common practice in order to facilitate deportation. In principle, the detention of asylum seekers outside exceptional circumstances (ie, threat to public security or public order) finds no legal justification. Whether at so-called international transit zone at airports[19] or in detention camps,[20] detention is unlawful if it is solely based on lack of the proper documents. Increasing use is also being made of fingerprints and photographs in order to prevent multiple or fraudulent applications. Comprehensive national filling systems of asylum claims are created with the same end[21] and, pursuant to the Schengen Convention, a parallel information system has also been introduced to facilitate the communication and use of data on persons and objects

---

[17] Interview (translated) with Mr. Von Arnim, December 1990 (*op. cit.*).

[18] Article 14. The European Parliament is, however, strongly against such provision and it has called for its suppression (MNS, May 1994, p. 1).

[19] See the French Law of 6 July 1992 and the Belgian Law of 6 May 1993. Both Belgium and France have used this concept despite strong criticism, particularly from the UNHCR. Michel Moussali, "Mémoire du HCR sur les questions d'actualité relatives à l'asile", Geneva, 13 March 1992, pp. 1–2.

[20] Britain has recently been subject to very strong criticism, particularly by Amnesty International. Not only are the living conditions of asylum seekers in immigration service detention centres, such as Campsfield centre, appalling but also the treatment of asylum seekers in prison detention (Pentoville prison) or when expulsion is taking place, has been considered dangerous and too often lethal (MNS, February 1994, p. 3, MNS, April 1994, p. 7 and Amnesty International, *Unlawful killing of Omasese Lumumba, op. cit.*).

[21] For instance, a computerized system of recording the fingerprints of asylum seekers is operating in Belgium since September 1993 and seems to be a real success in detecting fraudulent applications. MNS, April 1994, p. 10.

between the member states.[22] It is disconcerting that, currently, the secrecy and the confidentiality of data regarding asylum seekers are better protected outside the Schengen area (ie, in Sweden and Switzerland) than they are within that area (ie, in Belgium and France).

2. Few Are Recognized as Convention Refugees

Deterrent measures with effect in the country can be divided into three categories. The first kind of measures includes strong restrictions to, or even the abolition in some countries (ie, in France and in Belgium), of the right to work. The second category refers to heavy fines and/or imprisonment of persons directly or indirectly responsible for the entry and establishment of illegal aliens, in particular employers hiring illegal immigrants.[23] Finally, as a last step, European states have agreed to apply a restrictive interpretation of the definition of refugee, as provided in Article 1A(2) of the 1951 Convention. Rarely are asylum seekers granted the status of convention refugees because very few of them can prove persecution for political reasons alone. Credibility has become the key element of the whole asylum procedure. No country is willing to grant convention status to a refugee whose application does not appear credible. Furthermore, in Sweden, Switzerland and the United Kingdom, applications made by undocumented asylum seekers are presumed not to be credible. Though common to all the six countries, this restrictive interpretation is not, however, applied uniformly. At a comparative level, there is no doubt that Sweden provides the most restrictive interpretation of the definition of refugee, while France and Belgium offer the most liberal one. However, rejected applicants are not all required to leave, they are often granted some sort of residence rights as *de facto* refugees or humanitarian refugees for reasons based on humanitarian grounds.

3. Prospects for Harmonization

For a European refugee policy to be created, approximation of the laws and practices of states must exist and, wherever possible, harmonization must

---

[22] The Schengen Information System (SIS) is based in Strasbourg, at the CoE. See, Articles 92 to 119 of the Schengen Convention.

[23] For instance, in Belgium, refer to, Article 77 of the Aliens Law of 6 May 1993. See also, Conférence de Presse du Ministre de l'Intérieur, "Politique en matière d'asile: le point de la situation", 28 April 1993, pp. 5–8. In France, see, Law No. 91–1383 of 31 December 1991 and Law No. 93–1313 of 20 December 1993 (particularly, new Articles 21–24 of the 1945 Ordinance). In Germany, see, the Act to Control Illegal Employement of 15 December 1981. In Sweden, refer to, chap. 10, s.1 of the Aliens Law. In Switzerland, see, Federal Law on sojourn and establishment of aliens of 1931, as modified by Law of 9 October 1987, Article 23. In the UK, the Immigration Rules and the 1993 Asylum and Immigration Appeals Act are silent on this matter.

be achieved. Since the conflict started in the former Yugoslavia, a European refugee policy appears to be necessary and desirable, provided it is flexible enough to allow exceptional circumstances to be taken into account when these arise. At present, a proposal for the harmonization of the application of the definition of refugee is under intensive discussion; a harmonized definition has not yet been agreed but the possibility of a restrictive one seems to have been ruled out.[24] The harmonization of the definition of a refugee and of the definition of minimum guarantees afforded by asylum procedures could still be achieved by the end of 1994[25] yet obvious obstacles remain.

With regards to the definition of a refugee, while all the countries under review, except one, refer to the notion of 'refugee' and 'well-founded fear'[26] according to the 1951 Convention, the Federal Republic of Germany continues to adhere to the notion of 'politically persecuted' and 'political persecution', which is not in every aspect identical. With respect to the application, by national authorities and courts, of the definition of a refugee or of a politically persecuted individual, this book has shown that many divergences still exist amongst the states. The criteria for granting permanent residence permits or temporary authorizations to remain are not yet harmonized nor even near it. As for the status of convention refugee, as described in the 1951 Convention, if it appears to be applied harmoniously across Europe, a similar recognition for *de facto* refugees or refugees allowed to remain on humanitarian grounds seems to have little support. Moreover, discrepancies not only exist between states but also within some of them. This is particularly the case in the Federal Republic of Germany where it has proved quite common for courts to be divided on one issue over some time. A similar situation seems less likely to happen in Belgium and France because appeals against asylum decisions are dealt with a specialized commission but, like in Germany, there is no rule of precedent, and reversals of *jurisprudence* do exist. Sweden, Switzerland and the United Kingdom, thus, seem to provide the clearest and most uniform interpretation of the definition of refugees inside their jurisdiction: in Sweden, because important questions of interpretation rest on a decision of Government, in Switzerland, because the decision on appeal is essentially made by one authority and is almost always final, and, in the United Kingdom, because judicial authorities are bound by the rule of precedent, however, possibilities of judicial review exist.

Different national procedures for asylum place further obstacles to the harmonization of refugee policies within the EU. This book has demonstrated that states do not guarantee equally the protection of legal procedural rights throughout the whole procedure for asylum (ie, the right to be heard, the right to an interpreter and a counsel, the right to appeal and the principle of legal certainty). Common border controls, access to the territories and deportation measures are covered by the final draft of the Convention on External Borders;

---

[24] MNS, May 1994, p. 3.

[25] *Ibid.*

[26] The Swiss Asylum Law refers to "sérieux préjudices" (serious harm or fear).

harmonization on these areas should follow the ratification of the Convention. Nevertheless, the substantive law on asylum and refugees has still a long way to go before harmonization.

SUMMARY OF THE PRINCIPAL NATIONAL LEGISLATION

Belgium

Loi du 15 décembre 1980 sur l'accés au territoire, le séjour, l'établissement et l'éloignement des étrangers (as last modified on 6 May 1993)
    Arrêté royal du 8 octobre 1981 sur l'accés au territoire, le séjour, l'établissement et l'éloignement des étrangers (as last modified on 19 May 1993)
    Loi du 28 juin 1984 relative à certains aspects de la condition des étrangers et instituant le Code de la Nationalité belge
    Arrêté du Commissaire Général aux réfugiés et apatrides du 20 janvier 1988 portant délégation des pouvoirs du Commissaire Général en application de la loi du 14 juillet 1987 apportant des modifications, en ce qui concerne notamment les réfugiés, à la loi du 15 décembre 1980
    Arrêté ministèriel du 26 janvier 1988 modifiant l'arrêté ministèriel du 30 juin 1981 portant délégation des pouvoirs du Ministre en matière d'accés au territoire, séjour, établissement et éloignement des étrangers et désignant les fonctionnaires, les autorités communales et les autorités de police délégués (as last modified on 18 May 1993)

Federal Republic of Germany

Groundgesetz für die Bundesrepublik Deutschland vom 25 Mai 1949, Artikel 16a (as last modified on 1st July 1993)
    Ausländergesetz vom 28 April 1965 (as last modified on 1st January 1991)
    Arbeitsförderungsgesetz vom 25 Juni 1969
    Gesetz über Massnahmen für im Rahmen Humanitärer Hilfsaktionen aufgenommence Flüchtlinge vom 29 Juli 1980
    Arbeitserlaubnisverordnung vom 12 September 1980
    Asylverfahrensgesetz vom 16 Juli 1982 (as last modified on 1st July 1993)

France

Ordonnance no.45–2658 du 2 novembre 1945 relative aux conditions d'entrée et de séjour en France des étrangers et portant création de l'office national d'immigration (as last modified on 24 August 1993)

Loi no.52–893 du 25 juillet 1952 portant création d'un Office français de protection des réfugiés et apatrides (as last modified on 24 August 1993)

Décret no.53–377 du 2 mai 1953 relatif à l'Office français de protection des réfugiés et apatrides (as last modified on 30 July 1992)

Circulaire no.84–15 du 24 juin 1984 du ministère de la justice relative à l'état civil des réfugiés

Circulaire du 17 mai 1985 du Premier Ministre relative aux demandeurs d'asile

Loi no.90–550 du 2 juillet 1990 relative à l'OFPRA et à la Commission des Recours

Décret no.91–902 du 6 septembre 1991 portant publication de l'ordonnance du 2 novembre 1945

Circulaire du 26 septembre 1991 relative à la situation des demandeurs d'asile au regard du marché du travail

Loi no.91–1383 du 31 décembre 1991 renforçant la lutte contre le travail clandestin et la lutte contre l'organisation de l'entrée et du séjour irréguliers d'étrangers en France

Loi no.92–190 du 26 février 1992 sur l'entrée et le séjour en France et les mesures d'application de la Convention de Schengen du 19 juin 1990

Loi no.92–625 du 6 juillet 1992 sur la zone d'attente des ports et aéroports et décret no.92–1333 du 15 décembre 1992 fixant les modalités d'application de l'article 35 quater de l'ordonnance du 2 novembre 1945

Décret no.93–180 du 8 février 1993 sur la déclaration d'entrée sur le territoire français et la responsabilité des entreprises de transport

Loi no.93–933 du 22 juillet 1993 réformant le droit de la nationalité

Loi no.93–1027 du 24 août 1993 relative à la maîtrise de l'immigration et aux conditions d'entrée, d'accueil et de séjour des étrangers en France

Loi no.93–1417 du 30 décembre 1993 relative à la maîtrise de l'immigration et modifiant le code civil

Sweden

Act on legal aid of 1972

Aliens Act of 1st July 1989 (Utlänningslagen)

Aliens Ordinance of 8 June 1989 (Utlänningsförordning)

Act on special control of aliens of 1991

Ordinance on residence permits for aliens in special cases of 1991

Act on introductory remuneration for refugees and certain other aliens of 1992

Switzerland

Constitution fédérale du 29 mai 1874, article 69ter
  Loi fédérale sur le séjour et l'établissement des étrangers du 26 mars 1931
  Loi fédérale sur l'organisation judiciaire du 16 décembre 1943 (as last modified on 20 June 1978)
  Ordonnance fédérale relative à l'entrée et à l'enregistrement des étrangers du 10 avril 1946 (as modified on 25 November 1987)
  Ordonnance sur l'internement des étrangers du 14 août 1968
  Loi sur l'asile du 5 octobre 1979 (as last modified on 22 June 1990)
  Ordonnance sur l'asile du 12 novembre 1980 (as last modified on 2 October 1990)
  Ordonnance limitant le nombre des étrangers du 6 octobre 1986 (as modified on 5 October 1987)
  Arrêtés urgents sur la procédure d'asile du 22 juin 1990 portant modification de la loi sur l'asile du 5 octobre 1979 et de la loi fédérale sur le séjour et l'établissement des étrangers
  Arrêté fédéral du 18 décembre 1991 portant création de la Commission des Recours en matière d'Asile

United Kingdom

Immigration Act of 28 October 1971
  Immigration (Variation of Leave) Order of 1976
  British Nationality Act 1981
  (Statement of Changes in) Immigration Rules of 23 March 1990, as last modified on 5 July 1993
  Immigration Appeals (Procedure) Rules and (Notices) Regulations of 1984, as last modified on 5 July 1993
  Immigration (Carriers' Liability) Act of 1987
  Immigration (Overstaying and Deportation) Act of 1988
  Immigration (Variation of Leave) Order of 1989
  Asylum and Immigration Appeals Act of 5 July 1993

BIBLIOGRAPHY

Books and Monographs

BATAILLE, L.-M. and BERGER, J.-M., Aide Mémoire des C.P.A.S., *Recueil des principales dispositions légales relatives aux centres publics d'aide sociale*, Union des Villes et Communes belges, 1989.

BHABHA, J. and COLL, G. (Eds.), *Asylum and Practice in Europe and North America: A Comparative Analysis*, Federal Publications Inc., 1992.

BODART, S., *Les autres réfugiés. Le statut des réfugiés de facto en Europe*, Sybidi Papers 8, Academia, Edition et Diffusion, 1989.

BROWNLIE, I., *Basic Documents in International Law*, fourth edition, Clarendon Press, Oxford, 1992.

CARLIER, J.-Y., *Droits des réfugiés*, Editions Story-Scientia, 1989.

DRZEMEZEWSKI, A.Z., *European Human Rights Convention in domestic law – A Comparative Study*, Oxford, 1983.

EVANS, J.M., *Immigration Law*, Modern Legal Studies, London, Sweet & Maxwell, second edition, 1983.

FOSTER, N., *German Law and Legal System*, Blackstone Press Limited, 1993.

GOODWIN-GILL, G.S., *International Law and the Movement of Persons between States*, Clarendon Press, Oxford, 1978.

—— *The Refugee in International Law*, Clarendon Press, Oxford, 1985.

GRIFFITH, J.A.G., *The Politics of the Judiciary*, 1977.

HOLBORN, L.W., *Refugees: A Problem of Our Time. The Work of the UNHCR, 1951–1972*, the Scarecrow Press, 1975.

KANEIN and RENNER, *Ausländerrecht*, C.H.Beck'sche Verlagsbuchhandlung, München 1993.

MACDONALD, I.A., *Immigration Law and Practice in the United Kingdom*, Butterworths, 1983.

MARRUS, M.R., *The Unwanted: European Refugees in the Twentieth Century*, N.Y., Oxford University Press, 1985.

MAX PLANCK INSTITUTE for Comparative Public Law and International Law, *Encyclopedia of Public International Law*, Volume 8.

MELANDER, G., *Undocumented Asylum Seekers in Sweden*, An Independent Study, 1990.

MONK, S. and KLEINMAN, M., *Beyond Thatcherism*, Ed. Brown,P. and Sparks, R., Open University Press.

PATRNOGIC, J., *International Protection of Refugees in Armed Conflicts*, reprinted by the UNHCR Protection Division from "Annales de Droit International Médical", July 1981.

——, *Promotion, Dissemination and Teaching of International Refugee Law*, International Institute of Humaniatarian Law, Villa Nobel, San Remo, Italy, February 1984.

PLENDER, R., *International Migration Law*, Martinus Nijhoff Publishers, second revised edition, 1988.

QUERMONNE, J.-L., *Le gouvernement de la France sous la Vième République*, Etudes politiques économiques et sociales, Dalloz, 1987.

REDEKER, K. and VON OERTZEN, H.-J., *Verwaltungsgerichtsordnung – Kommentar*, Verlag W. Kohlhammer, Stuttgart Berlin Köln, 1994.

RESSLER, E.M., BOOTHBY, N. and STEINBOCK, D.J., *Unaccompanied children: care and protection in wars, natural disasters and refugee movements*, N.Y., Oxford, Oxford University Press, 1988.

SIMPSON, J.H.(Sir), *The Refugee Problem*, Oxford University Press, 1939.

SMITH, C., *Benefits, CHAR's guide to income support and housing benefit for single people without a permanent home*, the housing campaign for single people, 1989.

TIBERGHIEN, F., *La protection des réfugiés en France*, Presses Universitaires d'Aix-Marseilles, Ed.Economica, Collection droit public positif, 2e édition, 1988.

UNHCR, *The State of the World's Refugees, The Challenge of Protection*, Penguin Books, 1993.

VINCENZI, C. and MARRINGTON, D., *Immigration Law – The Rules Explained*, Sweet & Maxwell, 1992.

WEIS, P., *Nationality and Statelessness in International Law*, Sitjhoff & Noordhoff, 1979.

Journal Articles and Conference Papers

Alt SJ, J., *Comments on the increase in violent xenophobic attacks in Eastern Germany*, Paper presented in Geneva, 1989.

ARNOLD, H., *The Century of the Refugee, A European Century?*, Aussenpolitik, Volume 42, No.3, 1991.

AVERY, C.L., *Refugee Status Decision Making: The System of Ten Countrie*, Stanford Journal of International Law, 1984.

BARI, S., *Le droit des réfugiés en péril?*, Réfugiés, Août 1989.

BERGQUIST, P., *L'asile en Suède*, Documentation-Réfugiés, Août 1989.

BIACSKO, L., *Demandeurs d'asile en Belgique, les premiers effets de la loi Gol*, Réfugiés, Décembre 1988.

BOIS, P., *Procédures applicables aux requérants d'asile*, Revue Suisse de Jurisprudence, 1988.

BOVARD, A. *La procédure d'asile Suisse*, Documentation-Réfugiés, Supplément juridique, 1993.

CARLIER, J.-Y., *Réfugiés Refusés*, Revue des Droits des Etrangers, No.41, 1986.

CELS, J., *European responses to de facto refugees*, Refugees and International Relations, Ed. Gil Loescher and Laila Monahan, 1989.

COSTA-LASCOUX, J., *L'insertion sociale des réfugiés et demandeurs d'asile en Europe*, Revue Européenne des Migrations Internationales, Volume 3, No.3, 1987.

CRUZ, A., *Carrier sanctions in four community states*, Nederlands Juristedblad, 31 January 1991.

FULLERTON, M., *Persecution due to membership in a particular social group: jurisprudence in the Federal Republic of Germany*, Georgetown Immigration Law Journal, Vol.4, No.3, 1990.

FOUCART, R. and VANDAMME, G., *La place de la Commission Permanente de Recours des Réfugiés en droit belge*, Documentation-Réfugiés, Supplément au no.209, 1993.

GEIS, M.-E., *Neuregelung des Asylverfahrens*, JUS, Heft 2, 1993.

HAILBRONNER, K., *The concept of 'safe country' and expeditious asylum procedures: a Western European perspective*, IJRL, Oxford University Press, 1993.

HEILBRONNER, A., *La Commission de Recours des Réfugiés*, Etudes et Documents du Conseil d'Etat, 1978–79.

HELTON, A.C., *The Proper Role of Discretion in Political Asylum Determinations*, San Diego Law Review, Sept.–Oct. 1985.

——, *Asylum and Protection in Thailand*, IJRL, Oxford University Press, 1989.
HENKEL, J., *Das Neue Asylrecht*, NJW, Heft 42, 1993.
HUBER, B., *Prozessuale Besonderheiten asylrechtlicher Eilverfahren auf Gestattung der Einreise*, NVwZ, Heft 2, 1994.
KALIN, W., *Just another brick in the wall? A Swiss report on the use of computerized textual elements in substantiating negative asylum decisions*, IJRL, Oxford University Press, 1989.
——, *Refugees and civil wars: only a matter of interpretation?*, IJRL, Oxford University Press, 1991.
KJAERUM, M., *The concept of country of first asylum*, IJRL, Oxford University Press, 1992.
LEROUX, M.-C., *Vivre au 127*, Bulletin du Centre Social Protestant (Lausanne), No.275, September 1990.
LOESCHER, G., *The European Community and Refugees*, International Affairs, Volume 65, No.4, 1989.
LOVELAND, I., *Policing welfare: local authority responses to claimant fraud in the housing benefit scheme*, Journal of Law and Society, Basic Blackwell, Oxford, Volume 16, No.2.
MARX, R., *Study on the Treatment of Asylum Seekers at German Airports*, 30 March 1992.
——, *The criteria for determining refugee status in the Federal Republic of Germany*, IJRL, Oxford University Press, 1992.
NOBEL, P., *What happened with Sweden's refugee policies?*, IJRL, Oxford University Press, 1990.
O'KEEFFE, D., *The Schengen Convention: a suitable model for European integration?*, Yearbook of European Law, 1991.
——, *The free movement of persons and the single market*, European Law Review, 1992.
O'KEEFFE, D. and PIOTROWICZ, R.W., *National Report: asylum law in the United Kingdom*, Paper presented at the ERA Conference in Triers, March 1992.
RING, H., *Refugees in Sweden. Inclusion and exclusion in the welfare state*, Paper presented at the ECPR Conference, Leiden, April 1993.
ROOZE, T., *L'accueil à Anvers et dans les environs*, Réfugiés, Décembre 1988.
RUFF, A., *The Immigration (Carriers' Liability) Act 1987: its implications for refugees and airlines*, IJRL, Oxford University Press, 1989.
SCANNEL, R., *Recent developments in immigration law*, Legal Action, February 1993.
SCHUTTE, J.J.E., *Schengen: its meaning for the free movement of persons in Europe*, Common Market Law Review, 1991.
STUCKY, L., *Description du role de représentant de l'oeuvre d'entraide*, Le Jalon, Décembre 1987.
WEIS, P., *Le concept de réfugié en droit international*, Journal de Droit International, Clunet, 1960.
——, *The 1967 Protocol relating to the Status of refugees and some questions of the law of treaties*, B.Y.I.L., 1967.
——, *Refugees in Orbit*, Israel Yearbook on Human Rights, Volume 10, 1980.
WIKELEY, N., *Unemployment Benefit, the State and the Labour Market*, Journal of Law and Society, Basil Blackwell, Oxford, Volume 16, No.3.

Reports and Other Documentation

Accueil des Réfugiés, BILAN 1989, Le Cabinet du Secrétaire d'Etat à l'Emancipation Sociale, (Brussels).
Amnesty International, *Europe: Human Rights and the need for a fair asylum policy*, November 1991.
——, *Europe: Harmonization of asylum policy. Accelerated procedures for 'manifestly unfounded' asylum claims and the 'safe country' concept*, November 1992.

——, *United Kingdom – Unlawful killing of detained asylum seeker Omasese Lumumba*, November 1993.

——, *Passing the Buck: Deficient Home Office practice in 'safe third country" asylum cases*, 1993.

Asyl I Norden (Asylum in Nordic Countries), English Summary, Dansk Flygtingehjaelp, Denmark.

Les bénéficiaires du Minimex en Belgique, published by the Cabinet of the Secretary of State for Social Emancipation (Brussels), 1988–89.

British Refugee Council, *Settling for a future: proposals for a British policy on refugees*, London, The Council, 1987.

BRUTSCH, Y., *Memorandum relatif à l'application de la législation sur l'asile à l'intention du Parti Socialiste Suisse*, Geneva, 18 October 1990.

Bundesministerium des Innerns, *Das Neue Asylrecht – Fragen und Antworten*, Bonn, July 1993.

CRUZ, A., *Schengen, ad hoc Immigration Group and other European Intergovernmental bodies*, Churches Committee for Migrants in Europe, Briefing Paper 12, 1993.

DOSSIER: Vers une harmonisation du droit d'asile en Europe, Hommes et Migrations, No.1096, 15 October 1986.

European Conference on Reception of Asylum Seekers, *Final Report*, A Nordic Arrangement in Sweden at Orenäs Castle, 8–10 October 1991.

ECRE, *Asile en Europe, Guide à l'intention des associations de protection des réfugiés*, France Terre d'Asile, 1990.

Federal Minister of the Interior, *Survey of the Policy and Law regarding Aliens in the Federal Republic of Germany* (translation), January 1991.

FIELD, S., *Resettling Refugees: the lessons of research*, Home Office Research Study no.87.

First to Fifth Annual Reports of the General Commissioner for Refugees and Stateless Persons, Activity Years 1988 to 1992, Brussels.

FTDA, *Guide Pratique du Réfugié*, 1992.

GATTIKER, M., *Procédure d'asile et de renvoi*, Document de Travail pour représentants d'oeuvres d'entraide (OSAR), 1988.

HAMILTON, C.B. and STALVANT, C.-E., *A Swedish View of 1992*, the Royal Institute of International Affairs, Discussion Paper 13, 1989.

HOOGHIEMSTRA, R., *Comparative Study on the provision of publicly funded legal services to asylum seekers in the 12 Member States of the European Community*, Immigration Law Practitioners' Association, London.

Jesuit Refugee Service Lawyers Project, *Understanding the refugee status determination process*, Notes for Vietnamese Asylum Seekers awaiting refugee status determination, IJRL, Oxford University Press, 1993.

JONES, P.R., *Vietnamese refugees: a study of their reception and resettlement in the UK*, Research and Planning Unit, Paper 13, London, Home Office, 1982.

JONSSON, K. and DE GEER, S., *The rights of asylum seekers and accepted refugees in Sweden*, Röda Korset, 1993.

Ministre belge de l'Intérieur, *Politique en matière d'asile: le point de la situation*, Conférence de Presse, 28 April 1993.

MINORITY RIGHTS GROUP, *The Refugee Dilemma*, Report No.43, 1985.

——, *Refugees in Europe*, Report, October 1990.

MOUSSALI, M., *Mémoire du HCR sur les questions d'actualité relatives à l'asile*, Geneva, 13 March 1992.

Netherlands Interdisciplinary Demographic Institute (NIDI), *Draft Report on Asylum Seekers and Refugees in Germany*, 1993.

OSAR, *Points de repère. Cinquante ans d'aide aux réfugiés*, 1986.

——, Rapport Annuel de l'Office central Suisse d'Aide aux Réfugiés, Bern Lausanne, 1989.

Proceedings of the Sixteenth Colloquy on European Law, *The law of asylum and refugees: present tendencies and future perspectives*, Lund, September 1986, CoE, Legal Affairs, 1987.

Report on the problem of refugees and exiles in Europe, Volume II, Legal Report, International University Exchange Fund on behalf of the Working Group on Refugees and Exiles in Europe, Geneva, July 1974.

SCHOENI, H., *Refuge, Politique des Réfugiés, Politique d'Asile, Droit d'Asile*, Office Fédéral Suisse des Réfugiés, 1992.

SHUTTER, S., *Immigration and nationality law handbook*, Joint Council for the Welfare of Immigrants, 1992.

Swedish Ministry of Cultural Affairs, *Immigrant and Refugee Policy*, Stockholm, 1992 and 1993.

Statens Offentliga Utredningar (SOU), Kulturdepartementet, *Utvärdering av praxis asylären- den*, English Summary, Stockholm, 1994.

Statens Invandrarverk, *When you move to Sweden*, October 1991
(leaflets)
    Facts about Immigration, April 1992
    Immigrating to Sweden, September 1992
    Swedish Citizenship, August 1992
    To persons Seeking Asylum in Sweden, June 1992
    Immigration Controls, June 1992.

UNHCR, *Draft Protocol to the 1951 Convention: analysis of the present position*, Internal Memorandum, 26 May 1966.

——, *Handbook on Procedures and Criteria for Determining Refugee Status*, Geneva, January 1988 (first published in 1979, HCR/IP/4/FRE, Geneva, 1979).

——, *Collection of International Instruments concerning Refugees*, Geneva 1988.

——, *Conclusions on the International Protection of Refugees* adopted by the Executive Committee of the UNHCR Programme, Geneva, 1990.

——, *Information Paper*, Secretariat UNHCR, Geneva, March 1993.

Magazines and news sheets

ASYL, magazine for professionals, edited and published by Schweizerische Zentralstelle für Flüchtlingschilfe, Postfach 279, 8035 Zürich.

Bulletin C.E.D.R.I., published by Frédéric Furet, Association Imprimerie Ateliers Populaires. C.E.D.R.I.-France, BP 42, 04300 Forcalquier. C.E.D.R.I.-Suisse, Missionsstr.35, CP2780, 4002 Bâle.

DOCUMENTATION-REFUGIES, magazine specialized about information on refugees, 11, rue Ferdinand-Gambon, 75020 Paris.

The Economist.

The Guardian.

The Guardian Weekly.

The Independent.

Le JALON, Coordination pour la représentation des oeuvres d'entraide, OSAR, 3 rue Chaucrau, 1003 Lausanne.

Le Monde.

Migration News Sheet (MNS), edited by A. Cruz and published by the European Information Network, 172, rue Joseph II, B–1040 Brussels.

REFUGEES, published by the Public Information Service of the UNHCR; UNHCR, P.O. Box 2500, 1211 Geneva, Switzerland (in French, Réfugiés).

The Times.

Swedish Institute, *Fact Sheets on Sweden*, 1992 and 1993.

TABLE OF CASES

INDEX

International Studies in Human Rights

1. B. G. Ramcharan (ed.): *International Law and Fact-finding in the Field of Human Rights.* 1982
   ISBN 90-247-3042-2

2. B. G. Ramcharan: *Humanitarian Good Offices in International Law.* The Good Offices of the United Nations Secretary-General in the Field of Human Rights. 1983
   ISBN 90-247-2805-3

3. B. G. Ramcharan (ed.): *The Right to Life in International Law.* 1985
   ISBN 90-247-3074-0

4. P. Alston and K. Tomaševski (eds.): *The Right to Food.* 1984   ISBN 90-247-3087-2

5. A. Bloed and P. van Dijk (eds.): *Essays on Human Rights in the Helsinki Process.* 1985
   ISBN 90-247-3211-5

6. K. Törnudd: *Finland and the International Norms of Human Rights.* 1986
   ISBN 90-247-3257-3

7. H. Thoolen and B. Verstappen: *Human Rights Missions.* A Study of the Fact-finding Practice of Non-governmental Organizations. 1986   ISBN 90-247-3364-2

8. H. Hannum: *The Right to Leave and Return in International Law and Practice.* 1987
   ISBN 90-247-3445-2

9. J. H. Burgers and H. Danelius: *The United Nations Convention against Torture.* A Handbook on the Convention against Torture and Other Cruel, Inhuman or Degrading Treatment or Punishment. 1988   ISBN 90-247-3609-9

10. D. A. Martin (ed.): *The New Asylum Seekers: Refugee Law in the 1980s.* The Ninth Sokol Colloquium on International Law. 1988   ISBN 90-247-3730-3

11. C. M. Quiroga: *The Battle of Human Rights.* Gross, Systematic Violations and the Inter-American System. 1988   ISBN 90-247-3687-0

12. L. A. Rehof and C. Gulmann (eds.): *Human Rights in Domestic Law and Development Assistance Policies of the Nordic Countries.* 1989   ISBN 90-247-3743-5

13. B. G. Ramcharan: *The Concept and Present Status of International Protection of Human Rights.* Forty Years After the Universal Declaration. 1989
   ISBN 90-247-3759-1

14. A. D. Byre and B. Y. Byfield (eds.): *International Human Rights Law in the Commonwealth Caribbean.* 1991   ISBN 90-247-3785-0

15. N. Lerner: *Groups Rights and Discrimination in International Law.* 1991
   ISBN 0-7923-0853-0

16. S. Shetreet (ed.): *Free Speech and National Security.* 1991   ISBN 0-7923-1030-6

17. G. Gilbert: *Aspects of Extradition Law.* 1991   ISBN 0-7923-1162-0

18. P.E. Veerman: *The Rights of the Child and the Changing Image of Childhood.* 1991
   ISBN 0-7923-1250-3

19. M. Delmas-Marty (ed.): *The European Convention for the Protection of Human Rights.* International Protection versus National Restrictions. 1991   ISBN 0-7923-1283-X

International Studies in Human Rights

20. A. Bloed and P. van Dijk (eds.): *The Human Dimension of the Helsinki Process*. The Vienna Follow-up Meeting and its Aftermath. 1991   ISBN 0-7923-1337-2

21. L.S. Sunga: *Individual Responsibility in International Law for Serious Human Rights Violations*. 1992   ISBN 0-7923-1453-0

22. S. Frankowski and D. Shelton (eds.): *Preventive Detention*. A Comparative and International Law Perspective. 1992   ISBN 0-7923-1465-4

23. M. Freeman and P. Veerman (eds.): *The Ideologies of Children's Rights*. 1992
ISBN 0-7923-1800-5

24. S. Stavros: *The Guarantees for Accused Persons Under Article 6 of the European Convention on Human Rights*. An Analysis of the Application of the Convention and a Comparison with Other Instruments. 1993   ISBN 0-7923-1897-8

25. A. Rosas and J. Helgesen (eds.): *The Strength of Diversity*. Human Rights and Pluralist Democracy. 1992   ISBN 0-7923-1987-7

26. K. Waaldijk and A. Clapham (eds.): *Homosexuality: A European Community Issue*. Essays on Lesbian and Gay Rights in European Law and Policy. 1993
ISBN 0-7923-2038-7; Pb: 0-7923-2240-1

27. Y.K. Tyagi: *The Law and Practice of the UN Human Rights Committee*. 1993
ISBN 0-7923-2040-9

28. *In preparation*

29. L.A. Rehof: *Guide to the* Travaux Préparatoires *of the United Nations Convention on the Elimination of All Forms of Discrimination against Women*. 1993
ISBN 0-7923-2222-3

30. A. Bloed, L. Leicht, M. Novak and A. Rosas (eds.): *Monitoring Human Rights in Europe*. Comparing International Procedures and Mechanisms. 1993
ISBN 0-7923-2383-1

31. A. Harding and J. Hatchard (eds.): *Preventive Detention and Security Law*. A Comparative Survey. 1993   ISBN 0-7923-2432-3

32. Y. Beigbeder: *International Monitoring of Plebiscites, Referenda and National Elections*. Self-determination and Transition to Democracy. 1994 ISBN 0-7923-2563-X

33. F. de Varennes: *Language, Minorities and Human Rights*. 1994.   ISBN 0-7923-2728-4

34. D.M. Beatty (ed.): *Human Rights and Judicial Review*. A Comparative Perspective. 1994   ISBN 0-7923-2968-6

35. G. Van Bueren, *The International Law on the Rights of the Child*. 1995
ISBN 0-7923-2687-3

36. T. Zwart: *The Admissibility of Human Rights Petitions*. The Case Law of the European Commission of Human Rights and the Human Rights Committee. 1994
ISBN 0-7923-3146-X; Pb: 0-7923-3147-8

37. H. Lambert: *Seeking Asylum*. Comparitive Law and Practice in Selected European Countries. 1995   ISBN 0-7923-3152-4

International Studies in Human Rights

38. E. Lijnzaad: *Reservations to UN-Human Rights Treaties*. Ratify and Ruin? 1994
ISBN 0-7923-3256-3

39. L.G. Loucaides: *Essays on the Developing Law of Human Rights.* 1995
ISBN 0-7923-3276-8

40. T. Degener and Y. Koster-Dreese (eds.): *Human Rights and Disabled Persons*. Essays
and Relevant Human Rights Instruments. 1995   ISBN 0-7923-3298-9

This series is designed to shed light on current legal and political aspects of process and organization in the field of human rights.

MARTINUS NIJHOFF PUBLISHERS – DORDRECHT / BOSTON / LONDON